A TIME FOR ALL THINGS

COLLECTED ESSAYS AND SKETCHES

RUSKIN BOND

SPEAKING
TIGER

Speaking Tiger Publishing Pvt. Ltd
4381/4, Ansari Road, Daryaganj,
New Delhi–110002, India

Published by Speaking Tiger 2018

ISBN: 978-93-87693-12-8
eISBN: 978-93-87164-75-8

10 9 8 7 6 5 4 3 2 1

The moral right of the author has been asserted.

Typeset in Minon Pro by Jojy Philip, New Delhi
Printed at Sanat Printers, Kundli.

RUSKIN BOND has written novels, memoirs, short story collections and books of essays and poetry. His recent books include *Lone Fox Dancing: My Autobiography*, *I Was the Wind Last Night: New and Collected Poems*; *A Book of Simple Living: Brief Notes from the Hills*, *Friends in Wild Places: Birds, Beasts and Other Companions*, *A Little Book of Happiness*, *A Little Book of Serenity* and *A Little Book of Love and Companionship*, as well as the popular classics *Room on the Roof* (winner of the John Llewellyn Rhys Prize), *A Flight of Pigeons*, *The Blue Umbrella*, *Time Stops at Shamli*, *Night Train at Deoli*, *Our Trees Still Grow in Dehra* (winner of the Sahitya Akademi Award) and *Rain in the Mountains*. He has co-edited *Himalaya: Adventures, Meditations, Life* (with Namita Gokhale) and *Prankenstein: The Book of Crazy Mischief* (with Jerry Pinto). He was awarded the Padma Shri by the Government of India in 1999and the Padma Bhushan in 2014.

Contents

A Writer's Life

Family and Friends

The Further One Goes

India: People and Places

Humour

Thoughts from a Window

Introduction

The word 'essay' can be a little disconcerting to many readers, who will recall their schooldays and those dreaded exam papers in which they were asked to write an essay on some humdrum subject. Publishers also fight shy of publishing essays. Who would want to buy a book of them?

I, too, used to be reluctant to read essays—that is, until I discovered those by J.B. Priestly, George Orwell, Somerset Maugham and others—writers who had made their mark with the novel or play, but liked to dabble in essays from time to time; and often the essays were keener observations of life than their stories. Priestly took a friendly and optimistic view of the human race. Maugham was cynical but entertaining. Orwell thought we were by nature slavish, only too ready to submit to tyrants and dictators. (Much as I loved Priestly, I can't help feeling that the world is increasingly Orwellian.)

As one who has to make a living from his writing, most of my work has been in the field of fiction or, occasionally, autobiography or travel. But the essay has always been close to my heart. I have been writing essays of a sort for over sixty years. Not all were published. But the Sunday papers (especially *The Statesman* and the *Deccan Herald*) carried many of them, and in the 1970s my 'nature' pieces found a home in the Home Forum section of Boston's *Christian Science Monitor*, then a highly respected and widely read newspaper. Sadly, it has now shrunk, in both size and circulation.

Another revered publication was *Blackwood's*, a literary and political journal which had survived for over two hundred years (publishing Stevenson, Conrad, Jack London and others along the way) before finally succumbing to the advent of new forms of information and entertainment. It ran in the family for all those years, and G.D. Blackwood, its last editor, published several of my pieces on hill stations, leopards, rivers, cemeteries and railway stations—these were the things that interested me.

Much of my writing is nature-oriented, because I've spent most of my life in contemplation of the sky, the good earth and the waters of the earth, along with its inhabitants—humans, animals, birds and ladybirds. Windows and long walks have shown me beauty in the smallest things and in the most unexpected places, and recording these discoveries in short prose pieces, not in the service of a story, but complete in themselves, has brought me a lot of pleasure. I hope the essays and sketches in this collection will bring you some pleasure, too.

Ruskin Bond
Landour
20 January 2018

For All Seasons

A Mountain Stream

There is a brook at the bottom of the hill. From where I live I can always hear its murmur, but I am no longer conscious of the sound except when I return from a trip to the plains.

And yet I have grown so used to the constant music of water that when I leave it behind I feel naked and alone, bereft of my moorings. It is like getting accustomed to the friendly rattle of teacups every morning, and then waking one day to a deathly stillness and a fleeting moment of panic.

Below the house is a forest of oak and maple and rhododendron. A path twists its way down through the trees over an open ridge where red sorrel grows wild and then down steeply through a tangle of thorn bushes, creepers and ringal bamboo.

At the bottom of the hill the path leads on to a grassy verge, surrounded by wild rose. The stream runs close by the verge, tumbling over smooth pebbles over rocks worn yellow with age on its way to the plains and to the little Song river and finally to the sacred Ganga.

When I first discovered the stream it was April and the wild roses were flowering, small white blossoms lying in clusters. There were still pink and blue primroses on the hill slopes and an occasional late-flowering rhododendron provided a splash of red against the dark green of the hill.

A forktail, a bird of the Himalayan streams, was much in evidence during those early visits. It moved nimbly over the boulders with a fairy tread and continually wagged its tail. Both of us had a fondness for standing in running water. Once, while I stood in the stream. I saw a snake swim past, a slim brown snake, beautiful and lonely. A snake in water is a lovely creature.

In May and June, when the hills are always brown and dry, it remained cool and green near the stream where ferns and maidenhair and long grasses continued to thrive. Downstream, I found a small pool where I could bathe and a cave with water dripping from the roof, the water spangled gold and silver in the shafts of sunlight that pushed through the slits in the cave-roof.

Few people came here. Sometimes a milkman or a coalburner would cross the stream on his way to a village; but, the nearby hill station's summer visitors had not discovered this haven of wild and green things.

The monkeys—langurs with white and silver-grey fur, black faces and long swishing tails—had discovered the place but they kept to the trees and sunlit slopes. They grew quite accustomed to my presence and carried on about their work and play as though I did not exist— beautiful animals with slim waists and long sinewy legs and tails full of character. They were clean and polite, much nicer than the red monkeys of the plains.

During the rains the stream became a rushing torrent, and I did not visit the place too often. There were leeches in the long grass and they would fasten themselves onto my legs and feast on my blood.

But it was always worthwhile tramping through the forest to feast my eyes on the foliage that sprang up in tropical profusion—soft, spongy moss; great staghorn fern on the trunks of trees; mysterious and sometimes evil-looking lilies and orchids, wild dahlias and the climbing convolvulus opening its purple secrets to the morning sun.

And when the rains were over and it was October and the birds were in song again, I could lie in the sun on sweet-smelling grass and gaze up through a pattern of oak leaves into a blind-blue heaven. And I would thank my God for leaves and grass and the smell of things. The smell of mint and myrtle and bruised clover, and the touch of things, the touch of grass and air and sky, the touch of the sky's blueness.

And then after a November hail-storm it was winter and I could not lie on the frostbitten grass. The sound of the stream was the same but I missed the birds; and the grey skies came clutching at my heart and the rain and sleet drove me indoors.

It snowed—the snow lay heavy on the branches of the oak trees and piled up in the culverts—and the grass and the ferns and wild flowers were pressed to sleep beneath a cold white blanket, but the stream flowed on, pushing its way through and under the whiteness, towards another river, towards another spring.

A Marriage of the Waters

In summer the grass on the hills is still a pale yellowish green, tinged with brown, and that is how it remains until the monsoon rains bring new life to everything that subsists on the stony Himalayan soil. And then, for four months, the hills are deep and dark and emerald bright

But the other day, taking a narrow path that left the dry Mussoorie ridge to link up with Pari Tibba (Fairy Hill), I ran across a path of lush green grass, and I knew there had to be water there.

The grass was soft and springy, spotted with the crimson of small, wild strawberries. Delicate maidenhair, my favourite fern, grew from a cluster of moist, glistening rocks. Moving the ferns a little, I discovered the spring, a freshet of clear sparkling water.

I never cease to wonder at the tenacity of water—its ability to make its way through various strata of rock, zigzagging, back tracking, finding space, cunningly discovering faults and fissures in the mountain, and sometimes travelling underground for great distances before emerging into the open. Of course, there's no stopping water. For no matter how tiny that little trickle, it has to go somewhere!

Like this little spring. At first I thought it was too small to go anywhere; that it would dry up at the edge of the path. Then I discovered that the grass remained soft and green for some distance along the verge, and that there was moisture beneath the grass. This wet stretch ended abruptly; but, on looking further, I saw it continued on the other side of the path, after briefly going underground again.

I decided to follow its fortunes as it disappeared beneath a tunnel of tall grass and bracken fern. Slithering down a stony slope, I found myself in a small ravine and there I discovered that my little spring had grown, having been joined by the waters of another spring bubbling up from beneath a path of primroses.

A short distance away, a spotted forktail stood on a rock, surveying this marriage of the waters. His long, forked tail moved slowly up and down. He paid no attention to me, being totally absorbed in the movements of a water spider. A swift peck, and the spider vanished, completing the bird's breakfast. Thirsty, I cupped my hands and drank a little water. So did the forktail. We had a perennial supply of pure water all to ourselves!

There was now a rivulet to follow, and I continued down the ravine until I came to a small pool that was fed not only by my brook (I was already thinking of it as my very own!) but also by a little cascade of water coming down from a rocky ledge. I climbed a little way up the rocks and entered a small cave, in which there was just enough space for crouching down. Water dripped and trickled off its roof and sides. And most wonderful of all, some of these drops created tiny rainbows, for a ray of sunlight had struck through a crevice in the cave roof making the droplets of moisture radiant with all the colours of the spectrum.

When I emerged from the cave, I saw a pair of pine martens drinking at the pool. As soon as they saw me, they were up and away, bounding across the ravine and into the trees.

The brook was now a small stream, but I could not follow it much farther, because the hill went into a steep decline and the water tumbled over large, slippery boulders, becoming a waterfall and then a noisy little torrent as it sped toward the valley.

Climbing up the sides of the ravine to the spur of Pari Tibba, I could see the distant silver of a meandering river and I knew my little stream was destined to become part of it; and that the river would be joined by another that could be seen slipping over the far horizon, and that their combined waters would enter the great Ganga or Ganges farther downstream.

This mighty river would, in turn, wander over the rich alluvial plains of northern India, finally flowing into the ocean near the Bay of Bengal.

And the ocean, what was it but another droplet in the universe, in the greater scheme of things? No greater than the glistening drop of water that helped start it all, where the grass grows greener around my little spring on the mountain.

~

The Leopard

I first saw the leopard when I was crossing the small stream at the bottom of the hill. The ravine was so deep that for most of the day it remained in shadow. This encouraged many birds and animals to emerge from cover during the hours of daylight. Few people ever passed that way; only milkmen and charcoal-burners from the surrounding villages. As a result, the ravine had become a little haven of wildlife, one of the few natural sanctuaries left near Mussoorie.

Below my cottage was a forest of oak and maple and Himalayan rhododendron. A narrow path twisted its way down through the trees, over an open ridge where red sorrel grew wild, and then down steeply through a tangle of wild raspberries, creeping vines and the slender ringal bamboo. At the bottom of the hill, the path led on to a grassy verge, surrounded by wild dog roses. It is surprising how closely the flora of the lower Himalaya, between 5,000 to 8,000 feet, resembles that of the English countryside. The streams ran close by the verge, tumbling over smooth pebbles, over rocks worn yellow with age, on its way to the plains and to the little Song river and finally to the sacred Ganga.

When I first discovered the stream, it was early April and the wild roses were flowering, small white blossoms lying in clusters. There were still yellow and blue primroses on the hill slopes, saxifrage growing in the rocks, and an occasional late-flowering rhododendron providing a splash of crimson against the dark green of the hill.

I walked down to the stream almost every day, after I had done two or three hours of writing. I had lived in the cities far too long, and had returned to the hills to renew myself, physically and mentally, to get rid of some of the surplus flesh that had gathered about my waist, and, if possible, to write a novel.

Nearly every morning, and sometimes during the day, I heard the cry of the barking deer. And in the evening, walking through the forest, I disturbed parties of kaleej pheasant. The birds went gliding down the ravine on open, motionless wings. I saw pine martens and a handsome red fox; I recognized the footprints of a bear.

As I had not come to take anything from the jungle, the birds and animals soon 'grew accustomed to my face', as Mr Henry Higgins would have said. Or possibly they recognized my footsteps. After some time, my approach did not disturb them. A spotted forktail, which at first used to fly away, now remained perched on a boulder in the middle of the stream while I got across by means of other boulders only a few yards away. The forktail's plumage blended with the rocks and running water, so that the bird was difficult to spot at a distance, but the white 'Cross of St. Andrew' across its back eventually gave it away. Its tail moved gently up and down, in a slow, elegant movement, and its sharp, creaky call followed me up the hillside.

The langurs in the oak and rhododendron trees, who would at first go leaping through the branches at my approach, now watched me with some curiosity as they munched the tender green shoots of the oak. The young ones scuffled and wrestled like boys, while their parents groomed each other's coats, stretching themselves out on the sunlit hillside. But one evening, as I passed, I heard them chattering in the trees, and I was not the cause of their excitement.

As I crossed the stream and began climbing the hill, the grunting and chattering increased, as though the langurs were trying to warn me of some hidden danger. A shower of pebbles came rattling down the steep hillside, and I looked up to see a sinewy orange-gold leopard poised on a rock about twenty feet above me.

It was not looking towards me, but had its head thrust attentively forward in the direction of the ravine. But it must have sensed my presence, because slowly it turned its head and looked down at me. It seemed a little puzzled at my presence there; and when, to give myself courage, I clapped my hands sharply, the leopard sprang away into the thickets, making absolutely no sound as it melted into the shadows.

I had disturbed the animal in its quest for food. But a little later I heard the quickening cry of a barking deer as it fled through the forest; the hunt was still on.

The leopard, like other members of the cat family, is nearing extinction in India, and I was surprised to find one so close to Mussoorie. Probably the deforestation that had been taking place in the surrounding hills had driven the deer into this green valley; and the leopard, naturally, had followed.

It was some weeks before I saw the leopard again, although I was often made aware of its presence. A dry, rasping cough sometimes gave it away. At times I felt almost certain that I was being followed. And once, when I was late getting home, and the brief twilight gave way to a dark, moonless night, I was startled by a family of porcupines running about in a clearing. I looked around nervously and saw two bright eyes staring at me from a thicket. I stood still, my heart banging away against my ribs. Then the eyes danced away, and I realized that they were only fireflies.

In May and June, when the hills were brown and dry, it was always cool and green near the stream, where ferns and maidenhair and long grasses continued to thrive. Downstream I found a small pool where I could bathe, and a cave with water dripping from the roof, the water spangled gold and silver in the shafts of sunlight that pushed through the slits in the cave roof. 'He maketh me to lie down in green pastures; he leadeth me beside still waters.' Perhaps David had discovered a similar paradise when he wrote those words; perhaps I too would write good words. The hill station's summer visitors had not discovered this haven of wild and green things, I was beginning to feel that the place belonged to me, that dominion was mine.

The stream had at least one other regular visitor, the spotted forktail, and though it did not fly away at my approach, it became restless if I stayed too long, and then it would move from boulder to boulder uttering a long complaining cry. I spent an afternoon trying to discover the bird's nest, which I was certain contained her young, because I had seen the parent bird carrying grubs in her bill. The problem was that when the bird flew upstream I had difficulty in following her rapidly enough, as the rocks were sharp and slippery. Eventually I decorated myself with bracken fronds, and, slowly making my way upstream, hid myself in the hollow stump of a tree, at a spot where the forktail often disappeared. I had no wish to rob the bird of its young; I was simply curious to see its home.

By crouching down, I was able to command a view of a small stretch of the stream and the sides of the ravine; but I had done little to deceive the forktail, who continued to object strongly to my presence so near her home. I summoned up my reserves of patience, and sat perfectly still for about ten minutes, when the forktail quietened down. Out of sight, out of mind! But where had *she* gone? Probably into the walls of the ravine where, I felt sure, she was guarding her nest. So I decided on trying to take her by surprise, and jumped up like a jack-in-the-box, in time to see—not the forktail on her doorstep, but the leopard, bounding away with a grunt of surprise! Two urgent springs and it had crossed the stream and plunged into the forest.

Needless to say, I was as astonished as the leopard, and forgot all about the forktail and her nest. Had the leopard been following me again? I decided against this possibility. Only man-eaters follow humans, and, so far as I knew, there had never been a man-eater in the vicinity of Mussoorie.

During the monsoon the stream became a rushing torrent, bushes and small trees were swept away, and the friendly murmur of the water became a threatening boom. I did not visit too often, but it was always worthwhile tramping through the forest to feast my eyes on the foliage that sprang up in tropical profusion—soft, spongy moss; great stag-ferns on the trunks of trees; mysterious-looking lilies and orchids; wild dahlias, and the climbing convolvulus opening its purple secrets to the morning sun.

One day I found the remains of a barking deer which had been partially eaten. I wondered why the leopard had not hidden the remains of his meal, and decided that it must have been disturbed while eating. Then, climbing the hill, I met a party of shikaris resting beneath the oaks. They asked me if I had seen a leopard. I said I had not. They said they knew there was a leopard in the forest. Leopard-skins, they told me, were selling in Delhi at over a thousand rupees each! Of course there was a ban on the export of skins, but they gave me to understand that there were ways and means...

I thanked them for their information and walked on, feeling uneasy and disturbed.

The shikaris had seen the carcass of the deer, and they had seen the leopard's pug-marks, and they kept coming to the forest. Almost every evening I heard their guns banging away; for they were ready to fire at almost anything.

'There's a leopard about,' they always told me 'You should carry a gun.'

'I don't have one,' I said.

There were fewer birds to be seen, and even the langurs had moved on. The red fox did not show itself; and the pine martens, who had become quite bold, now dashed into hiding at my approach. The smell of one human is like the smell of any other.

And then the rains were over and it was October and I could lie in the sun, on sweet-smelling grass, and gaze up through a pattern of oak leaves into a blinding-blue heaven. And I would praise God for leaves and grass and the smell of things, the smell of mint and bruised clover, and the touch of things, the touch of grass and air and sky, the touch of the sky's blueness.

I thought no more of the men. I had seen them as their species *Homo Sapiens*, and not as individual personalities. My attitude to them was similar to the attitude of the denizens of the forest. They were men, unpredictable, and to be avoided if possible.

On the other side of the ravine rose Pari Tibba, Hill of the Fairies, a bleak, scrub-covered hill, where no one lived. It was said that in the previous century Englishmen had tried building their houses on the hill, but that the area had always attracted lightning, due either to the hill's situation or to its mineral deposits; and that, after several houses had been struck by lightning, the settlers had moved on to the next hill, where the hill station now stands. To the hill-men it is Pari Tibba, haunted by the spirits of a pair of ill-fated lovers who perished there in a storm; to others it is known as Burnt Hill, because of its scarred and stunted trees.

One day, after crossing the stream, I climbed Pari Tibba—a stiff undertaking, because there was no path to the top and I had to scramble up a precipitous rock-face with the help of rocks and roots that were apt to come away in my groping hand. But at the top was a plateau with a few pine trees, their upper branches catching the wind and humming softly. There I found the ruins of what must have been the houses of the first settlers—just a few piles of rubble, now overgrown with weeds, sorrel, dandelions and nettles.

As I walked through the roofless ruins, I was struck by the silence that surrounded me, the absence of birds and animals, the sense of complete desolation. The silence was so absolute that it seemed to be shouting in my ears. But there was something else of which I was becoming increasingly aware: the strong feline odour of one of the cat family.

I paused and looked about. I was alone. There was no movement of dry leaf or loose stone. The ruins were for the most part open to the sky. Their rotting rafters had collapsed and joined together to form a low passage like the entrance to a mine; and this dark cavern seemed to lead down into the ground.

The smell was stronger when I approached this spot, so I stopped again and waited there, wondering if I had discovered the lair of the leopard, wondering if the animal was now at rest after a night's hunt. Perhaps it crouched there in the dark, watching me, recognizing me, knowing me as the man who walked alone in the forest without a weapon. I like to think that he was there, that he knew me, and that he acknowledged my visit in the friendliest way: by ignoring me altogether.

Perhaps I had made him confident—too confident, too careless, too trusting of the human in his midst. I did not venture any further; I was not out of my mind. I did not seek physical contact, or even another glimpse of that beautiful sinewy body, springing from rock to rock. It was his trust I wanted, and I think he gave it to me.

But did the leopard, trusting one man, make the mistake of bestowing his trust on others? Did I, by casting out all fear—my own fear, and the leopard's protective fear—leave him defenceless?

Because next day, coming up the path from the stream, shouting and beating drums, were the shikaris. They had a long bamboo pole across their shoulders; and slung from the pole, feet up, head down, was the lifeless body of the leopard. It had been shot in the neck and in the head.

'We told you there was a leopard!' they shouted.

I walked home through the silent forest. It was very silent, almost as though the birds and animals knew that their trust had been violated.

I remembered the lines of a poem by D.H. Lawrence; and as I climbed the steep and lonely path to my home, the words beat out their rhythm in my mind: 'There was room in the world for a mountain-lion and me.'

~

A Place of Power

On the first clear day of a long-ago October, I visited the pine-knoll some distance from my cottage, my place of peace and power.

It was months since I had last been there. Trips to the plains, a crisis in my affairs, involvements with other people and their troubles, and an entire monsoon, had come between me and the grassy, pine-topped slope facing the eternal snows of the Himalaya. Now I tramped through autumn foliage—tall ferns, sky-blue commelina, wild balsam, purple and orange mushrooms, and bushes festooned with flowering convolvulus—crossed a stream by means of a little bridge of stones, and climbed the steep hill to the pine-knoll.

I felt that when the trees saw me, they made as if to turn in my direction. A puff of wind came across the valley from the distant snows. A long-tailed blue magpie took alarm and flew noisily out of an oak tree. The cicadas were suddenly silent. But yes, the trees remembered me. They bowed gently in the breeze and beckoned me nearer, welcoming me home. Three pines, a straggling oak and a wild cherry. I went among them, acknowledging their greeting with a touch of my hand against their trunks—the cherry's smooth and polished; the pine's patterned and whorled; the oak's rough, gnarled and full of experience. He has been there the longest, and the wind has beat his upper branches and twisted a few, so that he looks shaggy and undistinguished. But, like the philosopher who is careless about his dress and appearance, the oak has secret, hidden wisdom. He has been here longer than anyone else and he has learnt the art of survival. In a world where entire forests are being swept away, that is quite an achievement.

While the oak and the pine are much older than me, and have been here since the turn of the century, the cherry tree is exactly ten years old. I know, because I planted it.

One day I had this cherry seed in my hand, and on an impulse I thrust it into the soft earth and then went away and forgot all about it. A few months later I found a tiny cherry tree in the long grass. I did not expect it to survive. But the following year it was two feet tall. And then some goats ate the young leaves and a grasscutter's scythe injured the stem, and I was sure the tree would wither away. But it renewed itself, sprang up even faster. In three years, it was a healthy growing tree, about five feet tall.

I left the hills for a few years—forced by circumstances to make a living in the plains—but this time I did not forget the cherry tree. I thought about it quite often, even sent it telepathic messages of love and encouragement! And when, last year, I returned in the autumn, my heart did a somersault when I found the tree sprinkled with pale pink blossom. (The wild Himalayan cherry flowers in November and not in the spring.) Later, when the fruit was ripe, the tree was visited by finches, tits, bulbuls and other small birds, all coming to feast on the sour red cherries.

In the summer I spent a night on the pine-knoll, sleeping on the grass beneath the cherry tree. I lay awake for hours, listening to the chatter of the stream, the singing of crickets and the occasional chuckle of some night bird; and watching, through the branches overhead, the stars permanent and impartial in the sky and I felt the power of sky and earth, and the power of a small cherry seed.

And so, when the rains are over, this is where I come, that I might feel the peace and power of this magic place. It's a big world, and momentous events are taking place all the time. But this is where I have seen it all happen.

~~~

My Trees in the Himalayas

Living in a cottage at 7,000 feet in the Garhwal Himalayas, I am fortunate to have a big window that opens out on the forest so that the trees are almost within my reach. If I jumped, I could land quite neatly in the arms of an oak or horse chestnut. I have never made that leap, but the big langurs—silver-gray monkeys with long, swishing tails—often spring from the trees onto my corrugated tin roof, making enough noise to frighten all the birds away.

Standing on its own outside my window is a walnut tree, and truly this is a tree for all seasons. In winter the branches are bare, but beautifully smooth and rounded. In spring each limb produces a bright green spear of new growth, and by midsummer the entire tree is in leaf. Toward the end of the monsoon the walnuts, encased in their green jackets, have reached maturity. When the jackets begin to split, you can see the hard brown shells of the nuts, and inside each shell is the delicious meat itself.

Every year this tree gives me a basket of walnuts. But last year the nuts were disappearing one by one, and I was at a loss as to who had been taking them. Could it have been the milkman's small son? He was an inveterate tree climber, but he was usually to be found on the oak trees, gathering fodder for his herd. He admitted that his cows had enjoyed my dahlias, which they had eaten the previous week, but he stoutly denied having fed them walnuts.

It wasn't the woodpecker either. He was out there every day, knocking furiously against the bark of the tree, trying to pry an insect out of a narrow crack, but he was strictly non-vegetarian. As for the langurs, they ate my geraniums but did not care for the walnuts.

The nuts seemed to disappear early in the morning while I was still in bed, so one day I surprised everyone, including myself, by getting up before sunrise. I was just in time to catch the culprit climbing out of the walnut tree. She was an old woman who sometimes came to cut grass on the hillside. Her face was as wrinkled as the walnuts she so fancied, but her arms and legs were very sturdy.

'And how many walnuts did you gather today, Grandmother?' I asked.

'Just two,' she said with a giggle, offering them to me on her open palm. I accepted one, and thus encouraged, she climbed higher into the tree and helped herself to the remaining nuts. It was impossible for me to object. I was taken with admiration for her agility. She must have been twice my age, but I knew I could never get up that tree. To the victor, the spoils!

Unlike the prized walnuts, the horse chestnuts are inedible. Even the rhesus monkeys throw them away in disgust. But the tree itself is a friendly one, especially in summer when it is in full leaf. The lightest breeze makes the leaves break into conversation, and their rustle is a cheerful sound. The spring flowers of the horse chestnut look like candelabra, and when the blossoms fall, they carpet the hillside with their pale pink petals.

The deodar stands erect and dignified and does not bend with the wind. In spring the new leaves, or needles, are a tender green, while during the monsoon the tiny young cones spread like blossoms in the dark green folds of the branches. The deodar enjoys the company of its own kind: where one deodar grows, there will be others. A walk in a deodar forest is awe inspiring—surrounded on all sides by these great sentinels of the mountains, you feel as though the trees themselves are on the march.

I walk among the trees outside my window often, acknowledging their presence with a touch of my hand against their trunks. The oak has been there the longest, and the wind has bent its upper branches and twisted a few so that it looks shaggy and undistinguished. But it is a good tree for the privacy of birds. Sometimes it seems completely uninhabited until there is a whining sound, as of a helicopter approaching, and a party of long-tailed blue magpies flies across the forest glade.

Most of the pines near my home are on the next hillside. But there is a small Himalayan blue a little way below the cottage, and sometimes I sit beneath it to listen to the wind playing softly in its branches.

When I open the window at night, there is almost always something to listen to—the mellow whistle of a pygmy owlet, or the sharp cry of a barking deer. Sometimes, if I am lucky, I will see the moon coming up over the next mountain, and two distant deodars in perfect silhouette.

Some night sounds outside my window remain strange and mysterious. Perhaps they are the sounds of the trees themselves, stretching their limbs in the dark, shifting a little, flexing their fingers, whispering to one another. These great trees of the mountains. I feel they know me well, as I watch them and listen to their secrets, happy to rest my head beneath their outstretched arms.

Birdsong in the Hills

Bird-watching is more difficult in the hills than on the plains. It is hard to spot many birds against the dark trees of the varying shades of the hillside. There are few birds who remain silent for long, however, and one learns of their presence from their calls or songs. Birdsong is with you wherever you go in the Himalayas, from the foothills to the treeline; and it is often easier to recognize a bird from its voice than from its colourful but brief appearance.

The barbet is one of those birds which is heard more often than it is seen. It has a monotonous, far-reaching call, which carries for about a mile. These birds love listening to their own voices, and often two or three will answer each other from different trees, each trying to outdo the rest in a shrill shouting match. Some people like the barbet's call and consider it both striking and pleasant. Some just find it striking.

Hodgson's grey-headed flycatcher-warbler is the long name that ornithologists, in their infinite wisdom, have given to a very small bird. This tiny warbler is heard, if not seen, more often than any other bird throughout the western Himalayas. Its voice is heard in every second tree, and yet there are few who can say what it looks like. Its song (if you can call it that) is not very tuneful and puts me in mind of the notice that sometimes appeared in saloons out West: 'The audience is requested not to throw things at the pianist. He is doing his best.'

Our little warbler does his best, incessantly emitting four or five unmusical, but nevertheless joyful and penetrating notes.

Another tiny bird heard more often than it is seen is the green-backed tit, a smart little fellow about the size of a sparrow. It utters a sharp, rather metallic, but not unpleasant call which sounds like '*kiss me, kiss me, kiss me*'.

A real songster is the grey-winged ouzel, found here in the Garhwal hills. Throughout the early summer he makes the wooded hillsides ring with a melody that Nelson Eddy would have been proud of. Joining in sometimes with a sweet song of its own is the green pigeon. As though to mock their arias, the laughing thrushes, who are exponents of heavy rock, give vent to some weird calls of their own.

Nightjars are birds that lie concealed during the day in shady woods, coming out at dusk on silent wings to hunt for insects. The nightjar has a huge, frog-like mouth, but is best recognized by its unusual call—'*tonk-tonk, tonk-tonk*'—a noise like that produced by striking a plank with a hammer.

When I came to live in the hills, it was the song of the Himalayan whistling thrush that first caught my attention. It is a song that never fails to enchant me. The bird starts with a hesitant whistle, as though trying out the tune; then, confident of the melody, it bursts into full song, a crescendo of sweet notes and variations ringing clearly across the hillside. Suddenly the song breaks off, right in the middle of a cadenza, and I am left wondering what happened to make the bird stop. Nothing really, because the song is taken up again a few moments later.

It was a boy from the next village who acquainted me with the legend of the whistling thrush, or the kastura or kaljit, as the hill-men call the bird. According to the story, the young god Krishna fell asleep near a stream, and while he slept a small boy made off with Krishna's famous flute. Upon waking and finding his flute gone, Krishna was so angry that he changed the culprit into a bird. But having once played on the flute, the boy had learnt bits and pieces of the god's enchanting music. And so he continued, in his disrespectful way, to play the music of the gods, only stopping now and then (as the whistling thrush does) when he couldn't remember the tune.

The wild cherry tree, which grows just outside my bedroom window, attracts a great many small birds, both when it is in flower and when it is in fruit.

When it is covered with small pink blossoms, the most common visitor is a little yellow-backed sunbird, who emits a squeaky little song as she flits from branch to branch. She extracts the nectar from the blossoms with her long tubular tongue.

Amongst other visitors are the flycatchers, gorgeous birds, especially the paradise flycatcher with its long white tail and ghostlike flight. Basically an insect eater, it likes fruit for dessert, and will visit the tree when the cherries are ripening. While moving along the boughs of the tree, they utter twittering notes, with occasional louder calls, and now and then the male breaks into a sweet little song, thus justifying the name of shah bulbul (king of the nightingales), by which he is known in northern India.

The Song of the Whistling Thrush

I had been in the hills for only a few days when I heard the song of the Himalayan whistling thrush. I did not see the bird that day. It kept to the deep shadows of the ravine below the old stone cottage. I was sitting at the window, gazing out at the new leaves on the walnut and wild pear trees. All was still; the wind was at peace with itself, the mountains brooded massively under a darkening sky. Then, emerging from the depths of the forest like a dark sweet secret came the indescribably beautiful call of the whistling thrush.

At first the bird was heard but never seen. Then one day I found the whistling thrush perched on the broken garden fence. He was a glistening deep purple, his shoulders flecked with white; he had sturdy black legs and a strong yellow beak; rather a dapper fellow, who would have looked well in a top hat, dancing with Fred Astaire. When he saw me coming down the path, he uttered a sharp 'kreeee'— unexpectedly harsh when one remembered his singing—and flew off into the shadowed ravine.

But as the months passed, he grew used to my presence and became less shy. One of my drain pipes had blocked, resulting in an overflow of rainwater and a small permanent puddle under the stone steps. This became the whistling thrush's favourite bathing-place. On sultry summer afternoons, while I was taking a siesta upstairs, I would hear the bird flapping about in the rainwater pool. A little later, refreshed and sunning himself on the tin roof, he would treat me to a little concert, performed, I cannot help feeling, especially for my benefit.

It wasn't long before the thrush was joined by a female, who was exactly like him. (In fact, I have never been able to tell one from the other.) The pair did not sing together but preferred to give solo performances, waiting for each other to finish before bursting into a song. When, as sometimes happened, they started off together, the effect was not so pleasing to my human ear.

These were love-calls, no doubt, and it wasn't long before the pair were making forays into the rocky ledges of the ravine, looking for a suitable nesting site; but a couple of years were to pass before I saw any of their progeny.

After almost two years in the hills, I came to realize that the thrushes were birds 'for all seasons'. They were liveliest in midsummer; but even in the depths of winter, with snow lying on the ground, they would suddenly start singing, as they flitted from pine to oak to naked chestnut.

As I write, there is a strong wind rushing through the trees and bustling about in the chimney, while distant thunder threatens a summer storm. Undismayed, the whistling thrushes are calling to each other as they roam the wind-threshed forest. At other times I have heard them clearly above the sound of rushing water. And sometimes they leave the vicinity of the cottage and fly down to the stream, half a mile away, sending me little messages on the wind. Down there, they are busy snapping up snails and insects, the chief items on their menu.

Whistling thrushes usually nest on rocky ledges, near water; but my overtures of friendship may give my visitors other ideas. Recently I was away from Mussoorie for about a fortnight. When I returned, I was about to open my window when I noticed a large bundle of ferns, lichen, grass, mud and moss balanced outside on the window ledge.

Peering through the glass, I was able to recognize this untidy basket as a nest. Could such tidy birds make such an untidy nest? Indeed they could, because they arrived and proved their ownership a few minutes later.

Of course that meant I couldn't open the window again. (The nest would have gone over the ledge, if I had.) Fortunately, the room has another window, and I kept this one open to let in sunshine, fresh air, the music of birds and cicadas and the call of the ever-welcome postman.

And now, this very day, three pink, freckled eggs lie in the cup of moss that forms the nursery in this jumble of a nest. The parent birds, both male and female, come and go, bustling about very efficiently, fully prepared for the great day that's coming about a fortnight hence.

One small thought occurs to me. The song of one thrush was bright and cheerful. The song of two thrushes was loud and joyful. But won't a choir of *five* whistling thrushes be a little too much for a solitary writer trying to concentrate at his typewriter? Will I have to make a choice between writing and listening to the birds? Will I one day have to hand the cottage over to the denizens of the forest? Well, we shall have to wait and see. If readers do not hear from me again, they will know whom to blame!

All About My Walkabouts

All my life I've been a walking person. Up to this day, I have neither owned nor driven a car, bus, tractor, airplane, motorcycle, truck, or steamroller. Forced to make a choice, I would as soon drive a steamroller, because of its slow but solid progress and unhurried finality. And also because other vehicles don't try hustling steamrollers off the road.

For a brief period in my early teens I had a bicycle, until I rode into a bullock cart and ruined my new cycle. The bullocks panicked and ran away with the cart while the furious cart driver was giving me a lecture on road sense. I have never bumped into a bullock cart while walking.

My earliest memories are of a place called Jamnagar, a small port on the west coast of India, then part of a princely state. My father was an English tutor to several young Indian princes and princesses. This was where my walking really began, because Jamnagar was full of spacious palaces, lawns, and gardens. By the time I was four, I was exploring much of this territory on my own, with the result that I encountered my first snake. Instead of striking me dead as snakes are supposed to do, it allowed me to pass.

Living as it did so close to the ground, and sensitive to every footfall, it must have known instinctively that I presented no threat, that I was just another small creature discovering the use of his legs. Envious of the snake's swift gliding movements, I went indoors and tried crawling about on my belly. But I wasn't much good at it. Legs were better.

My father's schoolroom and our own residence were located on the grounds of one of the older palaces, which was full of turrets stairways and mysterious dark passages. Right on top of the building I discovered a glass-covered room, each pane of glass stained with a different colour. This room fascinated me as I could, by turn, look through the panes of glass at a green or rose-pink or orange or deep indigo world. It was nice to be able to decide for oneself what colour the world should be!

My father took his duties seriously and taught me to read and write long before I started attending a regular school. However, it would be true to say that I first learned to read upside down. is happened because I would sit on a stool in front of the three princesses, watching them read and write, and so the view I had of their books was an upside-down view. I still read that way occasionally, especially when a book becomes boring.

There was no boredom in the palace grounds. We were situated in the middle of a veritable jungle of a garden, where marigolds and cosmos grew, rampant in the long grass. An old disused well was the home of countless pigeons, their gentle cooing by day contrasting with the shrill cries of the brainfever bird (the hawk-cuckoo) at night. 'How very hot it's getting!' the bird seems to say. And then, in a rising crescendo, 'We feel it! *We feel it!* WE FEEL IT!'

Walking along a nearby beach, collecting seashells, I got into the habit of staring hard at the ground, a habit which has remained with me all my life. Apart from helping my thought processes, it also results in my picking up odd objects—coins, keys, broken bangles, marbles, pens, bits of crockery, pretty stones, feathers, ladybirds, seashells, snail shells! Not to speak of old nails and horseshoes. Looking at my collection of miscellaneous objects picked up on these walks, my friends insist that I must be using a metal detector. But it's only because I keep my nose to the ground like a bloodhound.

Occasionally, of course, this habit results in my walking some way past my destination (if I happen to have one). And why not? It simply means discovering a new and different destination, sights and sounds that I might not have experienced had I ended my walk exactly where it was supposed to end. And I am not looking at the ground *all* the time. Sensitive like the snake to approaching footfalls, I look up from time to time to take note of the faces of passers-by, just in case they have something interesting to say.

A bird singing in a bush or tree has my immediate attention, so does any familiar flower or plant, particularly if it grows in an unusual place such as a crack in a wall or rooftop, or in a yard full of junk—where once I found a rosebush blooming on the roof of an old, abandoned Ford car.

I like to think that I invented the zigzag walk. Tiring of walking in straight lines, or on roads that led directly to a destination, I took to going off at tangents—taking sudden unfamiliar turnings, wandering down narrow alleyways, following cart tracks or paths through fields instead of the main roads, and in general making the walk as complicated as possible.

In this way I saw much more than I would normally have seen. Here a temple, there a mosque; now an old church; a railway siding; follow the railway line; here's a pond full of buffaloes, there a peacock preening itself under a tamarind tree; and now I'm in a field of mustard, and soon I'm walking along a canal bank, and the canal leads me back into the town, and I follow the line of the mango trees until I am home.

The adventure is not in arriving, it's the on-the-way experience. It is not the expected; it's the surprise. You are not choosing what you shall see in the world, but are giving the world an even chance to see you.

It's like drawing lines from star to star in the night sky, not forgetting many dim, shy, out-of-the-way stars, which are full of possibilities. The first turning to the left, the next to the right! I am still on my zigzag way, pursuing the diagonal between reason and the heart.

~

The Trail to the Bank

Local residents have got fed up with offering me lifts on the road to our hilltop bank and post office. They typically drive up the steep road to Landour in third (or is it fourth?) gear, see me plodding along on foot, and out of the goodness of their hearts, stop and open the door for me.

Although I hate to disappoint them, I close the door, thank them profusely, and insist that I am enjoying my walk. They don't believe me, naturally; but with a shrug, the drivers get into gear again and take off, although sometimes they have difficulty getting started, the hill being very steep. As I don't wish to insult them by reaching the bank first, I sit on the parapet wall and make encouraging sounds until they finally take off. Then I renew my leisurely walk up the hill, taking note of the fact that the wild geraniums and periwinkles have begun to flower and that the whistling thrushes are nesting under the culvert over which those very cars pass everyday.

~

Most people, car drivers anyway, think I'm a little eccentric. So be it. I probably am eccentric! But having come to the Himalayan foothills over twenty-five years ago in order to enjoy walking among them, I am not about to stop now, just because everyone else has stopped walking. The hills are durable in their attractions, and my legs have proved durable too, so why should we not continue together as before?

The friends who once walked beside me now have their shiny new cars or capacious vans, and seldom emerge from them, unless it be to seek refreshment at some wayside tea shop or cafe.

Now, I'm no fitness freak. I don't jog either. If I did, I would almost certainly miss the latest wild flower to appear on the hillside, and I would not be able to stop awhile and talk to other people on the road—villagers with their milk and vegetables, all-weather postmen, cheeky schoolchildren, inquisitive tourists—or to exchange greetings with cats, dogs, stray cows and runaway mules.

Runaway mules are friendly creatures except towards their owners. I chat with the owners too, when they come charging up the road. I try to put them in good humour, so as to save the mules from a beating.

Most of the people I have mentioned are walkers from necessity. Those who walk for pleasure grow fewer by the day.

I don't mean long-distance trekkers or high-altitude climbers, who are almost professional in their approach to roads and mountains. I mean people such as myself who are not great athletes but who enjoy sauntering through the woods on a frosty morning, leaving the main road and slithering downhill into a bed of ferns, or following a mountain stream until you reach the small spring in the rocks where it begins… But, no—everyone must have a destination in mind, for this is the age of destinations, be it the Taj Mahal, the casino at Cannes, or the polar icecap. I glanced at a bestselling book of records the other day, and my eye lighted upon an entry stating that somebody's grandmother had knitted a scarf that was over twenty miles long. Where was it going, I wondered, and who would be wearing it? The book didn't say. It was just another destination, another 'first' to be recorded.

Personally I prefer people who come in second. I feel safer with them.

It takes a car less than five minutes up the hill to get to the bank. It takes me roughly twenty-five minutes. But there is never a dull minute. Apart from having interesting animal and human encounters, there are the changes that occur almost daily on the hill slopes: the ferns turning from green to gold, the Virginia creepers becoming a dark crimson, horse chestnuts falling to the ground.

On today's walk I spot a redstart, come down early from higher altitudes to escape the snow. He whistles cheerfully in a medlar tree. Wild ducks are flying south. There they go, high over the valley, heading for the lakes and marshlands.

If there's no one on the road, and I feel like a little diversion, I can always sing. I don't sing well, but there's no one to hear me except for a startled woodpecker, so I can go into my Nelson Eddy routine, belting out the songs my childhood gramophone taught me. 'Tramp, Tramp,

Tramp', 'Stouthearted Men', 'Song of the Open Road!' No one writes marching songs now, so I have to rely on the old ones.

Above me the blue sky, around me the green forest, below me the dusty plains.

~

Presently I am at Char-Dukaan—'Four Shops'—and the bank and post office.

Letters posted, I enter the bank, to be greeted effusively by the manager, Vishal Ohri—not because I have come to make a large deposit, but because he is that rarity among bank managers, a nature lover! When he learns that I have just seen the first redstart of the winter, he grows excited and insists that I take him to it. As we are nearing the office tea break, he sets off with me down the road and, to our mutual satisfaction and delight, the redstart is still in the medlar tree, putting on a special performance seemingly for our benefit.

The manager returns to his office, happy to be working at this remote hilltop branch. Both staff and customers will find him the most understanding and sympathetic of managers today, for has he not just seen the first white-capped redstart to fly into Landour for the winter? That's as good a 'first' as any in those books of records.

As long as there are nature-loving bank managers, I muse on my way home, there's still hope for this little old world. And for bank depositors, too!

~

When Cicadas Chorus

The barbet is one of those birds which are heard more often than they are seen. Summer visitors to Shimla, Mussoorie and other north-Indian hill resorts will be familiar with its monotonous, far-reaching call: *'pee-ho, pee-ho'*. It keeps to the tops of high trees, where it is not easily distinguished from the foliage.

Barbets love listening to their own voices, and often two or three birds answer each other from different trees, each trying to outdo the other in a shrill shouting match. Although most birds are noisy during the mating season, barbets are noisy all the year round.

Up here in the Garhwal Himalayas, there is a legend that the bird is the reincarnation of a moneylender who died of grief at the unjust termination of a law-suit. Eternally his plaintive cries rise to the heaven: *'unn-ee-ow, unn-ee-ow!'* which means 'injustice, injustice!' So the barbet's call can be interpreted in various ways. To me it always sounds like: *'pakaro, pakaro!'* or 'catch him, catch him!' And of course there's a story about how a barbet helped to catch a thief.

Now that the monsoon rains are here, the occasional snake, flooded out of its home, makes its appearance on the road or hillsides.

Most of the snakes up here are perfectly harmless, carrying only enough venom to paralyze their natural prey, which consists of frogs, rats, earthworms, small birds and smaller snakes.

Recently, I saw two pretty green and brown snakes on the hillside. I have no idea what they are called; I cannot pretend to be an expert on recognizing all the denizens of the wild, and never cease to wonder at the sharp-eyed observations of well-known naturalists who can tell a bullfinch from a chaffinch at a distance of 60 metres, or distinguish a pit viper from a saw-scaled viper in one hurried glance. I suspect some of them are just showing off. The experts, I mean. Snakes do not show off.

However, as regards the snakes on my hillside, I can say with certainty that one is brown and one is green, and personally I prefer the green one.

The postman, who almost trod on it the other day, wanted it killed; but I quoted the sayings of Buddha, Krishna and Confucius, and persuaded him to let it live. In some former incarnation it might well have been related to us, I said. Perhaps an aunt or distant cousin. Although he wasn't quite convinced (and nor was I), but the conversation gave the snake enough time to slip away. The postman no longer enters the gate, but leaves my letters in a hole in the wall.

During monsoon, our insect musicians are roused to their greatest activity. At dusk, the air seems to tinkle and murmur to their music. To the shrilling of the grasshopper is added the staccato notes of the crickets, while in the grass and on the trees, a myriad lesser artists are producing a variety of sounds.

As musicians, the cicadas are a class of their own. All through the monsoon, their screaming chorus rings through the forest. A shower of rain, far from dampening their ardour, only rouses them to a deafening crescendo of effort.

As with most insect musicians, the males do the performing, while the females remain silent. This moved one chauvinist Greek poet to exclaim: 'Happy the cicadas, for they have voiceless wives!' To which I would respond by saying: 'Pity the female cicadas, for they have singing husbands!'

Probably the most familiar and homely of insect singers are the crickets. I won't attempt to go into detail on how the cricket produces its music, except to say that its louder notes are produced by a rapid vibration of the wings, the right wing usually working over the left, the edge of one acting on the file of the other to produce a shrill, long-sustained note, like a violinist gone mad. Cicadas, on the other hand, use their abdominal muscles to produce their sound.

One of our best-known crickets is a large black fellow who lives underground and rarely comes to earth by day, except when the rains flood him out of his burrow. But when night falls, he sits on his doorstep and pours out his soul in strident song. This troubadour's name is as impressive as his sound—*Brachytrypes portentosus*.

The mole cricket is a genius by itself. Mole crickets are tillers of the soil. They use their powerful forelimbs for shovelling up the earth and their hard heads for butting into it.

Notwithstanding its earthly occupations, the mole cricket is sometimes moved to music. But as he repeats his note—a solemn deep-toned chirp (more burp than chirp) about a hundred times a minute—the performance can be monotonous.

The cone-headed katydids are probably the most notable performers. Katydids are trim, slender insects, much in evidence in the fresh green grass of the monsoon. In the fields, their loud shrill notes may be heard by day and night. Sometimes one of them comes into the house and treats us to a sudden outburst of high-pitched fiddling. In a room, it can be quite deafening, and the sound is always most difficult to locate—it seems to come from everywhere!

And finally there are the tree crickets, a band of willing artistes who commence their performance at dusk. Their sounds are familiar, but it is difficult to see the musicians. A tap on the bush upon which one of them sits will bring an immediate end to the performance.

I wish the tree crickets would duet, in the manner of Nelson Eddy and Jeanette Macdonald. But it is only the males who sing, in order to please their consorts.

And speaking of Nelson Eddy, this is the 100th anniversary of his birth. A fine baritone, unjustly neglected. When I listen to his songs (on tape or disk), the crickets and cicadas maintain a respectful silence. I'm sure they are listening.

Sounds I Like to Hear

All night the rain has been drumming on the corrugated tin roof. There has been no storm, no thunder, just the steady swish of a tropical downpour. It helps one to lie awake; at the same time, it doesn't keep one from sleeping.

It is a good sound to read by—the rain outside, the quiet within—and, although tin roofs are given to springing unaccountable leaks, there is in general a feeling of being untouched by, and yet in touch with, the rain.

Gentle rain on a tin roof is one of my favourite sounds. And early in the morning, when the rain has stopped, there are other sounds I like to hear—a crow shaking the raindrops from his feathers and cawing rather disconsolately; babblers and bulbuls bustling in and out of bushes and long grass in search of worms and insects; the sweet, ascending trill of the Himalayan whistling thrush; dogs rushing through damp undergrowth.

A cherry tree, bowed down by the heavy rain, suddenly rights itself, flinging pellets of water in my face.

Some of the best sounds are made by water. The water of a mountain stream, always in a hurry, bubbling over rocks and chattering, 'I'm late, I'm late!' like the White Rabbit, tumbling over itself in its anxiety to reach the bottom of the hill; the sound of the sea, especially when it is far away—or when you hear it by putting a seashell to your ear. The sound made by dry and thirsty earth, as it sucks at a sprinkling of water. Or the sound of a child drinking thirstily, the water running down his chin and throat.

Water gushing out of the pans on an old well outside a village while a camel moves silently round the well. Bullock-cart wheels creaking over rough country roads. The clip-clop of a pony carriage, and the tinkle of its bell, and the singsong call of its driver...

Bells in the hills. A school bell ringing, and children's voices drifting through an open window. A temple bell, heard faintly from across the valley. Heavy silver ankle-bells on the feet of sturdy hill-women. Sheep bells heard high up on the mountainside.

Do falling petals make a sound? Just the tiniest and softest of sounds, like the drift of falling snow. Of course big flowers, like dahlias, drop their petals with a very definite flop. These are showoffs, like the hawk-moth who comes flapping into the rooms at night instead of emulating the butterfly dipping lazily on the afternoon breeze.

One must return to the birds for favourite sounds, and the birds of the plains differ from the birds of the hills. On a cold winter morning in the plains of northern India, if you walk some way into the jungle you will hear the familiar call of the black partridge: 'Bhagwan teri qudrat' it seems to cry, which means: 'Oh God! Great is thy might.'

The cry rises from the bushes in all directions; but an hour later not a bird is to be seen or heard and the jungle is so very still that the silence seems to shout at you.

There are sounds that come from a distance, beautiful because they are far away, voices on the wind—they 'walked upon the wings of the wind'. The cries of fishermen out on the river. Drums beating rhythmically in a distant village. The croaking of frogs from the rainwater pond behind the house. I mean frogs at a distance. A frog croaking beneath one's window is as welcome as a motor horn.

But some people like motor horns. I know a taxi driver who never misses an opportunity to use his horn. It was made to his own specifications, and it gives out a resonant bugle-call. He never tires of using it. Cyclists and pedestrians always scatter at his approach. Other cars veer off the road. He is proud of his horn. He loves its strident sound—which only goes to show that some men's sounds are other men's noises!

Homely sounds, though we don't often think about them, are the ones we miss most when they are gone. A kettle on the boil. A door that creaks on its hinges. Old sofa springs. Familiar voices lighting up the dark. Ducks quacking in the rain.

And so we return to the rain, with which my favourite sounds began.

I have sat out in the open at night, after a shower of rain when the whole air is murmuring and tinkling with the voices of crickets and grasshoppers and little frogs. There is one melodious sound, a swift repeated trill, which I have never been able to trace to its source. Perhaps it is a little tree frog. Or it may be a small green cricket. I shall never know.

I am not sure that I really want to know. In an age when a scientific and rational explanation has been given for almost everything we see and touch and hear, it is good to be left with one small mystery, a mystery sweet and satisfying and entirely my own.

~

In Search of Sweet Peas

If someone were to ask me to choose between writing an essay on the Taj Mahal or on the last rose of the summer, I'd take the rose—even if it was down to its last petal. Beautiful, cold, white marble leaves me—well, just a little cold.... Roses are warm and fragrant, and almost every flower I know, wild or cultivated, has its own unique quality, whether it be subtle fragrance or arresting colour or liveliness of design. Unfortunately, winter has come to the Himalayas, and the hillsides are now brown and dry, the only colour being that of the red sorrel growing from the limestone rocks. Even my small garden looks rather forlorn, with the year's last dark-eyed nasturtium looking every bit like the Lone Ranger surveying the surrounding wilderness from his saddle. The marigolds have dried in the sun and tomorrow I will gather the seeds. The beanstalk that grew rampant during the monsoon is now down to a few yellow leaves and empty bean-pods.

'This won't do,' I told myself the other day. 'I must have flowers.' Prem, who had been to the valley town of Dehra the previous week, had made me even more restless, because he had spoken of masses of sweet peas in full bloom in the garden of one of the town's public schools. Down in the plains, winter is the best time for gardens, and I remembered my grandmother's house in Dehra, with its long rows of hollyhocks, neatly staked sweet peas and beds ablaze with red salvia and antirrhinum. Neither grandmother nor the house are there anymore. But surely there are other beautiful gardens, I mused, and maybe I could visit the school where Prem had seen the sweet peas. It was a long time since I had enjoyed their delicate fragrance.

So I took the bus down the hill, and throughout the two-hour journey, I dozed and dreamt of gardens—cottage gardens in the English countryside, tropical gardens in Florida, Mughal gardens in Kashmir, the Hanging Gardens of Babylon—what had they been like, I wondered.

And then we were in Dehra, and I got down from the bus and walked down the dusty, busy road to the school Prem had told me about.

It was encircled by a high wall, and, tip-toeing, I could see playing fields and extensive school buildings and, in the far distance, a dollop of colour which may have been a garden. Prem's eyesight was obviously better than mine.

Anyway, I made my way to a wrought-iron gate that would have done justice to a medieval fortress, and found it chained and locked. On the other side stood a tough looking guard with a rifle.

'May I enter?' I asked.

'Sorry, sir, today is holiday. No school today.'

'I don't want to attend classes, I want to see the sweet peas.'

'Kitchen is on the other side of the ground.'

'Not green peas. Sweet peas. I'm looking for the garden.'

'I am guard here.'

'Garden.'

'No garden, only guard.'

I tried telling him that I was an old boy of the school and that I was visiting the town after a long interval. This was true up to a point, because I had once been admitted to this very school, and after one day's attendance had insisted on going back to my old school. The guard was unimpressed. And perhaps it was poetic justice that the gates were barred to me now.

Disconsolate, I strolled down the main road, past a garage, a cinema, a row of cheap eating houses and tea shops. Behind the shops there seemed to be a park of sorts, but you couldn't see much of it from the road because of the buildings, the press of the people and the passing trucks and buses. But I found the entrance, unbarred this time, and struggled through patches of overgrown shrubbery until, like Alice after finding the golden key to the little door in the wall, I looked upon a lovely little garden.

There were no sweet peas, true, and the small fountain was dry. But around it, filling a large circular bed, were masses of bright yellow Californian poppies! They stood out like sunshine after the rain, and my heart leapt as Wordsworth's must have done when he saw his daffodils. I found myself oblivious to the sounds of the bazaar and the road, just as the people outside seemed oblivious to this little garden. It was as though it had been waiting here all the time. Waiting for me to come by and discover it.

I am very fortunate. Something like this is always happening to me. As grandmother often said, 'When one door closes, another door opens.' And while one gate had been closed upon the sweet peas, another had opened on Californian poppies.

~

Trees make you feel younger. And the older the tree, the younger you feel.

Whenever I pass beneath the old tamarind tree standing sentinel in the middle of Dehra's busiest street crossing, the years fall away and I am a boy again, sitting on the railing that circled the tree, while across the road, Granny ascended the steps of the Allahabad Bank, where she kept her savings.

The bank is still there, but the surroundings have changed, the traffic and the noise is far greater than it used to be, and I wouldn't dream of sauntering across the road as casually as I would have done in those days. The press of people is greater too, reflecting the tenfold increase in population that has taken place in this and other north Indian towns during the last forty years. But the old tamarind has managed to survive it all. As long as it stands, as long as its roots still cling to Dehra's rich soil, I shall feel confident that my own roots are well embedded in this old valley town.

There was a time when almost every Indian village had its spreading banyan tree, in whose generous shade, schoolteachers conducted open-air classes, village elders met to discuss matters of moment, and itinerant merchants spread out their wares. Squirrels, birds of many kinds, flying-foxes, and giant beetles, are just some of the many inhabitants of this gentle giant. Ancient banyan trees are still to be found in some parts of the country; but as villages grow into towns, and towns into cities, the banyan is gradually disappearing. It needs a lot of space for its aerial roots to travel and support it, and space is now at a premium.

If you can't find a banyan, a mango grove is a wonderful place for a quiet stroll or an afternoon siesta. In traditional paintings, it is often the haunt of young lovers. But if the mangoes are ripening, there is not much privacy in a mango grove. Parrots, crows, monkeys and small boys are all attempting to evade the watchman who uses an empty gasoline tin as a drum to frighten away these intruders.

The mango and the banyan don't grow above the foothills, and here in the mountains, the more familiar trees are the Himalayan oaks, horse chestnuts, rhododendrons, pines and deodars. The deodar (from the Sanskrit dev-dar, meaning tree of God) resembles the cedar of Lebanon, and can grow to a great height in a few hundred years. There are a number of giant deodars on the outskirts of Mussoorie, where I live, and they make the town seem quite young. Mussoorie is only 160 years old. The deodars are at least twice that age.

These are gregarious trees—they like being among their own kind—and a forest of deodars is an imposing sight. When a mountain is covered with them, they look like an army on the march: the only kind of army one would like to see marching over the mountains! Although the world has already lost over half its forest cover, these sturdy giants look as though they are going to be around a long time, given half a chance.

The world's oldest trees, a species of pine, grow in California and have been known to live up to five thousand years. Is that why Californians look so young?

The oldest tree I have seen is an ancient mulberry growing at Joshimath, a small temple town in the Himalayas. It is known as the Kalp Vriksha or Immortal Tree. The Hindu sage, Sankaracharya, is said to have meditated beneath it in the sixteenth century. These ancient sages always found a suitable tree beneath which they could meditate. The Buddha favoured a banyan tree, while Hindu ascetics are still to be found sitting cross-legged beneath peepul trees.

Personally, I prefer contemplation to meditation. I am happy to stand back from the great mulberry and study its awesome proportions. Not a tall tree, but it has an immense girth—my three-room apartment in Mussoorie would have fitted quite snugly into it. A small temple beside the tree looked very tiny indeed, and the children playing among its protruding roots could have been kittens.

As I said, I'm not one for meditating beneath trees, but that's really because something always happens to me when I try. I don't know how the great sages managed, but I find it difficult to concentrate when a Rhesus monkey comes up to me and stares me in the face. Or when a horse chestnut bounces off my head. Or when a cloud of pollen slides off the branch of a deodar and down the back of my shirt. Or when a woodpecker starts hammering away a few feet up the trunk from where I sit. I expect the great ones were immune to all this arboreal activity. I'm just a nature-lover, easily distracted by the caterpillar crawling up my leg.

And so I am happy to stand back and admire the 'good, green-hatted people', as a visitor from another planet described the trees in a story by R.L. Stevenson. Especially the old trees. They have seen a lot of odd humans coming and going, and they know I'm just a seventy-year-old boy without any pretensions to being a sage.

～⌒

Adventures in a Banyan Tree

Though the house and grounds of our home in India were Grandfather's domain, the magnificent old banyan tree was mine—chiefly because Grandfather, at the age of sixty-five, could no longer climb it. (Grandmother used to tease him about this, and would speak of a certain Countess of Desmond, an Englishwoman, who lived to the age of 117, and would have lived longer if she hadn't fallen while climbing an apple tree). The spreading branches of the banyan tree, which curved to the ground and took root again, forming a maze of arches, gave me endless pleasure. The tree was older than the house, older than Grandfather; as old as the town of Dehra, nestling in a valley at the foot of the Himalayas. I could hide myself in its branches, behind thick green leaves, and spy on the world below.

My first friend and familiar was a small grey squirrel. Arching his back and sniffing into the air, he seemed at first to resent my invasion of his privacy. But, when he found that I did not arm myself with a catapult or air gun, he became friendlier. And, when I started leaving him pieces of cake and biscuit, he grew bolder, and finally became familiar enough to take food from my hands.

Before long, he was delving into my pockets and helping himself to whatever he could find. He was a very young squirrel, and his friends and relatives probably thought him headstrong and foolish for trusting a human.

In the spring, when the banyan tree was full of small red figs, birds of all kinds would flock into its branches: the red-bottomed bulbul, cheerful and greedy; gossiping rosy pastors; parrots, and crows, squabbling with each other all the time. During the fig season, the banyan tree was the noisiest place on the road.

Halfway up the tree I had built a small platform where I would often spend the afternoons when it wasn't too hot. I could read there, propping myself up against the bole of the tree with cushions taken from the drawing room. *Treasure Island*, Huck Finn, the Mowgli stories and the novels of Edgar Wallace, Edgar Rice Burroughs and Louisa May Alcott made up my bag of very mixed reading.

When I didn't want to read, I could look down through the banyan leaves at the world below, at Grandmother hanging up or taking down the washing, at the cook quarrelling with a fruit vendor or at Grandfather grumbling at the hardy Indian marigolds which insisted on springing up all over his very English garden. Usually nothing very exciting happened while I was in the banyan tree, but on one particular afternoon I had enough excitement to last me through the summer.

That was the time I saw a mongoose and a cobra fight to death in the garden, while I sat directly above them in the banyan tree.

It was an April afternoon, and the warm breezes of approaching summer had sent everyone, including Grandfather, indoors. I was feeling drowsy myself and was wondering if I should go to the pond behind the house for a swim, when I saw a huge black cobra gliding out of a clump of cactus and making for some cooler part of the garden. At the same time a mongoose (whom I had often seen) emerged from the bushes and went straight for the cobra.

In a clearing beneath the tree, in bright sunshine, they came face to face.

The cobra knew only too well that the grey mongoose, three feet long, was a superb fighter, clever and aggressive. But the cobra was a skilful and experienced fighter too. He could move swiftly and strike with the speed of light; and the sacs behind his long, sharp fangs were full of deadly venom.

It was to be a battle of champions.

Hissing defiance, his forked tongue darting in and out, the cobra raised three of his six feet off the ground, and spread his broad, spectacled hood. The mongoose bushed his tail. The long hair on his spine stood up. (In the past, the very thickness of his hair had saved him from bites that would have been fatal to others.)

Though the combatants were unaware of my presence in the banyan tree, they soon became aware of the arrival of two other spectators. One was a myna, and the other a jungle crow (not the wily urban crow); they had seen these preparations for battle, and had settled on the cactus to watch the outcome. Had they been content only to watch, all would have been well with both of them.

The cobra stood on the defensive, swaying slowly from side to side, trying to mesmerize the mongoose into making a false move. But the mongoose knew the power of his opponent's glassy, unwinking eyes, and refused to meet them. Instead he fixed his gaze at a point just below the cobra's hood, and opened the attack.

Moving forward quickly until he was just within the cobra's reach, he made a feint to one side. Immediately the cobra struck. His great hood came down so swiftly that I thought nothing could save the mongoose. But the little fellow jumped neatly to one side, and darted in as swiftly as the cobra, biting the snake on the back and darting away again out of reach.

The moment the cobra struck, the crow and the myna hurled themselves at him, only to collide heavily in mid-air. Shrieking at each other, they returned to the cactus plant.

A few drops of blood glistened on the cobra's back.

The cobra struck again and missed. Again the mongoose sprang aside, jumped in and bit. Again the birds dived at the snake, bumped into each other instead, and returned shrieking to the safety of the cactus.

The third round followed the same course as the first, but with one dramatic difference. The crow and the myna, still determined to take part in the proceedings, dived at the cobra; but this time they missed each other as well as their mark. The myna flew on and reached its perch, but the crow tried to pull up in mid-air and turn back. In the second that it took him to do this, the cobra whipped his head back and struck with great force, his snout thudding against the crow's body.

I saw the bird flung nearly twenty feet across the garden, where, after fluttering about for a while, it lay still. The myna remained on the cactus plant, and when the snake and the mongoose returned to the fray, it very wisely refrained from interfering again!

The cobra was weakening, and the mongoose, walking fearlessly up to it, raised himself on his short legs, and with a lightning snap had the big snake by the snout. The cobra writhed and lashed about in a frightening manner, and even coiled itself about the mongoose, but all to no avail. The little fellow hung grimly on, until the snake had ceased to struggle. He then smelt along its quivering length, and gripping it round the hood, dragged it into the bushes.

The myna dropped cautiously to the ground, hopped about, peered into the bushes from a safe distance, and then, with a shrill cry of congratulation, flew away. When I had also made a cautious descent from the tree and returned to the house, I told Grandfather of the fight I had seen. He was pleased that the mongoose had won. He had encouraged it to live in the garden, to keep away the snakes, and fed it regularly with scraps from the kitchen. He had never tried taming it, because a wild mongoose was more useful than a domesticated one.

From the banyan tree I often saw the mongoose patrolling the four corners of the garden. Once I saw him with an egg in his mouth and knew he had been in the poultry house; but he hadn't harmed the birds, and I knew Grandmother would forgive him for stealing as long as he kept the snakes away from the house.

The banyan tree was also the setting for what we were to call the Strange Case of the Grey Squirrel and the White Rat.

The white rat was Grandfather's—he had bought it from the bazaar for four annas—but I would often take it with me into the banyan tree, where it soon struck up a friendship with one of the squirrels. They would go off together on little excursions among the roots and branches of the old tree.

Then the squirrel started building a nest. At first she tried building it in my pockets, and when I went indoors and changed my clothes, I would find straw and grass falling out. Then one day

Grandmother's knitting was missing. We hunted for it everywhere but without success.

Next day I saw something glinting in the hole in the banyan tree and, going up to investigate, saw that it was the end of Grandmother's steel knitting-needle. On looking further, I discovered that the hole was crammed with knitting. And amongst the wool were three baby squirrels—all of them white!

Grandfather had never seen white squirrels before, and we gazed at them in wonder. We were puzzled for some time, but when I mentioned the white rat's frequent visits to the trees, Grandfather told me that the rat must be the father. Rats and squirrels were related to each other, he said, and so it was quite possible for them to have offspring—in this case, white squirrels!

~

The Man Who Loved Trees

One morning, while I was sitting beside Grandfather on the verandah steps, I noticed the tendril of a creeping vine trailing nearby. As we sat there, in the soft sunshine of a north Indian winter, I saw the tendril moving very slowly towards Grandfather. We gazed at it in fascination. Twenty minutes later, it had crossed the step and was touching his feet.

There is probably a scientific explanation for the plant's behaviour—something to do with light or warmth perhaps—but I like to think that it moved across the steps simply because it wanted to be near Grandfather. One always felt like drawing close to him. Sometimes when I sat by myself beneath a tree, I would feel rather lonely, but as soon as Grandfather joined me, the garden became a happy place. Grandfather had served many years in the Indian Forest Service and it was natural that he would know and like trees. On his retirement, he built a bungalow on the outskirts of the town of Dehradun, planting trees all round: lime, mango, orange and guava; also eucalyptus, jacaranda and the Persian lilac. In the fertile Doon Valley, plants and trees grew tall and strong.

There were other trees in the compound before the house was built, including an old peepul that had forced its way through the walls of an abandoned outhouse, knocking the bricks down with its vigorous growth. Peepul trees are great show-offs. Even when there is no breeze, their broad-chested, slim-waisted leaves will spin like tops determined to attract your attention and invite you into their shade.

Grandmother had wanted the peepul tree cut down, but Grandfather said, 'Let it be; we can always build another outhouse.'

Grandmother didn't mind trees, but she preferred growing flowers and was constantly ordering seeds and catalogues. Grandfather helped her with the gardening, not because he was crazy about flower gardens but because he liked watching butterflies, and 'there's only one way to attract butterflies,' he said, 'and that's to grow flowers for them.'

Grandfather wasn't content with growing trees in our compound. During the rains, we would walk into the jungle beyond the riverbed, armed with cuttings and saplings, which we would plant in the forest.

'But no one ever comes here!' I protested, the first time we did this. 'Who's going to see them?'

'We're not planting them simply to improve the view,' replied Grandfather. 'We're planting for the forest and for the birds and animals who live here and need more food and shelter.'

'Of course men need trees too,' he added. 'For keeping the desert away; for attracting rain; for preventing the banks of rivers from being washed away; for fruit and flower, leaf and seed. Yes, and for timber too. But men are cutting down the trees without replacing them. And if we don't plant a few ourselves, there'll come a time when the world will be one great desert.'

The thought of a world without trees became a sort of nightmare to me, and I helped Grandfather in his tree-planting with greater enthusiasm. And while we went about our work, he taught me a poem by George Morris:

> *Woodman, spare that tree!*
> *Touch not a single bough!*
> *In youth it sheltered me,*
> *And I'll protect it now.*

'One day the trees will move again,' said Grandfather. 'They've been standing for thousands of years, but there was a time when they could walk about like people. Then along came an interfering busybody who cast a spell over them, rooting them to one place. But they're always trying to move. See how they reach out with their arms! And some of them, like the banyan tree with its travelling aerial roots, manage to get quite far!'

We found an island, a small rocky island in a dry riverbed. It was one of those riverbeds, so common in the foothills, which are completely dry in summer but flooded during the monsoon rains. A small mango tree was growing on the island. 'If a mango can grow here,' said Grandfather, 'so can other trees.'

As soon as the rains set in, and while the river could still be crossed, we set out with a number of tamarind, laburnum and coral tree saplings and cuttings, and spent the day planting them on the island.

The monsoon season was the time for rambling about. At every turn there was something new to see. Out of earth and rock and leafless bough, the magic touch of the rains had brought life and greenness. You could see the broad-leaved vines growing. Plants sprang up in the most unlikely places; a peepul would take root in the ceiling, a mango would sprout on the windowsill. We did not like to remove them, but they had to go if the house was to be kept from falling down.

'If you want to live in a tree, it's all right by me,' said Grandmother crossly. 'But I like having a roof over my own head, and I'm not going to have my roof brought down by the jungle.'

When World War II came, I was sent away to a boarding school and during the holidays I went to live with my father in Delhi. Meanwhile, my grandparents sold the house and went to England. Two or three years later I, too, went to England and I was away from India for several years.

Recently, however, I was in Dehradun again. After first visiting the old house—it hadn't changed much—I walked out of town towards the riverbed. It was February. As I looked across the dry watercourse, my eye was immediately caught by the spectacular red plumes of the coral blossom. In contrast with the dry riverbed, the island was a small green paradise. When I went up to the trees, I noticed that some squirrels were living in them, and a koel challenged me with a mellow 'who-are-you, who-are-you'.

But the trees seemed to know me; they whispered among themselves and beckoned me nearer. And looking around, I noticed that other smaller trees and wild plants and grasses had sprung up under their protection.

Yes, the trees we had planted long ago had multiplied. They were *walking* again. In one small corner of the world. Grandfather's dream had come true.

~~

A Little World of Mud

I had never imagined there was much to be found in the rainwater pond behind our house in north India except for large quantities of mud and sometimes a water buffalo. It was Grandfather who introduced me to the pond's diversity of life, so beautifully arranged that each individual gained some benefit from the well-being of the mass. To the inhabitants of the pond, the pond was the world; and to the inhabitants of the world, maintained Grandfather, the world was but a muddy pond.

When Grandfather first showed me the pond world, he chose a dry place in the shade of an old peepul tree, where we sat for an hour, gazing steadily at the thin, green scum on the water. The buffaloes had not arrived for their afternoon dip, and the surface of the pond was still.

~

For the first ten minutes we saw nothing. Then a small black blob appeared in the middle of the pond; gradually it rose higher, until at last we could make out a frog's head, its great eyes staring hard at us. He did not know if we were friend or enemy and kept his body out of sight. A heron, his mortal enemy, might have been wading about in search of him. When he had made sure we were not herons, he informed his friends and neighbours, and soon there were several big heads and eyes just above the surface of the water. Throats swelled, and a *wurk, wurk, wurk* began.

In the shallow water near the tree we could see a dark shifting shadow. When touched with the end of a stick, the dark mass immediately became alive. Thousands of little black tadpoles wriggled into life, pushing and hustling each other.

'What do tadpoles eat?' I asked.

'They eat each other most of the time,' said Grandfather. 'It may seem an unpleasant custom, but when you think of the thousands of tadpoles that are hatched, you'll realize what a useful system it is. If all the young tadpoles in this pond became frogs, they'd take up every inch of ground between here and the house!'

'Their croaking would certainly drive Grandmother crazy,'

All the same, I took home a number of frogs, placed them in a large glass jar, and left them on the windowsill of my bedroom.

At about four o'clock in the morning the entire household was awakened by a loud and fearful noise, and my grandparents, aunts and servants gathered on the verandah for safety. They were furious when they discovered that my frogs were the cause of the noise. Seeing the dawn breaking, the frogs had with one accord begun their morning song. Grandmother wanted to throw the frogs, bottle and all, out of the window; but Grandfather gave the bottle a good shaking and the frogs stayed quiet. Everyone went back to bed, but I was obliged to stay awake, to shake the bottle whenever the frogs showed signs of bursting into song. Long before breakfast, I had let them loose in the garden.

I was soon visiting the pond on my own, exploring its banks and shallows; and taking off my shoes, I would wade into the muddy water up to my knees, and pluck the water lilies floating on the surface.

One day, when I reached the pond, I found it occupied by buffaloes. Their owner, a boy a little older than me, was swimming about in the middle of the pond. He pulled himself up on the back of one of his buffaloes, stretched his slim brown body out on the animal's glistening back, and started singing to himself.

When the boy saw me staring at him, he smiled, showing gleaming white teeth in his dark, sun-burnished face. He invited me into the water for a swim. I told him I couldn't swim, and he offered to teach me. I hesitated, knowing that my Grandmother held strict and rather old-fashioned views about my mixing with village children; but, deciding that Grandfather—who sometimes smoked a hookah on the sly—would get me out of any trouble that might arise, I took the bold step of accepting the boy's offer. And once taken, the step did not seem so very bold.

He dived off the back of his buffalo and swam across to me. And I, having removed my shirt and shorts, followed his instructions until

I was floundering about among the water lilies. His name was Ramu, and he promised to give me swimming lessons every afternoon; and so it was during the afternoons—especially summer afternoons when everyone was asleep—that we met.

Before long I was able to swim across the pond to sit with Ramu astride a contented buffalo standing like an island in the middle of a muddy ocean. Sometimes we would try racing the buffaloes, Ramu and I sitting on different beasts. But they were lazy creatures and would leave one comfortable spot only to look for another; or, if they were in no mood for games, would simply roll over on their backs, taking us with them into the mud and green slime of the pond. I would emerge from the pond in shades of green and khaki, slip into the house through the bathroom, and bathe under the tap before getting into my clothes.

Ramu came from a family of low-caste farmers and had received no schooling. But he was well versed in folklore and knew a great deal about birds and animals.

'Many birds are sacred,' he told me, as a bluejay swooped down from the peepul tree and carried off a grasshopper. Ramu said that both the bluejay and the god Shiva were called Nilkanth. Shiva had a blue throat, like the bird, because out of compassion for the human race he had swallowed a deadly poison which was meant to destroy the world. Keeping the poison in his throat, he had not let it go further.

'Are squirrels sacred?' I asked.

'The god Krishna loved them,' said Ramu. 'He would take them in his arms and stroke them with his long fingers. That is why they have four dark lines down their back from head to tail. Krishna was very dark, and the lines are the marks of his fingers.'

Both Ramu and my grandfather felt that we should be more gentle with birds and animals, that we should not kill them indiscriminately.

'We must acknowledge their rights on the earth,' said Grandfather. 'Everywhere, birds and animals are finding it more difficult to live, because we are destroying their forests. They have to keep moving as the trees disappear.'

Ramu and I spent many long summer afternoons at the pond. We never saw each other again after I left my grandparents' house; he could not read or write, so we were unable to keep in touch.

No one knew of our friendship. Only the buffaloes and the frogs were our confidants. They had accepted us as part of their own world, their muddy but comfortable pond. And when I went away, both they and Ramu must have assumed that I would return again like the birds.

~⌐

Mountains in My Blood

It was while I was living in England, in the jostle and drizzle of London, that I remembered the Himalayas at their most vivid. I had grown up amongst those great blue and brown mountains; they had nourished my blood; and though I was separated from them by thousands of miles of ocean, plain and desert, I could not rid them from my system. It is always the same with mountains. Once you have lived with them for any length of time, you belong to them. There is no escape.

And so, in London in March, the fog became a mountain mist, and the boom of traffic became the boom of the Ganga emerging from the foothills.

I remembered a little mountain path which led my restless fret into a cool, sweet forest of oak and rhododendron, and then on to the windswept crest of a naked hilltop. The hill was called Cloud's End. It commanded a view of the plains on one side, and of the snow peaks on the other. Little silver rivers twisted across the valley below, where the rice fields formed a patchwork of emerald green. And on the hill itself, the wind made a *hoo-hoo-hoo* in the branches of the tall deodars where it found itself trapped.

During the rains, clouds enveloped the valley but left the hill alone, an island in the sky. Wild sorrel grew amongst the rocks, and there were many flowers—convolvulus, clover, wild begonia, dandelion— sprinkling the hillside.

On a spur of the hill stood the ruins of an old brewery. The roof had long since disappeared, and the rain had beaten the stone floors smooth and yellow. Some enterprising Englishman had spent a lifetime here making beer for his thirsty compatriots in the plains. Now, moss and ferns and maidenhair grew from the walls. In a hollow beneath a flight of worn stone steps, a wildcat had made its home. It was a beautiful grey creature, black-striped, with pale green eyes. Sometimes it watched me from the steps or the wall, but it never came near.

No one lived on the hill, except occasionally a coalburner in a temporary grass-thatched hut. But villagers used the path, grazing their sheep and cattle on the grassy slopes. Each cow or sheep had a bell suspended from its neck, to let the shepherd boy know of its whereabouts. The boy could then lie in the sun and eat wild strawberries without fear of losing his animals.

I remembered some of the shepherd boys and girls. There was a boy who played a flute. Its rough, sweet, straightforward notes travelled clearly across the mountain air. He would greet me with a nod of his head, without taking the flute from his lips. There was a girl who was nearly always cutting grass for fodder. She wore heavy bangles on her feet, and long silver earrings. She did not speak much either, but she always had a wide grin on her face when she met me on the path. She used to sing to herself, to the sheep, to the grass or to the sickle in her hand.

And there was a boy who carried milk into town (a distance of about five miles), who would often fall into step with me, to hold a long conversation. He had never been away from the hills, or in a large city. He had never been in a train. I told him about the cities, and he told me about his village; how they make bread from maize, how fish were to be caught in the mountain streams, how the bears came to steal his father's pumpkins.

These things I remembered—these, and the smell of pine needles, the silver of oak leaves and the red of maple, the call of the Himalayan cuckoo, and the mist, like a wet facecloth, pressing against the hills.

Odd, how some little incident, some snatch of conversation, comes back to one again and again, in the most unlikely places. Standing in the aisle of a crowded tube train on a Monday morning, my nose tucked into the back page of someone else's newspaper, I suddenly had a vision of a bear making off with a ripe pumpkin.

A bear and a pumpkin—and there, between Goodge Street and Tottenham Court Road stations, all the smells and sounds of the Himalayas came rushing back to me.

Bears of the Himalayas

Most Himalayan villages lie in the valleys, where there are streams, tolerably fertile soil, and protection from the biting winds that come through the mountain passes in winter. The houses are usually made of rough granite, and have sloping slate roofs that enable the heavy monsoon rain to run off easily. During the dry autumn months, the roofs are often covered with pumpkins, left there to ripen in the sun.

One October night, when I was sleeping in a friend's house in a village in Garhwal, I was woken by a rumbling and thumping on the roof. I woke my friend and asked him what was happening.

'It's only a bear,' he said.

'Is it trying to get in?' I asked.

'No—it's after the pumpkins.'

A little later we looked out of the small window and saw a black bear making off through a field, like a thief in the night, with a pumpkin held to his chest.

In winter, when snow covers the higher mountains, the brown and black Himalayan bears descend to lower altitudes in search of food. Sometimes they forage in fields. Because they are short-sighted and suspicious of anything that moves, they can be dangerous; but, like most wild animals, they will avoid men if they can, and are aggressive only when accompanied by their cubs.

Hill people are always advising me to run downhill if chased by a bear. They say that bears find it easier to run uphill than downhill.

Himalayan bears like pumpkins, maize, plums and apricots and, of course, honey. Once, while I was sitting in an oak tree, hoping to see a pair of pine martens who lived nearby, I heard the whining grumble of a bear, and presently saw one amble into the clearing near the tree.

At first he put his nose to the ground and sniffed his way along until he came to a large anthill. Here he began huffing and puffing, blowing rapidly in and out of his nostrils, so that the dust from the anthill flew in all directions. But he was a disappointed bear, because the anthill had been deserted long before. And so, grumbling, he made his way to a wild plum tree and, shinning rapidly up the smooth trunk, was soon perched in the topmost branches. It was only then that he saw me.

He at once scrambled several feet higher up the tree and laid himself out flat on a branch. It wasn't a very thick branch and left a large expanse of the bear showing on either side. He tucked his head away behind another branch and, so long as he could not, see me, was satisfied that he was well hidden, though he couldn't help grumbling with anxiety.

But, like all bears, he was full of curiosity. And slowly, inch by inch, his black snout appeared over the edge of the branch. As soon as his eyes came into view and met mine, he drew his head back with a jerk and hid his face.

He did this several times. I waited until he wasn't looking, then moved some way down the tree. When he looked up again and saw that I was missing, he was so pleased that he stretched right across to another branch and helped himself to a plum. My burst of laughter so startled him that he tumbled out of the tree, dropped through the branches for some 15 feet, and landed with a thud in a heap of dry leaves. He was quite unhurt but ran from the clearing, grunting and squealing with fright.

The inquisitiveness of bears was revealed to me on another occasion when, hearing that one had been active in a field of maize, I sat up for it at night in the company of one of my friends. We took up our position on a high promontory of rock which gave us a clear view of the moonlit field. A little after midnight a bear came down to the edge of the field, but he was suspicious and probably smelt that men had been about the place recently. He was, however, hungry; so, after standing up as high as possible on his hind legs and peering about to see if the field was empty, he came cautiously out of the forest and made his way toward the ripe corn.

About halfway there his attention was suddenly taken by some Buddhist prayer-flags which had been strung up between two small trees. (They had probably been placed there by Tibetans, some of whom had settled not far away.) On spotting the flags, the bear gave a little grunt of disapproval and began to get back into the forest; but the fluttering was a puzzle he felt he had to make out, so after a few backward steps he again stopped and watched them.

Not satisfied with this, he stood on his hind legs looking at the flags, first at one side and then at the other. Still unsatisfied, he advanced until he was a few yards away from them, again got on his hind legs and examined them from various points of view. Then, seeing that they did not attack him and did not appear dangerous, he approached warily, taking only two or three steps at a time, and having a good look each time before again advancing. Eventually he went confidently up to the flags and pulled them all down. After examining them carefully, he moved on into the field of corn.

But my friend (whose field it was) decided that he wasn't going to lose any more of his crop, so he started shouting, and the villagers woke up and came out of their houses beating drums and empty kerosene tins.

Deprived of his dinner, the bear made off in a bad temper. He ran downhill, and at a good speed too, and I was glad I wasn't in his path just then. Uphill or downhill, an angry bear is best given a very wide berth.

~~~

After the Monsoon

Towards the end of the year, those few monsoon clouds that still linger over the Himalayas are no longer burdened with rain and are able to assume unusual shapes and patterns, chasing each other across the sky and disappearing in spectacular sunset formations.

I have always found this to be the best time of the year in the hills. The sun-drenched hillsides are still an emerald green; the air is crisp, but winter's bite is still a month or two away; and for those who still like to take to the open road on foot, there are springs, streams and waterfalls tumbling over rocks that remain dry for most of the year. The lizard that basked on a sun-baked slab of granite last May is missing, but in his place the spotted forktail trips daintily among the boulders in a stream; and the strident sound of the cicadas is gradually replaced by the gentler trilling of the crickets and grasshoppers.

Now, more than at any other time of the year, the wild flowers come into their own.

The hillside is covered with flowers and ferns. Sprays of wild ginger, tangles of clematis, flat clusters of yarrow and lady's mantle. The datura grows everywhere with its graceful white balls and prickly fruits. And the wild woodbine provides the stems from which the village boys make their flutes.

Aroids are plentiful and attract attention by their resemblance to snakes with protruding tongues—hence the popular name, cobra lily. This serpent's tongue is a perfect landing stage for flies, who, crawling over the male flowers in their eager search for the liquor that lies at the base of the spike, succeed in fertilizing the female flowers.

One of the more spectacular cobra lilies, which rejoices in the name *Sauromotum guttatum*—ask your nearest botanist what that means—bears a solitary leaf and purple spike. When the seeds form, it withdraws the spike underground. And when the rains are over and the soil is not too damp, sends it up again covered with scarlet berries. In the opinion of the hill folk, the appearance of the red spike is more to be relied on as a forecast of the end of the monsoon than any meteorological expertise. Up here on the ranges that fall between the Jamuna and the Bhagirathi (known as the Rawain) we can be perfectly sure of fine weather a fortnight after that fiery spike appears.

But it is the commelina, more than any other Himalayan flower, that takes my breath away. The secret is in its colour; a pure pristine blue that seems to reflect the deepest blue of the sky. Towards the end of the rains it appears as if from nowhere, graces the hillside for the space of about two weeks, and disappears again until the following monsoon.

When I see the first commelina, I stand dumb before it, and the world stands still while I worship. So absorbed do I become in its delicate beauty that I begin to doubt the reality of everything else in the world.

But only for a moment. The blare of a truck's horn reminds me that I am still lingering on the main road leading out of the hill station. A cloud of dust and a blast of diesel fumes are further indication that reality takes many different forms, assailing all my senses at once! Even my commelina seems to shrink from the onslaught. But as it is still there, I take heart and leave the highway for a lesser road.

Soon I have left the clutter of the town behind. Wasn't it Lot's wife who was turned into a pillar of salt when she looked back at the doomed city that had been her home? I have an uneasy feeling that I will be turned into a pillar of cement if I look back, so I plod on along the road to Devasari, a kindly village in the valley. It will be some time before the 'developers' and big-money boys get here, for no one will go to live where there is no driveway!

A tea shop beckons. How would one manage in the hills without these wayside tea shops? I tackle some buns that have a pre-Independence look about them. They are rock hard, to match the environment, but I manage to swallow some of the jagged pieces with the hot sweet tea.

There is a small shrine here, right in front of the tea shop. It is no more than a slab of rock daubed with vermilion, strewn with offerings of wild flowers. Hinduism comes closest to being a nature religion. Rivers, rocks, trees, plants, animals and birds all play their part, both in mythology and in everyday worship. This harmony is most evident in remote places like this, and I hope it does not lose its unique character in the ruthless urban advance.

Fragrance to the Air

I would be the last person to belittle a flower for its lack of fragrance, because there are many spectacular blooms such as the dahlia and the gladioli which have hardly any scent and yet make up for it with their colour and appearance. But it does happen that my own favourite flowers are those with a distinctive fragrance and these are the flowers I would have around me.

The rose, of course, is the world's favourite, a joy to all—even to babies, who enjoy taking them apart, petal by petal. But there are other, less spectacular, less celebrated blooms which have a lovely, sometimes elusive fragrance all their own.

I have a special fondness for antirrhinums—or snapdragons, as they are more commonly known. If I sniff hard at them, I don't catch any scent at all. They seem to hold it back from me. But if I walk past a bed of snapdragons, or even a single plant, the gentlest of fragrance is wafted towards me. If I stop and try to take it all in, it has gone again! I find this quite tantalizing, but it has given me a special regard for this modest flower.

Another humble, even old-fashioned flower, is the wallflower which obviously takes its name from the fact that it thrives on walls.

I have seen wallflowers adorn a garden wall in an extravagant and delightful manner, making it a mountain of perfume. They are best grown so as to form dense masses which become literally solid with fiery flowers—blood-red, purple, yellow, orange or bronze, all sending a heady fragrance into the surrounding air.

Carnations, with their strong scent of cloves, are great showoffs. In India, the jasmine and the magnolia are both rather heady and overpowering. The honeysuckle too insists on making its presence known. A honeysuckle creeper flourished outside the window of my room in Mussoorie, and all through the summer its sweet, rather cloying fragrance drifted in through the open window. It was delightful at times, but at other times I had to close the window just so that I could give my attention to other, less intrusive smells like the soft, sweet scent of petunias (another of my favourites) growing near the doorstep, and great bunches of sweet peas in a bowl on my desk.

It is much the same with chrysanthemums and geraniums. The lemon geranium, for instance, is valued more for its fragrant leaves than for its rather indeterminate blue flowers. And I cannot truthfully say what ordinary mint looks like in flower. The refreshing fragrance of the leaves, when crushed, makes up for any absence of floral display. On the other hand, the multi-coloured loveliness of dahlias is unaccompanied by any scent. Its greenery, when cut or broken, does have a faintly acrid smell, but that's about all.

Not all plants are good to smell. Some leaves, when crushed, will keep strong men at bay! Crushed neem pods have a distinctive odour. Most people dislike the smell, but I find it quite refreshing.

Of course, one man's fragrance might well turn out to be another creature's bad smell. Geraniums, my grandmother insisted, kept snakes away because they couldn't stand the smell of the leaves. She surrounded her bungalow with pots of geraniums. As we never found a snake in the house, she may well have been right. But the evidence is purely circumstantial.

I suppose snakes like some smells, close to the ground, or by now they'd have taken to living in more elevated places. But, turning to a book on reptiles, I learnt that in the snake the sense of smell is rather dull. Perhaps it has an aversion to anything that it can smell—such as those aromatic geranium leaves!

Close to Mother Earth, there are many delightful smells, provided you avoid roadsides and freshly manured fields. When I lie on summer grass in some Himalayan meadow, I am conscious of the many good smells around me—the grass itself, redolent of the morning's dew, bruised clover, wild violets, tiny buttercups and golden stars and strawberry flowers and many others I shall never know the names of.

And the earth itself. It smells different in different places. But its loveliest fragrance is known only when it receives a shower of rain. And then the scent of the wet earth rises as though it would give something beautiful back to the clouds. A blend of all the fragrant things that grow upon it.

A Bush at Hand Is Good for Many a Bird

The thing I like most about shrubs and small bushes is that they are about my size or thereabouts. I can meet them on equal terms. Most trees grow tall, they overtake us after a few years, and we find ourselves looking up to them with a certain amount of awe and deference. And so we should.

A bush, on the other hand, may have been in the ground for a long time—thirty or forty years or more—while continuing to remain a bush, man-sized and approachable. A bush may spread sideways or gain in substance, but it seldom towers over you. This means that I can be on intimate terms with it, know its qualities—of leaf, bud, flower or fruit—and also its inhabitants, be they insects, birds, small mammals or reptiles.

Of course, we know that bushes are ideal for binding the earth together and preventing erosion. In this respect they are just as important as trees. Every monsoon I witness landslides all about me, but I know the hillside just above my cottage is well knit, knotted and netted, by bilberry and raspberry, wild jasmine, dog rose and bramble, and other shrubs, vines and creepers.

I have made a small bench in the middle of this civilized wilderness. And sitting here, I can look down on my own roof, as well as sideways and upward, into a number of bushes teeming with life throughout the year. This is my favourite place. No one can find me here, unless I call out and make my presence known. The buntings and sparrows grow 'accustomed to my face,' and welcoming the grain I scatter for them, flit about near my feet. One of them, bolder than the rest, alights on my shoe and proceeds to polish his beak on the leather. The sparrows are here all the year round. So are the whistling thrushes, who live in the shadow between the house and the hill, sheltered by a waterwood bush, so called because it likes cold, damp places.

Summer brings the fruit-eating birds, for now the berries are ripe. A pair of green pigeons, rare in these parts, scramble over the branches of a hawthorn bush, delicately picking off the fruit. The raspberry bush is raided by bands of finches and greedy, yellow-bottomed bulbuls. A flock of bright green parrots comes sweeping down on the medlar tree, but they do not stay for long. Taking flight at my approach, they wheel above, green and gold in the sunlight, and make for the plum trees further down the road.

The kingora, a native Himalayan shrub similar to the bilberry, attracts small boys as well as birds. On their way to and from school, the boys scramble up the hillside and help themselves to the small sweet and sour berries. Then, lips stained purple, they go their merry way. The birds return.

Other inhabitants of this shrubland include the skink, a tiny lizard-like reptile, quite harmless. It emerges from its home among stones or roots to sun itself or drink from a leaf-cup of water. I have to protect these skinks from a large prowling tabby cat who thinks the hillside and everything on it belongs to him.

From my bench, I can see him moving stealthily around the corner of my roof. He has his eye on the slow-moving green pigeons. I am sure, I shall have to watch out for him. There wouldn't be much point in encouraging the birds to visit my bushes if the main beneficiary is to be that handsome but single-minded cat.

There are flowering shrubs, too—a tangle of dog roses, the wild yellow jasmine, a buddleia popular with honey bees, and a spreading mayflower which today is covered with small saffron-winged butterflies.

The grass, straw-yellow in winter, is now green and sweet, sprinkled with buttercups and clover. I can abandon the bench and lie on the grass, studying it at close quarters while repeating Whitman's lines:

> *A child said, "What is the grass?"*
> *fetching it to me with full hands,*

how could I answer the child? I do not
know what it is any more than he.'

I am no wiser either, but grass is obviously a good thing, providing a home for crickets and ladybirds and other small creatures. It would not be much fun living on a planet where grass could not grow.

That cat agrees with me. He is flat on his stomach on the grass, inching closer to one of those defenceless little skinks. He has decided that a skink in hand is worth two birds in a bush. I get to my feet, and the skinks run away.

The green pigeon has also flown away. The smaller birds remain where they are; they know they are too swift for the prowler. I returned to my bench and the finches and coppersmith arrive and depart.

You might call my shrubbery an arrival and departure lounge for small birds but they are also free to take up residence if they want. Their presence adds stillness to my life. A bush in hand is good for many a bird.

～

Those Simple Things

It's the simple things in life that keep us from going crazy.

Like that pigeon in the skylight in the New Delhi Nursing Home where I was incarcerated for two or three days. Even worse than the illness that had brought me there were the series of tests that the doctors insisted I had to go through—gastroscopies, endoscopies, X-rays, blood tests, urine tests, probes into any orifice they could find, and, at the end of it all, a nice fat bill designed to give me a heart attack.

The only thing that prevented me from running into the street, shouting for help, was that pigeon in the skylight. It sheltered there at various times during the day, and its gentle cooing soothed my nerves and kept me in touch with the normal world outside. I owe my sanity to that pigeon.

Which reminds me of the mouse who shared my little bed-sitting room in London, when I was just seventeen and all on my own. Those early months in London were lonely times for a shy young man going to work during the day and coming back to a cold, damp, empty room late in the evening. In the morning I would make myself a hurried breakfast, and at night I'd make myself a cheese or ham sandwich. This was when I noticed the little mouse peeping out at me from behind the books I had piled up on the floor, there being no bookshelf. I threw some crumbs in his direction, and he was soon making a meal of them and a piece of cheese. After that, he would present himself before me every evening, and the room was no longer as empty and lonely as when I had first moved in. He was a smart little mouse and sometimes he would speak to me—sharp little squeaks to remind me it was dinner time.

Months later, when I moved to another part of London, I had to leave him behind—I did not want to deprive him of friends and family—but it was a fat little mouse I left behind.

During my three years in London I must have lived in at least half-a-dozen different lodging houses, and the rooms were usually dull and depressing. One had a window looking out on a railway track; another provided me with a great view of a cemetery. To spend my day off looking down upon hundreds of graves was hardly uplifting, even if some of the tombstones were beautifully sculpted. No wonder I spent my evenings watching old Marx Brothers films at the Everyman Cinema nearby.

Living in small rooms for the greater part of my life, I have always felt the need for small, familiar objects that become a part of me, even if sometimes I forget to say hello to them. A glass paperweight, a laughing Buddha, an old horseshoe, a print of Hokusai's *Great Wave*, a suitcase that has seen better days, an old school tie (never worn, but there all the same), a gramophone record (can't play it now, but when I look at it, the song comes back to me), a potted fern, an old address-book... Where have they gone, those old familiar faces? Not one address is relevant today (after some forty years), but I keep it all the same.

I turn to a page at the end, and discover why I have kept it all these years. It holds a secret, scribbled note to an early love: 'I did not sleep last night, for you had kissed me. You held my hand and put it to your cheek and to your breasts. And I had closed your eyes and kissed them, and taken your face in my hands and touched your lips with mine. And then, my darling, I stumbled into the light like a man intoxicated, and did not say or know what people were saying or doing...'

Gosh! How romantic I was at thirty! And reading that little entry, I feel like going out and falling in love again. But will anyone fall in love with an old man of seventy-five?

Yes! There's a little mouse in my room.

Sounds of the Sea

For years I had this large seashell, and by putting it to my ear I could hear the distant sob and hiss of the sea—or so I fancied, until this romantic notion was dispelled by twelve-year-old Mukesh, who told me that the same effect could be obtained by holding an empty cup to my ear. He was right, of course. In fact, the cup sounds better than the shell! And for years I'd gone on imagining that the sound of the sea was somehow trapped in my shell... But I still cling to it, for it takes me back to Jamnagar, on the west coast of India, and memories of sea and sand, small steamers and large Arab dhows plying across the Gulf of Kutch.

My small hand in my father's, I explored with him the little port's harbour and beach, bringing home shells of considerable variety, and even, on one occasion, a small crab, which lived in a spare bathtub for several days and was forgotten—until a visiting aunt, deciding on a tub-bath after a long train journey, found it keeping her company among the soapsuds. Amidst much clamour and consternation, it was evicted from the house and dropped into a nearby well. But my aunt was convinced that I had deliberately placed it in the tub, and refused to speak to me for the rest of her stay.

A small British steamer was often in port, and my father and I would visit the captain, a good-natured Welshman who gave me chocolates, a great treat in those days, for Jamnagar was too small a place for a Western confectionery shop. I was ready to go to sea with Captain Jenkins, convinced that chocolates were only to be found on tramp steamers.

We left Jamnagar when World War II broke out and my father joined the Royal Air Force. It was to be some ten years before I saw the sea again, for I went to boarding school in the hills. I was still in my teens, but now bereft of my father, when I set sail from Bombay in the S.S. *Strathnaver,* a beautiful P&O liner, one of a fleet, its sister ships being the *Strathaird* and *Stratheden.* Those were the days of the big passenger liners, before fast air travel put an end to leisurely ocean voyages. It took just over a fortnight to reach Southampton or London, but there was never a dull moment on the voyage. Apart from interesting shipboard acquaintances—the sort of mixed company that gave Somerset Maugham material for his stories—there were also colourful ports of call: Aden, Port Said, Marseilles, Gibraltar. At Marseilles, I decided to miss the coach tour and instead walk into the town. After three hours of walking along miles and miles of dockland, I finally reached the outskirts of the city—just in time to catch the coach back to the ship!

But later, living in London, I never tired of walking among the docks and wharfs along the Thames, for many of those places were associated with the novels of Dickens, which had inspired me to become a writer. Limehouse, Wapping, Shadwell Stairs, the Mile End Road, the East India Docks, these were all places I knew from *Bleak House, Dombey and Son* and *Our Mutual Friend.* And there was the fog, a thick peasouper, that seemed to have lingered on from the fog that had enveloped the characters and the action in *Bleak House,* setting the tone for that masterpiece. London, I am told, no longer has fogs—they are dispersed by modern and scientific means—and although the air no doubt is cleaner and healthier now, I feel sure some of the magic has gone—along with the East End of old.

From London's dockland to the Channel Islands was a short trip but a considerable change. I lived on the island of Jersey for two years. It had a number of bays and inlets of great charm and beauty, and it was here that I learnt to watch the tides advancing and retreating, and discovered that the tides make different sounds in different places.

Every tide has its own music, and those who live near lonely shores soon learn to recognize the familiar ripple, throb, sob or sigh. And sometimes the tide comes up from the deep against a steep sandbank and roars defiance.

The tide-rip which pushes through the Channel Islands off the Norman coast has a smoother thud than most, though it comes from the same Atlantic as the harsher-sounding waters among the

Orkneys. The difference may be that the channel tides move through purple waters which have drifted up from sunny Portugal, while the other has a shiver from the coast of Greenland.

The music of sea waters is wonderfully varied. Every bay and headland and strait has its note which the local fisherfolk recognize even in times of dense fog; a note which guides them home or which helps them locate the place for their fishing.

For many years I have been living far from the sea. Sometimes I feel the urge to go down to the sea again, all the way from the Himalayas to Cape Comorin. And maybe I will one day.

Meanwhile, if I wish to listen to the sound of the sea, there's always my seashell—or Mukesh's teacup.

Solitude

As far as I know, we do not have an anthology on solitude. It's a condition appreciated only by a small minority, I suppose.

It seems to me that most people are scared of solitude, for almost everything is carried out on a crowded scale. Clubs, wedding parties, sporting events, political meetings, victory parades, protests, religious events, melas, even prayer meetings—the bigger the crowd, the more successful the event. Let a man be seen walking about the hills or countryside alone, and he will be labelled an eccentric; for to most people loneliness is wrongly linked to unhappiness. Their minds are not deep enough to appreciate the sweetness and balm of solitude, they are afraid of life itself, of coming face to face with themselves.

Most of the time we are taken up with family life or working for a living. To get away from it all, just once in a while, into the hills or fields or by-lanes, where 'I am I', is to enjoy undisturbed serenity. It helps one to contemplate, to create a philosophy of life, to take the mind off the nagging pressures of this age of technological mayhem.

Probably the best book on solitude is *Robinson Crusoe*. Crusoe learnt to appreciate and value his enforced solitude. The arrival of Man Friday proved to be rather unsettling, and his subsequent conflict with savage intruders made him even more appreciative of his lost solitude.

Richard Jefferies, in *The Story of My Heart*, claims to be a pagan by nature, and avoids the haunts of men, escaping into the woods with a certain alacrity. He is happiest in the bosom of nature, and is a true solitary, with sun, moon and stars as his companions. An atheist, he does not even seek the companionship of a possible Creator; he simply accepts the natural world as he finds it.

But you do not have to turn your back on the world at large in order to find true solitude. A solitary spirit can move around with the crowd while still holding on to his innate reserve. Take Frobisher, the junior partner in a firm of solicitors in A.E.W. Mason's enjoyable novel, *The House of the Arrow*. 'He was a solitary person. Very few people up till now had mattered to him at all, and even those he could do without. It was his passion to feel that his life and the means of his life did not depend upon the purchased skill of other people... A half-decked sailing boat which one man could handle, an ice-axe, a rifle, an inexhaustible volume or two like *The Ring and the Book*—these with the stars and his own thoughts had been his companions on many lonely expeditions...'

Many of Conrad's characters have learnt to live with the solitude of the great oceans—Captain Lingard in *An Outcast of the Islands*, Captain Machheir in *Typhoon*, *Lord Jim*, Conrad himself in *The Secret Sharer, The Shadow Line*, and in the character of his narrator, Marlow.

T.E. Lawrence was another who chose the solitary life; indeed, he ended it in complete anonymity; but before that he had captured the solitude of the desert in his great work, *The Seven Pillars of Wisdom*.

The sea, the desert, the mountains—these underpopulated areas of the planet do seem to appeal to the solitary individual, whether writer or adventurer.

Some choose to sail around the world in small boats. Others, like Jefferies, remain in their own patch, yet see the world in a grain of sand.

~

In the Garden of My Dreams

The cosmos has all the genius of simplicity. The plant stands tall and erect; its foliage is uncomplicated, its inflorescence are bold, fresh, cheerful. Any flower, from a rose to a rhododendron, can be complicated. The cosmos is splendidly simple.

No wonder it takes its name from the Greek 'cosmos', meaning the universe as an ordered whole—the sum total of experience! For this unpretentious flower does seem to sum it all up: perfection without apparent striving for it, the artistry of the South American footballer! Needless to say, it came from tropical America.

And growing it is no trouble. A handful of seeds thrown in a waste patch or on a grassy hill slope, and a few months later there they are, en masse, doing their samba in the sunshine. They are almost wild, but not quite. They need very little attention, but if you take them too much for granted they will go away the following year. Simple they may be, but not insensitive. They need plenty of space. And as my own small apartment cannot accommodate them, they definitely belong to my dream garden.

My respect for the cosmos goes back to my childhood when I wandered into what seemed like a forest of these flowers, all twice my height (I must have been five at the time) but looking down on me in the friendliest way, their fine feathery foliage giving off a faint aroma. Now when I find them flowering on the Himalayan hillsides in mellow October sunshine, they are like old friends and I greet them accordingly, pressing my face to their petals.

Not everyone likes the cosmos. I have met some upper-class ladies (golf club members) who complain that it gives them hay fever, and they use this as an excuse to root out all cosmos from their gardens. I expect they are just being snobbish. There are other flowers which give off just as much pollen dust.

I have noticed the same snobbishness in regard to marigolds, especially the smaller Indian variety. 'Cultivated' people won't cultivate these humble but attractive flowers. Is it because they are used for making garlands? Or because they are not delicately scented? Or because they are so easily grown in the backyards of homes?

My grandparents once went to war with each other over the marigold. Grandfather had grown a few in one corner of the garden. Just as they began flowering, they vanished—Granny had removed them overnight! There was a row, and my grandparents did not speak to each other for several days. Then, by calling them 'French' marigolds, Grandfather managed to reintroduce them to the garden. Granny liked the idea of having something 'French' in her garden. Such is human nature!

Sometimes a wildflower can put its more spectacular garden cousins to shame. I am thinking now of the commelina, which I discover in secret places after the rains have passed. Its bright sky-blue flowers take my breath away. It has a sort of unguarded innocence that is beyond corruption.

Wild roses give me more pleasure than the sophisticated domestic variety. On a walk in the Himalayan foothills I have encountered a number of these shrubs and climbers—the ineptly named dog rose, sparkling white in summer; the sweet briar with its deep pink petals and bright red rosehips; the trailing rose, found in shady places; and the wild raspberry (the fruit more attractive than the flower) which belongs to the same family.

A sun-lover, I like plenty of yellow on the hillsides and in gardens—sunflowers, Californian poppies, winter jasmine, St John's Wort, buttercups, wild strawberries, mustard in bloom... But if you live in a hot place, you might prefer cooling blues and soft purples— forget-me-not, bluebells, cornflowers, lavender. I'd go far for a sprig of sweetly-scented lavender. To many older people the word lavender is charm; it seems to recall the plaintive strain of once familiar music—

> *Lavender blue, dilly dilly,*
> *Lavender green,*
> *When I am king, dilly dilly,*
> *You'll be my queen.*

This tame-looking, blue-green, stiff, sticky, and immovable shrub holds as much poetry and romance in its wiry arms as would fill a large book.

Most cultivated flowers were originally wild, and many take their names from the botanists who first 'tamed' them. Thus, the dahlia is named after Mr Dahl, a Swede; the rudbeckia after Rudbeck, a Dutchman; the zinnia after Dr Zinn, a German; and the lobelia after Monsieur Lobel, a Flemish physician. They, and others, brought to Europe many of the flowers found growing wild in tropical America, Asia and Africa.

But I am no botanist. I prefer to be the butterfly, perfectly happy in going from flower to flower in search of nectar.

~

Some Plants Become Friends

The little rose begonia: it has a glossy chocolate leaf, a pretty rose-pink flower, and it grows and flowers in my bedroom—almost all the year round. What more can one ask for?

Some plants become friends. Most garden flowers are fair-weather friends; gone in the winter when times are difficult up here in the mountains. Those who stand by you in adversity—plant or human—are your true friends; there aren't many around, so cherish them and take care of them in all seasons.

A loyal plant friend is the variegated ivy that has spread all over my bedroom wall. My small bedroom-cum-study gets plenty of light and sun, and when the windows are open, cool breeze from the mountains floats in, rustling the leaves of the ivy. (This breeze can turn into a raging blizzard in winter—on one occasion, even blowing the roof away—but right now, it's just a zephyr, gentle and balmy.) Ivy plants seem to like my room, and this one, which I brought up from Dehra, took an instant liking to my desk and walls, so that I now have difficulty keeping it from trailing over my typewriter when I am at work.

I like to take in other people's sick or discarded plants and nurse or cajole them back to health. This has given me a bit of a reputation as a plant doctor. Actually, all I do is give an ailing plant a quiet corner where it can rest and recuperate from whatever ails it—they have usually been ill-treated in some way. Plant abuse, no less! And its wonderful how quickly a small tree or plant will recover if given a little encouragement.

I rescued a dying asparagus fern from the portals of the Savoy Hotel, and now, six months later, its strong feathery fronds have taken over most of one window, so that I have no need of curtains. Nandu, the owner of the Savoy, now wants his fern back.

Maya Banerjee's sick geranium, never allowed to settle in one place—hence its stunted appearance—has, within a fortnight of being admitted to my plant ward, burst forth in such an array of new leaf and flower that I'm afraid it might pull a muscle or strain a ligament from too much activity.

Should I return these and other plants when they have fully recovered? I don't think they want to go back. And I should hate to see them suffering relapses on being returned to their former abodes. So I tell the owners that their plants need monitoring for a while… Perhaps, if I sent in doctor's bills, the demands for their return would not be so strident?

Loyalty in plants, as in friends, must be respected and rewarded. If dandelions show a tendency to do well on the steps of the house, then that is where they shall be encouraged to grow. If a sorrel is happier on the windowsill than on the hillside, then I shall let it stay, even if it means the window won't close properly. And if the hydrangea does better in my neighbour's garden than mine, then my neighbour shall be given the hydrangea. Among flower lovers, there must be no double standards: generosity, not greed; sugar, not spite.

And what of the rewards for me, apart from the soothing effect of fresh fronds and leaves at my place of work and rest? Well, the other evening I came home to find my room vibrating to the full-throated chorus of several crickets who had found the ivy to their liking. I thought they would keep me up all night with their music; but when I switched the light off, they immediately fell silent. So, crickets don't sing in the dark, I surmised, and switched the light on again. Once more, I was treated to symphonic variations on a theme by Tchaikovsky.

This reminded me that I hadn't listened to Tchaikovsky for some time, so I played a tape of 'The Dance of the Sugar Plum Fairy' from the *Nutcracker Suite*. The crickets maintained a respectful silence, even with the lights on.

~~◯

The Walkers' Club

Though their numbers have diminished over the years, there are still a few compulsive daily walkers around: the odd ones, the strange ones, who will walk all day, here, there and everywhere, not in order to get somewhere, but to escape from their homes, their lonely rooms, their mirrors, themselves...

Those of us who must work for a living and would love to be able to walk a little more don't often get the chance. There are offices to attend, deadlines to be met, trains or planes to be caught, deals to be struck, people to deal with. It's the rat race for most people, whether they like it or not. So who are these lucky ones, a small minority it has to be said, who find time to walk all over this hill station from morn to night?

Some are fitness freaks, I suppose; but several are just unhappy souls who find some release, some meaning, in covering miles and miles of highway without so much as a nod in the direction of others on the road. They are not looking at anything as they walk, not even at a violet in a mossy stone.

Here comes Miss Romola. She's been at it for years. A retired schoolmistress who never married. No friends. Lonely as hell. Not even a visit from a former pupil. She could not have been very popular.

She has money in the bank. She owns her own flat. But she doesn't spend much time in it. I see her from my window, tramping up the road to Lai Tibba. She strides around the mountain like the character in the old song 'She'll be coming round the mountain', only she doesn't wear pink pyjamas; she dresses in slacks and a shirt. She doesn't stop to talk to anyone. It's quick march to the top of the mountain, and then down again, home again, jiggety-jig. When she has to go down to Dehradun (too long a walk even for her), she stops a car and cadges a lift. No taxis for her; not even the bus.

Miss Romola's chief pleasure in life comes from conserving her money. There are people like that. They view the rest of the world with suspicion. An overture of friendship will be construed as taking an undue interest in her assets. We are all part of an international conspiracy to relieve her of her material possessions! She has no servants, no friends; even her relatives are kept at a safe distance.

A similar sort of character but even more eccentric is Mr Sen, who used to live in the US and walks from the Happy Valley to Landour (five miles) and back every day, in all seasons, year in and year out. Once or twice every week he will stop at the Community Hospital to have his blood pressure checked or undergo a blood or urine test. With all that walking he should have no health problems, but he is a hypochondriac and is convinced that he is dying of something or the other.

He came to see me once. Unlike Miss Romala, he seemed to want a friend, but his neurotic nature turned people away. He was convinced that he was surrounded by individual and collective hostility. People were always staring at him, he told me. I couldn't help wondering why, because he looked fairly nondescript. He wore conventional Western clothes, perfectly acceptable in urban India, and looked respectable enough except for a constant nervous turning of the head, looking to the left, right, or behind, as though to check on anyone who might be following him. He was convinced that he was being followed at all times.

'By whom?' I asked.

'Agents of the government,' he said.

'But why should they follow you?'

'I look different,' he said. 'They see me as an outsider. They think I work for the CIA.'

'And do you?'

'No, no!' He shied nervously away from me. 'Why did you say that?'

'Only because you brought the subject up. I haven't noticed anyone following you.'

'They're very clever about it. Perhaps you're following me too.'

'I'm afraid I can't walk as fast or as far as you,' I said with a laugh, but he wasn't amused. He never smiled, never laughed. He did not feel safe in India, he confided. The saffron brigade was after him!

'But why?' I asked. 'They're not after me. And you're a Hindu with a Hindu name.'

'Ah yes, but I don't look like one!'

'Well, I don't look like a Taoist monk, but that's what I am,' I said, adding, in a more jocular manner: 'I know how to become invisible, and you wouldn't know I'm around. That's why no one follows me! I have this wonderful cloak, you see, and when I wear it I become invisible!'

'Can you lend it to me?' he asked eagerly.

'I'd love to,' I said, 'but it's at the cleaners right now. Maybe next week.'

'Crazy,' he muttered. 'Quite mad.' And he hurried on.

A few weeks later he returned to New York and safety. Then I heard he'd been mugged in Central Park. He's recovering, but doesn't do much walking now.

Neurotics do not walk for pleasure, they walk out of compulsion. They are not looking at the trees or the flowers or the mountains; they are not looking at other people (except in apprehension); they are usually walking away from something—unhappiness or disarray in their lives. They tire themselves out, physically and mentally, and that brings them some relief.

Like the journalist who came to see me last year. He'd escaped from Delhi, he told me. He had taken a room in Landour Bazaar and was going to spend a year on his own, away from family, friends, colleagues, the entire rat race. He was full of noble resolutions. He was planning to write an epic poem or a great Indian novel or a philosophical treatise. Every fortnight I meet someone who is planning to write one or the other of these things, and I do not like to discourage them, just in case they turn violent!

In effect he did nothing but walk up and down the mountain, growing shabbier by the day. Sometimes he recognized me. At other times there was a blank look on his face, as though he were on some drug, and he would walk past me without a sign of recognition. He discarded his slippers and began walking about barefoot, even on the stony paths. He did not change or wash his clothes. Then he disappeared; that is, I no longer saw him around.

I did not really notice his absence until I saw an ad in one of the national papers, asking for information about his whereabouts. His family was anxious to locate him. The ad carried a picture of the gentleman, taken in happier, healthier times; but it was definitely my acquaintance of that summer.

I was sitting in the bank manager's office, up in the cantonment, when a woman came in, making inquiries about her husband. It was the missing journalist's wife. Yes, said Mr Ohri, the friendly bank manager, he'd opened an account with them; not a very large sum, but there were a few hundred rupees lying to his credit. And no, they hadn't seen him in the bank for at least three months

He couldn't be found. Several months passed, and it was presumed that he had moved on to some other town; or that he'd lost his mind or his memory. Then some milkmen from Kolti Gaon discovered bones and remnants of clothing at the bottom of a cliff.

In the pocket of the ragged shirt was the journalist's press card.

How he'd fallen to his death remains a mystery. It's easy to miss your footing and take a fatal plunge on the steep slopes of this range. He may have been high on something or he may simply have been trying out an unfamiliar path. Walking can be dangerous in the hills if you don't know the way or if you take one chance too many.

And here's a tale to illustrate that old chestnut that truth is often stranger than fiction.

Colonel Parshottam had just retired and was determined to pass the evening of his life doing the things he enjoyed most: taking early morning and late evening walks, afternoon siestas, a drop of whisky before dinner, and a good book on his bedside table.

A few streets away, on the fourth floor of a block of flats, lived Mrs L, a stout, neglected woman of forty, who'd had enough of life and was determined to do away with herself.

Along came the Colonel on the road below, a song on his lips, strolling along with a jaunty air; in love with life and wanting more of it.

Quite unaware of anyone else around, Mrs L chose that moment to throw herself out of her fourth-floor window. Seconds later she landed with a thud on the Colonel. If this was a Ruskin Bond story, it would have been love at first flight. But the grim reality was that he was crushed beneath her and did not recover from the impact. Mrs L, on the other hand, survived the fall and lived on into a miserable old age.

There is no moral to the story, any more than there is a moral to life. We cannot foresee when a bolt from the blue will put an end to the best-laid plans of mice and men.

~

Death of the Trees

The peace and quiet of the hillside above Maplewood Cottage disappeared forever one winter. The powers-that-be decided to build another new road into the mountains and the PWD saw fit to take it right past the cottage, about six feet from the window which overlooked the forest.

In my journal I wrote—Already they have felled most of the trees.

The walnut was one of the first to go. A tree I had lived with for over ten years, watching it grow as I had watched Prem's small son Rakesh grow up, looking forward to its new leaf-buds, the broad green leaves or summer turning to spears of gold in September when the walnuts were ripe and ready to fall. I knew this tree better than the others. It was just below the window where a buttress for the road is going up.

Another tree I will miss is the young deodar, the only one growing in this stretch of the woods. Some years back it was stunted from lack of sunlight. The oaks covered it with their shaggy branches, so I cut away some of the overhanging ones and after that the deodar grew much faster. It was just coming into its own this year—now cut down in its prime like my young brother on the road to Delhi last month. Both victims of the roads—the tree killed by the PWD, my brother by a truck.

Twenty oaks have been felled just in this small stretch near the cottage. By the time this bypass reaches Jabai Khet, about six miles from here, over a thousand oaks will have been slaughtered, besides many other fine trees—maples, deodars and pines—most of them unnecessarily as they grow some fifty or sixty yards from the roadside.

The trouble is, hardly anyone (with the exception of the contractor who buys the felled trees) really believes that trees and shrubs are necessary. They get in the way so much, don't they? According to my milkman, the only useful tree is the one which can be picked clean of its leaves for fodder! And a young man remarked to me, 'You should come to Pauri. The view is terrific, there's not a tree in the way!'

Well he can stay here now and enjoy the view of the ravaged hillside. But as the oaks have gone, the milkman will have to look further afield for his fodder.

Rakesh calls the maples butterfly trees because when the winged seeds fall, they flutter like butterflies in the breeze. No maples now. No bright red leaves to flame against the sky No birds! That is to say, no birds near the house. No longer will it be possible for me to open the window and watch the scarlet minivets flitting through the dark green foliage of the oaks; the long-tailed magpies gliding through the trees, the barbet calling insistently from his perch on the top of the deodar. Forest birds, all of them, they will now be in search of some other stretch of surviving forest. The only visitors will be the crows who have learnt to live with and off humans and seem to multiply along with roads, houses and people. And even when all the people have gone, the crows will still be there.

Other things to look forward to—trucks thundering past in the night, perhaps a tea and pakora shop around the corner. The grinding of gears, the music of motor horns. Will the whistling thrush be heard above them? The explosions that continually shatter the silence of the mountains as thousand-year-old rocks are dynamited have frightened away all but the most intrepid of birds and animals. Even the bold langurs haven't shown their faces for over a fortnight.

Somehow, I don't think we shall wait for the tea shop to arrive. There must be some other quiet corner, possibly on the next mountain where new roads have yet to come into being. No doubt this is a negative attitude and if I had any sense I'd open my own tea shop. To retreat is to be a loser. But the trees are losers too and when they fall, they do so with a certain dignity.

Never mind. Men come and go, the mountains remain.

***

The Open Road

As the years go by, I do not walk as far or as fast as I used to; but speed and distance were never my forte. Like J. Krishnamurti, I believe that the journey is more important than the destination. But, then, I have never really had a destination. The glory that comes from conquering the Himalayan peaks is not for me. My greatest pleasure lies in taking a path—any old path will do—and following it until it leads me to a forest glade or village or stream or windy hilltop.

This sort of tramping (it does not even qualify as trekking) is a compulsive thing with me. You could call it my vice, since it is stronger than the desire for wine, women or song. To get on to the open road fills me with joie de vivre, gives me an exhilaration not found in other, possibly more worthy, pursuits.

Only this afternoon I had one of my more enjoyable tramps. I had been cooped up in my room for several days, while outside it rained and hailed and snowed and the wind blew icily from all directions. It seemed ages since I'd taken a long walk. Fed up with it all, I pulled on my overcoat, banged the door shut and set off up the hillside.

I kept to the main road, but because of the heavy snow there were no vehicles on it. Even as I walked, flurries of snow struck my face, and collected on my coat and head. Up at the top of the hill, the deodars were clothed in a mantle of white. It was fairyland: everything still and silent. The only movement was the circling off an eagle over the trees. I walked for an hour, and passed only one person, the milkman on his way back to his village. His cans were crowned with snow. He looked a little tipsy. He asked me the time, but before I could tell him he shook me by the hand and said I was a good fellow because I never complained about the water in the milk. I told him that as long as he used clean water, I'd contain my wrath.

On my way back, I passed a small group. It consisted of a person in some sort of uniform (because of the snow I couldn't really make it out), who was hurling epithets at several small children who were busy throwing snowballs at him. He kept shouting: 'Do you know who I am? Do you know who I am?' The children did not want to know. They were only interested in hitting their target, and succeeded once in every five or six attempts.

I came home exhilarated and immediately sat down beside the stove to write this piece. I found some lines of Stevenson's which seemed appropriate:

> *And this shall be for music when no one else is near,*
> *The fine song for singing, the rare song to hear!*
> *That only I remember, that only you admire,*
> *Of the broad road that stretches, and the roadside fire.*

He speaks directly to me, across the mists of time: R.L. Stevenson, prince of essayists. There is none like him today. We hurry, hurry in a heat of hope—and who has time for roadside fires, except, perhaps, those who must work on the roads in all weathers?

Whenever I walk into the hills, I come across gangs of road workers breaking stones, cutting into the rocky hillsides, building retaining walls. I am not against more roads—especially in the hills, where the people have remained impoverished largely because of the inaccessibility of their villages. Besides, a new road is one more road for me to explore, and in the interests of progress I am prepared to put up with the dust raised by the occasional bus. And if it becomes too dusty, one can always leave the main road. There is no dearth of paths leading off into the valleys.

On one such diversionary walk, I reached a village where I was given a drink of curd and a meal of rice and beans. That is another of the attractions of tramping to nowhere in particular—the finding of somewhere in particular; the striking up of friendships; the discovery of new springs and waterfalls, unusual plants, rare flowers, strange birds. In the hills, a new vista opens up at every bend in the road.

That is what makes me a compulsive walker—new vistas, and the charm of the unexpected.

In the Darkness of the Night

No night is so dark as it seems.

Here in Landour, on the first range of the Himalayas, I have grown accustomed to the night's brightness—moonlight, starlight, lamplight, firelight! Even fireflies and glow-worms light up the darkness.

Over the years, the night has become my friend. On the one hand, it gives me privacy; on the other, it provides me with limitless freedom.

Not many people relish the dark. There are some who will even sleep with their lights burning all night. They feel safer that way. Safer from the phantoms conjured up by their imaginations. A primeval instinct, perhaps, going back to the time when primitive man hunted by day and was in turn hunted by night.

And yet, I have always felt safer by night, provided I do not deliberately wander about on cliff tops or roads where danger is known to lurk. It's true that burglars and lawbreakers often work by night, their principal object being to get into other people's houses and make off with the silver or the family jewels. They are not into communing with the stars. Nor are late-night revellers, who are usually to be found in brightly lit places and are thus easily avoided. The odd drunk stumbling home is quite harmless and probably in need of guidance. I have often helped drunks find their way home, although I have yet to be thanked for it!

I feel safer by night, yes, but then I do have the advantage of living in the mountains, in a region where crime and random violence are comparatively rare. I know that if I were living in a big city in some other part of the world, I would think twice about walking home at midnight, no matter how pleasing the night sky.

Walking home at midnight in Landour can be quite eventful, but in a different sort of way. One is conscious all the time of the silent life in the surrounding trees and bushes. I have smelt a leopard without seeing it. I have seen jackals on the prowl. I have watched foxes dance in the moonlight. I have seen flying squirrels flit from one treetop to another. I have observed pine martens on their nocturnal journeys, and listened to the calls of nightjars and owls and other birds who live by night.

Not all on the same night, of course. That would be a case of too many riches all at once. Some night walks can be uneventful. But usually there is something to see or hear or sense. Like those foxes dancing in the moonlight. One night, when I got home, I sat down and wrote these lines:

> As I walked home last night,
> I saw a lone fox dancing
> In the bright moonlight.
> I stood and watched; then
> Took the low road, knowing
> The night was his by right.
> Sometimes, when words ring true,
> I'm like a lone fox dancing
> In the morning dew.

Who else, apart from foxes, flying squirrels, and night-loving writers, are at home in the dark? Well, there are the nightjars, not much to look at, although their large, lustrous eyes gleam uncannily in the light of a lamp. But their sounds are distinctive. The breeding call of the Indian nightjar resembles the sound of a stone skimming over the surface of a frozen pond; it can be heard for a considerable distance. Another species utters a loud grating call which, when close at hand, sounds exactly like a whiplash cutting the air. 'Horsfield's nightjar' (with which I am more familiar in Mussoorie) makes a noise similar to that made by striking a plank with a hammer.

During the day the bird spends long hours sitting motionless on the ground, where it is practically invisible, only springing into life when an intruder approaches. It is also called the 'Goatsucker' because of its huge mouth and the legend spread in many countries that it feeds from the udders of cows and goats. Because of this erroneous belief, it is considered a bird of ill omen. Night-flying insects, such as moths and beetles, are its preferred meals.

I must not forget the owls, those most celebrated of night birds, much maligned by those who fear the night.

Most owls have very pleasant calls. The little jungle owlet has a note which is both mellow and musical. One misguided writer has likened its call to a motorcycle starting up, but this is a libel. If only motorcycles sounded like the jungle owl, the world would be a more peaceful place to live and sleep in.

Then there is the little scops owl, who speaks only in monosyllables, occasionally saying 'Wow' softly but with great deliberation. He will continue to say 'Wow' at intervals of about a minute, for several hours throughout the night.

Probably the most familiar of Indian owls is the spotted owlet, a noisy bird who pours forth a volley of chuckles and squeaks in the early evening and at intervals all night. Towards sunset, I watch the owlets emerge from their holes one after another. Before coming out, each puts out a queer little round head with staring eyes. After they have emerged they usually sit very quietly for a time as though only half awake. Then, all of a sudden, they begin to chuckle, finally breaking out in a torrent of chattering. Having in this way 'psyched' themselves into the right frame of mind, they spread their short, rounded wings and sail off for the night's hunting.

I wind my way homewards. 'Night with her train of stars' is always enticing. The poet Henley found her so. But he also wrote of 'her great gift of sleep', and it is this gift that I am now about to accept with gratitude and humility. For it is also good to be up and dancing in the morning dew.

A Writer's Life

Good Morning

Quite often, I'm up with the lark—more often, with the sound of monkeys jumping on my tin roof. I've often wondered why hill station houses must have these rusty red tin roofs, apart from an understandable human desire to make them look like battered old biscuit tins. Well, now I know. They're there for the benefit of monkeys, langurs, field-rats, cats, crows, mynas, spiders and scorpions.

I don't mind the spiders—they seem harmless enough. The scorpions are evil-looking but sluggish—unlike the dashing red scorpions of the Rajasthan desert. The other day I found a scorpion enjoying a nap on my pillow. I like to have my pillow to myself, so I tipped the slumbering creature out of the window and returned to my afternoon siesta. I do not take the lives of fellow creatures if I can help it. Cats are not so squeamish. At night they get between the tin roof and the wooden ceiling and create havoc among the rats and mice who dwell there. And early morning, if I leave a window open, the monkeys will finish anything they find on the breakfast table.

In spite of occasional rude awakenings, I enjoy sleeping late, especially on winter mornings when the sun struggles to penetrate banks of cloud or mist or drizzle. The bed is one of my favourite places. And even if I am wide awake, I can lie there under the blanket and razai and enjoy the view without rising. The window in front of me looks out on the clouds or the clear sky; the window beside it gives me a view of upper Landour and the houses on the slopes; and the far window looks out on a thicket of oak trees. And if I sit up in bed, I can see the road and some of the people on it.

But to start with my bed, for that's where the day begins and ends. There's something to be said for beds. After all, we spend roughly half our lives stretched out upon them. The amount of time spent in sleep varies from one individual to another. 'Five hours sleepeth a traveller, seven a scholar, eight a merchant, and eleven every knave.'

So goes an old proverb, and there is much truth in proverbs. I must fall somewhere between merchant and knave. There are times when I like to rise early and times when I enjoy sleeping late. If I fall asleep before midnight, I will rise early. One hour's sleep before midnight is worth two after. When the moon is up, the night has its magic; but at two or three in the morning there is very little to offer, because by ten even cats, bats and field-rats are asleep. In summer, birdsong starts at dawn, somewhere between four and five o'clock and that's a good time to be up and about, exercising mind or body.

The other morning I was up at five; wrote a couple of pages, opened my window and swallowed a portion of cloud; closed it, conscience clear, and returned to bed where presently a cup of tea materialized, prepared by Beena or Dolly or some other member of the family. But for that morning cup of tea, would I have survived all these years? Without it, the mornings would be one long, endless wasteland. Without it, I would not get up. I would refuse breakfast, lunch and dinner, and waste away. Looking back upon my life from the vantage point of seventy years, I cannot remember a time when I was deprived of that morning cup of tea. Except for when I was in boarding school. Now you know why I ran away.

Getting up and making my own tea is no fun either. It has to be brought to me by some gentle soul—man, woman or child who has got up before everyone else in order to ensure that I get up too.

The best tea I've ever drunk was made by an ex-convict who worked for my landlady in Dehradun, many years ago. He told me that while he was in jail he was assigned to the task of making the warden's tea. It was appreciated so much that they wouldn't let him go even after he'd served his sentence. How, then, did he gain his freedom? Well, my landlady was the wife of the jail superintendent. So you see how well the system worked!

For a while in London, I had a Jewish landlady who brought me my breakfast on a tray. I don't know if such civilized courtesies still exist. Back in the 1950s, English food was not very exciting; it had yet to be enriched by Indian curries and Chinese noodles. But breakfasts were always good—far superior to the skimpy fare served out by the French. Bacon and eggs, marmalade on toast, occasionally a kipper, a sausage, a slice of ham, grapefruit...what more could anyone ask for at the start of a busy day. And even now, when the days aren't quite so busy, I might skip lunch or dinner but I'll breakfast well.

So finally I'm out of bed and enjoying my breakfast. The children have gone to school and silence has descended on the house. A day in the life of Ruskin Bond is about to commence. I am at liberty to write a poem or a story or fill these pages with inconsequential thoughts. But first I must get dressed.

I am not fond of clothes, but I wouldn't care to start the day's work without at least wearing a clean shirt. When I was a struggling young writer, I did not possess more than two shirts at one time, but I would wash one every night in the hope that it would be dry by morning. Even today I don't have a large wardrobe. It isn't possible, not with all these monkeys around. If you see a large red monkey wearing a blue and yellow check bush-shirt, please try and retrieve it for me— it's my favourite shirt. Putting clothes out on the roof to dry is fairly common practice in hill stations, but not to be recommended. Only the other day, when a strong wind came up from the east, I saw my pyjamas floating away downhill to end up entangled in the branches of an oak tree. Fortunately the milkman's son, who is good at climbing oak trees, rescued them for me. The milkman's son does not pass his exams, but us long as he can climb trees, he'll be a success in life. All of us need just one good accomplishment in order to get by. Obviously he can't spend the rest of his life climbing trees, but it's the agility and enterprise involved in the act that will make him a survivor.

Enough of bed and breakfast and getting ready for the long morning's journey into day. When does this ageing writer sit down to write? Or does he simply dictate to a secretary or into a machine of some kind? Well, I wish that was the case, because I'm a lazy sort of writer, better in bed than out of it. Unfortunately, I get tongue-tied when I try to tell a story, make a speech, or conduct something as simple as a telephone or cell phone conversation.

Recently Dolly made me buy a mobile phone; it would make me more efficient and up-to-date, she said. I tried making a call, and when nothing happened, she said, 'Dada, you're holding it upside down!' I got it the right way up and tried again, and when nothing happened, she said, 'Not here. You have to go to the window.'

I dutifully walked over and tried again. No luck. 'Open the window,' ordered Dolly. I opened the window. Just a crackle on the cell phone.

'Now look out of the window!' I looked out, and there were all these schoolgirls gazing up at me, wondering why I was staring down at them. 'Good morning girls,' I called out, and gave them a friendly wave. 'No girls here,' said a gruff voice on the cell phone. 'This is your local thana.'

I gave the mobile to Dolly. She has no difficulty in getting through to her friends, or hearing from them. I'm no good at these things, except to pay the bill.

I'm strictly a man of the written word. Give me pen and paper and I manage to get something down, even if it's only for my own amusement. An elderly reader once remarked, 'How do you manage to write so much about nothing?' to which I could only reply: 'Well, it's better than writing nothing about everything!'

That small red ant walking across my desk may mean nothing to the world at large, but to me it represents the world at large. It represents industry, single-mindedness, intricacy of design, the perfection of nature, the miracle of creation. So much so, that it inspires me to poetic composition:

> *You stride through the wasteland of my desk,*
> *Pressing on over books and papers,*
> *Down the wall and across the floor—*
> *Small red ant, now crossing a sea of raindrops At my open door.*
> *Your destiny, your task*
> *To carry home*
> *That heavy sunflower seed,*
> *Waving it like a banner*
> *Of victory!*

Nothing is insignificant; nothing is without consequence in the intricate web of life.

~

Among the Maples and Oaks

It isn't many years since I left Maplewood, but I wouldn't be surprised to hear that the cottage has disappeared. Already, during my last months there, the trees were being cut and the new road was being blasted out of the mountain. It would pass just below the old cottage. There were (as far as I know) no plans to blow up the house; but it was already shaky and full of cracks, and a few tremors, such as those produced by passing trucks, drilling machines and bulldozers, would soon bring the cottage to the ground.

If it has gone, don't write and tell me: I'd rather not know.

When I moved in, it had been nestling there among the oaks for over seventy years. It had become a part of the forest. Birds nestled in the eaves; beetles burrowed in the woodwork. Some denizens remained, even during my residence. And I was there—how long? Eight, nine years, I'm not sure; it was a timeless sort of place. Even the rent was paid only once a year, at a time of my choosing.

I first saw the cottage in late spring, when the surrounding forest was at its best—the oaks and maples in new leaf, the oak leaves a pale green, the maple leaves red and gold and bronze; this is the Himalayan maple, quite different from the North American maple; only the winged seed-pods are similar, twisting and turning in the breeze as they fall to the ground, so that the Garhwalis call it the Butterfly Tree.

There was one very tall, very old maple above the cottage, and this was probably the tree that gave the house its name. A portion of it was blackened where it had been struck by lightning, but the rest of it lived on, a favourite haunt of woodpeckers: the ancient peeling bark seemed to harbour any number of tiny insects, and the woodpeckers would be tapping away all day. A steep path ran down to the cottage. During heavy rain, it would become a watercourse and the earth would be washed away to leave it very stony and uneven. I first took this path to see Miss Mackenzie, an impoverished old lady who lived in two small rooms on the ground floor and who was acting on behalf of the owner. It was she who told me that the cottage was to-let provided she could remain in the portion downstairs.

Actually, the path ran straight across a landing and up to the front door of the first floor. It was the ground floor that was tucked away in the shadow of the hill; it was reached by a flight of steps, which also took the rush of water when the path was in flood.

Miss Mackenzie was eighty-six. I helped her up the steps and she opened the door for me. It led into an L-shaped room. There were two large windows, and when I pushed the first of these open, the forest seemed to rush upon me. From below, from the ravine, the deep-throated song of the whistling thrush burst upon me.

I told Miss Mackenzie I would take the place. She grew excited; it must have been lonely for her during the past several years, with most of the cottage lying empty, and only her old bearer and a mongrel dog for company. Her own house had been mortgaged to a moneylender. Her brothers and sisters were long dead.

I told her I would move in soon: my books were still in Delhi. She gave me the keys and I left a cheque with her. It was all done on an impulse—the decision to give up my job in Delhi, find a cheap house in a hill station and return to freelance writing. It was a dream I'd had for some time; lack of money had made it difficult to realize. But then, I knew that if I was going to wait for money to come, I might have to wait until I was old and grey and full of sleep. I was thirty-five—still young enough to take a few risks. If the dream was to become reality, this was the time to do something about it.

I don't know what led me to Maplewood; it was the first place I saw, and I did not bother to see any others. The location was far from being ideal. It faced east and stood in the shadow of the Balahissar Hill, so that while it received the early morning sun, it went without the evening sun.

There was no view of the snows and no view of the plains. In front stood Burnt Hill. But the forest below the cottage seemed full of possibilities, and the windows opening on to it probably decided the issue. In my romantic frame of my mind, I was susceptible to magic casements opening wide. I would make a window-seat and lie there on a summer's day, writing lyric poetry…

But long before that could happen I was opening tins of sardines and sharing them with Miss Mackenzie. And then Prem came along. And there were others, like Binya. I went away at times, but returned as soon as possible. Once you have lived with mountains, there is no escape. You belong to them.

In Praise of Older Women

Some of my autobiographical work may have given the impression that I am something of a misogynist. This is not the case. While the path of true love and romance proved rather stony and while I may have faltered at the altar or backed away from the registrar's office, I have always enjoyed the friendship and company of women. Older women, in particular, have always been stimulating, in the nicest sense of the word.

I was only twelve when I was smitten by a girl of eighteen, a kind and beautiful Anglo-Indian girl who broke many hearts before she went on to marry a Sergeant-Major in the British Army. But that was puppy love, and I soon recovered from the condition.

What I really want to do here is to recall some of the women who helped me along the way, or who were simply good companions. If you really want to know what I mean by Companionship, you must get hold of J.B. Priestley's classic novel, *The Good Companions*—a wonderful tale of friendship growing out of shared experience, as an incongruous group of eccentric but talented people take to the road performing in little theatres across England.

Well, my own performances are limited to putting words on paper, and occasionally travelling about India, reading and talking to children in numerous schools, where almost all the principals and teachers are women. Having grown up in a boarding school dominated by male teachers who were more interested in getting us on to the sports field, it's refreshing to find schools where the children are encouraged to read and write and not only as a part of their curriculum. In spite of the rival attractions of television and the Internet, the number of book-lovers is on the increase, and this is due largely to the efforts of enlightened schoolteachers—and just occasionally enlightened parents!

Certainly my father encouraged me to read and I wish all fathers would do the same for their children. But when I became a writer, my first editors were women—Diana Athill, who encouraged me to write my first novel, and Kaye Webb, who published my stories in *Young Elizabethan*. Diana became a good friend and helped to make life tolerable for me during those lonely years in London. She was fifteen years older than me, but somehow I never noticed this. We had so much to talk about (books, films, music) and so many places to visit (the theatre, cinemas, restaurants, parks). When, finally, I left London to return to India, she was the only person I really missed.

A woman of similar intellectual attainments, but not as close to me, was Marie Seton, who I knew in Delhi in the early 1960s. Today, Marie Seton is probably best remembered for her biography of Satyajit Ray. She spent many years studying his cinematic art, knew him personally and was a true enthusiast for his work.

Even before she became a devotee of Ray's work, she had been a film enthusiast, and I'd come across her name when I was a raw youth in London, in 1953. A lonely boy who had grown up on films, I would haunt the small cinemas such as the Academy, off Leicester Square, and the Everyman in Hampstead, taking in everything from silent classics to the lyrical films of Jean Renoir and the comedies of Jacques Tati. There was a season of Eisenstein, I remember. *Battleship Potemkin*, of course. And an edited version of the unfinished *Que Viva Mexico;* edited by a certain Marie Seton, of whom I knew absolutely nothing. But I remembered the name because the film had been memorable and I'd been to see it several times.

Seven years later, when I was living and working in New Delhi, I met the person behind the name. I don't remember how I met her. I was never one for going to parties, and in any case parties were a rarity in Delhi in the 1950s and '60s.

I was working for CARE at the time, and it's possible that I was introduced to her by Oden Meeker, the Chief of CARE who was an author in his own right. I had written just one novel till then—*The Room on the Roof*—and he would very kindly give it to people he knew and urge them to read it. That's how Marie Seton got a copy. And when, quite by chance, I bumped into her somewhere or the other, she said, 'I've read your book—it's absolutely marvellous!' and when she introduced herself to me as Marie Seton, I was able to say, 'But not as marvellous as your work on *Que Viva Mexico!*'

There's nothing like a little mutual admiration to set off an enduring relationship.

Marie Seton enjoyed a good conversation, provided she did most of the talking. When she found I was a good listener, she would ask me to meet her in the evenings at Nirula's coffee cafe at Connaught Circus. It was never boring listening to her, but I soon learnt to sit across the table from her because, if I sat beside her, I would get a crick in my neck from having to keep my head turned constantly in her direction.

Apart from her vast knowledge of films, mostly European, she was also well up on all the latest authors, artists and musicians and seemed to be an expert on the British Royal family. She was not averse to imparting tidbits of scandal in regard to princes and princesses, dukes and duchesses. I loved listening to her gossip, although I must admit that I can't remember much of it now. She also knew several famous film stars and gave me confidential asides on who was gay, who was straight, who was sexless and the many who were having extra-marital affairs. Gary Cooper, she told me, was the best-hung man in Hollywood; Charlie Chaplin was a sex maniac; Tyrone Power was gay; and ladies' man Errol Flynn really had nothing to write home about.

All the gossip was not without a solid foundation in fact, as I was to find out in time to come. It was Marie who told me that Somerset Maugham had disowned his daughter; that Richard Burton was an alcoholic; and that Merle Oberon, the actress, had been born in Calcutta and not in Tasmania as she claimed. All true, of course!

Marie Seton was an independent woman who moved about a good deal, so I was not surprised when, a few months later, I bumped into her on the Mall in Darjeeling. No time for coffee and gossip because she was busy watching Satyajit Ray make his new film, *Kanchenjunga*.

When Marie spotted me on the road, she called out: 'Have you got my Henry Green?'

'No,' I said, 'I've never read Henry Green.' And haven't done so till this day. But she seemed to think she'd lent me one of his books and continued to press me about it.

When, finally, I'd convinced her that I was not a Henry Green abductor, she took the trouble to introduce me to the great man himself, Satyajit Ray.

Mr Ray was, as always, courteous and friendly and invited me to watch the shooting of some of their outdoor scenes. I did so but couldn't see Marie again as she seemed to be having an affair with a still photographer.

I was in Darjeeling on business for CARE and was staying at the Everest Hotel, where two film crews were in residence—Mr Ray and his unit, and Shammi Kapoor and his crew who were working on a film called *Professor*, if my memory serves me right.

These two production units provided a sharp contrast in their approach to filming—Ray making his film entirely on location, the Bollywood lot using the hill station merely as a backdrop for several song-and-dance routines, one of them on the railway-tracks! While Ray symbolized the natural in cinematic art, Kapoor and Co. stood for the artificial.

After this encounter, I did not see Marie Seton again. I left Delhi for a somewhat reclusive life in the hills, while she continued with her multifarious activities, especially her excellent biography of Satyajit Ray.

~

While on the subject of older women who charmed or fascinated me, I cannot forget Lillian, or Lily as we called her, who was some twelve years my senior. Her mother was a friend of my grandmother's and Lily had grown up in Dehradun. She was a pretty, fun-loving girl who, at the age of eighteen, accepted a proposal of marriage from a British soldier who was stationed in Dehra during World War II. I was invited to be a page-boy at the wedding, my reward being a large slice of wedding cake, and my duty was to fling endless supplies of confetti on the wedding guests—something I did with great gusto, being only six at the time.

She was given a wonderful wedding cake, tier upon tier of icing, spangled with all sorts of colourful sugary appendages, and within the edifice an assortment of raisins and dried fruits embedded in a scrumptious base. I can still wax poetic about such creations!

As a page-boy I was given an extra-large helping, and as a result I was as enthusiastic as anyone in giving Lily and her pink-cheeked soldier boy an enthusiastic send-off.

I am writing about Lily not because I had a crush on her, but because I was to encounter her at various periods of her life and mine, and on each occasion she was married to a different person. In the course of a turbulent life, Lily went through five husbands. I admired her for her resilience, tenacity and optimism—for she went through life in the hope that she would one day find the perfect man, partner and lover and everything else, and of course there is no such thing, man being a very imperfect creation.

Eleven years after attending Lily's marriage in Dehra, I was in Jersey, in the Channel Islands, where I met her again. The soldier boy had vanished, leaving her with a small son. She was now married to a greengrocer, who had given her two strapping daughters. Unfortunately, the greengrocer could not live up to Lily's high standards of husbandry and soon began hitting the bottle. If he was too inebriated, she would lock him out of the house. On one occasion he climbed up a drainpipe to attempt an entry through a second-floor window. She pushed him out and he landed in some hydrangea bushes and had to be hospitalized. I did not see much of her during this period but got all the inside information from her aunt, who was fond of me and often had me over for meals.

After my return to India, I heard (from the same aunt) that Lily had divorced the greengrocer and left the children with the aunt. She had then proceeded to Rhodesia (now Zimbabwe) where she had married a wealthy white farmer who had two grown sons from his previous marriage, the first wife having succumbed to yellow fever. Lily remained in Rhodesia for three or four years surviving all forms of fever, but finally grew bored with the lonely farm life, and left the land and her husband in order to return to India for a short spell.

This was where I met her again, shortly after her fourth marriage to a former big-game hunter who had now, in his early sixties, taken up fishing. Lily could not get excited about fishing but while dear Frank was away on his trips, she entertained quite lavishly at the old family home, and as an old family friend I was invited to these junkets. Lily would occasionally drop in at my place for a gin and tonic and to talk about old times in Dehra. We joined a few picnic parties— those were the days when picnics were still in vogue—and had some great times. She was a fun-loving person who seemed to have fallen into the bad habit of marrying individuals whose temperaments were totally opposed to hers.

Finally, tiring of the quiet hill station life, she told Frank he could spend the rest of his life fishing and took off for America, where she worked as a private nurse. She married one of her patients, a wealthy man who lived on a large estate in New Orleans, who was swept away in his wheelchair when Hurricane Katrina flooded the city. Hurricane Lily inherited his fortune.

This brief sketch does not do justice to Lily. She deserves an epic novel to herself. And it would have to include her family history, which is equally fascinating. Her grandfather, a British Civil Servant stationed in old Madras, with a wife and children in England, fell in love with a fourteen-year-old Muslim girl and insisted on marrying her. As a result, he had to give up his job and leave Madras. The couple settled in Dehradun, where they started a family of their own. They had two sons and two daughters, and each of the children was given a house in Dehra and Mussoorie, for their father had an independent income. I never saw him because he died before I was born, but I saw his widow when she was an old woman in her late seventies—a tiny little lady with dark smouldering eyes, who must have used them to bewitch the Englishman who had thrown up career, family and social standing in order to marry her.

One of the children (Lily's aunt) had wanted to adopt me when I was a toddler but my parents would not part with me. Had they done so, I might have inherited one of the houses, quite possibly The Parsonage, later owned by my friend Victor Banerjee, the well-known thespian.

Victor is no parson, but we like to call him the Vicar. There is an aura of sanctity around his dwelling, surrounded as it is by sacred deodars, flying squirrels and retired company executives.

~

Someone who did go into a novel—my first—was 'Meena', the older woman with whom young Rusty falls in love in *The Room on the Roof.*

In the novel she is the mother of Kishen, who befriends the runaway Rusty. As many readers have inferred, the novel is autobiographical in essence, and Rusty is the author as a boy. It's true that I was infatuated with Meena (not her real name), who was some fifteen years older than me, the mother of three children, Kishen being the eldest. Her husband, a PWD engineer who had been suspended on a corruption charge, was hitting the bottle in a big way.

Tea and sympathy were the order of the day. Meena gave me tea and I gave her sympathy. She also made wonderful pakoras and I have always believed that the best way to a young man's heart is through his stomach.

Apart from that, she was a beautiful woman, and I was quite smitten, ready to carry out her slightest wish. I ran errands for her, typed out her husband's appeals for reinstatement, gave English lessons to her ten-year-old son and even held the baby when she was busy with other things. This dog-like devotion was rewarded with amusement, affection and even companionship, but she was ever faithful to her husband who seldom emerged from a drunken stupor.

In the novel, Meena dies, killed in a road accident; the alcoholic husband staggers on. This was because of the exigencies of the plot. In reality, it was my friend's father who succumbed to cirrhosis. Meena lived on to a healthy old age.

I did not see her again, but I am told that she remained beautiful into her later years. She had that classical type of Indian beauty, personified in screen stars such as Kamini Kaushal and Nargis, that does not fade with time.

At a book reading in the capital not long ago, a student stood up and asked me: 'How could you fall in love with a married woman who was much older than you?

To which I could only reply: 'I just couldn't help it!'

Meena was not in love with me, that would have been expecting too much; but she was not displeased with my attention. She was like the character in Wilde's *A Woman of No Importance* who says: 'Men always want to be a woman's first love. That is their clumsy vanity. We women have a more subtle instinct about things. What we like is to be a man's last romance.'

And yet it was Meena who set me on the road to romance. For the next ten years I was writing love stories. But in none of them did the lovers live happily ever after.

∽

All You Need Is Paper

'Writing is very easy. All you have to do is sit in front of the typewriter until little drops of blood appear on your forehead.' These immortal words of Red Smith, a forgotten freelance writer, sum up the agony and the ecstasy of those who have made writing their profession.

And it's one reason why I prefer pen and paper to typewriter or computer. A machine in front of me is rather daunting. A pen is more personal and that gives me some control over it, a feeling of power as the words flow with the electric thrill that runs down my arm, through my fingers and onto the clean white page. It is a sensuous act, writing by hand. The feel of the paper, as my hand glides over it, its touch and its texture. The flow of ink, the gliding motion of the pen, the letters themselves as they appear as if by magic in my individual script. No two people have the same handwriting. Your character, your personality is revealed the minute you put pen to paper.

I'm a compulsive writer of course, and I'll write with whatever is handy. Even crayons will do.

The other night I woke up at about two in the morning, having had a vivid dream about discovering a town where the sun never penetrated, the valley being so deep and precipitous; and yet, apparently, people lived there. There was even a bus service bringing in tourists who wanted to look at the town where people lived in a perpetual shadow. In the dream I left, or rather woke up, before it could get too depressing. But I wanted to remember the dream, as I thought it had the makings of a good story, so I switched on the night light and groped around for a pen or pencil. Both were missing, having been commandeered by Siddharth, Shrishti and Gautam the previous evening. Two in the morning is no time for typing, so I looked around for other means of notation and found Gautam's box of coloured crayons lying on my desk.

I selected a bright orange crayon—a psychological choice, as I wished to disperse the gloom of that sunless town—and made my notes on the back of a large envelope. This is one page of notes that I won't misplace, it stands out so vividly; and someday I might even write the story.

I should use crayons more often!

Desperate writers like me will seize upon any bit of writing material when in need. And I recall that my first literary production was inscribed on sheets of toilet paper.

I was at Prep School in Shimla, and in those days boarders were provided, not with rolls of toilet paper, but with flat packets of tissue. As there was a wartime paper shortage, boys would often use these bits of tissue for writing letters, doing rough work or simply making paper aeroplanes. There were no spare exercise books.

Feeling the urge to write a detective story (inspired by a film about the Brighton Strangler), I used up an entire packet of toilet paper in penning my masterpiece. In my story, the mysterious strangler got a job as games' master in our school and went about eliminating all the teachers we disliked. He met his match in the food matron who sprinkled rat poison on his cornflakes.

Unfortunately, one of my friends was overcome by the call of nature. He grabbed my sheets of manuscript and rushed to the toilet, bolting the door, and a little later, when I heard the flush in action, I knew that my story would not reach a publisher.

There have been other lost stories over the years. I don't think any of them have been a great loss to literature, but for personal reasons I would have liked to preserve one or two of them. Like the one about the tikkee-eating contest behind Dehradun's clock tower back in 1956. I wasn't just a spectator, I was a participant, and came a close second, having consumed twenty-six fried potato tikkees to Sahib Singh's thirty-two. Sahib was a young Sikh friend who went to England a few years later and did much to popularize samosas, tikkees and chaat in the UK, making a fortune in the process.

I wrote a story about the contest and published it in *The Tribune*, which appeared from Ambala in those far-off days; Chandigarh was only just coming into existence. A clipping of the story went into my scrapbook, but that particular scrapbook was lost when I moved to Delhi and with it several of my early stories. *The Great Tikkee-Eating Contest* was not one of my more memorable works, but it was fun writing it.

As Gautam says, with inexorable logic, 'You can always write it again!'

That is, if it's worth the effort…

Another runaway story was *The Runway Bus*, which appeared in *Sport and Pastime* at about the same time. A bus driver in the metropolis spots his wife riding pillion on a scooter with a stranger, and gives chase, heedless of the convenience of his passengers. He catches up with them near the Qutub Minar, only to find that he has been chasing his wife's double. The bus passengers beat him up.

Then there was *Gone Fishing*, in which the narrator (me) meets a village boy and promises to go fishing with him the next day. But he has to leave town suddenly to take up a job in the capital. As his train passes over a small bridge, he catches a glimpse of the boy sitting on the banks of a stream, rod and line in hand, fishing by himself. The narrator feels that he has missed something—something more than just a day's fishing—and knows that happiness can be as elusive as a small fish darting away in a mountain stream.

That's a story that I might like to write again.

The invention of the Xerox copying machine meant that I could make as many copies as I wished and the days of lost clippings and typescripts were (almost) over. In my early freelancing days, when I had to use a typewriter, you could take a couple of carbon copies but you could hardly submit these to publishers. Of course, in those days publishers took the trouble to return unwanted manuscripts, so you did not always lose your fair copy. Like most writers, I collected my fair share of rejection slips. Some editors were kind enough to make helpful comments such as 'try again' or 'shows promise', and thus encouraged, I would bombard them with articles, stories and poems.

Most publications paid the writer for his work if it was accepted. The sums may have been small but they came in on time. This is not the case today; many successful publications will avoid making payments if they can get away with it.

Many of my rejects (written when I was in my teens) would end up in the pages of a little magazine called *My Magazine of India*, published from Chennai (then called Madras). They would send me a five-rupee money order for every item published. I looked forward to these money orders. With five rupees I could see three films or buy a couple of paperbacks or indulge in a bottle of beer.

If a writer is any good he should expect to be paid for his work. Those who go to vanity publishers and pay to have their books published are doomed to disappointment; they will end up forcing their books upon their unfortunate friends, who will wish they could have had something better for Christmas.

'I have brought you a present!' boomed a retired Brigadier-General the other day, shaking me vigorously by the hand.

'Ah,' I thought, 'perhaps he's brought me a bottle of whisky.' And aloud: 'Do sit down, sir. It's so kind of you to drop in.' And with a flourish he produced two volumes of his memoirs, all done up in handloom cloth, and with a frontispiece showing the General with a tremendous moustache which would have scared the wits out of me twenty years ago. He still scares the wits out of me, although the moustache has lost much of its early elasticity.

The books are presented to me with a flourish, with a request, or rather order, that I have them reviewed in *Outlook*, *India Today* and the *New York Times*. I promise to do my best and place the books reverently in the most prominent place in my sitting room. As soon as he leaves, I take them down and put them out of sight; they will make good doorstops. But he is too crafty this old General. Suddenly he is back in in the room.

'I forgot to autograph them for you,' he says, taking out his fountain pen.

For a few seconds I am at a loss. Then little Gautam appears in the doorway.

'Gautam!' I scold. 'Why did you take those books down from the shelf?' I retrieve them quickly and hold them out for his autograph. Perhaps his signature will be worth something.

Now I can't use his books as doorstops. He is bound to pop in again, expecting to see them prominently displayed.

A strange thing is human vanity. We all succumb to it from time to time.

I was pleased when the boy from the ration-shop asked me for one of my books. At last, a reader! I presented him with a large format children's book. Lots of pages, good strong paper.

Two or three days later, when I was passing his shop, I noticed a pile of paper bags on the counter. They had all been made from the pages of my book! The boy's father was even then filling one of the bags with channa for one of his customers.

'And what do you require, sir?' he asked me.

'Two rupees worth of peanuts,' I said.

He filled a bag with peanuts and handed them to me. Humbly, I walked away with two pages of my book neatly pasted together to hold peanuts.

I gave the peanuts to Gautam and told him what had happened to the book.

He was quite philosophical about it.

'I suppose the world needs peanuts more than it needs books,' he said.

I couldn't argue with that. Gautam's worldly wisdom and advice is always on a par with Mr Dick's in *David Copperfield*.

We strolled into the sitting room and I surveyed my shelves of books. The General's memoirs immediately caught my eye. I took the two large volumes down from the shelf. Gautam noticed the wicked glint in my eyes.

'What are you going to do?' he asked.

'Come,' I said. 'We are going to make paper bags.'

A Year with Suzie

Suzie came into my life when she was just three weeks old—really too small a baby to be adopted by an inexperienced bachelor. Perhaps I should make it clear at the start that Suzie is a Siamese cat.

I had told a friend that I needed a pet to share my rather lonely life on the outskirts of a north Indian hill station. I had expected to receive a dog; but when the kitten arrived, its small questing head with the chocolate-tipped ears thrust out of a friend's coat pocket, I fell in love at first sight. And, taking its sex for granted, I named the kitten Suzie.

Suzie spent her first night curled up in a tea cosy. She showed her good breeding right from the start by selecting a commodious pot of geraniums for her morning ablutions. A puppy, I reflected, would have been less discriminating.

Like most Siamese cats, she showed a dislike for milk, and I was faced with the problem of obtaining a regular supply of meat. As I lived two miles from the nearest butcher, I took meat only once or twice a week; but Suzie disdained a vegetarian diet. I solved the problem by purchasing a month's supply of tinned sardines and feeding her exclusively on fish. She liked butter too, and used it to polish her coat. All this proved expensive, but I was hoping that as she grew older her natural instincts would result in her bringing in her own supplies.

I was not disappointed. She was barely a month old when she snapped up a large moth that flew in through the open windows on a balmy September night. With all the savage artistry of her species, Suzie dissected this choice morsel and devoured it with relish. A few days later I found, on the kitchen floor, the head and tail of a mouse. The bright innocence of Suzie's sky-blue eyes told me where the rest of the mouse was now lodged.

Cats rarely answer to their names; but Suzie often did. Moreover, I had tied a little bell to her neck, and this generally told me where she is. Her favourite haunt was a cherry tree. When a pair of thrushes were building a nest, Suzie learnt to climb this tree beautifully and the birds went elsewhere. There is truth in the saying that the cat is the aunt of the tiger, and taught the tiger everything except how to climb a tree.

If a cat and a dog are properly introduced to each other, they make the best of friends. It did not take Suzie long to develop a playful, nose-tapping relationship with my neighbour's Peke. Another dog, a rather doleful, good-natured Cocker, permitted Suzie to sleep beneath her on cold days. Such was Suzie's charm that she was soon being fed by my neighbours, and this generosity solved my food problems. People took pity on us. Bachelors and kittens are suitable objects for compassion.

Suzie must have been about five months old when I discovered, to my dismay and embarrassment, that my cat was really a male. But I scorned all suggestions for a change of name: he had been Suzie from his infancy, and he would keep his girl's name for the rest of his time with me.

I had been warned that as soon as Suzie was eight months old he would start staying out late at nights, or even remaining away for several days in his search for a suitable mate. But Suzie was not like other males. He stayed at home, and the queens came to him. There was a beautiful black creature with yellow eyes, straight out of Edgar Allan Poe, and a handsome wild cat from the forest, who came to the front door on alternate nights (never together). Suzie would go out and meet his admirers, and frolic with them in the long, dew-drenched monsoon grass, before returning indoors to sleep deeply and sweetly at the foot of my bed.

Suzie likes people. I think he finds them comfortable. If there are guests, he will always choose the one with the broadest, most accommodating lap. At night he usually sleeps on my tummy (he likes its rise and fall, as I breathe) and if it gets cold, he curls up in the hollow behind my knees.

In the house, during the day, he is unobtrusive. Outside, he has his own pursuits and pleasures, whether it be stalking garden lizards or too familiar myna birds and crows. Sometimes I find him curled up on my typewriter, reminding me that I have not been working regularly of late. He likes music (or is it just the vibrations from the set?) and a favourite spot of his, ever since childhood, has been beside the radio.

At the time of writing Suzie is in the garden, among the marigolds. I doubt if he will find any lizards there. But perhaps this time he is only looking for fairies.

Running for Cover

The right to privacy is a fine concept and might actually work in the West, but in Eastern lands it is purely notional. If I want to be left alone, I have to be a shameless liar—pretend that I am out of town or, if that doesn't work, announce that I have measles, mumps or some new variety of Asian 'flu.

Now I happen to like people and I like meeting people from all walks of life. If this were not the case I would have nothing to write about. But I don't like too many people all at once. They tend to get in the way. And if they arrive without warning, banging on my door while I am in the middle of composing a poem or writing a story, or simply enjoying my afternoon siesta, I am inclined to be snappy or unwelcoming. Occasionally I have even turned people away.

As I get older, that afternoon siesta becomes more of a necessity and less of an indulgence. But it's strange how people love to call on me between two and four in the afternoon. I suppose it's the time of day when they have nothing to do.

'How do we get through the afternoon?' one of them will say.

'I know! Lets go and see old Ruskin. He's sure to entertain us with some stimulating conversation, if nothing else.' Stimulating conversation in mid-afternoon? Even Socrates would have balked at it.

'I'm sorry I can't see you today,' I mutter. 'I don't feel at all well.' (In fact, extremely unwell at the prospect of several strangers gaping at me for at least half an hour.)

'Not well? We're so sorry. My wife here is a homeopath.' It's amazing the number of homeopaths who turn up at my door. Unfortunately they never seem to have their little powders on them, those miracle cures for everything from headaches to hernias.

The other day a family burst in—uninvited of course. The husband was an ayurvedic physician, the wife was a homeopath (naturally), the eldest boy a medical student at an allopathic medical college.

'What do you do when one of you falls ill?' I asked, 'Do you try all three systems of medicine?'

'It depends on the ailment,' said the young man. 'But we seldom fall ill. My sister here is a yoga expert.'

His sister, a hefty girl in her late twenties (still single) looked more like an all-in wrestler than a supple yoga practitioner. She looked at my tummy. She could see I was in bad shape.

'I could teach you some exercises,' she said. 'But you'd have to come to Ludhiana.'

I felt grateful that Ludhiana was a six-hour drive from Mussoorie.

'I'll drop in some day,' I said. 'In fact, I'll come and take a course.'

We parted on excellent terms. But it doesn't always turn out that way.

There was this woman, very persistent, in fact downright rude, who wouldn't go away even when I told her I had bird-flu.

'I have to see you,' she said, 'I've written a novel, and I want you to recommend it for a Booker Prize.'

'I'm afraid I have no influence there,' I pleaded. 'I'm completely unknown in Britain.'

'Then how about the Nobel Prize?'

I thought about that for a minute. 'Only in the science field,' I said. 'If it's something to do with genes or stem cells?' She looked at me as though I was some kind of worm. 'You are not very helpful,' she said.

'Well, let me read your book.'

'I haven't written it yet.'

'Well, why not come back when it's finished? Give yourself a year—two years—these things should never be done in a hurry.' I guided her to the gate and encouraged her down the steps.

'You are very rude,' she said. 'You did not even ask me in. I'll report you to Khushwant Singh. He's a friend of mine. He'll put you in his column.'

'If Khushwant Singh is your friend,' I said, 'why are you bothering with me? He knows all the Nobel and Booker Prize people. All the important people, in fact.'

I did not see her again, but she got my phone number from someone, and now she rings me once a week to tell me her book is coming along fine. Any day now, she's going to turn up with the manuscript.

Casual visitors who bring me their books or manuscripts are the ones I dread most. They ask me for an opinion, and if I give them a frank assessment they resent it. It's unwise to tell a would-be writer that his memoirs or novel or collected verse would be better off unpublished. Murders have been committed for less. So I play safe and say, 'Very promising. Carry on writing.' But this is fatal. Almost immediately I am asked to write a foreword or introduction, together with a letter of recommendation to my publisher—or any publisher of standing. Unwillingly I become a literary agent; unpaid of course.

I am all for encouraging the arts and literature, but I do think writers should seek out their own publishers and write their own introductions.

The peril of doing this sort of thing was illustrated when I was prevailed upon to write a short introduction to a book about a dreaded man-eater who had taken a liking to the flesh of the good people of Dogadda, near Lansdowne. The author of the book could hardly write a decent sentence, but he managed to string together a lengthy account of the leopard's depredations. He was so persistent, calling on me or ringing me up that I finally did the introduction. He then wanted me to edit or touch up his manuscript; but this I refused to do. I would starve if I had to sit down and rewrite other people's books. But he prevailed upon me to give him a photograph.

Months later, the book appeared, printed privately of course. And there was my photograph, and a photograph of the dead leopard after it had been hunted down. But the local printer had got the captions mixed up. The dead animal's picture earned the line: 'Well-known author Ruskin Bond.' My picture carried the legend: 'Dreaded man-eater, shot after it had killed its 26th victim.' The printer's devil had turned me into a serial killer.

Now you know why I'm wary of writing introductions.

'Vanity' publishers thrive on writers who are desperate to see their work in print. They will print and deliver a book at your doorstep and then leave you with the task of selling it; or to be more accurate, disposing of it.

One of my neighbours, Mrs Santra—may her soul rest in peace—paid a publisher forty thousand rupees to bring out a fancy edition of her late husband's memoirs. During his lifetime he'd been unable to get it published, but before he died he got his wife to promise that she'd publish it for him. This she did, and the publisher duly delivered 500 copies to the good lady. She gave a few copies to friends, and then passed away, leaving the books behind. Her heir is now saddled with 450 hardbound volumes of unsaleable memoirs.

I have always believed that if a writer is any good he will find a publisher who will print, bind, and sell his books, and even give him a royalty for his efforts. A writer who pays to get published is inviting disappointment and heartbreak.

~

Many people are under the impression that I live in splendour in a large mansion, surrounded by secretaries and servants. They are disappointed to find that I live in a tiny bedroom-cum-study and that my living-room is so full of books that there is hardly space for more than three or four visitors at a time.

Sometimes thirty to forty school children turn up, wanting to see me. I don't turn away children, if I can help it. But if they come in large numbers I have to meet and talk to them on the road, which is inconvenient for everyone.

If I had the means, would I live in a splendid mansion in the more affluent parts of Mussoorie, with a film star or TV personality as my neighbour? I rather doubt it. All my life I've been living in one or two rooms and I don't think I could manage a bigger establishment. True, my extended family takes up another two rooms, but they see to it that my working space is not violated. And if I am hard at work (or fast asleep) they will try to protect me from unheralded or unwelcome visitors.

And I have learnt to tell lies. Especially when I'm asked to attend school functions as a chief guest or in some formal capacity. To spend two or three hours listening to speeches (and then being expected to give one) is my idea of hell. It's hell for the students and its hell for me. The speeches are usually followed (or preceded) by folk dances, musical interludes or class plays, and this only adds to the torment. Sports' days are just as bad. You can skip the speeches (hopefully), but you must sit out in the hot sun for the greater part of the day, while a loudspeaker informs you that little Parshottam has just broken the school record for the under-nine high jump, or that Pamela Highjinks has won the hurdles for the third year running. You don't get to see the events because you are kept busy making polite conversation with the other guests. The only occasion when a sports' event really came to life was when a misdirected discus narrowly missed decapitating the headmaster's wife.

Former athletes and sportsmen seldom visit me. They have difficulty making it up my steps. Most of them have problems with their knees before they are fifty. They *hobble* (for want of a better word). Once their playing days are over, they start hobbling. Nandu, a former tennis champion, can't make it up my steps, nor can Chand—a former wrestler. Too much physical activity when young has resulted in an early breakdown of the body's machinery As Nandu says, 'Body can't take it any more.' I'm not too agile either, but then, I was never much of a sportsman. Second last in the marathon was probably my most memorable achievement.

Oddly enough, some of the most frequent visitors to my humble abode are honeymooners.

Why, I don't know, but they always ask for my blessing even though I am hardly an advertisement for married bliss. A seventy-year-old bachelor blessing a newly married couple? Maybe they are under the impression that I'm a brahmachari? But how would that help them? They are going to have babies sooner or later.

It is seldom that they happen to be readers or book-lovers, so why pick an author, and that too one who does not go to places of worship? However, since these young couples are inevitably attractive, and full of high hopes for their future and the future of mankind, I am happy to talk to them, wish them well. And if it's a blessing they want, they are welcome…. My hands are far from being saintly but at least they are well-intentioned.

I have, at times, been mistaken for other people.

'Are you Mr Pickwick?' asked a small boy. At least he'd been reading Dickens. A distant relative, I said, and beamed at him in my best Pickwickian manner.

I am at ease with children, who talk quite freely except when accompanied by their parents. Then it's mum and dad who do all the talking.

'My son studies your book in school,' said one fond mother, proudly exhibiting her ten-year-old. 'He wants your autograph.' 'What's the name of the book you're reading?' I asked. 'Tom Sawyer,' he said promptly

So I signed Mark Twain in his autograph book. He seemed quite happy.

I have signed books in the names of Enid Blyton, R.K. Narayan, Ian Botham, Daniel Defoe, Harry Potter and the Swiss Family Robinson. No one seems to mind...

Let me not cavil at my unexpected visitors. Sometimes they turn out to be very nice people—like the gentleman from Pune who brought me a bottle of whisky and then sat down and drank most of it himself.

~

The Postman Knocks

As a freelance writer, most of my adult life has revolved around the coming of the postman. 'A cheque in the mail,' is something that every struggling writer looks forward to. It might, of course, arrive by courier, or it might not come at all. But for the most part, the acceptances and rejections of my writing life, along with editorial correspondence, readers' letters, page proofs and author's copies—how welcome they are!—come through the post.

The postman has always played a very real and important part in my life, and continues to do so. He climbs my twenty-one steps every afternoon, knocks loudly on my door—three raps, so that I know it's him and not some inquisitive tourist—and gives me my registered mail or speed-post with a smile and a bit of local gossip. The gossip is important. I like to know what's happening in the bazaar—who's getting married, who's standing for election, who ran away with the headmaster's wife, and whose funeral procession is passing by. He deserves a bonus for this sort of information.

The courier boy, by contrast, shouts to me from the road below and

I have to go down to him. He's mortally afraid of dogs and there are three in the building. My postman isn't bothered by dogs. He comes in all weathers, and he comes on foot except when someone gives him a lift. He turns up when it's snowing, or when it's raining cats and dogs, or when there's a heat wave, and he's quite philosophical about it all. He meets all kinds of people. He has seen joy and sorrow in the homes he visits. He knows something about life. If he wasn't a philosopher to begin with, he will certainly be one by the time he retires.

Of course, not all postmen are paragons of virtue. A few years ago, we had a postman who never got further than the country liquor shop in the bazaar. The mail would pile up there for days, until he sobered up and condescended to deliver it. In due course he was banished to another route, where there were no liquor shops.

We take the postman for granted today, but there was a time, over a hundred years ago, when the carrying of the mails was a hazardous venture, and the mail-runner, or hirkara as he was called, had to be armed with sword or spear. Letters were carried in leather wallets on the backs of runners, who were changed at stages of eight miles. At night, the runners were accompanied by torch-bearers—in wilder parts, by drummers called dug-dugi wallas—to frighten away wild animals.

The tiger population was considerable at the time, and tigers were a real threat to travellers or anyone who ventured far from their town or village. Mail-runners often fell victim to man-eating tigers. The mail-runners (most of them tribals) were armed with bows and arrows, but these were seldom effective.

In the Hazaribagh district (through which the mail had to be carried, on its way from Calcutta to Allahabad) there appears to have been a concentration of man-eating tigers. There were four passes through this district, and the tigers had them well covered. Williamson, writing in 1810, tells us that the passes were so infested with tigers that the roads were almost impassable. 'Day after day, for nearly a fortnight, some of the dak people were carried off at one or other of these passes.'

In spite of these hazards, a letter sent by dak runner used to take twelve days to reach Meerut from Calcutta. It takes about the same time today, unless you use speed-post.

At up-country stations the Collector of Land Revenue was the

Postmaster. He was given a small postal establishment, consisting of a munshi, a matsaddi or sorter, and thirty or forty runners whose pay, in 1804, was five rupees a month. The maintenance of the dak cost the government (i.e., the East India Company) twenty-five rupees a month for each stage of eight miles. Postage stamps were introduced in 1854.

My father was an enthusiastic philatelist, and when I was a small boy I could sit and watch him pore over his stamp collection, which included several early and valuable Indian issues. He would grumble at the very dark and smudgy postmarks which obliterated most of Queen Victoria's profile from the stamps. This was due to the composition of the ink used for cancelling the earlier stamps. It was composed of two parts lamp-black, four parts linseed oil and three-and-a-half of vinegar.

Letter-distributing peons, or postmen, were always smartly turned out: 'A red turban, a light green chapkan, a small leather belt over the breast and right shoulder, with a chaprass attached showing the peon's number and having the words "Post Office Peon" in English and in two vernaculars, and a bell suspended by a leather strap from the left shoulder.'

Today's postmen are more casual in their attire, although I believe they are still entitled to uniforms. The general public doesn't care how they are dressed, as long as they turn up with those letters containing rakhis or money orders from soldier sons and husbands. This is where the postman still scores over the fax and e-mail.

To return to our mail-runners, they were eventually replaced by the dak-ghari the equivalent of the English 'coach and pair'—which gradually established itself throughout the country.

A survivor into the 1940s, my Great-aunt Lillian recalled that in the late nineteenth century, before the coming of the railway, the only way of getting to Dehradun was by the dak-ghari or Night Mail. Dak-ghari ponies were difficult animals, she told me—'always attempting to turn around and get into the carriage with the passengers!' But once they started there was no stopping them. It was a gallop all the way to the first stage, where the ponies were changed to the accompaniment of a bugle blown by the coachman, in true Dickensian fashion.

The journey through the Siwaliks really began—as it still does— through the Mohand Pass. The ascent starts with a gradual gradient which increases as the road becomes more steep and winding. At this stage of the journey, drums were beaten (if it was day) and torches lit (if it was night) because sometimes wild elephants resented the approach of the dak-ghari and, trumpeting a challenge, would throw the ponies into confusion and panic, and send them racing back to the plains.

After 1900, Great-aunt Lillian used the train. But the mail bus from Saharanpur to Mussoorie still uses the old route, through the Siwaliks. And if you are lucky, you may see a herd of wild elephants crossing the road on its way to the Ganga.

And even today, in remote parts of the country, in isolated hill areas where there are no motorable roads, the mail is carried on foot, the postman often covering five or six miles every day. He never runs, true, and he might sometimes stop for a glass of tea and a game of cards en route, but he is a reminder of those early pioneers of the postal system, the mail-runners of India.

Mountains Are Kind to Writers

It's hard to realize that I've been here all these years—twenty-five summers and monsoons and winters and Himalayan springs (there is no spring in the plains)—because, when I look back to the time of my first coming here, it does seem like yesterday.

That probably sums it all up. Time passes, and yet it doesn't pass; people come and go, the mountains remain. Mountains are permanent things. They are stubborn, they refuse to move. You can blast holes out of them for their mineral wealth; or strip them of their trees and foliage; or dam their streams and divert their currents; or make tunnels and roads and bridges; but no matter how hard they try, humans cannot actually get rid of their mountains. That's what I like about them; they are here to stay.

I like to think that I have become a part of this mountain, this particular range, and that by living here for so long, I am able to claim a relationship with the trees, wild flowers, even the rocks that are an integral part of it. Yesterday, at twilight, when I passed beneath a canopy of oak leaves, I felt that I was a part of the forest. I put out my hand and touched the bark of an old tree, and as I turned away, its leaves brushed against my face as if to acknowledge me.

One day, I thought, if we trouble these great creatures too much, and hack away at them and destroy their young they will simply uproot themselves and march away—whole forests on the move—over the next range and the next, far from the haunts of man. I have seen many forests and green places dwindle and disappear. Now there is an outcry. It is suddenly fashionable to be an environmentalist. That's all right. Perhaps it isn't too late to save the little that's left. They could start by curbing the property developers who have been spreading their tentacles far and wide.

The sea has been celebrated by many great writers—Conrad, Melville, Stevenson, Masefield—but I cannot think of anyone comparable for whom the mountains have been a recurring theme. I must turn to the Taoist poets from old China to find a true feeling for mountains. Kipling does occasionally look to the hills but the Himalayas do not appear to have given rise to any memorable Indian literature, at least not in modern times. By and large, writers have to stay in the plains to make a living. Hill people have their work cut out just trying to wrest a livelihood from their thin, calcinated soil. And as for mountaineers, they climb their peaks and move on, in search of other peaks; they do not take up residence in the mountains.

But to me, as a writer, the mountains have been kind.

They were kind from the beginning, when I left a job in Delhi and rented a small cottage on the outskirts of the hill station. Today, most hill stations are rich men's playgrounds, but twenty-five years ago they were places where people of modest means would live quite cheaply. There were few cars and everyone walked about. The cottage was on the edge of the oak and maple forest and I spent eight or nine years in it, most of them happy, writing stories, essays, poems and books for children. It was only after I came to live in the hills that I began writing for children.

I think this had something to do with Prem's children. He and his wife had taken on the job of looking after the house and all practical matters (I remain helpless with fuses, clogged cisterns, leaking gas cylinders, ruptured water pipes, tin roofs that blow away when there's a storm and the do-it-yourself world of small-town India). They made it possible for me to write. Their sons Rakesh and Mukesh, and daughter Savitri, grew up in Maplewood Cottage and then in other houses when we moved.

Naturally I grew attached to them and became a part of the family, an adopted grandfather. For Rakesh I wrote a story about a cherry tree that had difficulty in growing up; for Mukesh, who liked upheavals, I wrote a story about an earthquake and put him in it; and for Savitri, I wrote rhymes and poems.

One seldom ran short of material. There was a stream at the bottom of the hill and this gave me many subjects in the way of small (occasionally large) animals, wild flowers, birds, insects, ferns. The nearby villages and their good-natured people were of absorbing interest. So were the old houses and old families of the Landour and Mussoorie hill stations. There were walks into the mountains and along the pilgrim trails, and sometimes I slept at a roadside tea shop or a village school.

'Who goes to the Hills, goes to his Mother.' So wrote Kipling, and he seldom wrote truer words. For, living in the hills was like living in the bosom of a strong, sometimes proud, but always comforting mother. And every time I went away, the homecoming would be more tender and precious. It became increasingly difficult for me to go away.

It has not always been happiness and light. There were times when money ran out. Freelancing can be daunting at times, and I never could make enough to buy a house like almost everyone else I know. Editorial doors sometimes close; but when one door closes, another has, for me, almost immediately, miraculously opened. I could perhaps have done a little better living in London, or in Canada like my brother; or even in a city like Bombay. But given the choice, I would not have done differently. When you have received love from people, and the freedom that only the mountains can give, then you have come very near the borders of heaven.

~~

Upon an Old Wall Dreaming

It is time to confess that at least half my life has been spent in idleness. My old school would not be proud of me. Nor would my Aunt Muriel.

'You spend most of your time sitting on that wall, doing nothing,' scolded Aunt Muriel, when I was seven or eight. 'Are you *thinking* about something?'

'No, Aunt Muriel.'

'Are you *dreaming*?'

'I'm awake!'

'Then what on earth are you doing there?'

'Nothing, Aunt Muriel.'

'He'll come to no good,' she warned the world at large. 'He'll spend all his life sitting on walls, doing nothing.'

And how right she proved to be! Sometimes I bestir myself, and bang out a few sentences on my old typewriter, but most of the time I'm still sitting on that wall, preferably in the winter sunshine. Thinking? Not very deeply. Dreaming? But I've grown too old to dream. Meditation, perhaps. That's been fashionable for some time. But it isn't that either. Contemplation might come closer to the mark.

Was I born with a silver spoon in my mouth that I could afford to sit in the sun for hours, doing nothing? Far from it; I was born poor and remained poor, as far as worldly riches went. But one has to eat and pay the rent. And there have been others to feed too. So I have to admit that between long bouts of idleness there have been short bursts of creativity. My typewriter, after more than thirty years of loyal service, has finally collapsed, proof enough that it has not lain idle all this time.

Sitting on walls, apparently doing nothing, has always been my favourite form of inactivity. But for these walls, and the many idle hours I have spent upon them, I would not have written even a fraction of the hundreds of stories, essays and other diversions that have been banged out on the typewriter over the years. It is not the walls themselves that set me off or give me ideas, but a personal view of the world that I receive from sitting there.

Creative idleness, you could call it. A receptivity to the world around me—the breeze, the warmth of the old stone, the lizard on the rock, a raindrop on a blade of grass—these and other impressions impinge upon me as I sit in that passive, benign condition that makes people smile tolerantly at me as they pass. 'Eccentric writer', they remark to each other, as they drive on, hurrying in a heat of hope, towards the pot of gold at the end of their personal rainbows.

It's true that I am eccentric in many ways, and old walls bring out the essence of my eccentricity.

I do not have a garden wall. This shaky tumbledown house in the hills is perched directly above a motorable road, making me both accessible and vulnerable to casual callers of all kinds—inquisitive tourists, local busybodies, schoolgirls with their poems, hawkers selling candy-floss, itinerant sadhus, scrap merchants, potential Nobel prize winners…

To escape them, and to set my thoughts in order, I walk a little way up the road, cross it, and sit down on a parapet wall overlooking the Woodstock spur. Here, partially shaded by an overhanging oak, I am usually left alone. I look suitably down and out, shabbily dressed, a complete nonentity—not the sort of person you would want to be seen talking to!

Stray dogs sometimes join me here. Having been a stray dog myself at various periods of my life, I can empathize with these friendly vagabonds of the road. Far more intelligent than your inbred Pom or Peke, they let me know by their silent companionship that they are on the same wavelength. They sport about on the road, but they do not yap at all and sundry.

Left to myself on the wall, I am soon in the throes of composing a story or poem. I do not write it down—that can be done later. I just work it out in my mind, memorize my words, so to speak, and keep them stored up for my next writing session.

Occasionally a car will stop, and someone I know will stick his head out and say, 'No work today, Mr Bond? How I envy you! Not a care in the world!'

I travel back in time some fifty years to Aunt Muriel asking me the same question. The years melt away and I am a child again, sitting on the garden wall, doing nothing.

'Don't you get bored sitting there?' asks the latest passing motorist, who has one of those half beards which are in vogue with TV news readers. 'What are you doing?'

'Nothing, aunty,' I reply.

He gives me a long hard stare.

'You must be dreaming. Don't you recognize me?'

'Yes, Aunt Muriel.'

He shakes his head sadly, steps on the gas, and goes roaring up the hill in a cloud of dust.

'Poor old Bond,' he tells his friends over evening cocktails. 'Must be going round the bend. This morning he called me Aunty.'

The Typewriter

Working at nights in an attic room provided by my aunt, I took six months to complete my first book, a novel. I was eighteen at the time, and though the novel was about growing up in India, I was living in Jersey, in the Channel Islands, earning about £4 a week as a Public Works' clerk.

I hadn't been away from India for as much as a year, but I was very homesick, and writing the book helped to take me back to the people and places I had known and loved.

Working in the same office was a sympathetic soul, a senior clerk whose name was Mr Bromley. He came from good Lancashire stock. His wife and son had predeceased him, and he lived alone in lodgings near the St Helier seafront. As I lived not far away, I would sometimes accompany Mr Bromley home after work, walking with him along the sea wall, watching the waves hissing along the sandy beaches or crashing against the rocks.

I gathered from some of his remarks that he had an incurable disease, and that he had come to live and work in Jersey in the hope that a sunnier climate would help him to get better. He sensed that we were, in a way, both exiles, our real homes far from this small, rather impersonal island in the Channel.

He had read widely, and sympathized with my ambitions to be a writer. He had tried it once himself, and failed.

'I didn't have the perseverance, lad,' he said. 'I wasn't inventive enough, either. It isn't enough to be able to write well—you have to know how to tell a good story... Those who could do both, like Conrad and Stevenson, those are the ones we still read today. The critics keep telling us that Henry James was a master stylist, and so he was, but who reads Henry James?'

Mr Bromley rather admired my naive but determined attempt to write a book.

On a Sunday afternoon I was standing in front of a shop, gazing wistfully at a baby portable typewriter on display. It was just what I wanted. My book was nearly finished but I knew I'd have to get it typed before submitting it to a publisher.

'Buying a typewriter, lad?' Mr Bromley had stopped beside me.

'I wish I could,' I said. 'But it's £19 and I've only got £6 saved up. I'll have to hire some old machine.'

'But a good-looking typescript can make a world of difference, lad. Editors are jaded people. If they find a dirty manuscript on the desk, they feel like chucking it in the wastepaper basket—even if it is a masterpiece!'

'There's an old typewriter-belonging to my aunt,' I said, 'but it should be in a museum. The letter b is missing. She must have used that one a lot—or perhaps it was my uncle. Anyway, when I type my stories on it, I have to go through them again and ink in all the missing bs.'

'That won't do, lad. I tell you what, though. Give me your £6 and I'll add £13 to it, and we'll buy the machine. Then you can pay me back out of your wages—a pound every week. How would that suit you?'

I accepted his offer and walked down the street in a state of euphoria, the gleaming new typewriter in my hand. I sat up late that night, hammering out the first chapter of my book.

It was midsummer then, and by the end of the year I had paid £6 back to Mr Bromley. It was then that I received a letter from a publisher (the third to whom I had submitted the book) saying that they had liked my story, but had some suggestions to make, and could I call on them in London?

I took a few days' leave and crossed the Channel to England.

London swept me right off my feet. The theatres and bookshops exerted their magic on me. And the publishers said they would take my book if only I'd try writing it again.

At eighteen, I was prepared to rewrite a book a dozen times, so I took a room in Hampstead, and grabbed the first job that came my way. I would have to keep working until I established myself as a writer. I did not know, then, how long this would take, but life was only just beginning, and I fell in love with someone, and someone fell in love with me, and both loves were unrequited; but all the same I was very happy.

For some time I was unable to send any money to Mr Bromley. My wage was small, and London was expensive. I meant to write to him, explaining the situation, but kept putting it off, telling myself that I would write as soon as I had some money to send him.

Several months passed, I wrote the book a third time, and this time it was accepted and I received a modest advance. I opened an account with Lloyd's, and the first cheque I made out was in the name of Mr Bromley.

But it was never to be cashed. It came back in the post with my letter, and along with it was a letter from my former employer saying that Mr Bromley had gone away and left no address. It seemed to me that he had given up his quest for better health, and had gone home to his own part of the country.

And so my debt was never paid.

The typewriter is still with me. I have used it for over ten years, and it is now old and battered. But I will not give it away. It's like a guilty conscience, always beside me, always reminding me to pay my debts in time.

~

When Time Stands Still

If there be a heaven on earth, it is this, it is this.

These words are inscribed on the wall of the Diwan-i-Khas, or the Hall of Private Audience, in the royal gardens of the Red Fort at Delhi, built by Shah Jahan in the seventeenth century. It is a beautiful pavilion, the walls inlaid with jade and other semi-precious stones, and from the latticed windows one sees the waters of the Jamuna winding placidly across the plain.

In Shah Jahan's time, the river ran much closer to the fort and I like to think that the Emperor, when he found time to be alone, strolled along the ramparts of his palace while it was being constructed; and that one evening, while he gazed at the river, something happened to make him feel at peace with the world and he was so moved by his surroundings that he decided to build his private pavilion at that spot, inscribing on its walls the words, or rather the poetry, that came to him that moment of truth: *If there be a heaven on earth, it is this, it is this…*

Such moments come to each of us, moments when we feel deeply moved or inspired, moments when time seems to stand still, or when we become acutely aware of the benediction of sun and wind and trees. These moments of great wonder and delight are, for me, rare. They come as small miracles, like the fragrance of the first summer rain on the parched earth, or the song of the whistling thrush emerging like a sweet secret from a dark forest—moments when heaven is here, compensating for the irritations and disasters that we build around ourselves each day.

When I was seventeen, I wanted desperately to be a writer but my early efforts did not meet much success and my relatives threw cold water on my aspirations. At that time I was living and working in Jersey, in the Channel Islands. Late one evening, when I was feeling particularly depressed, I went out for a walk along the seafront. The tide was in, the sea was rough, and the wind which was almost a gale came pouring in from the darkness like a mad genie just released from his bottle. Great waves crashed against the sea-wall and the wind whipped the salt spray into my face, I was alone in a wild wasteland of wind and water. And then something touched me, something from the elements took hold of my heart, and all the stuffing went out of my head, and I felt as free and as virile as the wind. I spoke to the genie in the swirling darkness and said; 'I will be writer, I am going to write, and no one can stop me.'

A week later, with a capital of five pounds and ten shillings (then equal to about a hundred rupees), I left my astonished relatives and went to live in London, where the writing began again. It is still going on, and it is still a struggle. But whenever I feel like giving up, I try to recapture that moment when heaven and earth and I were all one, and when I remember, the writing begins again.

~

Heaven seems to turn up when we least expect it. I gave up a good job in Delhi and came to live in a hill station, partly because I love mountains and forests, and partly because I wanted to devote more time to writing. I live at the edge of a forest of oak and maple. I am happy among trees but the full magic of a tree was only brought home to me some time ago when I was in the plains.

I was walking through a stretch of wasteland, a desert that seemed to stretch endlessly across a wide, flat plain. Just as I was beginning to find the heat and the glare a little discouraging, I saw a tree, just one small, crooked tree shimmering in the distance. And seeing it there all by itself, but growing stubbornly where other trees would not grow, I was filled with love and admiration for it. When I reached the tree, I found that it had given shelter to other small plants from the sun. A pair of parrots emerged from a hole in the tree trunk and flew across the plain, flashes of red and green and gold. Finding that tree there, struggling on its own but giving life to other things, was like finding a bit of heaven where I least expected it.

I decided that people, even in large numbers, could be good to live with and that Thoreau must have missed a lot when he turned his back on people and went to live alone in the woods.

Almost always, it's the unexpected that delights us, that takes us by the throat and gives us a good shaking, leaving us gaping in wonder. It may only be a shaft of sunlight slanting through the pillars of a banyan tree or dewdrops caught in a spider's web or, in the stillness of the mountains, the sudden chatter of a mountain stream as you round the bend of a hill. Or an emperor's first glimpse of a winding river and the world beyond.

Written By Hand

Amongst the current fraternity of writers, I must be that very rare person—an author who actually writes by hand!

Soon after the invention of the typewriter, most editors and publishers understandably refused to look at any mansucript that was handwritten. A decade or two earlier, when Dickens and Balzac had submitted their hefty manuscrips in longhand, no one had raised any objection. Had their handwriting been awful, their manuscripts would still have been read. Fortunately for all concerned, most writers, famous or obscure, took pains over their handwriting. For some, it was an art in itself, and many of those early manuscripts are a pleasure to look at and read.

And it wasn't only authors who wrote with an elegant hand. Parents and grandparents of most of us had distinctive styles of their own. I still have my father's last letter, written to me when I was at boarding school in Shimla some fifty years ago. He used large, beautifully formed letters, and his thoughts seemed to have the same flow and clarity as his handwriting.

In his letter he advises me (then a nine-year-old) about my own handwriting; 'I wanted to write before about your writing. Ruskin.... Sometimes I get letters from you in very small writing, as if you wanted to squeeze everything into one sheet of letter paper. It is not good for you or for your eyes, to get into the habit of writing too small... Try and form a larger style of handwriting—use more paper if necessary!'

I did my best to follow his advice, and I'm glad to report that after nearly forty years of the writing life, most people can still read my handwriting!

Word processors are all the rage now, and I have no objection to these mechanical aids any more than I have to my old Olympia typewriter, made in 1956 and still going strong. Although I do all my writing in longhand, I follow the conventions by typing a second draft. But I would not enjoy my writing if I had to do it straight on to a machine. It isn't just the pleasure of writing longhand. I like taking my notebooks and writing-pads to odd places. This particular essay is being written on the steps of my small cottage facing Pari Tibba (Fairy Hill). Part of the reason for sitting here is that there is a new postman on this route, and I don't want him to miss me.

For a freelance writer, the postman is almost as important as a publisher. I could, of course, sit here doing nothing, but as I have pencil and paper with me, and feel like using them, I shall write until the postman comes and maybe after he has gone, too! There is really no way in which I could set up a word processor on these steps.

There are a number of favourite places where I do my writing. One is under the chestnut tree on the slope above the cottage. Word processors were not designed keeping mountain slopes in mind. But armed with a pen (or pencil) and paper, I can lie on the grass and write for hours. On one occasion, I did take my typewriter into the garden, and I am still trying to extricate an acorn from under the keys, while the roller seems permanently stained yellow with some fine pollen-dust from the deodar trees.

My friends keep telling me about all the wonderful things I can do with a word processor, but they haven't got around to finding me one that I can take to bed, for that is another place where I do much of my writing—especially on cold winter nights, when it is impossible to keep the cottage warm.

While the wind howls outside, and snow piles up on the windowsill, I am warm under my quilt, writing-pad on my knees, ballpoint pen at the ready. And if, next day, the weather is warm and sunny, these simple aids will accompany me on a long walk, ready for instant use should I wish to record an incident, a prospect, a conversation or simply a train of thought.

When I think of the great eighteenth- and nineteenth-century writers, scratching away with their quill pens, filling hundreds of pages every month, I am amazed to find that their handwriting did not deteriorate into the sort of hieroglyphics that often make up the average doctor's prescription today. They knew they had to write legibly, if only for the sake of the typesetters.

Both Dickens and Thackeray had good, clear, flourishing styles. (Thackeray was a clever illustrator, too.) Somerset Maugham had an upright, legible hand. Churchill's neat handwriting never wavered, even when he was under stress. I like the bold, clear, straightforward hand of Abraham Lincoln; it mirrors the man. Mahatma Gandhi, another great soul who fell to the assassin's bullet, had many similarities of both handwriting and outlook.

Not everyone had a beautiful hand. King Henry VIII had an untidy scrawl, but then, he was not a man of much refinement. Guy Fawkes, who tried to blow up the British Parliament, had a very shaky hand. With such a quiver, no wonder he failed in his attempt! Hitler's signature is ugly, as you would expect. And Napoleon's doesn't seem to know where to stop; how much like the man!

I think my father was right when he said handwriting was often the key to a man's character, and that large well-formed letters went with an uncluttered mind. Florence Nightingale had a lovely handwriting, the hand of a caring person. And there were many like her, amongst our forebears.

───

Joyfully I Write

I am a fortunate person. For over fifty years I have been able to make a living by doing what I enjoy most—writing.

Sometimes I wonder if I have written too much. One gets into the habit of serving up the same ideas over and over again; with a different sauce perhaps, but still the same ideas, themes, memories, characters. Writers are often chided for repeating themselves. Artists and musicians are given more latitude. No one criticized Turner for painting so many sunsets at sea, or Gauguin for giving us all those lovely Tahitian women; or Husain, for treating us to so many horses, or Jamini Roy for giving us so many identical stylized figures.

In the world of music, one Puccini opera is very like another, a Chopin nocturne will return to familiar themes, and in the realm of lighter, modern music the same melodies recur with only slight variations. But authors are often taken to task for repeating themselves. They cannot help this, for in their writing they are expressing their personalities. Hemingway's world is very different from Jane Austen's. They are both unique worlds, but they do not change or mutate in the minds of their author-creators. Jane Austen spent all her life in one small place, and portrayed the people she knew. Hemingway roamed the world, but his characters remained much the same, usually extensions of himself.

In the course of a long writing career, it is inevitable that a writer will occasionally repeat himself, or return to themes that have remained with him even as new ideas and formulations enter his mind. The important thing is to keep writing, observing, listening and paying attention to the beauty of words and their arrangement. And like artists and musicians, the more we work on our art, the better it will be.

Writing, for me, is the simplest and greatest pleasure in the world. Putting a mood or an idea into words is an occupation I truly love. I plan my day so that there is time in it for writing a poem, or a paragraph, or an essay, or part of a story or longer work; not just because writing is my profession, but from a feeling of delight.

The world around me—be it the mountains or the busy street below my window—is teeming with subjects, sights, thoughts, that I wish to put into words in order to catch the fleeting moment, the passing image, the laughter, the joy, and sometimes the sorrow. Life would be intolerable if I did not have this freedom to write every day. Not that everything I put down is worth preserving. A great many pages of manuscript have found their way into my waste-paper basket or into the stove that warms the family room on cold winter evenings. I do not always please myself. I cannot always please others because, unlike the hard professionals, the Forsyths and the Sheldons, I am not writing to please everyone, I am really writing to please myself!

My theory of writing is that the conception should be as clear as possible, and that words should flow like a stream of clear water, preferably a mountain stream! You will, of course, encounter boulders, but you will learn to go over them or around them, so that your flow is unimpeded. If your stream gets too sluggish or muddy, it is better to put aside that particular piece of writing. Go to the source, go to the spring, where the water is purest, your thoughts as clear as the mountain air.

I do not write for more than an hour or two in the course of the day. Too long at the desk, and words lose their freshness.

Together with clarity and a good vocabulary, there must come a certain elevation of mood. Sterne must have been bubbling over with high spirits when he wrote *Shandy*. The sombre intensity of *Wuthering Heights* reflects Emily Bronte's passion for life, fully knowing that it was to be brief. Tagore's melancholy comes through in his poetry. Dickens is always passionate; there are no half measures in his work. Conrad's prose takes on the moods of the sea he knew and loved.

A real physical emotion accompanies the process of writing, and great writers are those who can channel this emotion into the creation of their best work.

'Are you a serious writer?' a schoolboy once asked.

'Well, I try to be *serious*,' I said, 'but cheerfulness keeps breaking in!'

Can a cheerful writer be taken seriously? I don't know. But I was certainly serious about making writing the main occupation of my life.

In order to do this, one has to give up many things—a job, security, comfort, domesticity—or rather, the pursuit of these things. Had I married when I was twenty-five, I would not have been able to throw up a good job as easily as I did at the time; I might now be living on a pension! God forbid. I am grateful for continued independence and the necessity to keep writing for my living, and for those who share their lives with me and whose joys and sorrows are mine too. An artist must not lose his hold on life. We do that when we settle for the safety of a comfortable old age.

Normally writers do not talk much, because they are saving their conversation for the readers of their books—those invisible listeners with whom we wish to strike a sympathetic chord. Of course, we talk freely with our friends, but we are reserved with people we do not know very well. If I talk too freely about a story I am going to write, chances are it will never be written. I have talked it to death.

Being alone is vital for any creative writer. I do not mean that you must live the life of a recluse. People who do not know me are frequently under the impression that I live in lonely splendour on a mountaintop, whereas in reality, I share a small flat with a family of twelve—and I'm the twelfth man, occasionally bringing out refreshments for the players!

I love my extended family, every single individual in it, but as a writer I must sometimes get a little time to be alone with my own thoughts, reflect a little, talk to myself, laugh about all the blunders I have committed in the past and ponder over the future. This is contemplation, not meditation. I am not very good at meditation, as it involves remaining in a passive state for some time. I would rather be out walking, observing the natural world, or sitting under a tree contemplating my novel or navel! I suppose the latter is a form of meditation.

When I casually told a journalist that I planned to write a book consisting of my meditations, he reported that I was writing a book on Meditation *per se,* which gave it a different connotation. I shall go along with the simple dictionary meaning of the verb *meditate*—to plan mentally, to exercise the mind in contemplation.

So I was doing it all along!

~

I am not, by nature, a gregarious person. Although I love people, and have often made friends with complete strangers, I am also a lover of solitude. Naturally, one thinks better when one is alone. But I prefer walking alone to walking with others. That ladybird on the wild rose would escape my attention if 1 was engaged in a lively conversation with a companion. Not that the ladybird is going to change my life. But by acknowledging its presence, stopping to admire its beauty, I have paid obeisance to the natural scheme of things of which I am only a small part.

It is upon a person's power of holding fast to such undimmed beauty that his or her inner hopefulness depends. As we journey through the world, we must inevitably encounter meanness and selfishness. As we fight for our survival, the higher visions and ideals often fade. It is then that we need ladybirds! Contemplating that tiny creature, or the flower on which it rests, gives one the hope—better, the certainty that there is more to life than interest rates, dividends, market forces and infinite technology.

As a writer, I have known hope and despair, success and failure; some recognition but also long periods of neglect and critical dismissal. But I have had no regrets. I have enjoyed the writer's life to the full, and one reason for this is that living in India has given me certain freedoms which I would not have enjoyed elsewhere. Friendship when needed. Solitude when desired. Even, at times, love and passion. It has tolerated me for what I am—a bit of a drop-out, unconventional, idiosyncratic. I have been left alone to do my own thing. In India, people do not censure you unless you start making a nuisance of yourself. Society has its norms and its orthodoxies, and provided you do not flaunt all the rules, society will allow you to go your own way. I am free to become a naked ascetic and roam the streets with a begging bowl; I am also free to live in a palatial farmhouse if I have the wherewithal. For twenty-five years, I have lived in this small, sunny second-floor room looking out on the mountains, and no one has bothered me, unless you count the neighbour's dog who prevents the postman and courier boys from coming up the steps.

~

I may write for myself, but as I also write to get published, it must follow that I write for others too. Only a handful of readers might enjoy my writing, but they are my soul mates, my alter egos, and they keep me going through those lean times and discouraging moments.

Even though I depend upon my writing for a livelihood, it is still, for me, the most delightful thing in the world.

I did not set out to make a fortune from writing; I knew I was not that kind of writer. But it was the thing I did best, and I persevered with the exercise of my gift, cultivating the more discriminating editors, publishers and readers, never really expecting huge rewards but accepting whatever came my way. Happiness is a matter of temperament rather than circumstance, and I have always considered myself fortunate in having escaped the tedium of a nine-to-five job or some other form of drudgery.

Of course, there comes a time when almost every author asks himself what his effort and output really amounts to? We expect our work to influence people, to affect a great many readers, when in fact, its impact is infinitesimal. Those who work on a large scale must feel discouraged by the world's indifference. That is why I am happy to give a little innocent pleasure to a handful of readers. This is a reward worth having.

As a writer, I have difficulty in doing justice to momentous events, the wars of nations, the politics of power; I am more at ease with the dew of the morning, the sensuous delights of the day, the silent blessings of the night, the joys and sorrows of children, the strivings of ordinary folk, and of course, the ridiculous situations in which we sometimes find ourselves.

We cannot prevent sorrow and pain and tragedy. And yet, when we look around us, we find that the majority of people are actually enjoying life! There are so many lovely things to see, there is so much to do, so much fun to be had, and so many charming and interesting people to meet... How can my pen ever run dry?

Love Thy Critic

Having just read a nasty review of my last book in *India Today*, I take heart by recalling Hemingway's direct action against critic **Mark** Eastman in 1937. Eastman had questioned Hemingway's manhood in his review of *Death in the Afternoon*, which he had sarcastically titled 'Bull in the Afternoon'.

When Hemingway saw Eastman, he bashed him over the head with a copy of the book and then wrestled him to the ground. Trouble is, my critic is a woman. I'd lose the wrestling match.

This sort of response is rare, but exchanges between authors and critics can get nasty, with reputations maligned and genuine talents belittled. The worst sort of reviewers are those who make personal attacks on authors, usually a sign of envy coupled with malice. Thomas Carlyle called Emerson a hoary-headed and toothless baboon' and wrote of Charles Lamb: 'a more pitiful, rickety, gasping, staggering Tomfool I do not know.' But we still read and enjoy Lamb and Emerson; who reads Carlyle?

Of Walt Whitman, one reviewer said: 'Whitman is as unacquainted with art as a hog is with mathematics.' Swift was accused of having 'a diseased mind' and Henry James was called an 'idiot and a Boston idiot to boot, than which there is nothing lower in the world'. Their critics have long been forgotten, but just occasionally an author turns critic with equal virulence. There was the classic Dorothy Parker review which read: 'This is not a novel to be tossed aside lightly. It should be thrown with great force.'

When brickbats are flung at an author it is usually a sign that he or she is successful, has reached the top. No one received more abuse than Shakespeare. *Hamlet was* described by Voltaire as 'the work of a drunken savage', and Pepys said *A Midsummer Night's Dream* was 'the most insipid, ridiculous play that I ever saw in my life'. Macaulay sneered at Wordsworth's 'crazy mystical metaphysics, the endless wilderness of dull, flat, prosaic twaddle', a description that would aptly describe Macaulay's own meandering and monotonous style.

Should authors really have to put up with this sort of thing? Politicians do, and actors and sportsmen, so why not writers? As E.M. Forster once said: 'No author has the right to whine. He was not obliged to be an author. He invited publicity, and he must take the publicity that comes along.'

Of course, some reviewers do go a little too far, like the one who once referred to 'that well-known typist Harold Robbins'. That was a remark truly deserving a bash over the head, on behalf of typists everywhere.

People do ask funny questions. Recently, I was accosted on the road by a stranger, who proceeds to cross-examine me, starting with: 'Excuse me, are you a good writer?' For once, I'm stumped for an answer. Writing for a living; it's a battlefield!

~⁓

Adventures of a Book-Lover

My father died when I was ten, and for the next few years books became a scarce commodity in my life, for my mother and stepfather were not great readers. In my rather lonely early teens I was to discover that books could be good friends, reliable companions and I seized upon almost any printed matter that came my way, whether it was a girls' classic like *Little Women,* or a *Hotspur* or *Champion* comic, or a detective story or *The Naturalist on the River Amazon* by Henry Walter Bates. The only books I balked at reading were collections of sermons (amazing how often they turned up in those early years) and self-improvement books, since I hadn't the slightest desire to improve myself in any way.

I think it all began in that forest rest house in the Siwalik Hills, a sub-tropical range cradling the Doon valley in northern India. Here my stepfather and his gun-toting friends were given to hunting birds and animals that roamed those forests. He was a poor shot, so he cannot really be blamed for the absence of wildlife today; but he did his best to eliminate every creature that came within his sights.

On one of these shikar trips, we were staying in a rest house near the Timli Pass. My stepfather and his friends were 'after tiger' (you were out of fashion if you weren't after big game) and set out every morning with an army of paid villagers to 'beat' the jungle, that is, to make enough noise with drums, whistles, tin trumpets and empty kerosene tins, to disturb the tiger and drive the unwilling beast into the open where he could conveniently be dispatched. Truly bored by this form of sport, I stayed behind in the rest house, and in the course of a morning's exploration of the bungalow, discovered a dusty but crowded bookshelf half-hidden in a corner of the back verandah.

Who had left them there? A literary forest officer? A memsahib who had been bored by her husband's camp-fire boasting? Or someone like me who had no enthusiasm for the 'manly' sport of slaughtering wild animals, and brought his library along to pass the time?

Possibly the poor fellow had gone into the jungle one day, as a gesture towards his more bloodthirsty companions, and been trampled by an elephant or gored by a wild boar, or (more likely) accidentally shot by one of his companions—and they had taken his remains away and left his books behind. Anyway, there they were, a shelf of some fifty volumes, obviously untouched for several years. I wiped the dust off the covers and examined the titles. As my reading taste had not yet formed, I was ready to try anything. The bookshelf was varied in its contents—and my own interests have remained equally wide-ranging.

On that fateful day in the forest rest house, I discovered two very funny books. One was P. G. Wodehouse's *Love among the Chickens,* an early Ukridge story and still one of my favourites. The other was *The Diary of a Nobody* by George and Weedon Grossmith, who spent more time on the stage than in the study but are now remembered mainly for this hilarious book. It isn't everyone's cup of tea. Recently I lent my copy to a Swiss friend, who could see nothing funny about it. I must have read it a dozen times; I pick it up whenever I'm feeling low, and on one occasion it even cured me of a peptic ulcer!

Anyway back to the rest house. By the time the perspiring hunters came back late in the evening, I had started on M. R. James' *Ghost Stories of an Antiquary,* which had me hooked on ghost stones for the rest of my life. It kept me awake most of the night, until the oil in the kerosene lamp had finished.

Next morning, fresh and optimistic again, the shikaris set out for a different area, where they hoped to locate their tiger. All day I could hear the beaters' drums throbbing in the distance. This did not prevent me from finishing James or a collection of stories called *The Big Karoo* by Pauline Smith—wonderfully evocative of the life of the pioneering Boers in South Africa.

My concentration was disturbed only once, when I looked up and saw a spotted deer crossing the open clearing in front of the bungalow. The deer disappeared into the forest and I returned to my book.

Dusk had fallen when I heard the party returning from the hunt. The great men were talking loudly and seemed excited. Perhaps they had got their tiger! I came out on the verandah to meet them.

'Did you shoot the tiger?' I asked.

'No, Ruskin,' said my stepfather. 'I think we'll catch up with it tomorrow. But you should have been with us—we saw a spotted deer!'

There were three days left and I knew I would never get through the entire bookshelf. So I chose *David Copperfield*—my first encounter with Dickens—and settled down in the verandah armchair to make the acquaintance of Mr Micawber and his family, along with Aunt Betsy Trotwood, Mr Dick, Peggotty and a host of other larger-than-life characters. I think it would be true to say that *Copperfield* set me off on the road to literature; I identified with young David and wanted to grow up to be a writer like him.

But on my second day with the book an event occurred which interrupted my reading for a little while.

I had noticed, on the previous day, that a number of stray dogs—some of them belonging to watchmen, villagers and forest rangers—always hung about the bungalow, waiting for scraps of food to be thrown away. It was about ten in the morning (a time when wild animals seldom come into the open), when I heard a sudden yelp coming from the clearing. Looking up, I saw a large, full-grown leopard making off with one of the dogs. The other dogs, while keeping their distance, set up a furious barking, but the leopard and its victim had soon disappeared. I returned to *Copperfield*, and it was getting late when the shikaris returned. They looked dirty, sweaty and disgruntled. Next day we were to return to the city, and none of them had anything to show for a week in the jungle.

'I saw a leopard this morning,' I said modestly.

No one took me seriously. 'Did you really?' said the leading shikari, glancing at the book in my hands. 'Young Master Copperfield says he saw a leopard!'

'Too imaginative for his age,' said my stepfather. 'Comes from reading so much, I expect.'

I went to bed and left them to their tales of 'good old days' when rhinos, cheetahs and possibly even unicorns were still available for slaughter. Camp broke up before I could finish *Copperfield*, but the forest ranger said I could keep the book. And so I became the only member of the expedition with a trophy to take home.

After that adventure, I was always looking for books in unlikely places. Although I never went to college, I think I have read as much, if not more, than most collegiates, and it would he true to say that I received a large part of my education in second-hand bookshops. London had many, and Calcutta once had a large number of them, but I think the prize must go to a small town in Wales called Hay-on-Wye, which has twenty-six bookshops and over a million books. It's in the world's quiet corners that book-lovers still flourish—a far from dying species!

One of my treasures is a little novel called *Sweet Rocket* by Mary Johnston. It was a failure when it was first published in 1920. It has only the thinnest outline of a story but the author lets out her ideas in lyrical prose that seduces me at every turn of the page. Miss Johnston was a Virginian. She did not travel outside America. But her little book did. I found it buried under a pile of railway timetables at a bookstall in Simla, the old summer capital of India almost as though it had been waiting there for me, these seventy years!

I have collected a number of 'little' books, like my father's *Finger Prayer Book*, which is the size of a small finger but is replete with Psalms and the complete Book of Common Prayer. Another is *The Pocket Trivet: An Anthology for Optimists*, published by *The Morning Post* newspaper in 1932 and designed to slip into the waistcoat pocket.

But what is a trivet, one might well ask. Well it's a stand for a small pot or kettle, fixed securely over a grate. To be right as a trivet is to be perfectly and thoroughly right—just right, like the short sayings in this tiny anthology which range from Emerson's 'Hitch your wagon to a star!' to the Japanese proverb: 'In the market place there is money to be made, but under the cherry tree there is rest.'

It helps me forget the dilapidated old building in which I live and work, and to look instead at the ever-changing cloud patterns as seen from my small window. There is no end to the shapes made by the clouds, or to the stories they set off in my head.

Swallows Are Free

A few years ago I found myself under arrest. A story I had written had offended the guardians of our morals, and the result was a criminal charge.

But this is not an account of how I was pursued by the law because of my literary style. Unpleasant experiences are best forgotten if one is not to become an embittered old cynic. And in any case, I was finally acquitted.

No one who is under arrest is likely to enjoy the experience. Warrants make bad reading, except in detective stories. So how does a writer of essays and light verse take it? A nervous breakdown would not have been surprising, and did in fact seem likely. But I was saved from one by the swallows.

Yes, the swallows.

There I was, sitting on a hard bench on the police station verandah, waiting for a couple of friends to arrive and stand bail for me, when I noticed the swallows wheeling in and out of the verandah, busily building a nest in the eaves of the old building. Nothing unusual about that. Swallows love old police stations. But just because it *was* so usual, so commonplace, I took heart.

The right word is *reassuring*. That is what we all need when we are in a tight corner—a little reassurance. Like a friendly, familiar face. Or the sleepy drone of a cricket commentary in the background. Or someone whistling cheerfully in a gloomy corridor.

Something to let you know that even if things seem to be getting out of hand for a while, the rest of the world is still going on quite normally.

And for me, nothing could have been more reassuring than the sight of several swallows—all oblivious of the terrors of the thana—going about their business as usual.

Business as usual. That's what reassures. It bucked me up tremendously, just watching those little birds.

Presently an official came along, took me into his office, and asked me to fill in a form.

I remarked, 'Have you noticed that the swallows are nesting in the verandah?' He looked at me blankly. He hadn't noticed any swallows. What were swallows, anyway? Obviously I was deranged—a candidate for an asylum if not for a jail.

But I knew, then, watching the blank look on his face, that I was equal to the situation—that I was dealing with a human being whose plight was worse than mine, because he would never be able to find reassurance so quickly or so easily.

◦∼ ∽

When the Lamp Is Lit

'Love thy art, poor as it may be, which thou hast learned, and be content with it; and pass through the rest of life like one who has entrusted to the gods with his whole soul and all that he has, making thyself neither the tyrant nor the slave of any man.'

Marcus Aurelius (121–180), the last of the great Antonine emperors, speaks to us across the centuries through his *Meditations*, those nuggets of wisdom jotted down during a crowded and adventurous life.

Being unable to find much comfort or wisdom in the utterances of present-day teachers, preachers or godmen (be they of the Eastern or Western variety), I frequently turn for advice and reassurance to the early Greek and Roman philosophers—Epicurus, Epictetus, Marcus Aurelius, Seneca and others—those Stoics and Epicureans whose precepts are as relevant today as they were during the finest flowering of the Greek and Roman civilizations.

'Love thy art, poor as it may be...' I have never regretted following this precept; for, no matter how skilful one is with words, it is only drudgery to have to use them in the more mundane spheres of journalism. I have tried to use words creatively and lovingly. The gift for putting together words and sentences to make stories or poems or essays has carried me through life with a certain serenity and inner harmony which could not have come from any unloved vocation.

Within my own 'art' I think I have known my limitations and worked within them, thus sparing myself the bitter disappointment that comes to those whose ambitions stretch far beyond their talents. Do what you know best, and do it well. Act impeccably. Everything will then fall into place.

I was looking for a living example to try and illustrate this precept, and came across it in the persons of Mahboob Khan and Ramji Mai, stonemasons who were engaged in restoring Shah Jahan's Hall of Mirrors in the Agra Fort. They had been at work for ten years, slowly but deftly bringing their epic task to completion.

The restoration work was so intricate that these two skilled craftsmen could restore only about six inches in a day. In recreating the original stucco work on walls and ceiling, everything had to be done impeccably: millions of pieces of tiny mirrors and coloured glass had to find their exact place in order to reflect just the right amount of light and, at the same time, conform to a certain pattern.

It is a small art, theirs, but it requires infinite patience, skill and dedication. No fame for them, no great material reward. Their greatest reward comes from the very act of taking pains in the pursuit of perfection.

Surely they must be happy, or at least contented men. In truth, I am yet to meet a neurotic carpenter or stonemason or clay worker or bangle maker or master craftsman of any kind. Those who work with wood or stone or glass are usually well-balanced people. Working with the hands is in itself a therapy. Those of us who work with our minds—composers or artists or writers—must try to emulate these craftsmen's methods, paying attention to every detail and working with loving care.

The trouble is that creative people are cerebral creatures with fluctuations of mood that make life exhilarating at one moment and depressing the next. And this is often reflected in their work unless they have become mechanical, turning out books or paintings like samosas.

Yet there are times when I do love my art. And because I have loved it, I think I have been able to pass through life without being any man's slave or tyrant. I doubt if I have ever written a story or essay or workaday article unless I have really wanted to write it. And in this way I have probably suffered materially, because I have never attempted a blockbuster of a novel, or a biography of a celebrity, or a soap opera that goes on for ever. The prospect of spinning out thousands of words of little or no consequence seems a dull and dreary way of earning a living.

'Writing is easy,' said Red Smith. 'All you have to do is sit at your typewriter till little drops of blood appear on your forehead.' That's true for some of us. But I refuse to suffer. At the first sign of drops of blood or perspiration, I get up from my desk and do something totally different—make myself a sandwich, water my ferns, take a walk, or discuss politics with the milkman. If the writing isn't easy, if I'm not enjoying it, I know I'm better off doing something else.

And yet writing is easy if I'm happy with my theme. Ask me to write a piece on petunias, and I'll turn out an enthusiastic essay on this underrated flower. I might even write a story about someone who grows petunias, because such a person must obviously have sterling qualities. I might even delve into the love life of a petunia grower because those who love flowers must, by their very nature, be loving, even sensual and passionate people. From *The Rose Garden of Sa'adi* to Wordsworth's sea of golden daffodils, love poetry and song has been enriched by flowers—the rose, the jasmine, the lily, the daffodil, the honeysuckle... No sweeter scent than the honeysuckle's. No more inviting name. Come, suckle up to your honey, it seems to say; and under my bower you'll kiss the fleeting hours away.

Of flowers, lovers, melons and moonbeams, I can write reams. But ask me to write the life story of a great leader or media tycoon or matchbox maker, and I'm stumped and stymied. Those little drops of blood threaten to appear. I cannot breathe life into these subjects, noble though they might be. Their true personalities, the essence of their natures, somehow eludes me. It is not that they are too complicated, but rather that one has to peel off too many layers of protective armour to get at the flesh and blood that lies beneath the skin. In the case of the great leader, all those speeches—no matter how many fat volumes they may occupy—are just so many layers of onion peel. And the more you peel the less you find. We come no nearer to the heart and mind of our hero.

As for the captains of industry, we have even less to go on. Factory chimneys, figures, television satellites, song charts, all go into your computers and come out neatly sanitized yet somehow faceless. What they felt like in their darker moments remains well hidden from posterity. It took the genius of Shakespeare to reach into the darker recesses of the human mind, and he got no help from his subjects either; they were long dead when he wrote of their personal tragedies—for tragedy is usually the lot of those whose grasp exceeds their reach. Alexander, Caesar, Napoleon and other conquerors, when they forget that they are mortals must reckon with the gods: the gods being the self-destructive elements in their own natures.

Why is humility so hard to come by? Most religions teach the wisdom of humility, but who listens? We all know that life is finite, that human civilization, for what it's worth, is self-limiting. And yet the most educated of men will strut about their little world like actors on a stage; they assume the mantle of immortals, deluding themselves into thinking they are indispensable, until eventually they join all those other indispensables who have reached perfection in the form of dust or ashes.

Why so much pride when a little humility can get us far more by way of love and peace and happiness? Better to efface yourself like the cricket who is heard but seldom seen than to flap your wings and crow like a cockbird before ending up as someone's tandoori dinner.

Happiness is an elusive state of mind, not to be gained by clumsy pursuit. It is given to those who do not sue for it: to be unconcerned about a desired good is probably the only way to possess it.

'I enjoy life,' said Seneca, 'because I am ready to leave it.'

If we can disencumber ourselves of nine-tenths of our worldly goods, it should not be difficult to leave the rest behind. But it's amazing how most of us hang on to our bric-a-brac, hoping maybe that it will be treasured and valued by those who come after us. Yes, the Duke and Duchess of Windsor's slice of wedding cake, preserved for over fifty years, recently fetched over thirty thousand dollars at an auction in New York. But did the original royal owners have that end in mind when they decided to hang on to a slice of the cake that symbolized their bittersweet romance? It certainly wasn't put away as an investment. As a symbol of the sacrifice that Edward made in giving up the throne of England in exchange for Mrs Simpson, it certainly meant something to the ex-king and his wife; but to its subsequent and present owners it is merely a curiosity which has cost them a lot of money. Perhaps they will put it on display. There are always people who will gaze in awe and wonder at such a thing. But I would like to see one of them eat it.

'How weary, stale, flat and unprofitable!' sighed Hamlet in another context, although he might well have been commenting on the values of our own time, which sets more store on a pop singer's toothbrush or a dead princess's wardrobe than on the legacy of the truly great. It's a world in which we elevate the second rate above the first rate. Will posterity set the record straight? Seedy politicians, swelling with self-importance, and the men who pull their strings, the medieval robber barons of today, will do their best to promote the second best, because that's where the money lies, but Time has a way of taking the stuffing out of the bully, the braggart and, of course, the stuffed shirt.

Recently a publishing giant and media tycoon refused to publish a book because he was afraid it would offend his customers in China. In doing so, he had curtailed his own freedom, made himself the victim of his own overriding ambitions. As his empire grows, his personal freedom shrinks. There is too much to lose. He is stuck on the point of his own glittering star, as he channels the second rate into the homes of helpless millions.

Not long ago there was another media mogul (name forgotten now, as such names must be) who found his success so stale, flat and in the end unprofitable, that he threw himself off the stern of his expensive yacht, seeking oblivion in the ocean. His body was never found. A great many decent people lost their savings because of him, otherwise the world was no worse for his exit.

Let us, for a change, turn to someone of real worth, whose name is imperishable. She made no money and did not live long enough to enjoy her fame. Riddled with tuberculosis she clung on to life until she finished her single masterpiece, *Wuthering Heights*, thereby giving to the world her very lifeblood along with the creative urge that justified her existence. Emily Bronte's indifference to wealth, fame, and personal comfort would be rare in today's world of high-powered literary agents and media hype. For her, writing was ecstasy. It was emancipation wrought in the soul. She and her sisters and others like them held only a brief tenure on this earth—no time to think of getting to the top of the ladder!—but their words, their thoughts, their songs are still with us. At least with those of us who would listen...

And there are many brave and good Indian writers, who work in their own language—be it Bengali or Oriya or Telugu or Marathi or fifteen to twenty others—and plough their lonely furrow without benefit of agent or media blitz or Booker prize. Some of them may despair. But even so, they work on in despair. Their rewards may be small, their readers few, but it is enough to keep them from turning off the light. For they know that the pen, in honest and gifted hands, is mightier than the grave.

And these are my parting words to you, dear reader: *May you have the wisdom to be simple, and the humour to be happy.*

Family and Friends

Remember This Day

If you can get an entire year off from school when you are nine years old, and can have a memorable time with a great father, then that year has to be the best time of your life even if it is followed by sorrow and insecurity.

It was the result of my parents' separation at a time when my father was on active service in the R.A.F. during World War II. He managed to keep me with him for a summer and winter, at various locations in New Delhi—Hailey Road, Atul Grove Lane, Scindia House—in apartments he had rented, as he was not permitted to keep a child in the quarters assigned to service personnel. This arrangement suited him perfectly, and I had a wonderful year in Delhi, going to the cinema, quaffing milkshakes, helping my father with his stamp collection…but this idyllic situation could not continue for ever, and when my father was transferred to Karachi, he had no option but to put me in a boarding school.

This was the Bishop Cotton Preparatory School in Simla—or rather, Chhota Simla—where boys studied up to Class 4, after which they moved on to the senior school.

Although I was a shy boy, I had settled down quite well in the friendly atmosphere of this little school, but I did miss my father's companionship, and I was overjoyed when he came up to see me during the midsummer break. He had a couple of days' leave, and he could only take me out for a day, bringing me back to school in the evening.

I was so proud of him when he turned up in his dark blue R.A.F. uniform, a Flight Lieutenant's stripes very much in evidence as he had just been promoted. He was already forty, engaged in Codes and Ciphers and not flying much. He was short and stocky, getting bald, but smart in his uniform. I gave him a salute—I loved giving salutes—and he returned the salutation and followed it up with a hug and a kiss on my forehead.

'And what would you like to do today, son?'

'Let's go to Davico's,' I said.

Davico's was the best restaurant in town, famous for its meringues, marzipans, curry-puffs and pastries.

So to Davico's we went, where of course I gorged myself on confectionery as only a small schoolboy can do.

'Lunch is still a long way off, so let's take a walk,' suggested my father. And provisioning ourselves with more pastries, we left the Mall and trudged up to the Monkey Temple at the top of Jakko Hill. Here we were relieved of the pastries by the monkeys, who simply snatched them away from my unwilling hands, and we came downhill in a hurry before I could get hungry again. Small boys and monkeys have much in common.

My father suggested a rickshaw ride around Elysium Hill, and this we did in style, swept along by four sturdy young rickshaw-pullers. My father took the opportunity of relating the story of Kipling's 'Phantom Rickshaw' (this was before I discovered it in print), and a couple of other ghost stories designed to build up my appetite for lunch. We ate at Wenger's (or was it Clark's?) and then—

'Enough of ghosts, Ruskin. Let's go to the pictures.'

I loved going to the pictures. I know the Delhi cinemas intimately, and it hadn't taken me long to discover the Simla cinemas. There were three of them—the Regal, the Ritz and the Rivoli.

We went to the Rivoli. It was down near the ice-skating ring and the old Blessington Hotel. The film was about an ice-skater and starred Sonja Henie, a pretty young Norwegian Olympic champion who appeared in a number of Hollywood musicals. All she had to do was skate and look pretty, and this she did to perfection. I decided to fall in love with her. But by the time I'd grow up and finished school, she'd stopped skating and making films! Whatever happened to Sonja Henie?

After the picture, it was time to return to school. We walked all the way to Chhota Simla, talking about what we'd do during the winter holidays, and where we would go when the War was over.

'I'll be in Calcutta now,' said my father. 'There are good bookshops there. And cinemas. And Chinese restaurants. And we'll buy more gramophone records, and add to the stamp collection.'

It was dusk when we walked slowly down the path to the school gate and playing-field. Two of my friends were waiting for me—Bimal and Riaz. My father spoke to them, asked about their homes. A bell started ringing. We said goodbye.

'Remember this day, Ruskin,' said my father.

He patted me gently on the head and walked away.

I never saw him again.

Three months later I heard that he had passed away in the military hospital in Calcutta.

I dream of him sometimes, and in my dream he is always the same, caring for me and leading me by the hand along old familiar roads.

And of course I remember that day. Over sixty-five years have passed, but it's as fresh as yesterday.

~

The Regimental Myna

In my grandfather's time, British soldiers stationed in India were very fond of keeping pets, and there were few barrack-rooms where pets were not to be found. Dogs and cats were the most common, but birds were also great favourites.

In one instance, a bird was not only the pet of a barrack-room but of a whole regiment. His owner was my grandfather, Private Bond, a soldier of the line who had come out to India with the King's Own Scottish Rifles.

The bird was a myna, common enough in India, and Grandfather named it Dickens after his favourite author. Dickens came into Grandfather's possession when quite young, and he was soon a favourite with all the men in the barracks at Meerut, where the regiment was stationed. Meerut was hot and dusty; the curries were hot and spicy; the General in command was hot-tempered and crusty. Keeping a pet was almost the sole recreation for the men in barracks.

Because he was tamed so young, Dickens (or Dicky for short) never learned to pick up food for himself. Instead, just like a baby bird, he took his meals from Grandfather's mouth. And other men used to feed him in the same way. When Dickens was hungry, he asked for food by sitting on Grandfather's shoulders, flapping his wings rapidly and opening his beak.

Dicky was never caged, and as soon as he was able to fly he attended all parades, watched the rations being issued, and was present on every occasion which brought the soldiers out of their barracks. When out in the country, he would follow the regiment or party, flying from shoulder to shoulder, or from tree to tree, always keeping a sharp look-out for his enemies, the hawks.

Sometimes he would choose a mounted officer as a companion; but after the manoeuvres were over he would return to Grandfather's shoulder.

One day there was to be a General's inspection, and the Colonel gave orders that Dicky was to be confined, so that he wouldn't appear on parade.

'Lock him away somewhere, Bond,' the Colonel snapped. 'We can't have him flapping all over the parade-ground.'

Dickens was put into a storeroom, with the windows closed and the door locked. But while the General's inspection was going on, the mess orderly, who wanted something from the storeroom and knew where to find the key, opened the door.

Out flew Dickens. He made straight for the parade-ground, greatly excited at being let out and chattering loudly.

Dicky must have thought the General had something to do with his detention, or else he may have felt an explanation was due to him. Whatever his reasoning, he chose to alight on the General's pith helmet, between the plumes.

Here he chattered faster than ever, much to the surprise of the General, who was obliged to take his helmet off before he could dislodge the bird.

'What the dickens!' exclaimed the General, going purple in the face for Dicky had discharged his breakfast between the plumes of the helmet.

Meanwhile, Dicky had flown to the Colonel's shoulder to make further complaints, to the great delight of the men.

'Fall out, Bond!' the Colonel screamed. 'Take this bird away—for good! I don't want to see it again!'

A crestfallen Private Bond returned to the barracks with Dicky, wondering what to do next. To part with Dicky, or even to cage him, was out of the question.

But Grandfather was not the only one who loved Dickens. He was also highly popular with the entire battalion. In the end, Grandfather decided to ask his Captain to bring him before the Colonel so he could ask forgiveness for Dicky's behaviour.

The Colonel gave Private Bond and his Captain a patient hearing. Then the Colonel consulted his officers and decided that the bird could stay—provided he was taken on as a serving member of the regiment!

Dickens' popularity was not surprising, as he was highly intelligent. He knew the men of his own regiment from those of others, and would only associate with the Scottish Rifles. Even in the drill season, when there were as many as twenty regiments in camp, Dicky never made a mistake.

Dickens had a unique method of getting from one part of the camp to another. Instead of flying over the top of the camp, he would go in stages from tent to tent, flying very low, sheltering in each one, then peeping out and looking carefully for hawks before moving on to the next.

One day Grandfather was admitted to hospital with malaria. Dicky couldn't find him anywhere, and searched and searched all over the camp in great distress. The hospital was a couple of kilometres away from the barracks, and it wasn't until the third day of searching that Dickens finally discovered Grandfather lying there.

From then on, for as long as Grandfather was on the sick list, Dicky spent his time at the hospital. An upturned helmet was placed on a shelf for him near Grandfather's bed, and Dickens spent the night inside it. As soon as Grandfather was discharged from the hospital, Dickens left as well, and never returned, not even for a visit.

In 1888, the regiment got orders to proceed to Calcutta, en route for Burma, where it was to take part in the Chin Lushai Expedition. All pets had to be left behind, and Dickens was no exception.

But Dicky had his own views on the subject.

The regiment travelled in stages, marching along the Grand Trunk Road, moving at night and going into rest camps for the day.

Dickens caught up on the third day. He arrived in camp after a journey of more than three hundred kilometers—dull, dejected and starving, as he still depended on being fed from Grandfather's mouth.

Route-marching and travelling by train (the railway was just beginning to spread across India), the battalion finally reached

Calcutta. From there, contrary to orders, Dickens embarked for Burma along with the soldiers.

On board the ship, Dickens would amuse himself by peeping from the portholes, and flapping from one to the other. He would also go up on deck, and sometimes even took experimental flights out to sea. But one day he was caught in a gale and had such difficulty getting back to the ship that he gave up that kind of adventuring.

Dickens stayed with his regiment all through the expedition and the campaign. Many of his soldier friends lost their lives, but Grandfather and Dickens survived the fighting and returned safely to Calcutta.

Grandfather, now a Corporal, was given six months' home leave, along with the rest of the regiment. This meant sailing home to England.

During the first part of the voyage, Dicky was his usual cheerful self. But when the ship left the Suez Canal, the weather grew cold, and he was no longer to be seen on the yardarms or on the bridge with the captain. He even lost interest in going on deck with Grandfather, preferring to stay with the parrots on the waste deck.

After the ship passed Gibraltar, Dickens went below. He never came on deck again.

Dickens was laid out in a Huntley and Palmer's biscuit tin, and buried at sea. Not, perhaps, with full military honours, but certainly to the sound of Grandfather's bagpipes, playing *The Last Post*.

The Old Gramophone

It was a large square mahogany box, well polished, and there was a handle you had to wind, and lids that opened top and front. You changed the steel needle every time you changed the record.

The records were kept flat in a cardboard box to prevent them from warping. If you didn't pack them flat, the heat and humidity turned them into strange shapes which would have made them eligible for an exhibition of modern sculpture.

The winding, the changing of records and needles, the selection of a record were boyhood tasks that I thoroughly enjoyed. I was very methodical in these matters. I hated records being scratched, or the turntable slowing down in the middle of a record, bringing the music of the song to a slow and mournful stop: this happened if the gramophone wasn't fully wound. I was especially careful with my favourites, such as Nelson Eddy singing 'The Mounties' and 'The Hills of Home', various numbers sung by the Ink Spots, and a medley of marches.

All this musical activity (requiring much physical exertion on the part of the listener!) took place in a little-known port called Jamnagar, on the west coast of our country, where my father taught English to the young princes and princesses of the state. The gramophone had been installed to amuse me and my mother, but my mother couldn't be bothered with all the effort that went into playing it.

I loved every aspect of the gramophone, even the cleaning of the records with a special cloth. One of my first feats of writing was to catalogue all the records in our collection—only about fifty to begin with—and this cataloguing I did with great care and devotion. My father liked 'grand opera'—Caruso, Gigli, and Galli-Curci—but I preferred the lighter ballads of Nelson Eddy, Deanna Durbin, Grade Fields, Richard Tauber, and 'The Street Singer' (Arthur Tracy). It may seem incongruous, to have been living within sound of the Arabian Sea and listening to Nelson sing most beautifully of the mighty Missouri river, but it was perfectly natural to me. I grew up with that music, and I love it still.

I was a lonely boy, without friends of my own age, so that the gramophone and the record collection meant a lot to me. My catalogue went into new and longer editions, taking in the names of composers, lyricists and accompanists.

When we left Jamnagar, the gramophone accompanied us on the long train journey (three days and three nights, with several changes) to Dehradun. Here, in the spacious grounds of my grandparents' home at the foothills of the Himalayas, songs like 'The Hills of Home' and 'Shenandoah' did not seem out of place.

Grandfather had a smaller gramophone and a record collection of his own. His tastes were more 'modern' than mine. Dance music was his passion, and there were any number of foxtrots, tangos and beguines played by the leading dance bands of the 1940s. Granny preferred waltzes and taught me to waltz. I would waltz with her on the broad verandah, to the strains of *The Blue Danube* and *The*

Skater's Waltz, while a soft breeze rustled in the banana fronds. I became quite good at the waltz, but then saw Gene Kelly tap-dancing in a brash, colourful MGM musical, and—base treachery!—forsook the waltz and began tap-dancing all over the house, much to Granny's dismay.

All this is pure nostalgia, of course, but why be ashamed of it? Nostalgia is simply an attempt to try and preserve that which was good in the past.... The past has served us: why not serve the past in this way?

When I was sent to boarding school and was away from home for nine long months, I really missed the gramophone. How I looked forward to coming home for the winter holidays! There were, of course, some new records waiting for me. And Grandfather had taken to the Brazilian rumba, which was all the rage just then. Yes, Grandfather did the rumba with great aplomb.

I believe he'd moved on to the samba and then the calypso, but by then I'd left India and was away for five years. A great deal had changed in my absence. My grandparents had moved on, and my mother had sold the old gramophone and replaced it with a large radiogram. But this wasn't so much fun: I wanted something I could wind!

I keep hoping our old gramophone will turn up somewhere—maybe in an antique shop or in someone's attic or store-room, or at a sale. Then I shall buy it back, whatever the cost, and install it in my study and have the time of my life winding it up and playing the old records. I now have tapes of some of them, but that won't stop me listening to the gramophone. I have even kept a box of needles in readiness for the great day.

A Boy and a River

Between the boy and the river was a mountain. I was a small boy, and it was a small river, but the thickly forested mountain was big and hid the river. Yet I knew it was there and what it looked like. I had never seen the river with my own eyes, but from the villagers I had heard of it, of the fish in its waters, of its rocks and currents and waterfalls; and it only remained for me to touch the water and know it personally.

I stood in front of our house on the hill opposite the mountain, and gazed across the valley, dreaming of the river. I was barefooted; not because I couldn't afford shoes, but because I felt free with my bare feet, because I liked the feel of warm stones and cool grass, because not wearing shoes saved me the trouble of taking them off.

It was eleven o'clock and I knew my parents wouldn't be home till evening. There was a loaf of bread I could take with me, and on the way I might find some fruit. Here was the chance I had been waiting for: it would not come again for a long time, because it was seldom my father and mother visited friends for the entire day. If I came back before dark, they wouldn't even know where I had been.

I went into the house and wrapped the loaf of bread in a newspaper. Then I closed all the doors and windows.

~

The path to the river dropped steeply into the valley, then rose and went round the big mountain. It was frequently used by the villagers— woodcutters, milkmen, shepherds, mule-drivers—but there were no villages beyond the mountain or near the river.

I passed a woodcutter and asked him how far it was to the river. He was a short, powerful man, with a creased and weathered face and muscles that stood out in hard lumps.

'Seven miles,' he said. 'Why do you want to know?'

'I am going there,' I said.

'Alone?'

'Of course.'

'It will take you three hours to reach it, and then you have to come back. It will be getting dark, and it is not an easy road.'

'But I'm a good walker,' I said, though I had never walked farther than the two miles between our house and my school.

I left the woodcutter on the path and continued down the hill. It was a dizzy, winding path, and I slipped once or twice and slid into a bush or down a slope of slippery pine needles. The hill was covered with lush green ferns, the trees were entangled in creepers, and a great wild dahlia would suddenly rear its golden head from the leaves and ferns.

Soon I was in the valley, and the path straightened out and then began to rise. I met a girl who was coming from the opposite direction.

She held a long curved knife with which she had been cutting grass, and there were rings in her nose and ears, and her arms were covered with heavy bangles. The bangles made music when she moved her wrists. It was as though her hands spoke a language of their own.

'How far is it to the river?' I asked.

The girl had probably never been to the river, or she may have been thinking of another one, because she said, without any hesitation, 'Twenty miles.'

I laughed and ran down the path. A parrot screeched suddenly and flew low over my head, a flash of blue and green. It took the course of the path, and I followed its dipping flight, running until the path rose and the bird disappeared amongst the trees.

A trickle of water came down the hillside, and I stopped to drink. The water was cold and sharp and very refreshing. But I was soon thirsty again. The sun was striking the side of the hill, and the dusty path became hotter, the stones scorching my feet. I was sure I had covered half the distance: I had been walking for over an hour.

Presently I saw a boy ahead of me, driving a few goats down the path.

'How far is it to the river?' I asked.

The village boy smiled and said, 'Oh, not far, just round the next hill and straight down.'

Feeling hungry, I unwrapped my loaf of bread and broke it in two, offering one half to the boy. We sat on the hillside and ate in silence. When we finished, we walked on together and began talking; and, talking, I did not notice the smarting of my feet and the heat of the sun and the distance I had covered and the distance I had yet to cover. But after some time my companion had to take another path, and once more I was on my own.

I missed the village boy; I looked up and down the mountain path but no one else was in sight. My own home was hidden from view by the side of the mountain, and there was no sign of the river. I began to feel discouraged. If someone had been with me, I would not have faltered; but alone, I was conscious of my fatigue and isolation.

I had come more than halfway, and I couldn't turn back; I had to see the river. If I failed, I would always be a little ashamed of the experience. So I walked on, along the hot, dusty, stony path, past stone huts and terraced fields, until there were no more fields or huts, only forest and sun and loneliness. There were no men, and no sign of man's influence—only trees and rocks and grass and small flowers—and silence...

The silence was impressive and a little frightening. There was no movement, except for the bending of grass beneath my feet, and the circling of a hawk against the blinding blue of the sky.

Then, as I rounded a sharp bend, I heard the sound of water.

I gasped with surprise and happiness, and began to run. I slipped and stumbled, but I kept on running, until I was able to plunge into the snow-cold mountain water.

And the water was blue and white and very wonderful.

Friends of My Youth

1
SUDHEER

Friendship is all about doing things together. It may be climbing a mountain, fishing in a mountain stream, cycling along a country road, camping in a forest clearing or simply travelling together and sharing the experiences that a new place can bring.

On at least two of these counts, Sudheer qualified as a friend, albeit a troublesome one, given to involving me in his adolescent escapades.

I met him in Dehra soon after my return from England. He turned up at my room, saying he'd heard I was a writer and did I have any comics to lend him?

'I don't write comics,' I said; but there were some comics lying around, left over from my own boyhood collection so I gave these to the lanky youth who stood smiling in the doorway, and he thanked me and said he'd bring them back. From my window I saw him cycling off in the general direction of Dalanwala.

He turned up again a few days later and dumped a large pile of new-looking comics on my desk. 'Here are all the latest,' he announced. 'You can keep them for me. I'm not allowed to read comics at home.'

It was only weeks later that I learnt he was given to pilfering comics and magazines from the town's bookstores. In no time at all, I'd become a receiver of stolen goods!

My landlady had warned me against Sudheer and so had one or two others. He had acquired a certain notoriety for having been expelled from his school. He had been in charge of the library, and before a consignment of newly acquired books could be registered and library stamped, he had sold them back to the bookshop from which they had originally been purchased. Very enterprising but not to be countenanced in a very pukka public school. He was now studying in a municipal school, too poor to afford a library.

Sudheer was an amoral scamp all right, but I found it difficult to avoid him, or to resist his undeniable and openly affectionate manner. He could make you laugh. And anyone who can do that is easily forgiven for a great many faults.

One day he produced a couple of white mice from his pockets and left them on my desk.

'You keep them for me,' he said. 'I'm not allowed to keep them at home.'

There were a great many things he was not allowed to keep at home. Anyway, the white mice were given a home in an old cupboard where my landlady kept unwanted dishes, pots and pans, and they were quite happy there, being fed on bits of bread or chapatti, until one day I heard shrieks from the storeroom, and charging into it, found my dear stout landlady having hysterics as one of the white mice sought refuge under her blouse and the other ran frantically up and down her back.

Sudheer had to find another home for the white mice. It was that, or finding another home for myself.

Most young men, boys and quite a few girls used bicycles. There was a cycle hire shop across the road, and Sudheer persuaded me to hire cycles for both of us. We cycled out of town, through tea gardens and mustard fields, and down a forest road until we discovered a small, shallow river where we bathed and wrestled on the sand. Although I was three or four years older than Sudheer, he was much the stronger, being about six feet tall and broad in the shoulders. His parents had come from Bhanu, a rough-and-ready district on the North West Frontier, as a result of the Partition of the country. His father ran a small press situated behind the Sabzi Mandi and brought out a weekly newspaper called *The Frontier Times*.

We came to the stream quite often. It was Sudheer's way of playing truant from school without being detected in the bazaar or at the cinema. He was sixteen when I met him, and eighteen when we parted, but I can't recall that he ever showed any interest in his school work.

He took me to his home in the Karanpur bazaar, then a stronghold of the Bhanu community. The Karanpur boys were an aggressive lot and resented Sudheer's friendship with an angrez. To avoid a confrontation, I would use the back alleys and side streets to get to and from the house in which they lived. Sudheer had been overindulged by his mother, who protected him from his father's wrath. Both parents felt I might have an 'improving' influence on their son, and encouraged our friendship. His elder sister seemed more doubtful. She felt he was incorrigible, beyond redemption, and that I was not much better, and she was probably right.

The father invited me to his small press and asked me if I'd like to work with him. I agreed to help with the newspaper for a couple of hours every morning. This involved proofreading and editing news agency reports. Uninspiring work, but useful.

Meanwhile, Sudheer had got hold of a pet monkey, and he carried it about in the basket attached to the handlebar of his bicycle. He used it to ingratiate himself with the girls. 'How sweet! How pretty!' they would exclaim, and Sudheer would get the monkey to show them its tricks.

After some time, however, the monkey appeared to be infected by Sudheer's amorous nature, and would make obscene gestures which were not appreciated by his former admirers. On one occasion, the monkey made off with a girl's dupatta. A chase ensued, and the dupatta retrieved, but the outcome of it all was that Sudheer was accosted by the girl's brothers and given a black eye and a bruised cheek. His father took the monkey away and returned it to the itinerant juggler who had sold it to the young man.

Sudheer soon developed an insatiable need for money. He wasn't getting anything at home, apart from what he pinched from his mother and sister, and his father urged me not to give the boy any money. After paying for my boarding and lodging I had very little to spare, but Sudheer seemed to sense when a money order or cheque arrived, and would hang around, spinning tall tales of great financial distress until, in order to be rid of him, I would give him five to ten rupees, (In those days, a magazine payment seldom exceeded fifty rupees.)

He was becoming something of a trial, constantly interrupting me in my work, and even picking up confectionery from my landlady's small shop and charging it to my account. I had stopped going for bicycle rides. He had wrecked one of the cycles and the shopkeeper held me responsible for repairs.

The sad thing was that Sudheer had no other friends. He did not go in for team games or for music or other creative pursuits which might have helped him to move around with people of his own age group. He was a loner with a propensity for mischief. Had he entered a bicycle race, he would have won easily. Forever eluding a variety of pursuers, he was extremely fast on his bike. But we did not have cycle races in Dehra.

And then, for a blessed two or three weeks, I saw nothing of my unpredictable friend.

I discovered later that he had taken a fancy to a young schoolteacher, about five years his senior, who lived in a hostel up at Rajpur. Hs cycle rides took him in that direction. As usual, his charm proved irresistible, and it wasn't long before the teacher and the acolyte were taking rides together down lonely forest roads. This was all right by me, of course, but it wasn't the norm for the middle-class matrons of small-town India, at least not in 1957. Hostel wardens, other students and naturally Sudheer's parents were all in a state of agitation. So 1 wasn't surprised when Sudheer turned up in my room to announce that he was on his way to Nahan, to study at an Inter college there.

Nahan was a small hill town about sixty miles from Dehra. Sudheer was banished to the home of his mama, an uncle who was a sub-inspector in the local police force. He had promised to see that Sudheer stayed out of trouble.

Whether he succeeded or not, I could not tell, for a couple of months later I gave up my rooms in Dehra and left for Delhi. I lost touch with Sudheer's family, and it was only several years later, when I bumped into an old acquaintance, that I was given news of my erstwhile friend.

He had apparently done quite well for himself. Taking off for Calcutta, he had used his charm and his fluent English to land a job as an assistant on a tea estate. Here he had proved quite efficient, earning the approval of his manager and employers. But his roving eye soon got him into trouble. The women working in the tea gardens became prey to his amorous and amoral nature. Keeping one mistress was acceptable. Keeping several was asking for trouble. He was found dead early one morning with his throat cut.

2
THE ROYAL CAFE SET

Dehra was going through a slump in those days, and there wasn't much work for anyone—least of all for my neighbour, Suresh Mathur, an income tax lawyer, who was broke for two reasons. To begin with, there was not much work going around, as those with taxable incomes were few and far between. Apart from that, when he did get work, he was slow and half-hearted about getting it done. This was because he seldom got up before eleven in the morning, and by the time he took a bus down from Rajpur and reached his own small office (next door to my rooms), or the income tax office a little further on, it was lunchtime and all the tax officials were out. Suresh would then repair to the Royal Cafe for a beer or two (often at my expense) and this would stretch into a gin and tonic, after which he would stagger up to his first-floor office and collapse on the sofa for an afternoon nap. He would wake up at six, after the income tax office had closed.

I occupied two rooms next to his office, and we were on friendly terms, sharing an enthusiasm for the humorous works of P.G. Wodehouse. I think he modelled himself on Bertie Wooster, for he would often turn up wearing mauve or yellow socks or a pink shirt and a bright green tie—enough to make anyone in his company feel quite liverish. Unlike Bertie Wooster, he did not have a Jeeves to look after him and get him out of various scrapes. I tried not to be too friendly, as Suresh was in the habit of borrowing lavishly from all his friends, conveniently forgetting to return the amounts. I wasn't well off and could ill afford the company of a spendthrift friend. Sudheer was trouble enough.

Dehra, in those days, was full of people living on borrowed money or no money at all. Hence, the large number of disconnected telephone and electric lines. I did not have electricity myself, simply because the previous tenant had taken off, leaving me with outstandings of over a thousand rupees, then a princely sum. My monthly income seldom exceeded 500 rupees. No matter. There was plenty of kerosene available and the oil lamp lent a romantic glow to my literary endeavours.

Looking back, I am amazed at the number of people who were quite broke. There was William Matheson, a Swiss journalist, whose remittances from Zurich never seemed to turn up; my landlady, whose husband had deserted her two years previously; Mr Madan, who dealt in second-hand cars which no one wanted; the owner of the corner restaurant, who sat in solitary splendour surrounded by empty tables; and the proprietor of the Ideal Book Depot, who was selling off his stock of unsold books and becoming a departmental store. We complain that few people buy or read books today, but I can assure you that there were even fewer customers in the 1950s and '60s. Only doctors, dentists and the proprietors of English schools were making money.

Suresh spent whatever cash came his way, and borrowed more. He had an advantage over the rest of us—he owned an old bungalow inherited from his father, up at Rajpur in the foothills, where he lived alone with an old manservant. And owning a property gave him some standing with his creditors. The grounds boasted of a mango and litchi orchard, and these he gave out on contract every year, so that his friends did not even get to enjoy some of his produce. The proceeds helped him to pay his office rent in town, with a little left over to give on account to the owner of the Royal Cafe.

If a lawyer could be hard up, what chance had a journalist? And yes, William Matheson had everything going for him from the start, when he came out to India as an assistant to Von Hesseltein, correspondent for some of the German papers. Von Hesseltein passed on some of the assignments to William, and for a time, all went well. William lived with Von Hesseltein and his family, and was also friendly with Suresh, often paying for the drinks at the Royal Cafe. Then William committed the folly (if not the sin) of having an affair with Von Hesseltein's wife. Von Hesseltein was not the understanding sort. He threw William out of the house and stopped giving him work.

William hired an old typewriter and set himself up as a correspondent in his own right, living and working from a room in the Doon Guest House. At first he was welcome there, having paid a three-month advance for room and board. He bombarded the Swiss and German papers with his articles, but there were very few takers. No one in Europe was really interested in India's five-year plans, or Corbusier's Chandigarh, or the Bhakra Nangal Dam. Book publishing in India was confined to textbooks, otherwise William night have published a vivid account of his experiences in the French Foreign Legion. After two or three rums at the Royal Cafe, he would regale us with tales of his exploits in the Legion, before and after the siege of Dien Bien Phu. Some of his stories had the ring of truth, others (particularly his sexual exploits) were obviously tall tales; but I was happy to pay for the beer or coffee in order to hear him spin them out.

Those were glorious days for an unknown freelance writer. I was realizing my dream of living by my pen, and I was doing it from a small town in north India, having turned my back on both London and New Delhi. I had no ambitions to be a great writer, or even a famous one, or even a rich one. All I wanted to do was *write*. And I wanted a few readers and the occasional cheque so I could carry on living my dream.

The cheques came along in their own desultory way—fifty rupees from the *Weekly* or thirty-five from *The Statesman* or the same from *Sport and Pastime*, and so on—just enough to get by, and to be the envy of Suresh Mathur, William Matheson and a few others, professional people who felt that I had no business earning more than they did. Suresh even declared that I should have been paying tax, and offered to represent me, his other clients having gone elsewhere.

And there was old Colonel Wilkie, living on a small pension in a corner room of the White House Hotel. His wife had left him some years before, presumably because of his drinking, but he claimed to have left her because of her obsession with moving the furniture—it seems she was always shifting things about, changing rooms, throwing out perfectly sound tables and chairs and replacing them with fancy stuff picked up here and there. If he took a liking to a particular easy chair and showed signs of settling down in it, it would disappear the next day to be replaced by something horribly ugly and uncomfortable.

'It was a form of mental torture,' said Colonel Wilkie, confiding in me over a glass of beer on the White House verandah. 'The sitting room was cluttered with all sorts of ornamental junk and flimsy side tables, so that I was constantly falling over the damn things. It was like a minefield! And the mines were never in the same place. You've noticed that I walk with a limp?'

'First World War?' I ventured. 'Wounded at Ypres? Or was it Flanders?'

'Nothing of the sort,' snorted the Colonel. 'I did get one or two flesh wounds but they were nothing as compared to the damage inflicted on me by those damned shifting tables and chairs. Fell over a coffee table and dislocated my shoulder. Then broke an ankle negotiating a stool that was in the wrong place. Bookshelf fell on me. Tripped on a rolled-up carpet. Hit by a curtain rod. Would you have put up with it?'

'No,' I had to admit.

'Had to leave her, of course. She went off to England. Send her an allowance. Half my pension! All spent on furniture!'

'Its a superstition of sorts, I suppose. Collecting things.'

The Colonel told me that the final straw was when his favourite spring bed had suddenly been replaced by a bed made up of hard wooden slats. It was sheer torture trying to sleep on it, and he had left his house and moved into the White House Hotel as a permanent guest.

Now he couldn't allow anyone to touch or tidy up anything in his room. There were beer stains on the tablecloth, cobwebs on his family pictures, dust on his books, empty medicine bottles on his dressing table, and mice nesting in his old, discarded boots. He had gone to the other extreme and wouldn't have anything changed or moved in his room.

I didn't see much of the room because we usually sat out on the verandah, waited upon by one of the hotel bearers, who came over with bottles of beer that I dutifully paid for, the Colonel having exhausted his credit. I suppose he was in his late sixties then. He never went anywhere, not even for a walk in the compound. He blamed this inactivity on his gout, but it was really inertia and an unwillingness to leave the precincts of the bar, where he could cadge the occasional drink from a sympathetic guest. I am that age now, and not half as active as I used to be, but there are people to live for, and tales to tell, and I keep writing. It is important to keep writing.

Colonel Wilkie had given up on life. I suppose he could have gone off to England, but he would have been more miserable there, with no one to buy him a drink (since he wasn't likely to reciprocate), and the possibility of his wife turning up again to rearrange the furniture.

3
'BIBIJI'

My landlady was a remarkable woman, and this little memoir of Dehra in the 1950s would be incomplete without a sketch of hers.

She would often say, 'Ruskin, one day you must write my life story,' and I would promise to do so. And although she really deserves a book to herself, I shall try to do justice to her in these few pages.

She was, in fact, my Punjabi stepfather's first wife. Does that sound confusing? It was certainly complicated. And you might well ask, why on earth were you living with your stepfather's first wife instead of your stepfather and mother?

The answer is simple. I got on rather well with this rotund, well-built lady, and sympathized with her predicament. She had been married at a young age to my stepfather, who was something of a playboy, and who ran the photographic saloon he had received as part of her dowry. When he left her for my mother, he sold the saloon and gave his first wife part of the premises. In order to sustain herself and two small children, she started a small provision store and thus became Dehra's first lady shopkeeper.

I had just started freelancing from Dehra and was not keen on joining my mother and stepfather in Delhi. When 'Bibiji'—as I called her—offered me a portion of her flat on very reasonable terms, I accepted without hesitation and was to spend the next two years above her little shop on Rajpur Road. Almost fifty years later, the flat in still there, but it is now an ice cream parlour! Poetic justice, perhaps.

'Bibiji' sold the usual provisions. Occasionally, I lent a helping hand and soon learnt the names of the various lentils arrayed before us—moong, malka, masoor, arhar, channa, rajma, etc. She bought her rice, flour and other items wholesale from the mandi, and sometimes I would accompany her on an early morning march to the mandi (about two miles distant) where we would load a handcart with her purchases. She was immensely strong and could lift sacks of wheat or rice that left me gasping. I can't say I blame my rather skinny stepfather for staying out of her reach.

She had a helper, a Bihari youth, who would trundle the cart back to the shop and help with the loading and unloading. Before opening the shop (at around 8 a.m.) she would make our breakfast—parathas with my favourite shalgam pickle, and in winter, a delicious kanji made from the juice of red carrots. When the shop opened, I would go upstairs to do my writing while she conducted the day's business. Sometimes she would ask me to help her with her accounts, or in making out a bill, for she was barely literate. But she was an astute shopkeeper; she knew instinctively who was good for credit and who was strictly nakad (cash). She would also warn me against friends who borrowed money without any intention of returning it; warnings that I failed to heed. Friends in perpetual need there were aplenty—Sudheer, William, Suresh and a couple of others—and I am amazed that I didn't have to borrow too, considering the uncertain nature of my income. Those little cheques and money orders from magazines did not always arrive in time. But sooner or later something *did* turn up. I was very lucky.

~

Bibiji had a friend, a neighbour, Mrs Singh, an attractive woman in her thirties who smoked a hookah and regaled us with tales of ghosts and churels from her village near Agra. We did not see much of her husband who was an excise inspector. He was busy making money.

Bibiji and Mrs Singh were almost inseparable, which was quite understandable in view of the fact that both had absentee husbands. They were really happy together. During the day Mrs Singh would sit in the shop, observing the customers. And afterwards she would entertain us to clever imitations of the more odd or eccentric among them. At night, after the shop was closed, Bibiji and her friend would make themselves comfortable on the same cot (creaking beneath their combined weights), wrap themselves in a razai or blanket and invite me to sit on the next charpai and listen to their yarns or tell them a few of my own. Mrs Singh had a small son, not very bright, who was continually eating laddoos, jalebis, barfis and other sweets. Quite appropriately, he was called Laddoo. And I believe he grew into one.

Bibiji's son and daughter were then at a residential school. They came home occasionally. So did Mr Singh, with more sweets for his son. He did not appear to find anything unusual in his wife's intimate relationship with Bibiji. His mind was obviously on other things.

Bibiji and Mrs Singh both made plans to get me married. When I protested, saying I was only twenty-three, they said I was old enough.

Bibiji had an eye on an Anglo-Indian schoolteacher who sometimes came to the shop, but Mrs Singh turned her down, saying she had very spindly legs. Instead, she suggested the daughter of the local padre, a glamourous-looking, dusky beauty, but Bibiji vetoed the proposal, saying the young lady used too much make-up and already displayed too much fat around the waistline. Both agreed that I should marry a plain-looking girl who could cook, use a sewing machine and speak a little English.

'And be strong in the legs,' I added, much to Mrs Singh's approval.

They did not know it, but I was enamoured of Kamla, a girl from the hills, who lived with her parents in quarters behind the flat. She was always giving me mischievous glances with her dark, beautiful, expressive eyes. And whenever I passed her on the landing, we exchanged pleasantries and friendly banter; it was as though we had known each other for a long time. But she was already betrothed, and that too to a much older man, a widower, who owned some land outside the town. Kamla's family was poor, her father was in debt and it was to be a marriage of convenience. There was nothing much I could do about it—landless, and without prospects—but after the marriage had taken place and she had left for her new home, I befriended her younger brother and through him sent her my good wishes from time to time. She is just a distant memory now, but a bright one, like a forget-me-not blooming on a bare rock. Would I have married her, had I been able to? She was simple, unlettered; but I might have taken the chance.

Those two years on Rajpur Road were an eventful time, what with the visitations of Sudheer, the company of William and Suresh, the participation in Bibiji's little shop, the evanescent friendship with Kamla. I did a lot of writing and even sold a few stories here and there; but the returns were modest, barely adequate. Everyone was urging me to try my luck in Delhi. And so I bid goodbye to sleepy little Dehra (as it then was) and took a bus to the capital. I did no better there as a writer, but I found a job of sorts and that kept me going for a couple of years.

Owls in the Family

One winter morning, my grandfather and I found a baby spotted owlet by the verandah steps of our home in Dehradun. When Grandfather picked it up the owlet hissed and clacked its bill but then, after a meal of raw meat and water, settled down under my bed.

Spotted owlets are small birds. A fully grown one is no larger than a thrush and they have none of the sinister appearance of large owls. I had once found a pair of them in our mango tree and by tapping on the tree trunk had persuaded one to show an enquiring face at the entrance to its hole. The owlet is not normally afraid of man nor is it strictly a night bird. But it prefers to stay at home during the day as it is sometimes attacked by other birds who consider all owls their enemies.

The little owlet was quite happy under my bed. The following day we found a second baby owlet in almost the same spot on the verandah and only then did we realize that where the rainwater pipe emerged through the roof, there was a rough sort of nest from which the birds had fallen. We took the second young owl to join the first and fed them both.

When I went to bed, they were on the window ledge just inside the mosquito netting and later in the night, their mother found them there. From outside, she crooned and gurgled for a long time and in the morning, I found she had left a mouse with its tail tucked through the netting. Obviously she put no great trust in me as a foster parent.

The young birds thrived and ten days later, Grandfather and I took them into the garden to release them. I had placed one on a branch of the mango tree and was stooping to pick up the other when I received a heavy blow on the back of the head. A second or two later, the mother owl swooped down on Grandfather but he was quite agile and ducked out of the way.

Quickly, I placed the second owl under the mango tree. Then from a safe distance we watched the mother fly down and lead her offspring into the long grass at the edge of the garden. We thought she would take her family away from our rather strange household but next morning I found the two owlets perched on the hat stand in the verandah.

I ran to tell Grandfather and when we came back we found the mother sitting on the birdbath a few metres away. She was evidently feeling sorry for her behaviour the previous day because she greeted us with a soft 'whoo-whoo'.

'Now there's an unselfish mother for you,' said Grandfather. 'It's obvious she wants us to keep an eye on them. They're probably getting too big for her to manage.'

So the owlets became regular members of our household and were among the few pets that Grandmother took a liking to. She objected to all snakes, most monkeys and some crows—we'd had all these pets from time to time—but she took quite a fancy to the owlets and frequently fed them spaghetti!

They loved to sit and splash in a shallow dish provided by Grandmother. They enjoyed it even more if cold water was poured over them from a jug while they were in the bath. They would get thoroughly wet, jump out and perch on a towel rack, shake themselves and return for a second splash and sometimes a third. During the day they dozed on a hat stand. After dark, they had the freedom of the house and their nightly occupation was catching beetles, the kitchen quarters being a happy hunting ground. With their razor sharp eyes and powerful beaks, they were excellent pest-destroyers.

Looking back on those childhood days, I carry in my mind a picture of Grandmother in her rocking chair with a contented owlet sprawled across her aproned lap. Once, on entering a room while she was taking an afternoon nap, I saw one of the owlets had crawled up her pillow till its head was snuggled under her ear.

Both Grandmother and the owlet were snoring.

~

Coaxing a Garden from Himalayan Soil

I wouldn't go so far as to say that a garden is the answer to all problems, but it's amazing how a little digging and friendly dialogue with the good earth can help reactivate us when we grow sluggish.

Whenever I'm stuck in the middle of a story or an essay, I go into my tiny hillside garden and get down to the serious business of transplanting or weeding or pruning or just plucking off dead blooms, and in no time at all I'm struck with a notion of how to proceed with the stalled story, reluctant essay, or unresolved poem.

Not all gardeners are writers, but you don't have to be a writer to benefit from the goodness of your garden. Baldev, who heads a large business corporation in Delhi, tells me that he wouldn't dream of going to his office unless he'd spent at least half an hour in his garden that morning. If you can start the day by looking at the dew on your antirrhinums, he tells me, you can face the stormiest of board meetings.

Or take Cyril, an old friend.

When I met him, he was living in a small apartment on the first floor of a building that looked over a steep, stony precipice. The house itself appeared to be built on stilts, although these turned out to be concrete pillars. Altogether an ugly edifice. 'Poor Cyril,' I thought. 'There's no way he can have a garden.'

I couldn't have been more wrong. Cyril's rooms were surrounded by a long verandah that allowed in so much sunlight and air, resulting in such a profusion of leaf and flower, that at first I thought I was back in one of the greenhouses at Kew Gardens, where I used to wander during a lonely sojourn in London.

Cyril found a chair for me among the tendrils of a climbing ivy, while a coffee table materialized from behind a plant. By the time I had recovered enough from taking in my arboreal surroundings, I discovered that there were at least two other guests—one concealed behind a tree-sized philodendron, the other apparently embedded in a pot of begonias.

Cyril, of course, was an exception. We cannot all have sunny verandahs; nor would I show the same tolerance as he does towards the occasional caterpillar on my counterpane. But he was a happy man until his landlord, who lived below, complained that water was cascading down through the ceiling.

'Fix the ceiling,' said Cyril, and went back to watering his plants. It was the end of a beautiful tenant-landlord relationship.

So let us move on to the washerwoman who lives down the road, a little distance from my own abode. She and her family live at the subsistence level. They have one square meal at midday, and they keep the leftovers for the evening. But the steps to their humble quarters are brightened by geraniums potted in large tin cans, all ablaze with several shades of flower.

Hard as I try, I cannot grow geraniums to match hers. Does she scold her plants the way she scolds her children? Maybe I'm not firm enough with my geraniums. Or has it something to do with the washing? Anyway, her abode certainly looks more attractive than some of the official residences here in Mussoorie.

Some gardeners like to specialize in particular flowers, but specialization has its dangers. My friend, Professor Saili, an ardent admirer of the nature poetry of William Wordsworth, decided he would have his own field of nodding daffodils, and planted daffodil bulbs all over his front yard. The following spring, after much waiting, he was rewarded by the appearance of a solitary daffodil that looked like a railway passenger who had gotten off at the wrong station. This year he is specializing in 'easy-to-grow' French marigolds. They grow easily enough in France, I'm sure; but the professor is discovering that they are stubborn growers on our stony Himalayan soil.

Not everyone in this Indian hill station has a lovely garden. Some palatial homes and spacious hotels are approached through forests of weeds, clumps of nettles and dead or dying rose bushes. The owners are often plagued by personal problems that prevent them from noticing the state of their gardens. Loveless lives, unloved gardens.

On the other hand, there was Annie Powell, who, at the age of ninety, was up early every morning to water her lovely garden. Watering can in hand, she would move methodically from one flower bed to the next, devotedly giving each plant a sprinkling. She said she loved to see leaves and flowers sparkling with fresh water; it gave her a new lease of life every day.

And there were my maternal grandparents, whose home in Dehra in the valley was surrounded by a beautiful, well-kept garden. How I wish I had been old enough to prevent that lovely home from passing into other hands. But no one can take away our memories.

Grandfather looked after the orchard, Grandmother looked after the flower garden. Like all people who have lived together for many years, they had the occasional disagreement.

Grandfather would proceed to sulk on a bench beneath the jack-fruit tree while, at the other end of the garden, Grandmother would start clipping a hedge with more than her usual vigour. Silently, imperceptibly, they would make their way towards the centre of the garden, where the flower beds gave way to a vegetable patch. This was neutral ground. My cousins and I looked on like UN observers. And there among the cauliflowers, conversation would begin again, and the quarrel would be forgotten. There's nothing like home-grown vegetables for bringing two people together.

Red roses for young lovers. French beans for long-standing relationships!

The Further One Goes

Nandprayag: Where Rivers Meet

It's a funny thing, but long before I arrive at a place I can usually tell whether I am going to like it or not.

Thus, while I was still some twenty miles from the town of Pauri, I felt it was not going to be my sort of place; and sure enough, it wasn't. On the other hand, while Nandprayag was still out of sight, I knew I was going to like it. And I did.

Perhaps it's something on the wind—emanations of an atmosphere—that are carried to me well before I arrive at my destination. I can't really explain it, and no doubt it is silly to make judgements in advance. But it happens and I mention the fact for what it's worth.

As for Nandprayag, perhaps I'd been there in some previous existence, I felt I was nearing home as soon as we drove into this cheerful roadside hamlet, some little way above the Nandakini's confluence with the Alakananda river. A prayags is a meeting place of two rivers, and as there are many rivers the Garhwal Himalayas, all linking up to join either the Ganga or the Jamuna, it follows that there are numerous prayags, in themselves places of pilgrimage as well as wayside halts en route to the higher Hindu shrines at Kedarnath and Badrinath. Nowhere else in the Himalayas are there so many temples, sacred streams, holy places and holy men.

Some little way above Nandprayag's busy little bazaar, is the tourist rest house, perhaps the nicest of the tourist lodges in this region. It has a well-kept garden surrounded by fruit trees and is a little distance from the general hubbub of the main road.

Above it is the old pilgrim path, on which you walked. Just a few decades ago, if you were a pilgrim intent on finding salvation at the abode of the gods, you travelled on foot all the way from the plains, covering about 200 miles in a couple of months. In those days people had the time, the faith and the endurance. Illness and misadventure often dogged their footsteps, but what was a little suffering if at the end of the day they arrived at the very portals of heaven? Some did not survive to make the return journey. Today's pilgrims may not be lacking in devotion, but most of them do expect to come home again. Along the pilgrim path are several handsome old houses, set among mango trees and the fronds of the papaya and banana. Higher up the hill the pine forests commence, but down here it is almost subtropical. Nandprayag is only about 3,000 feet above sea level—a height at which the vegetation is usually quite lush provided there is protection from the wind.

In one of these double-storeyed houses lives Mr Devki Nandan, scholar and recluse. He welcomes me into his house and plies me with food till I am close to bursting. He has a great love for his little corner of Garhwal and proudly shows me his collection of clippings concerning this area. One of them is from a travelogue by Sister Nivedita—an Englishwoman, Margaret Noble, who became an interpreter of Hinduism to the West. Visiting Nandprayag in 1928, she wrote:

Nandprayag is a place that ought to be famous for its beauty and order. For a mile or two before reaching it we had noticed the superior character of the agriculture and even some careful gardening of fruits and vegetables. The peasantry also, suddenly grew handsome, not unlike the Kashmiris. The town itself is new, rebuilt since the Gohna flood, and its temple stands far out across the fields on the shore of the Prayag. But in this short time a wonderful energy has been at work on architectural carvings, and the little place is full of gemlike beauties. Its temple is dedicated to Naga Takshaka. As the road crosses the river, I noticed two or three old Pathan tombs, the only traces of Mohammedanism that we had seen north of Srinagar in Garhwal.

Little has changed since Sister Nivedita's visit, and there is still a small and thriving Pathan population in Nandprayag. In fact, when I called on Mr Devki Nandan, he was in the act of sending out Id greetings to his Muslim friends. Some of the old graves have disappeared, in the debris from new road cuttings: an endless business, this road-building. And as for the beautiful temple described by Sister Nivedita, I was sad to learn that it had been swept away by a mighty flood in 1970, when a cloudburst and subsequent landslide on the Alakananda resulted in great destruction downstream.

Mr Nandan remembers the time when he walked to the small hill station of Pauri to join the old Messmore Mission School, where so many famous sons of Garhwal received their early education. It would take him four days to get to Pauri. Now it is just four hours by bus. It was only after the Chinese invasion of 1962 that there was a rush of road-building in the hill districts of northern India. Before that, everyone walked and thought nothing of it!

Sitting alone that same evening in the little garden of the rest house, I heard innumerable birds break into song. I did not see any of them, because the light was fading and the trees were dark, but there was the rather melancholy call of the hill dove, the insistent ascending trill of the koel and much shrieking, whistling and twittering that I was unable to assign to any particular species.

Now, once again, while I sit on the lawn surrounded by zinnias in full bloom, I am teased by that feeling of having been here before, on this lush hillside, among the pomegranates and oleanders. Is it some childhood memory asserting itself? But as a child I never travelled in these parts.

True, Nandprayag has some affinity with parts of the Doon valley before it was submerged by a tidal wave of humanity. But in the Doon there is no great river running past your garden. Here there are two, and they are also part of this feeling of belonging. Perhaps in some former life I did come this way, or maybe I dreamed about living here. Who knows? Anyway, mysteries are more interesting than certainties. Presently the room-boy joins me for a chat on the lawn. He is in fact running the rest house in the absence of the manager. A coach-load of pilgrims is due at any moment but until they arrive the place is empty and only the birds can be heard. His name is Janakpal and he tells me something about his village on the next mountain, where a leopard has been carrying off goats and cattle. He doesn't think much of the conservationists' law protecting leopards: nothing can be done unless the animal becomes a man-eater!

A shower of rain descends on us, and so do the pilgrims. Janakpal leaves me to attend to his duties. But I am not left alone for long. A youngster with a cup of tea appears. He wants me to take him to Mussoorie or Delhi. He is fed up, he says, with washing dishes here.

'You are better off here,' I tell him sincerely. 'In Mussoorie you will have twice as many dishes to wash. In Delhi, ten times as many.'

'Yes, but there are cinemas there,' he says, 'and television and videos.' I am left without an argument. Birdsong may have charms for me but not for the restless dish-washer in Nandprayag.

The rain stops and I go for a walk. The pilgrims keep to themselves but the locals are always ready to talk. I remember a saying (and it may have originated in these hills), which goes: 'All men are my friends. I have only to meet them.' In these hills, where life still moves at a leisurely and civilized pace, one is constantly meeting them.

〜

Ganga Descends
(1989)

There has always been a mild sort of controversy as to whether the true Ganga (in its upper reaches) is the Alaknanda or the Bhagirathi. Of course, the two rivers meet at Deoprayag and then both are Ganga. But there are some who assert that geographically the Alaknanda is the true Ganga, while others say that tradition should be the criterion, and traditionally the Bhagirathi is the Ganga.

I put the question to my friend Dr Sudhakar Misra, from whom words of wisdom sometimes flow; and, true to form, he answered, 'The Alaknanda is the Ganga, but the Bhagirathi is Gangaji.'

One sees what he means. The Bhagirathi is beautiful, almost caressingly so, and people have responded to it with love and respect, ever since Shiva released the waters of the goddess from his tangled locks and she sped plains-wards in the tracks of Prince Bhagirath's chariot.

> He held the river on his head,
> And kept her wandering, where,
> Dense as Himalayas woods were spread,
> The tangles of his hair.

Revered by Hindus, and loved by all, the goddess Ganga weaves her spell over all who come to her. Moreover, she issues from the very heart of the Himalayas. Visiting Gangotri in 1820, the writer and traveller Baillie Fraser noted: 'We are now in the centre of the Himalayas, the loftiest and perhaps the most rugged range of mountains in the world.'

Perhaps it is this realization that one is at the very centre and heart of things, that gives one an almost primeval sense of belonging to these mountains and to this river valley in particular. For me, and for many who have been in the mountains, the Bhagirathi is the most beautiful of the four main river valleys of Garhwal. It will remain so provided we do not pollute its waters and strip it of its virgin forests.

The Bhagirathi seems to have everything—people of a gentle disposition, deep glens and forests, the ultra vision of an open valley graced with tiers of cultivation leading up by degrees to the peaks and glaciers at its head.

From some twenty miles above Tehri, as far as Bhatwari, a distance of about 55 miles along the valley, there are extensive forests of pine. It covers the mountains on both sides of the river and its effluents, filling the ravines and plateaus up to a height of about 5,000 feet. Above Bhatwari, forests of box yew and cypress commence, and if we leave the valley and take the roads to Nachiketa Tal or Dodi Tal—little lakes at around 9,000 feet above sea level—we pass through dense forests of oak and chestnut. From Gangnani to Gangotri the deodar is the principal tree. The excelsia pine also extends eight miles up the valley above Gangotri, and birch is found in patches to within half a mile of the glacier.

On the right bank of the river, above Sukhi, the forest is nearly pure deodar, but on the left bank, with a northern aspect, there is a mixture of silver-fir, spruce and birch. The valley of the Jad-ganga is also full of deodar, and towards its head the valuable pencil-cedar is found. The only other area of Garhwal where the deodar is equally extensive is the Jaunsar-Bawar tract to the west.

It was the valuable timber of the deodar that attracted the adventurer Frederick 'Pahari' Wilson to the valley in the 1850s. He leased the forests from the Raja of Tehri in 1859, and in a few years, he had made a fortune.

The old forest rest houses at Dharasu, Bhatwari and Harsil were all built by Wilson as staging-posts, for the only roads were narrow tracks linking one village to another. Wilson married a local girl, Gulabi, from the village of Mukhba, and the portraits of Mr and Mrs Wilson (early examples of the photographer's art) still hang in these sturdy little bungalows. At any rate, I found their pictures at Bhatwari. Harsil is now out of bounds to civilians, and I believe part of the old house was destroyed in a fire a few years ago.*

Amongst other things, Wilson introduced the apple into this area, and 'Wilson apples'—large, red and juicy—are sold to travellers and pilgrims on their way to Gangotri. This fascinating man also acquired an encyclopaedic knowledge of the wildlife of the region, and his articles, which appeared in *Indian Sporting Life* in the 1860s, were later plundered by so-called wildlife experts for their own writings.

Bridge-building was another of Wilson's ventures. These bridges were meant to facilitate travel to Harsil and the shrine at Gangotri. The most famous of them was a 350-foot suspension bridge over the Jad-ganga at Bhaironghat, over 1,200 feet above the young Bhagirathi where it thunders through a deep defile. This rippling contraption of a bridge was at first a source of terror to travellers, and only a few ventured across it. To reassure people, Wilson would often mount his horse and gallop to and fro across the bridge. It has long since collapsed but local people will tell you that the hoofbeats of Wilson's horse can still be heard on full moon nights! The supports of the old bridge were complete tree trunks, and they can still be seen to one side of the new motor-bridge put up by engineers of the Northern Railway.

Wilson's life is fit subject for a romance; but even if one were never written, his legend would live on, as it has done for over a hundred years. There has never been any attempt to commemorate him, but people in the valley still speak of him in awe and admiration, as though he had lived only yesterday. Some men leave a trail of legend behind them, because they give their spirit to the place where they have lived, and remain forever a part of the rocks and mountain streams.

In the old days, only the staunchest of pilgrims visited the shrines of Gangotri and Jamnotri. The roads were rocky and dangerous, winding along in some places, ascending and descending the faces of deep precipices and ravines, at times leading along banks of loose earth where landslides had swept the original path away. There are still no large towns above Uttarkashi, and this absence of large centres

---

* Wilson inspires one of my brief forays into historical fiction in the opening chapters to *Rosebud*.

of population may be one reason why the forests are better preserved than, say, those in the Alaknanda valley, or further downstream.

Gangotri is situated at just a little over 10,300 feet and on the right bank of the river is the Gangotri temple. It is a small neat building without too much ornamentation, built by Amar Singh Thapa, a Nepali general, early in the nineteenth century. It was renovated by the Maharaja of Jaipur in the 1920s. The rock on which it stands is called Bhagirath Shila and is said to be the place where Prince Bhagirath did penance in order that Ganga be brought down from her abode of eternal snow.

Here the rocks are carved and polished by ice and water, so smooth that in places they look like rolls of silk. The fast-flowing waters of this mountain torrent look very different from the huge sluggish river that finally empties its waters into the Bay of Bengal 1,500 miles away.

The river emerges from beneath a great glacier, thickly studded with enormous loose rocks and earth. The glacier is about a mile in width and extends upwards for many miles. The chasm in the glacier, through which the stream rushes into the light of day, is named Gaumukh, the cow's mouth, and is held in deepest reverence by Hindus. The regions of eternal frost in the vicinity were the scenes of many of their most sacred mysteries.

The Ganga enters the world no puny stream, but bursts from its icy womb a river thirty or forty yards in breadth. At Gauri Kund (below the Gangotri temple) it falls over a rock of considerable height, and continues tumbling over a succession of small cascades until it enters the Bhaironghati gorge.

A night spent beside the river, within sound of the fall, is an eerie experience. After some time it begins to sound, not like one fall but a hundred, and this sound permeates both one's dreams and walking hours. Rising early to greet the dawn proved rather pointless at Gangotri, for the surrounding peaks did not let the sun in till after 9 a.m. Everyone rushes about to keep warm, exclaiming delightedly at what they call gulabi thand—literally, rosy cold. Guaranteed to turn the cheeks a rosy pink! A charming expression, but I prefer a rosy sunburn—and remained beneath a heavy quilt until the sun came up to throw its golden shafts across the river.

This is mid-October, and after Diwali the shrine and the small township will close for the winter, the pandits retreating to the relative warmth of Mukhba. Soon snow will cover everything, and even the hardy purple-plumaged whistling thrushes, lovers of deep shade, will move further down the valley. And down below the forest-line, the Garhwali farmers go about harvesting their ripening paddy, as they have done for centuries; their terraced fields form patterns of yellow, green and gold above the deep green of the river.

Yes, the Bhagirathi is a green river. Although deep and swift, it does not lose its serenity. At no place does it look hurried or confused—unlike the turbulent Alaknanda, fretting and frothing as it goes crashing down its boulder-strewn bed. The Alaknanda gives one a feeling of being trapped, because the river itself is trapped. The Bhagirathi is free-flowing, easy. At all times and places it seems to find its true level.

Uttarkashi, though a large and growing town, is as yet uncrowded. The seediness of over-populated towns like Rishikesh and Dehradun is not yet evident here. One can take a leisurely walk through its long (and well-supplied) bazaar, without being jostled by crowds or knocked over by three-wheelers. Here, too, the river is always with you, and you must live in harmony with its sound, as it goes rushing and humming along its shingly bed.

Uttarkashi is not without its own religious and historical importance, although all traces of its ancient capital called Barahat appear to have vanished. There are four important temples here, and on the occasion of Makar Sankranti, early in January, a week-long fair is held, when thousands from the surrounding areas throng the roads to the town. To the beating of drums and blowing of trumpets, the Gods and Goddesses are brought to the fair in gaily decorated palanquins. The surrounding villages wear a deserted look that day as everyone flocks to the temples and bathing-ghats and to the entertainment of the fair itself.

We have to move far downstream to reach another large centre of population, the town of Tehri, and this is a very different place from Uttarkashi. Tehri has all the characteristics of a small town in the plains—crowds, noise, traffic congestion, dust and refuse, scruffy dhabas—with this difference, that here it is all ephemeral, for Tehri is destined to be submerged by the waters of the Bhagirathi when the Tehri dam is finally completed.

The rulers of Garhwal often changed their capitals, and when, after the Gurkha Wars (1811–15) the former capital of Srinagar became part of British Garhwal, Raja Sundershan Shah established his new capital at Tehri. It is said that when he reached this spot, his horse refused to go any further. This was enough for the king, it seems; or so the story goes.

Perhaps Prince Bhagirath's chariot will come to a halt here too, when the dam is built. The 246-metre high earthen dam, with 42 square miles of reservoir capacity, will submerge the town and about thirty villages.

As we leave the town and cross the narrow bridge over the river, a mighty blast from above sends rocks hurtling down the defile, just to remind us that work is in progress.

Unlike the Raja's horse, I have no wish to be stopped in my tracks at Tehri. There are livelier places upstream.

Falling for Mandakini

To see a river for the first time at its confluence with another great river is, for me, a special moment in time. And so it was with the Mandakini at Rudraprayag, where its waters were joined with the waters of the Alaknanda, the one having come from the glacial snows above Kedarnath, the other from the Himalayan heights beyond Badrinath. Both sacred rivers, both destined to become the holy Ganga further downstream.

I fell in love with the Mandakini at first sight. Or was it the valley that I fell in love with? I am not sure, and it doesn't really matter. The valley is the river.

While the Alaknanda valley, especially in its higher reaches, is a deep and narrow gorge where precipitous outcrops of rock hang threateningly over the traveller, the Mandakini valley is broader, gentler, the terraced fields wider, the banks of the river a green sward in many places.

Rudraprayag is hot. It is probably a pleasant spot in winter, but at the end of June it is decidedly hot. Perhaps its chief claim to fame is that it gave its name to the dreaded man-eating leopard of Rudraprayag who, in the course of seven years (1918-25), accounted for more than 300 victims. It was finally shot by the fifty-one-year-old

Jim Corbett, who recounted the saga of his long hunt for the killer in his fine book, *The Man-eating Leopard of Rudraprayag*.

The place at which the leopard was shot was the village of Gulabrai, two miles south of Rudraprayag. Under a large mango tree stands a memorial raised to Jim Corbett by officers and men of the Border Roads Organisation. It is a happy gesture to one who loved Garhwal and India. Unfortunately several buffaloes are gathered close by, and one has to wade through slush and buffalo-dung to get to the memorial-stone. A board tacked on to the mango tree attracts the attention of motorists who might pass without noticing the memorial, which is off to one side.

The killer-leopard was noted for its direct method of attack on humans; and, in spite of being poisoned, trapped in a cave and shot at innumerable times, it did not lose its contempt for man. Two English sportsmen covering both ends of the old suspension bridge over the Alaknanda fired several times at it but to little effect.

It was not long before the leopard acquired a reputation among the hill folk for being an evil spirit. A sadhu was suspected of turning into the leopard by night, and was only saved from being lynched by the ingenuity of Philip Mason, then Deputy Commissioner of Garhwal. Mason kept the sadhu in custody until the leopard made his next attack, thus proving the man innocent. Years later, when Mason turned novelist and (using the pen-name Philip Woodruff) wrote *The Wild Sweet Witch,* he had as his main character a beautiful young woman who turns into a man-eating leopard by night.

Corbett's host at Gulabrai was one of the few who survived an encounter with the leopard. It left him with a hole in his throat.

Apart from being a superb storyteller, Corbett displayed great compassion for people from all walks of life and is still a legend in Garhwal and Kumaon amongst people who have never read his books.

In June, one does not linger long in the steamy heat of Rudraprayag. But as one travels up the river, making a gradual ascent of the Mandakini valley, there is a cool breeze coming down from the snows, and the smell of rain is in the air.

The thriving little township of Agastmuni spreads itself along the wide riverbanks, and further upstream, near a little place called Chanderpuri, we cannot resist breaking our journey to sprawl on the tender green grass that slopes gently down to the swiftly flowing river. A small rest house is in the making. Around it, banana fronds sway and poplar leaves dance in the breeze.

This is no sluggish river of the plains, but a fast-moving current, tumbling over rocks, turning and twisting in its efforts to discover the easiest way for its frothy snow-fed waters to escape the mountains. Escape is the word! For the constant plaint of many a Garhwali is that, while his hills abound in rivers, the water runs down and away, and little if any reaches the fields and villages above it. Cultivation must depend on the rain and not on the river.

The road climbs gradually, still keeping to the river. Just outside Guptkashi my attention is drawn to a clump of huge trees sheltering a small but ancient temple. We stop here and enter the shade of the trees.

The temple is deserted. It is a temple dedicated to Shiva, and in the courtyard are several river-rounded stone lingams on which leaves and blossoms have fallen. No one seems to come here, which is strange, since it is on the pilgrim route. Two boys from a neighbouring field leave their yoked bullocks to come and talk to me, but they cannot tell me much about the temple except to confirm that it is seldom visited. 'The buses do not stop here.' That seems explanation enough. For where the buses go, the pilgrims go, and where the pilgrims go, other pilgrims will follow. Thus far and no further.

The trees seem to be magnolias, judging by the scent and shape of the flowers, and the boys call them champa, Hindi for magnolia blossom. But I have never seen magnolia trees grow to such huge proportions. Perhaps they are something else. Never mind; let them remain a sweet-scented mystery.

Guptkashi in the evening is all a bustle. A coach-load of pilgrims (headed for Kedarnath) has just arrived, and the tea shops near the bus stand are doing brisk business. Then the local bus—from Okhimath, across the river—arrives, and many of the passengers head for a tea shop famed for its samosas. The local bus is called the bhook-hartal— the 'hunger strike' bus.

'How did it get that name?' I ask one of the samosa-eaters.

'Well, it's an interesting story. For a long time we had been asking the authorities to provide a bus service for the local people and for the villagers who live off the roads. All the buses came from Srinagar or Rishikesh, and were taken up by pilgrims. The locals couldn't find room in them. But our pleas went unheard until the whole town—or most of it, anyway—decided to go on hunger-strike. That worked. And so the bus is named after our successful hunger-strike.'

'They nearly put me out of business too,' said the tea shop owner cheerfully. 'Nobody ate any samosas for two days!'

There is no cinema or public place of entertainment at Guptkashi, and the town goes to sleep early. And wakes early.

At six, the hillside, green from recent rain, sparkles in the morning sunshine. Snow-capped Chaukhamba (23,400 ft.) is dazzling. The air is clear, no smoke or dust up here. The climate, I am told, is mild all the year round, Okhimath, on the other side of the river, lies in shadow. It gets the sun at nine. In winter it must wait till afternoon. And yet it seems a bigger place, and by tradition the temple priest from Kedarnath passes winter there when the snows cover that distant shrine.

Guptkashi has not yet been rendered ugly by the barrack-type architecture that has come up in some growing hill towns. The old double-storeyed houses are built of stone, with grey slate roofs. They blend well with the hillside. Cobbled paths meander through the old bazaar.

One of these takes us to the famed Guptkashi temple, tucked away above the old part of the town. Here, as in Benares, Shiva is worshipped as Vishwanath, and two underground streams representing the sacred Yamuna and Bhagirathi rivers feed the pool sacred to the god. This temple gives the town its name—Guptkashi, the 'Invisible Benares,' just as Uttarkashi on the Bhagirathi is 'Upper Benares.'

Guptkashi and its environs have so many lingams that the saying *jitne kankar itne Sankar*—'As many stones, so many Shivas'—has become a proverb to describe its holiness.

From Guptkashi, pilgrims proceed north to Kedarnath, and the last stage of their journey—about a day's march—must be covered on foot or horseback. The temple of Kedarnath, situated at a height of 11,753 feet, is encircled by snowcapped peaks, and Atkinson has conjectured that 'the symbol of the linga may have arisen from the pointed peaks around his [God Shiva's] original home.'

The temple is dedicated to Sadashiva, the subterranean form of the god, who, 'fleeing from the Pandavas took refuge here in the form of a he-buffalo.'

We leave the Mandakini to visit Tungnath on the Chandrashila range. But I will return to this river. It has captured my mind and heart.

~⌒

The Magic of Tungnath

The mountains and valleys of Uttaranchal never fail to spring surprises on the traveller in search of the picturesque. It is impossible to know every corner of the Himalaya, which means that there are always new corners to discover; forest or meadow, mountain stream or wayside shrine.

The temple of Tungnath, at a little over 12,000 feet, is one of the highest shrines on the inner Himalayan range. It lies just below the Chandrashila peak. Some way off the main pilgrim routes, it is less frequented than Kedarnath or Badrinath, although it forms a part of the Kedar temple establishment. The priest here is a local man, a Brahmin from the village of Maku; the other Kedar temples have South Indian priests, a tradition begun by Sankaracharya, the eighth-century Hindu reformer and revivalist.

Tungnath's lonely eminence gives it a magic of its own. To get there (or beyond), one passes through some of the most delightful temperate forest in the Garhwal Himalaya. Pilgrim, or trekker, or just plain rambler such as myself, one comes away a better person, forest-refreshed, and more aware of what the world was really like before mankind began to strip it bare.

Duiri Tal, a small lake, lies cradled on the hill above Okhimath, at a height of 8,000 feet. It was a favourite spot of one of Garhwal's earliest British Commissioners, J.H. Batten, whose administration continued for twenty years (1836–56). He wrote:

The day I reached there, it was snowing and young trees were laid prostrate under the weight of snow; the lake was frozen over to a depth of about two inches. There was no human habitation, and the place looked a veritable wilderness. The next morning when the sun appeared, the Chaukhamba and many other peaks extending as far as Kedarnath seemed covered with a new quilt of snow, as if close at hand. The whole scene was so exquisite that one could not tire of gazing at it for hours. I think a person who has a subdued settled despair in his mind would all of a sudden feel a kind of bounding and exalting cheerfulness which will be imparted to his frame by the atmosphere of Duiri Tal.

This feeling of uplift can be experienced almost anywhere along the Tungnath range. Duiri Tal is still some way off the beaten track, and anyone wishing to spend the night there should carry a tent; but further along this range, the road ascends to Dugalbeta (at about 9,000 feet) where a PWD rest house, gaily painted, has come up like some exotic orchid in the midst of a lush meadow topped by excelsia pines and pencil cedars. Many an official who has stayed here has rhapsodized on the charms of Dugalbeta; and if you are unofficial (and therefore not entitled to stay in the bungalow), you can move on to Chopta, lusher still, where there is accommodation of a sort for pilgrims and other hardy souls. Two or three little tea shops provide mattresses and quilts. The Garhwal Mandal is putting up a rest house. These tourist rest houses of Garhwal are a great boon to the traveller; but during the pilgrim season (May/June) they are filled to overflowing, and if you turn up unexpectedly you might have to take your pick of tea shop or 'dharamshala': something of a lucky dip, since they vary a good deal in comfort and cleanliness.

The trek from Chopta to Tungnath is only 3.5 miles, but in that distance one ascends about 3,000 feet, and the pilgrim may be forgiven for feeling that at places he is on a perpendicular path. Like a ladder to heaven, I couldn't help thinking.

In spite of its steepness, my companion, the redoubtable Ganesh Saili, insisted that we take a shortcut. After clawing our way up tufts of alpine grass, which formed the rungs of our ladder, we were stuck and had to inch our way down again; so that the ascent of Tungnath began to resemble a game of Snakes and Ladders.

A tiny guardian-temple dedicated to the god Ganesh spurred us on. Nor was I really fatigued; for the cold fresh air and the verdant greenery surrounding us was like an intoxicant. A myriad wildflowers grow on the open slopes—buttercups, anemones, wild strawberries, forget-me-not, rock-cress—enough to rival Bhyundar's 'Valley of Flowers' at this time of the year.

But before reaching these alpine meadows, we climb through rhododendron forest, and here one finds at least three species of this flower: the red-flowering tree rhododendron (found throughout the Himalaya between 6,000 feet and 10,000 feet); a second variety, the almatta, with flowers that are light red or rosy in colour; and the third chimul or white variety, found at heights ranging from between 10,000 and 13,000 feet. The chimul is a brushwood, seldom more than twelve feet high and growing slantingly due to the heavy burden of snow it has to carry for almost six months in the year.

These brushwood rhododendrons are the last trees we see on our ascent, for as we approach Tungnath the tree line ends and there is nothing between earth and sky except grass and rock and tiny flowers. Above us, a couple of crows dive-bomb a hawk, who does his best to escape their attentions. Crows are the world's great survivors. They are capable of living at any height and in any climate; as much at home in the back streets of Delhi as on the heights of Tungnath.

Another survivor, up here at any rate, is the pika, a sort of mouse-hare, who looks like neither mouse nor hare but rather a tiny guinea-pig—small ears, no tail, grey-brown fur and chubby feet. They emerge from their holes under the rocks to forage for grasses on which to feed. Their simple diet and thick fur enable them to live in extreme cold, and they have been found at 16,000 feet, which is higher than any other mammal lives. The Garhwalis call this little creature the runda—at any rate, that's what the temple priest called it, adding that it was not averse to entering houses and helping itself to grain and other delicacies. So perhaps there's more in it of mouse than of hare.

These little rundas were with us all the way from Chopta to Tungnath, peering out from their rocks or scampering about on the hillside, seemingly unconcerned by our presence. At Tungnath they live beneath the temple flagstones. The priest's grandchildren were having a game discovering their burrows; the rundas would go in at one hole and pop out at another—they must have had a system of underground passages.

When we arrived, clouds had gathered over Tungnath, as they do almost every afternoon. The temple looked austere in the gathering gloom.

To some, the name 'tung' indicates 'lofty', from the position of the temple on the highest peak outside the main chain of the Himalaya; others derive it from the word 'tunga', that is 'to be suspended'—an allusion to the form under which the deity is worshipped here. The form is the Swayambhu Ling. On Shivratri the true believer may, 'with the eye of faith', see the lingam increase in size; but 'to the evil-minded no such favour is granted'.

The temple, though not very large, is certainly impressive, mainly because of its setting and the solid slabs of grey granite from which it is built. The whole place somehow puts me in mind of Emily Bronte's *Wuthering Heights*—bleak, windswept, open to the skies. And as you look down from the temple at the little half-deserted hamlet that serves it in summer, the eye is met by grey slate roofs and piles of stones, with just a few hardy souls in residence—for the majority of pilgrims now prefer to spend the night down at Chopta.

Even the temple priest, attended by his son and grandsons, complains bitterly of the cold. To spend every day barefoot on those cold flagstones must indeed be hardship. I wince after five minutes of it, made worse by stepping into a puddle of icy water. I shall never make a good pilgrim; no rewards for me, in this world or the next. But the pandit's feet are literally thick-skinned; and the children seem oblivious to the cold. Still in October they must be happy to descend to Maku, their home village on the slopes below Dugalbeta.

It begins to rain as we leave the temple. We pass herds of sheep huddled in a ruined dharamshala. The crows are still rushing about the grey weeping skies, although the hawk has very sensibly gone away. A runda sticks his nose out from his hole, probably to take a look at the weather. There is a clap of thunder and he disappears, like the white rabbit in *Alice in Wonderland*. We are halfway down the Tungnath 'ladder' when it begins to rain quite heavily. And now we pass our first genuine pilgrims, a group of intrepid Bengalis who are heading straight into the storm. They are without umbrellas or raincoats, but they are not to be deterred. Oaks and rhododendrons flash past as we dash down the steep, winding path. Another short cut, and Ganesh Saili takes a tumble, but is cushioned by moss and buttercups. My wrist-watch strikes a rock and the glass is shattered. No matter. Time here is of little or no consequence. Away with time! Is this, I wonder, the 'bounding and exalting cheerfulness' experienced by Batten and now manifesting itself in me?

The tea shop beckons. How would one manage in the hills without these wayside tea shops? Miniature inns, they provide food, shelter and even lodging to dozens at a time. We sit on a bench between a

Gujar herdsman and a pilgrim who is too feverish to make the climb to the temple. He accepts my offer of an aspirin to go with his tea. We tackle some buns—rock-hard, to match our environment—and wash the pellets down with hot sweet tea.

There is a small shrine here, too, right in front of the tea shop. It is a slab of rock roughly shaped like a lingam, and it is daubed with vermilion and strewn with offerings of wildflowers. The mica in the rock gives it a beautiful sheen.

I suppose Hinduism comes closest to being a nature religion. Rivers, rocks, trees, plants, animals and birds, all play their part, both in mythology and in everyday worship. This harmony is most evident in these remote places, where gods and mountains co-exist. Tungnath, as yet unspoilt by a materialistic society, exerts its magic on all who come here with open mind and heart.

~

On the Road to Badrinath

If you have travelled up the Mandakini valley, and then cross over into the valley of the Alaknanda, you are immediately struck by the contrast. The Mandakini is gentler, richer in vegetation, almost pastoral in places; the Alaknanda is awesome, precipitous, threatening—and seemingly inhospitable to those who must live, and earn a livelihood, in its confines.

Even as we left Chamoli and began the steady, winding climb to Badrinath, the nature of the terrain underwent a dramatic change. No longer did green fields slope gently down to the riverbed. Here they clung precariously to rocky slopes and ledges that grew steeper and narrower, while the river below, impatient to reach its confluence with the Bhagirathi at Deoprayag, thundered along the narrow gorge.

Badrinath is one of the four dhams, or four most holy places in India. (The other three are Rameshwaram, Dwarka and Jagannath Puri.) For the pilgrim travelling to this holiest of holies, the journey is exciting, possibly even uplifting; but for those who live permanently on these crags and ridges, life is harsh, a struggle from one day to the next. No wonder so many young men from Garhwal find their way into the Army. Little grows on these rocky promontories; and what does, is at the mercy of the weather. For most of the year the fields lie fallow. Rivers, unfortunately, run downhill and not uphill.

The harshness of this life, typical of much of Garhwal, was brought home to me at Pipalkoti, where we stopped for the night. Pilgrims stop here by the coach load, for the Garhwal Mandal Vikas Nigam's rest house is fairly capacious, and small hotels and dharamshalas abound. Just off the busy road is a tiny hospital, and here, late in the evening, we came across a woman keeping vigil over the dead body of her husband. The body had been laid out on a bench in the courtyard. A few feet away the road was crowded with pilgrims in festival mood; no one glanced over the low wall to notice this tragic scene.

The woman came from a village near Helong. Earlier that day, finding her consumptive husband in a critical condition she had decided to bring him to the nearest town for treatment. As he was frail and emaciated, she was able to carry him on her back for several miles, until she reached the motor road. Then, at some expense, she engaged a passing taxi and brought him to Pipalkoti. But he was already dead when she reached the small hospital. There was no morgue; so she sat beside the body in the courtyard, waiting for dawn and the arrival of others from the village. A few men arrived next morning and we saw them wending their way down to the cremation ground. We did not see the woman again. Her children were hungry and she had to hurry home to look after them.

Pipalkoti is hot (and peepul trees are conspicuous by their absence), but Joshimath, the winter resort of the Badrinath temple establishment, is about 6,000 feet above sea level and has an equable climate. It is now a fairly large town, and although the surrounding hills are rather bare, it does have one great tree that has survived the ravages of time. This is an ancient mulberry, known as the Kalpa Vriksha, beneath which the great Sankaracharya meditated, a few centuries ago. It is reputedly over two thousand years old, and is certainly larger than my modest four-roomed flat in Mussoorie. Sixty pilgrims holding hands might just about encircle its trunk.

I have seen some big trees, but this is certainly the oldest and broadest of them. I am glad the Sankaracharya meditated beneath it and thus ensured its preservation. Otherwise it might well have gone the way of other great trees and forests that once flourished in this area.

A small boy reminds me that it is a Wishing Tree, so I make my wish. I wish that other trees might prosper like this one.

'Have you made a wish?' I ask the boy.

'I wish that you will give me one rupee,' he says.

His wish comes true with immediate effect. Mine lies in the uncertain future. But he has given me a lesson in wishing.

Joshimath has to be a fairly large place, because most of Badrinath arrives here in November, when the shrine is snowbound for six months. Army and PWD structures also dot the landscape. This is no carefree hill resort, but it has all the amenities for making a short stay quite pleasant and interesting. Perched on the steep mountainside above the junction of the Alaknanda and Dhauli rivers, it is now vastly different from what it was when Frank Smythe visited it fifty years ago and described it as 'an ugly little place…straggling unbeautifully over the hillside. Primitive little shops line the main street, which is roughly paved in places and in others has been deeply channelled by the monsoon rains. The pilgrims spend the night in single-storeyed rest houses, not unlike the hovels provided for the Kentish hop-pickers of former days, some of which are situated in narrow passages running off the main street and are filthy and evil-smelling.'

Those were Joshimath's former days. It is a different place today, with small hotels, modern shops, a cinema; and its growth and comparative modernity date from the early 1960s, when the old pilgrim footpath gave way to the motor road which takes the traveller all the way to Badrinath. No longer does the weary, footsore pilgrim sink gratefully down in the shade of the Kalpa-Vriksha. He alights from his bus or luxury coach and drinks a Cola or a Thums-up at one of the many small restaurants on the roadside.

Contrast this comfortable journey with the pilgrimage fifty years ago. Frank Smythe again: 'So they venture on their pilgrimage… Some borne magnificently by coolies, some toiling along in rags, some almost crawling, preyed on by disease and distorted by dreadful deformities… Europeans who have read and travelled cannot conceive what goes on in the minds of these simple folk, many of them from the agricultural parts of India; wonderment and fear must be the prime ingredients. So the pilgrimage becomes an adventure. Unknown dangers threaten the broad well-made path, at any moment the gods, who hold the rocks in leash, may unloose their wrath upon the hapless passerby. To the European it is a walk to Badrinath, to the Hindu pilgrim it is far, far more.'

Above Vishnuprayag, Smythe left the Alaknanda and entered the Bhyunder valley, a botanist's paradise, which he called the Valley of Flowers. He fell in love with the lush meadows of this high valley, and made it known to the world. It continues to attract the botanist and trekker. Primulas of subtle shades, wild geraniums, saxifrages clinging to the rocks, yellow and red potentillas, snow-white anemones, delphiniums, violets, wild roses, all these and many more flourish there, capturing the mind and heart of the flower-lover.

'Impossible to take a step without crushing a flower.' This may not be true any more, for many footsteps have trodden the Bhyundar in recent years. There are other areas in Garhwal where the hills are rich in flora—the Harki-doon, Harsil, Tungnath and the Khiraun valley where the balsam grows to a height of eight feet—but the Bhyundar has both a variety and a concentration of wild flowers, especially towards the end of the monsoon. It would be no exaggeration to call it one of the most beautiful valleys in the world.

The Bhyundar is a digression for lovers of mountain scenery; but the pilgrim keeps his eyes fixed on the ultimate goal—Badrinath, where the gods dwelt and where salvation is to be found.

There are still a few who do it the hard way—mostly those who have taken sanyas and renounced the world. Here is one hardy soul doing penance. He stretches himself out on the ground, draws himself up to a standing position, then flattens himself out again. In this manner he will proceed from Badrinath to Rishikesh, oblivious of the sun and rain, the dust from passing buses, the sharp gravel of the footpath.

Others are not so hardy. One saffron-robed scholar, speaking fair English, asks us for a lift to Badrinath, and we find a space for him. He rewards us with a long and involved commentary on the Vedas, which lasts through the remainder of the journey. His special field of study, he informs us, is the part played by aeronautics in Vedic literature.

'And what,' I ask him, 'is the connection between the two?'

He looks at me pityingly.

'It is what I am trying to find out,' he replies.

The road drops to Pandukeshwar and rises again, and all the time I am scanning the horizon for the forests of the Badrinath region

I had read about many years ago in Fraser's *Himalaya Mountains*. Walnuts growing up to 9,000 feet, deodars and 'Bilka' up to 9,500 feet, and 'Amesh' and 'Kiusu' fir up a similar height—but, apart from stands of long-leaved excelsia pine, I do not see much, certainly no deodars. What has happened to them, I wonder. An endless variety of trees delighted us all the way from Dugalbeta to Mandal, a well-protected area but here on the high ridges above the Alaknanda, little seems to grow; or, if ever they did, have long since been despoiled or swept away.

Finally we reach the wind-swept, barren valley which harbours Badrinath—a growing township, thriving, lively, but somewhat dwarfed by the snow-capped peaks that tower above it. As at Joshimath, there is no dearth of hostelries and dharamshalas. Even so, every hotel or rest house is filled to overflowing. It is the height of the pilgrim season, and pilgrims, tourists and mendicants of every description throng the riverfront.

Just as Kedar is the most sacred of the Shiva temples in the Himalayas, so Badrinath is the supreme place of worship for the Vaishnav sects.

According to legend, when Sankaracharya in his digvijaya travels visited the Mana valley he arrived at the Narada-Kund and found fifty different images lying in its waters. These he rescued, and when he had done so, a voice from Heaven said, 'These are the images for the Kaliyug, establish them here.' Sankaracharya accordingly placed them beneath a mighty tree which grew there and whose shade extended from Badrinath to Nandprayag, a distance of over eighty miles. Close to it was the hermitage of Nar-Narayana (or Arjuna and Krishna), and in course of time temples were built in honour of these and other manifestations of Vishnu. It was here that Vishnu appeared to his followers in person, as the four-armed, crested and adorned with pearls and garlands. The faithful, it is said, can still see him on the peak of Nilkantha, on the great Kumbha day. It is, in fact, the Nilkantha peak that dominates this crater-like valley where a few hardy thistles and nettles manage to survive. Like cacti in the desert, the pricklier forms of life seem best equipped to live in a hostile environment.

Nilkantha means blue-necked, an allusion to the god Shiva's swallowing of a poison meant to destroy the world. The poison remained in his throat, which was rendered blue thereafter. It is a majestic and awe-inspiring peak, soaring to a height of 21,640 feet. As its summit is only five miles from Badrinath, it is justly held in reverence. From its ice-clad pinnacle three great ridges sweep down, of which the southern one terminates in the Alaknanda valley.

On the evening of our arrival we could not see the peak, as it was hidden in clouds. Badrinath itself was shrouded in mist. But we made our way to the temple, a gaily decorated building about 50 feet high, with a gilded roof. The image of Vishnu, carved in black stone, stands in the centre of the sanctum, opposite the door, in a Dhyana posture. An endless stream of people passes through the temple to pay homage and emerge the better for their proximity to the divine.

From the temple, flights of steps lead down to the rushing river and to the hot springs which emerge just above it. Another road leads through a long but tidy bazaar where pilgrims may buy mementos of their visit—from sacred amulets to pictures of the gods in vibrant technicolour. Here at last I am free to indulge my passion for cheap rings, with none to laugh at my foible. There are all kinds, from rings designed like a coiled serpent (my favourite) to twisted bands of copper and iron and others containing the pictures of gods, gurus and godmen. They do not cost more than two or three rupees each, and so I am able to fill my pockets. I never wear these rings. I simply hoard them away. My friends are convinced that in a previous existence I was a jackdaw, seizing upon and hiding away any kind of bright and shiny object: So be it....

Even those who have renounced the world appear to be cheerful—like the young woman from Gujarat who had taken sanyas and who met me on the steps below the temple. She gave me a dazzling smile and passed me an exercise book. She had taken a vow of silence; but being, I think, of an extrovert nature, she seemed eager to remain in close communication with the rest of humanity, and did so by means of written questions and answers. Hence the exercise book.

Although at Badrinath I missed the sound of birds and the presence of trees, it was good to be part of the happy throng at its colourful little temple, and to see the sacred river close to its source. And early next morning I was rewarded with the liveliest experience of all.

Opening the window of my room, and glancing out, I saw the rising sun touch the snow-clad summit of Nilkantha. At first the snows were pink; then they turned to orange and gold. All sleep vanished as I gazed up in wonder at that magnificent pinnacle in the sky. And had Lord Vishnu appeared just then on the summit, I would not have been in the least surprised.

Flowers on the Ganga

Flowers floating down the river: yellow and scarlet cannas, roses, jasmine, hibiscus. They are placed in boats made of broad leaves, then consigned to the waters with a prayer. The strong current carries them swiftly downstream, and they bob about on the water for fifty, sometimes a hundred yards, before being submerged in the river. Do the prayers sink too, or do they reach the hearts of the many gods who have favoured Hardwar—'Door of Hari, or Vishnu'—these several hundred years?

The river issues through a gorge in the mountains with a low booming sound. It does not break its banks until it levels out over the flat plains of Uttar Pradesh and Bihar. It is fast and muddy; but this does not deter thousands from descending the steps of the bathing-ghats, and plunging into the cold, snowfed waters. For the Ganga washes away all sin.

Says the *Mahabharata*: 'To repeat her name brings purity, to see her secures prosperity, to bathe in or drink her waters saves seven generations of our race... There is no place of pilgrimage like the Ganga, no god like Vishnu...'

Almost every child knows the story of how the Ganga descended from heaven. For 1,000 years King Sagara's great-grandson stood with his hands upraised, praying for water to enable him to make the funeral oblations for the ashes of his 60,000 grand-uncles. Almost all the gods were involved in the affair. Finally, when the waters of the Ganga were released from heaven and the river reached the earth, the prince mounted his chariot and drove towards the spot where the ashes of his kinsmen lay. Wherever he went, the Ganga meekly followed. Gods, nymphs, demons, giants, sages and great snakes, all

joined in the procession, and as the river followed in the footsteps of
the prince, the whole multitude of created beings bathed in her sacred
waters and washed away their sins.

~

The multitude that followed the prince could be the same multitude
that throngs the riverfront today. I see no one who is not delighted at
the prospect of entering the water. *'Ganga-Mai ki jai!'* The cry goes up
mostly from the older people who have come here, many for the last
time, to make their peace with the gods. Only their ashes will make
the trip again.

It is a big crowd, although this is just an ordinary day of the week
and not an occasion of special religious significance. Every day is a
good day for bathing in the Ganga. But at the time of major festivals,
such as Baisakhi, elaborate arrangements have to be made, including
special trains and police reinforcements, to take care of the great
influx of pilgrims. The number of pilgrims at the Baisakhi festival
usually exceeds 100,000. During the Kumbh Mela, held every twelve
years, there may be as many as 500,000 present on the great bathing-
day. This is ten times the normal population of Hardwar. And when
one realizes that the town is bounded by the steep Siwalik hills on
one side and the river on the other, and has one main street leading
to the riverfront, it is not surprising that in the past large numbers of
people were crushed to death in stampedes at the narrow entrance to
the ghats.

Fortunately the main street is a broad and pleasant thoroughfare.
Although Hardwar is ancient (the Chinese traveller, Hiuen Tsang,
records a visit made in the seventh century), little remains of earlier
settlements. There are only two or three old temples. But the present
buildings—tall, balconized structures put up in the 1920s and '30s
have a certain old-world charm. Even new houses follow the same
pattern. This isn't conscious planning; it is simply that Hardwar is a
conservative town and clings to its traditions.

Most of the buildings along the road are dharamsalas. The road is
shaded by tall old peepul and banyan trees. In some places the trees
reach right across the street to touch the roofs of the three-storey
buildings on the other side. At several places I find small peepul
saplings growing out of the walls of buildings. One young peepul

has sprung up in the fork of an adult kadam tree and will probably throttle it in time. No one fells the sacred peepul. It is better that walls should crumble or kadam trees wither. At least this guarantees the survival of one species of tree in a world where forests are rapidly disappearing.

Peepuls live for hundreds of years, and Hardwar's oldest trees must have been here before the present town reached maturity. Some will be as old as the eleventh-century Maya-devi temple, which is probably the oldest temple in Hardwar. On a sultry day there can be no pleasanter spot than the shade of a peepul tree; the leaves are perpetually in motion, even when there is no breeze, and spin around in currents of their own making. It is no wonder that the man who plants a peepul is blessed by generations of Hindus to come.

While I stand beneath one of these giant trees, a devout and elderly man approaches with a watering-can, and, circling the tree, waters the soil around the base of the trunk. I move out of the way of his sprinkler watching the ritual in some surprise. It has been raining steadily for some days, and the tree should have no need of water.

'Why are you watering it?' I ask.

'Why does one water anything?' asks the old man. 'So that it may grow and flourish, of course.'

'But it's been raining almost every day.'

'Rain is something else,' he says. 'I am not responsible for the rain; this is water from the Ganga, and I have fetched it myself. That makes a lot of difference.'

I cannot argue. He waters the tree with love; and his love for the tree, as much as rainwater or river-water, is what makes it flourish.

Leaving the main street, I enter the bazaar.

The Hardwar bazaar is a long, narrow, winding street, probably the oldest part of the town, and free of all vehicular traffic. The road is no more than four yards wide. The small shops are spilling over with sweets, pickles, bead-necklaces, sacred texts, ritual designs, festival images and pictures of the gods in vibrant technicolour. There is something in these naive, gaudy prints that acts as a transformer, making the more abstract Hindu philosophies comprehensible to anxious farmer or acquisitive taxi-driver.

The bazaar winds and turns back upon itself, and eventually I find myself back at the riverfront, gazing out across the river at the forested foothills. Few of the pilgrims on the bathing-steps can realize that sometimes at night a tiger stands on the opposite bank watching the bright illuminations of the temples, or that elephants listen to the rumbling of the trains bringing pilgrims to Hardwar from all parts of India.

It is evening now, and there are fewer people at the ghats. Most of the bathers are family people—farmers and small shopkeepers with their women and children and aged parents. One does not see many students, or young people in Western clothes. Hardwar is old-fashioned, and so are most of the people who come here.

~

Charity, too, is old-fashioned, and Hardwar thrives on charity: donations to the temples and alms to the beggars, mendicants and itinerant ash-smeared sadhus. The beggars do not follow one about, as in the larger cities. They are confident of receiving coins from the pilgrims who pass by on the steps to the river. They simply sit there, occasionally calling out, but preferring to listen to the music of small coins dropping into brass begging-bowls.

Close by are the money changers, squatting before baskets which are brimming over with small change. In the rest of the country there is a shortage of small coins, and shopkeepers often decline to provide change; but in Hardwar you can change any number of notes for small coins. You are going to leave all the coins here anyway, when you distribute it along the riverfront.

As the pilgrims leave the ghats, the joy of having accomplished their mission bursts forth in songs of praise: 'Henceforth no more pain, no more sickness; all will be well in future; *Ganga-mai ki jai.*'

More flowers are being sold; and now the leaf-boats are lit by diyas. The little boats are swept away, sometimes travelling a considerable distance before being upset by submerged rocks or inquisitive fish.

I, too, send an offering downstream, but my boat sails beneath the legs of a late bather, and disappears beneath the pilgrim. My boat is lost; but my rose petals still float on the Ganga.

It has been said that if the Ganga ran dry, all life in India would cease. There is no likelihood of that happening. The Ganga is overgenerous as the annual floods will testify. So long as the Himalayas stand, this river will flow to the sea, and millions will come to immerse their bodies, their sins and their prayers in its sacred waters.

~

Mathura's Hallowed Haunts

Mathura, most sacred of cities, stands on the right bank of the Yamuna northwest of Agra. All men speak of Mathura with reverence, and it has been said that 'if a man spend in Banaras all his lifetime, he has earned less merit than if he passes but a single day in the sacred city of Mathura.'

It is difficult to pierce the fog which hides the date of the city's birth; but sacred it has always been, as the capital of the kingdom of Braj and the birthplace of Lord Krishna: 'Teacher and Soul of the Universe. Destroyer of the earth's tyrant kings, and the First of the Spirits...'

I went to Mathura at the end of the rains. The fields and the trees were alive with strange, beautiful birds: the long-tailed king crow; innumerable doves in shades of blue and green; kingfishers and bluejays and weaver-birds; and, resting on a telegraph pole, the great white-headed kite, which, some say, was Garuda, Vishnu's famous steed. Resplendent, too, were the green and gold parrots, from among whom Kamadeva, the god of love, chose his steed. Armed with his sugarcane bow with its string made of bees, Kamadeva still rides at night over the plains of Mathura. Many are the journeys he makes on nights approaching the full moon. He knows the ways of men and women, and his bow, like Cupid's, is always ready to assist the ardent lover.

In the tanks and 'jheels' around Mathura I saw a variety of game birds—wild duck, herbits, cranes and snipe—but all life is sacred for many miles around Mathura, and not even the bird trapper is permitted to lay his snares.

Strutting under an old tamarind tree are Krishna's birds, the brilliant peacocks. Centuries ago, they gave the city their name, and today Mathura is still known as the Peacock City. The peacocks seem to know that they are the chosen of Krishna. Spreading out their many-hued fantails, they glance at us drab mortals with an air of disdain.

Near Mathura is Brindavan in whose forests—they have gone now—the boy Krishna and his brother Balram ran wild, playing on their shepherds' pipes. The neighbours found Krishna very mischievous. He was extremely fond of butter and, going by stealth one day to the house of a neighbour, climbed onto a shelf to get at a large jar of butter. He ate the butter as far as he could reach, and then got into the jar. The owner, on returning, found him there and putting a cover on the jar to prevent the boy from escaping went to Krishna's father to make a complaint. But when he arrived at the house it was not the father who met him but the little butter-thief.

There is another story which tells us of the day Krishna stole his mother's curds, and finished them while no one was looking. 'O, you wicked one!' exclaimed his mother when she discovered what had happened. 'Come, let me see your mouth.' And when she looked into his mouth, she saw the Universe—the earth, sea and heavens; the sun and the moon, the planets and all the stars...

Brindavan stands on a tongue of land surrounded by the river, which has curved here in a strange fashion. Legend tells us that Balram who was very strong, once led a dance on the Yamuna's bank, but moved his giant limbs so clumsily that the river laughed aloud and taunted him, saying: 'Enough, my clumsy child! How can you hope to dance as Krishna, who is divine?' Balram was very angry with the river, and taking his great plough he traced a furrow from the brink of the river; but so deep was the furrow that the river fell into it and was led far astray.

When the tyrant king Kamsa heard of the unusual exploits of Krishna and Balram, he planned to have them killed in case they became a danger to his power. He sent a message to the brothers, inviting them to a contest of arms in the royal city of Mathura. Krishna and Balram accepted the challenge.

On the day of the contest, King Kamsa sat on a lofty throne near the arena. As Krishna and Balram entered, a mighty elephant was sent against them. But Krishna, seizing the animal by the tail, swung it around his head and threw it to the ground. Then each of the brothers taking a tusk, they slew Kamsa's mightiest champions. Kamsa ordered his army to kill the boys, but Krishna sprang up the steps of the throne, seized the king by his hair and hurled him into a deep ravine.

Visitors to Mathura are still shown the mound where Kamsa's throne once stood. And still venerated is that part of the riverfront where the two boys rested after dragging the body of Kamsa down to the funeral pyre.

I wandered in the streets of the city past shops gleaming with brasswork or piled high with pedas, Mathura's famous sweets. From the bridge, I could see the riverfront with its innumerable temples. And below, hundreds of majestic tortoises watched the bathers and the boatmen with speculative eyes. Sometimes a boatman seized one of these longnecked creatures and held it up to view. The tortoise would immediately draw its legs into its shell—a vivid illustration of the theory that nothing is annihilated but only disappears, the effect being absorbed in the cause!

Footloose in Agra

The cycle-rickshaw is the best way of getting about Agra. Its smooth gliding motion and leisurely rate of progress are in keeping with the pace of life in this old-world city. The rickshaw-boy juggles his way through the crowded bazaars, exchanging insults with tonga-drivers, pedestrians and other cyclists; but once on the broad Mall or Taj Road, his curses change to carefree song and he freewheels along the tree-lined avenues. Old colonial-style bungalows still stand in large compounds shaded by peepul, banyan, neem and jamun trees,

Looking up, I notice a number of bright paper kites that flutter, dip and swerve in the cloudless sky. I cannot recall seeing so many kites before.

'Is it a festival today?' I ask.

'No, sahib,' says the rickshaw-boy, 'not even a holiday.'

'Then why so many kites?'

He does not even bother to look up. 'You can see kites every day, sahib.'

'I don't see them in Delhi.'

'Ah, but Delhi is a busy place. In Agra, people still fly kites. There are kite-flying competitions every Sunday, and heavy bets are sometimes placed on the outcome.'

As we near the city, I notice kites stuck in trees or dangling from electric wires; but there are always others soaring up to take their place. I ask the rickshaw-boy to tell me something about the kite-fliers and the kitemakers, but the subject bores him.

'You had better see the Taj today, sahib.'

All right take me to it. I can lunch afterwards.'

It is difficult to view the Taj at noon. The sun strikes the white marble, and there is a great dazzle of reflected light. I stand there with averted eyes, looking at everything—the formal gardens, the surrounding walls of red sandstone, the winding river—everything except the monument I have come to see.

It is there, of course, very solid and real, perfectly preserved, with every jade, jasper or lapis lazuli playing its part in the overall design; and after a while, I can shade my eyes and take in a vision of shimmering white marble. The light rises in waves from the paving-stones, and the squares of black and white marble create an effect of running water. Inside the chamber it is cool and dark but rather musty, and I waste no time in hurrying out again into the sunlight.

I walk the length of a gallery and turn with some relief to the river scene. The sluggish Yamuna winds past Agra on its way to its union with the Ganga. I know the Yamuna well. I know it where it emerges from the foothills near Kalsi, cold and blue from the melting snows; I know it as it winds through fields of wheat and sugarcane and mustard, across the flat plains of Uttar Pradesh, sometimes placid, sometimes in flood. I know the river at Delhi, where its muddy banks are a patchwork of clothes spread out by the hundreds of washermen who serve the city and I know it at Mathura, where it is alive with huge turtles; Mathura, sacred city, whose beginnings are lost in antiquity.

And then the river winds its way to Agra, to this spot by the Taj, where parrots flash in the sunshine, kingfishers swoop low over the water and a proud peacock struts across the lawns surrounding the monument.

I follow the peacock into a shady grove. It is quite tame and does not fly away. It leads me to a small boy who is sitting in the shade of a tree, feasting on a handful of small green fruit.

I have not seen the fruit before, and I ask the boy to tell me what it is. He offers me what looks like a hard green plum.

'It is the fruit from the Ashoke tree,' says the boy. There are many such trees in the garden.'

'Are you allowed to take the fruit?'

'I am allowed,' he says, grinning. 'My father is the head gardener.'

I bite into the fruit. It is hard and sour but not unpleasant.

'Do you live here?' I ask.

'Over the wall,' he says. 'But I come here every day, to help my father and to eat the fruit.'

'So you see the Taj Mahal every day?'

'I have seen it every day for as long as I can remember.'

'And I am seeing it for the first time...you're very lucky.'

He shrugs. 'If you see it once, or a hundred times, it is the same. It doesn't change.'

'Don't you like looking at it, then?'

'I like looking at the people who come here. They are always different. In the evening there will be many people.'

'You must have seen people from almost every country in the world.'

That is so. They all come here to look at the Taj. Kings and Queens and Presidents and Prime Ministers and film stars and poor people too. And I look at them. In that way it isn't boring.'

'Well, you have the Taj to thank for that.'

He gazes thoughtfully at the shimmering monument. His eyes are accustomed to the sharp sunlight. He sees the Taj every day, but at this moment he is really looking at it, thinking about it, wondering what magic it must possess to attract people from all comers of the earth, to bring them here walking through his father's well-kept garden so that he can have something new and fresh to look at each day.

A cloud—a very small cloud—passes across the face of the sun; and in the softened light I too am able to look at the Taj without screwing up my eyes.

As the boy said, it does not change. Therein lies beauty. For the effect on the traveller is the same today as it was three hundred years ago when Bernier wrote: 'Nothing offends the eye.... No part can be found that is not skilfully wrought, or that has not its peculiar beauty.'

And so, for a few moments, this poem in marble is on view to two unimportant people—the itinerant writer and the gardener's boy.

We say nothing; there is really nothing to be said. (But now, a few months later, when I try to recapture the essence of that day, it is not the monument that I remember most vividly. The Taj is there of course; I still see it as a mirror for the sun. But what remains with me, more than anything else, is the passage of the river and the sharp flavour of the Ashoke fruit.)

~

In the afternoon I walk through the old bazaars which lie to the west of Akbar's great red sandstone fort, and I am not surprised to find a small street which is almost entirely taken up by kite shops. Most of them sell the smaller, cheaper kites, but one small dark shop has in it a variety of odd and fantastic creations. Stepping inside, I find myself face to face with the doyen of Agra's kite-makers, Hosain Ali, a feeble old man whose long beard is dyed red with mehendi leaves. He has just finished making a new kite from bamboo, paper and thin silk, and it lies outside in the sun, firming up. It is a pale pink kite, with a small green tail.

The old man is soon talking to me, for he likes to talk and is not very busy. He complains that few people buy kites these days (I find this hard to believe), and tells me that I should have visited Agra twenty-five years ago, when kite-flying was the sport of kings and even grown men found time to spend an hour or two every day with these gay, dancing strips of paper. Now, he says, everyone hurries, hurries in a heat of hope, and delicate things like kites and daydreams are trampled underfoot. 'Once I made a wonderful kite,' says Hosain Ali nostalgically. 'It was unlike any kite seen in Agra. It had a number of small, very light paper discs trailing on a thin bamboo frame. At the end of each disc I fixed a sprig of grass, forming a balance on both sides. On the first and largest disc I painted a face and gave it eyes made of two small mirrors. The discs, which grew smaller from head to tail, gave the kite the appearance of a crawling serpent. It was very difficult to get this great kite off the ground. Only I could manage it.

'Of course, everyone heard of the Dragon Kite I had made, and word went about that there was some magic in its making. A large crowd arrived on the maidan to watch me fly the kite.

'At first the kite would not leave the ground. The discs made a sharp wailing sound, the sun was trapped in the little mirrors. My kite had eyes and tongue and a trailing silver tail. I felt it come alive in my hands. It rose from the ground, rose steeply into the sky, moving farther and farther away, with the sun still glinting in its dragon eyes. And when it went very high, it pulled fiercely on the twine, and my son had to help me with the reel.

'But still the kite pulled, determined to be free—yes, it had become a living thing—and at last the twine snapped, and the wind took the kite, took it over the rooftops and the waving trees and the river and the far hills for ever. No one ever saw where it fell. Sahib, are you listening? The Dragon Kite is lost, but for you I'll make a bright new poem to fly.'

'Make me one,' I say, moved by his tale, or rather by the manner of its telling. 'I will collect it tomorrow, before I leave Agra. Let it be a beautiful kite. I won't fly it. I'll hang it on my wall, and will not give it a chance to get away.'

It is evening, and the winter sun comes slanting through the intricate branches of a banyan tree, as a cycle-rickshaw—a different one this time—brings me to a forgotten corner of Agra that I have always wanted to visit. This is the old Roman Catholic cemetery where so many early European travellers and adventurers lie buried.

Although it is quite probably the oldest Christian cemetery in northern India, it has none of that overgrown, crumbling look that is common to old cemeteries in monsoon lands. It is a bright, even cheerful place, and the jingle of tonga-bells and other street noises can be heard from any part of the grounds. The grass is cut, the gravestones are kept clean, and most of the inscriptions are still readable.

The caretaker takes me straight to the oldest grave—this is the oldest known European grave in northern India—and it happens to be that of an Englishman, John Mildenhall. The lettering stands out clearly:

Here lies John Mildenhall, Englishman, who left London in 1599 and travelling to India through Persia, reached Agra in 1605 and spoke with the Emperor Akbar. On a second visit in 1614 he fell ill at Lahore, died at Ajmere, and was buried here through the good offices of Thomas Kerridge Merchant.

During the seventeenth and eighteenth centuries, the Agra cemetery was considered blessed ground by Christians, and the dead were brought here from distant places. Thomas Kerridge must have put himself to considerable expense to bury his friend in Agra.

Mildenhall was a romantic, who styled himself an envoy of Queen Elizabeth. Unfortunately he left no account of his travels, although a couple of his letters are quoted in the writings of Purchas, another English merchant, who lies buried in the Protestant cemetery a couple of furlongs away.

Nearby is the grave of the Venetian, Jerome Veronio, who died at Lahore. According to some old records, he had a hand in designing the Taj, modelling it on Humayun's tomb in Delhi. There had for long been a belief that this 'architect' of the Taj lay buried in the cemetery but no one knew where. Then in 1945, Father Hyacinth, Superior Regular of Agra, scraped the moss off a tombstone, revealing the simple epitaph: 'Here lies Jerome Veronio, who died at Lahore.'

Actually, there is no evidence that Veronio designed the Taj, and even if he had something to do with it, he was only one of a number of artists and architects who worked on its construction. The chief architect was Muhammed Sharif of Samarkand. Each drew a salary of one thousand rupees per month. Ismail Khan of Turkey was the dome-maker. A number of inlay workers, sculptors and masons were Hindus, including Manohar Singh of Lahore and Mohan Lai of Kanauj, both famous inlay-workers.

A man of more authentic accomplishments was the Italian lapidary, Horten Bronzoni, whose grave lies at a short distance from Veronio's. He died on 11 August 1677. According to Tavernier, it was Bronzoni who cut the Koh-i-noor diamond; and, says Tavernier, he cut the stone very badly.

Bronzoni is again mentioned as having manufactured a model ship of war for Aurangzeb, who had been annoyed by the depredations of Portuguese pirates and was anxious to create a navy. The ship was floated in a huge tank and manoeuvred by a number of European artillery-men. It made a ridiculous sight and convinced the Emperor that a navy was out of the question.

There are over eighty old Armenian graves in the cemetery, but the only one that interests me is the tomb of Shah Azar Khan, an expert in the art of moulding a heavy cannon. One of these, 'Zamzamah', earned a measure of immortality in Kipling's *Kim*. Who hold *Zam-Zammah*, that 'fire-breathing dragon', hold the Punjab; for the great green-bronze piece is always first of the conqueror's loot. The gun was 14.6 feet long, and is still at Lahore.

Other historic tombs lie scattered about the cemetery, but the most striking and curious of them is the grave of Colonel Jon Hessing, who died in 1803. It is a miniature Taj Mahal, built of red sandstone. Although small compared to a Mughal tomb, it is large for a Christian grave, and could easily accommodate a living family of moderate proportions. Hessing came to India from Holland, and was one of a colourful band of freelance soldiers (most of them deserters) who served in Sindhia's Maratha army. Hessing, we are told, was a good, benevolent man and a great soldier. The tomb was built by his wife Alice, who it must be supposed, felt as tenderly towards the Colonel as Shah Jahan felt towards his queen. She could not afford marble. Even so, her 'Taj' cost a lakh of rupees.

Outside, in the street, people move about with casual unconcern. Street-vendors occupy the pavement, unwilling that their rivals should take advantage of a brief absence. In the banyan tree, the sparrows and bulbuls are settling down for the night. A kite lies entangled in the upper branches.

On the Highway

Once or twice a year, in self-indulgent mood, I give myself a treat, if you can call it that: a seven-hour drive to Delhi from Mussoorie, in an old but sturdy Ambassador taxi. Winter is the best time for such a visit. The hot winds of summer are best avoided, for once you have descended from the hills, the road becomes dusty, and in places something of an obstacle race.

I have known this highway over the years and I have seen it change imperceptibly. There wasn't much traffic on it in the 1940s, apart from the familiar bullock carts stacked high with sugarcane. The carts are still used, although the wooden wheels have given way to heavy tyres, and the bullocks to buffaloes. Most of the cane is now carried in trucks, and these 'kings of the road' have made it difficult for others to drive smoothly by day or safely by night. The trucks and the sugarcane keep the economy going, so we shouldn't grumble too much. This is one of the wealthiest agricultural areas in the land— Shamli, in its heartland, has the highest per capita income in the country, according to my bank manager—and from field to factory, and factory to town, the truckers are the ones to do the job.

Shamli is not one of the places you normally pass through on the way to Delhi. Not unless you are the actor Tom Alter and your driver takes the wrong turning in the middle of the night.

Tom got into his favourite Mussoorie taxi, leaving town after dinner as he had to be in Delhi early next morning. The driver fortified himself with a couple of drinks while Tom, who doesn't drink, settled into the back seat for a nap. He woke up to find himself in Shamli instead of Roorkee; but they eventually returned to the main highway and, having completed half the journey, the driver felt the need for further refreshment and stopped at a wayside inn where he fell in with some of his buddies. Tom got out of the car to stretch his legs. He crossed the road and gazed out across the moonlit mustard fields. When he turned back to the taxi, he found it had vanished! The inebriated driver had returned to the wheel and, without glancing back to see if his passenger was still in the back seat, had driven on. An hour later, on reaching the outskirts of Meerut, the driver discovered that Tom was missing. Crestfallen, he was about to turn back in search of his lost passenger when Tom himself arrived, having hitched a ride on an early-morning milk van.

Although I have been up and down the Delhi road two or three times a year, for the last forty years, I have been fortunate in that I have experienced relatively few mishaps. And when my nature-loving bank manager, Vishal Ohri, decided to give me a treat some years ago by taking a shortcut from Hardwar through the Rajaji Sanctuary and out at the Mohand Pass, I did not demur, I'm the ideal front-seat passenger, as I cannot drive and simply put my faith in God and the travelling public in general. Vishal Ohri enjoys his driving, especially in rough conditions; unfortunately his ancient Fiat was in poor condition, and halfway through the Sanctuary, while we were crossing a boulder-strewn rao (a semi-dry riverbed) the door on my side fell off and I very nearly went with it. For the rest of the journey, I had an uninterrupted view of the wildlife in the sanctuary—two peahens, a startled porcupine and a herd of tame buffaloes.

~

Driving by night is not always so risible. Most accidents on the main highway road occur in the early hours when drivers fall asleep at the wheel: their vehicles overturn, or run into trees and ditches, or collide with other vehicles. Before dawn breaks, the road has taken its toll of several lives.

It was late Christmas Eve in the 1970s, when my thirty-year-old half-brother Harold set out from Dehra in his father's car, to try and get to Delhi in time for a party at the Anglo-Indian Club. Although he was a good driver, having taken part in car rallies and other tests of speed and endurance, he had become a heavy drinker and he was in no condition to undertake a long and arduous drive late at night. He was alone, and as he was killed instantly (or so it appeared), we never knew all the circumstances of the accident. Apparently his car had been caught and crushed between two trucks, which had speedily disappeared into the night.

What can one say about Harold? He was attractive to women, but they had a hard time looking after him. And he wrecked their lives in addition to his own.

Harold's interests and mine were very different, but we did not get in each other's way. He left me to my books and long walks; I left him to his motorcycles and dance parties. Our mother indulged him; his father left him to his own devices.

Our mother died a year or two before Harold's fatal accident, and so she was spared a lot of heartbreak—double heartbreak, because a few months later my second half-brother died in a motorcycle accident. He was the careful one, who seldom took risks, so I don't suppose there are any lessons to be learnt.

~

I haven't driven through Meerut for many years, because most cars now take the bypass. Back in the 1960s it would provide an escape from Delhi, and I would spend an occasional weekend there, staying with old Captain Saulez in the cantonment and attending the Meerut races. The Meerut races were always a shade superior to the Delhi races, as they were patronized by the Army. Captain Saulez, a legendary racehorse owner and trainer, was a familiar figure in Meerut, moving about in his little pony trap. His daughter had married a Swiss journalist, William Matheson, much disliked by the Captain. It was at William's invitation that I first went to stay at their bungalow in its sprawling grounds on Centre Road. The Captain paid no attention to me. This meant he approved of me, according to William; most other visitors weren't allowed in at the gate. On summer nights I slept out of doors, kept awake for long hours by a brainfever bird screaming at me from a gulmohur tree. There were many trees in the compound, as well as lots of open space for the horses to exercise.

Captain Saulez died many years ago, mourned by jockeys and racing people if not by his relatives. William and his wife left the country. I wonder if the house and grounds have gone too, swallowed up by the march of time and the pressures of population. It is unlikely that I will go that way again. It is good to remember the past, but to return to places associated with one's youth can often be disappointing. An old school friend of mine visited Saharanpur after fifty years, hoping to find the house where he had grown up. Instead he found a crowded bus stand. And in Delhi, the bungalow and garden where I spent a year or two of my childhood has vanished and in its place has risen a massive high-rise building, with hundreds of cars parked where sweet peas and roses once flourished.

> You may break, you may shatter the vase if you will,
> But the scent of the roses will linger there still.

Rishikesh

'*Ganga Mai ki jai!*' Everyone raised the cry as the Hardwar bus moved out of Meerut. Most of the passengers, including Kamal and I, were going to take darshan of Mother Ganga. But while many were bound for Hardwar, we were going to Rishikesh, a more secluded temple town, situated on the banks of the Ganga at the point where the river emerges from the mountains and, hemmed in no longer by rocks and trees, stretches itself across the plains of Uttar Pradesh and Bihar, flowing past great cities like Kanpur, Allahabad, Benares and Patna, and into Bengal.

Just next to us sat a well-built woman with three small children. The eldest, a boy of about six, took a fancy to Kamal, and was soon lolling about on his knees. In front of us, obliterating the view, sat a stout 'lala' and his devoted wife. Lalaji proved to be an impatient and ill-tempered man. He quarrelled with the conductor, the driver and the ticket seller. In order to travel in comfort he had reserved three front seats, but was unwilling to pay toll on the third seat which, he insisted, would only be occupied by his and his wife's feet. They gave in to him eventually. An urchin who inadvertently touched the sleeve of his kurta received a stinging slap. But he became more tolerant as time went on, and once, when engaged in an argument with a passenger at the other end of the bus, favoured me with a smile.

The countryside was monotonous up to Roorkee.

Then the road took us along the Ganga canal, and Kamal sat up and began to look at things. We changed buses at Hardwar, and got into a very old and wheezy contraption which surprised us by going much faster than the government roadways bus. Probably the driver was trying to make up for time lost in stopping every five minutes to pick up some acquaintance on the road. We stopped for ten minutes at the Sat Narain temple, once famous for the tiger that used to visit it every evening. Rattling through the Motichur forest block, we saw two elephants—tame ones, possibly—and a variety of monkeys.

We left the bus at Rishikesh and went in search of my friend Jhardari, with whom we were to stay. He lived at Muni-ki-Reti, two miles upstream, where the wealthier ashrams were situated. His rooms, adjoining Swami Sivananda's Ashram, were on the right-hand bank of the Ganga.

Jhardhari was away, on a routine trip to Devprayag. As Secretary of the Tehri-Garhwal Motor Mazdoor Sangh Workers' Union, he has to travel all over the district to keep in touch with the men who drive the trucks and buses on the dangerous hill roads. The buses are privately owned; the government only nationalizes those services that use first-class roads. The state is very cautious about taking over the responsibility of transporting people to remote hill towns like Tehri and Pipalkoti, where pilgrims on the way to Gangotri or Badrinath must start their journey on foot. The motor roads in the interior are narrow, precipitous and unmetalled. To mention this is not to condemn them. Till a few years ago many of these regions had no roads at all. And Garhwalis are excellent drivers—many have experience of Army trucks—and serious accidents are uncommon.

Jhardhari's roommate made us at home, and prepared hot, strong tea. Garhwalis drink more tea than Englishmen, and seldom take water. We were to become accustomed to drinking tea at almost hourly intervals.

One of the first things we did was to dip ourselves in the river. The water was icy cold, and it was impossible to stay in for more than ten minutes. Shivering, we climbed on to the bathing steps to dry ourselves. Our clothes felt hot against our bodies.

Down at the Rishikesh bathing ghat, hundreds of people would be dipping themselves in the sacred waters; but at Muni-ki-reti (which is in Tehri-Garhwal district, while the town of Rishikesh is in Dehradun district) there were only a few people by the river—a few pilgrims from Bengal, Andhra and Madras; disciples from Swami Sivananda's Ashram; and a number of boys who work in the area.

Logs were always floating downstream, and boys would get across them, lying flat on their stomachs and paddling the planks through the water. Two of the more daring youths paddled their logs right across the river, to the temples on the opposite bank. They were good swimmers, but had they been parted from their floats they would have been carried away by the current and quite possibly drowned.

We walked down to Rishikesh in the evening, and saw over a hundred sadhus emerging from an ashram where they were given their evening meal. In their saffron robes, they flooded the dusty road, talking animatedly amongst themselves. Many of them were young men, probably novices. One was a strapping youth of about twenty, a Hercules gracefully wearing the robe of renunciation.

They looked well fed and contented. Most of them spoke a little English. What had brought them to Rishikesh, I wondered, to live as recluses and ascetics? Personal tragedy, the stress of modern city life, or the failure of material pursuits… Or did the career of a religious mendicant hold out profitable prospects? Later on I was told that some of the novitiates should really have been in prison. But perhaps the rigours of their monastic existence rid them of early criminal tendencies; and if that was so, then surely ashrams were better places for them than jails.

Little shacks lined the river banks and though few people bathed late in the evening, hundreds were beside the water. Offerings of flowers in little leaf boats went sailing downstream. They were lighted by wicks dipped in oil, and went bobbing up and down on the water, sometimes for a considerable distance. Kamal sent an offering downstream, and requested Mother Ganga to grant him success as an artist. His boat, though, did not go very far.

Undeterred, Kamal fed little balls of flour to the fish. They were huge, completely tame, and came to the bank in shoals to be fed by the bathers. Sometimes they fought amongst themselves, and a few of them were a raw pink where they had been savagely bitten.

That night we slept in the open, on a wide ledge above the riverbed. The lights from the temples and ashrams on the opposite bank reflected gently on the water. There was a human quietness everywhere. The sounds were of the river—the distant roar of the rapids, the nearby lapping of water on the bathing steps.

We bathed again in the river, as the sun came up over the mountain known as Manikoot Parbat. There is an unbroken ridge along the top of this mountain, stretching all the way to the snows of Badrinath, some two hundred miles away. Only a few hermits live on the mountain. It belongs to the elephants who sometimes visit the river in herds, to bathe and drink.

Jhardhari had returned, looking quite fresh after a 150-mile bus journey; and he offered to take us up to Narindernagar, a little town on a hilltop, which, though smaller and less central than Tehri, is the capital of the district. The former Maharaja had preferred it to the less congenial valley town of Tehri on the banks of the Bhagirathi; and Narindernagar became the Maharaja's summer capital.

The buses were all full, and we had to travel up separately, one to each bus. First Kamal, then I, and last of all Jhardhari.

~

Narindernagar is only ten miles from Rishikesh, but it is also two thousand feet higher, and the bus has to climb a dizzy, winding road on which there can be no two-way traffic. But the buses go faster than their counterparts in the plains. With speedometers conveniently out of order, buses and trucks come downhill at a speed of thirty to thirty-five miles an hour. But, as I have said before, Garhwalis are very good drivers. Along the main highways of the Punjab are the wrecks of numerous trucks, some jammed up against trees, others in head-on collisions. But in the hills there is no driving at night, and the drivers prefer smoking bidis to drinking rum or country liquor. Mechanical failure is usually the cause of the few accidents that do occur.

From Narindernagar we went on for another eight miles, and eventually got down at Agra-khal, a pass in the mountains at a height of about 5,000 feet. The motor road, soon becoming kachcha, continues to Tehri and Dharasu, and from the latter, pilgrims must proceed on foot to the shrines and temples of Gangotri.

After eating some hot puris, we walked back to Narindernagar, leaving the main road, and hiking through a forest of oak and pine. Kamal, who was seeing real mountains for the first time, was very excited and asked me innumerable questions about plants and streams and trees and rocks. He chattered away until Jhardhari said something flattering about his many and varied interests, and this embarrassed Kamal so much that he stopped talking altogether. I enjoyed the shade of the gnarled, untidy oaks, and the soft, slippery carpet of pine needles.

But after the forest there was bare hillside, the sun was scorching hot, and we had soon emptied the water bottle. So we rejoined the main road and stopped a truck going down to Rishikesh.

It was the first time Kamal and I had sat in the back of a truck travelling at speed down a mountain. It was impossible to anchor oneself on the floor. A kindly sadhu, also at the back, placed his blanket on a tyre and invited us to share it with him; but at every hairpin bend the tyre slid violently about the floor and we were pitched off it. Kamal and I clung to each other to avoid being thrown against the sides of the truck; Jhardhari hung on to an iron bar; we were all feeling quite sick. Only the sadhu appeared unperturbed. He retained his seat on the tyre, even when it went skidding from one end of the truck to the other.

When we reached Rishikesh we went straight to the river. Never had Mother Ganga's waters been so refreshing. The giddiness disappeared. Then we lay down on the sand, and Kamal, like the sleepy giant Kumbhakarna in the *Ramayana*, did not come to life until it was time to eat.

We slept well that night. In the morning we would go to Lachhman Jhula and, passing the suspension bridge, walk a little way up Manikoot Parbat.

As the sun rose, turning the river to gold, we climbed into the boat that took pilgrims across to the temples on the other bank. The oarsmen sat in the prow, straining against the current, and the people in the boat raised the same ageless cry: '*Ganga Mai ki jai!*'

Climbing ashore, we passed through groves of mango trees, planted by rich pilgrims for the benefit of the sadhus. Then, leaving behind Lachhman Jhula, we walked along the pilgrim route to Badrinath until we came to a dharamshala called Garur Chatti. Here we drank tea, the inevitable but welcome tea, and set off up the hillside in search of a waterfall Jhardhari had told us about

It did not take us long to reach the waterfall. Set amidst rocks and ferns, it fell about thirty feet onto a platform of smooth yellow rocks and pebbles. Here it formed a small pool, about waist deep, into which we leapt without hesitation. The water wasn't as cold as the Ganga's, and we could splash about for as long as we liked, while the waterfall sprayed down on our heads. The water was very clear and fresh, though it had a slightly bitter taste, evidence, I suppose, of a strong mineral content.

Further down the stream we found a lot of old bones, which Kamal insisted were the remains of a tiger's kill; as, indeed, they might have been, tigers having been seen on the mountain. But no tiger troubled us; only a band of langurs, swinging from tree to tree, seemed resentful of our presence and urged us to leave.

This we did at our leisure and, after more tea at Garur Chatti, and a visit to a small temple, where the courtyard floor was so hot to our bare feet that we had to skip about in agony, we trudged back to Muni-ki-Reti.

It was our last night sleeping beside the Ganga, and we rested with our chins in our hands, watching the river move silently past us, surging onward, India's lifeblood, inexorable and irresistible.

Jaipur

As we still had a few days left of our holiday, and a little money, and as neither Kamal nor I was anxious to return to Delhi earlier than was necessary, we decided to sneak off to Jaipur for a day or two. We had both been to Jaipur before, but it is a city that one can visit again and again without ever tiring of its charm.

There is an atmosphere about Jaipur—once the most beautiful city in India, and one of the earliest planned cities in the world which even to the casual visitor distinguishes it from other towns. This is probably due to the almost entire absence of any European or Western influence in the architecture and planning of the town.

Founded in 1728 by the brilliant astronomer-king Maharaja Jai Singh II, it is quite unlike any other town in India or Asia: no tortuous gloomy streets or squalid overcrowded bazaars. Its six main streets are very wide and straight, one running the whole length of the town, the others crossing it at right angles, dividing the city into rectangular blocks. These are enclosed by a high wall, its parapets loopholed for musketry, into which are set seven entrance gates.

On the north-west side the hills rise sheer beyond the city, bearing on their summit the Nahargarh or Tiger Fort. Not needed now for purposes of war, it houses much of the wealth of this former state's ruler. Guarded not by troops but by men of the robber caste, this wealth lay hoarded for centuries, potential but never used capital, typical of the ways of the East.

In the city itself, narrow streets are found in plenty, for a network of them connects the wide main roads. So narrow are some, that the bougainvillea sprawls from the upper storey of one building to its opposite across the way. But curiously enough, they are nearly all straight, and a passing glimpse from the main street reveals their whole length. Sometimes these lanes are full of little shops, but many of them contain only private houses, where occasionally a half-open door reveals a glimpse of the grass and fountain of a garden or courtyard beyond.

The great attraction of the main streets is their spaciousness and the beautiful facade of the tall buildings which line them, most colour-washed in a dull, pale old-rose tone, some showing the soft amber or grey of the original limestone. In some of them the plain walls are varied with beautiful little chhattris, while here and there the old carved domes of some Jain temple break the flat line of roofs.

The street walls of these houses—which are really only the walls of the outer courtyard, the main building being behind and cut off from the street altogether—can boast of only the smallest windows, for these were meant to conceal, and not reveal, the zenana quarters behind. The quaint figures of elephants and other animals painted on the walls give them the appearance of dolls' houses when seen from the road below, though many of them are three or four storeys in height and from a distance look very imposing.

The streets themselves are a feast of colour and interest. Every mode of progression can be seen here, from ambling bullock carts and ekkas, with their quaintly shaped and brightly coloured hoods, to buses and streamlined motor cars. There are strings of camels bearing fodder, and elephants that amble up the road to the Amber Palace, and here and there wanders the ubiquitous Brahmani bull. All along the streets and around the squares throng hundreds of pigeons—sacred birds throughout Rajasthan—being fed by the passers-by or helping themselves to food on the stalls.

All along the ground floor of the buildings, and cut off from them by a small projecting tin roof along which the langurs run up and down in play, are the bazaar shops, little hives of industry doing a brisk trade. Busier still are the wide pavements in front; they are chock-a-block with stalls and with groups of artisans plying their trade in the midst of the passers-by.

We saw great piles of yellow maize and corn, of jawar and bajra, heaped upon the pavement, while to one side people were busy making the grain on primitive grindstones, laughing and singing as they ceaselessly wound the handle, three of them often working at one grinder. A little further on, what seemed at a distance to be a rich Herati rug flung down resolved itself into masses of chillies spread for yards along the pavement to dry in the sun. Then came the vegetables and fruit piled high in baskets, the countrywomen who had brought them squatting in the midst, sorting and selling and often nursing their babies at the same time.

Next came a little colony of brass workers sitting at the pavement's edge, engraving patterns on brass trays, plates and vessels, and then inlaying them with sticks of coloured enamel. Unlike them, the dyers generally work within their shops. In one of these we saw a whole family variously employed, from the old grandfather, who was mixing brilliant dyes in great brass cauldrons, to the latest infant, sitting in the middle and watching the others with an open mouth, while the family goat and attendant kid ambled in and out at will. Two of the family, a pugree-length of gaudy cloth just freshly dyed between them, walked up and down the pavement, waving it in the air to dry. The street had the appearance of being hung with bunting.

Most amusing of all, we came suddenly on three rows of little boys standing on the pavement with their slates at their feet. To one side stood the enterprising schoolmaster, while in front a small urchin with head craned forward loudly chanted the words of some lesson, which the class, in a medley of hoarse and squeaky voices, repeated after him. The intense concentration of this determined little group seemed in no way upset by the surrounding bustle and confusion.

There are few palaces in India to surpass the grandeur of the famous old palace of Amber. It lies north-west of the city, approached by a narrow pass in the hills which shuts off all view of Jaipur and opens on a little valley almost entirely closed by hills. Above a small lake, built on the barren hillside, stand the still perfect walls of this majestic fortress-palace. Their limestone blocks are mellowed to a soft amber colour, and the marble is now a rich cream.

The palace, now deserted except for its temple to the goddess Kali, is still in perfect condition. Its sun-soaked courtyards are open to the sky, and its empty pillared halls are full of echoes.

～ා

The Further One Goes

In the good old, bad old days, before the First World War, no one bothered about passports and immigration procedures. The hazards of travel were disincentives in themselves. But now that travel has become swift, comfortable and relatively painless, new obstacles arise in the form of travel documents, income-tax and health certificates, foreign exchange regulations, and other diabolical trappings of the twentieth century.

We need concern ourselves no longer about the reliability of camels or the safety of canoes, the seaworthiness of sailing-ships or the hazards of the stagecoach. But, there is the slight possibility of our plane being hijacked, or of crashing into the sea and saving our relatives the cost of a funeral. (Even so, one can have the satisfaction of plunging to one's doom strapped into a well-padded seat, with a glass of Scotch clutched in one's trembling hand, while someone makes an announcement that everything is under control. Our forefathers died the hard way.)

Travel, it used to be said, broadened the mind. I'm not certain that it ever did, but it certainly doesn't do so any more. Undoubtedly it broadens the bottom. Most of the time—in plane, airport lounge, all-night bar or luxury coach—one is sitting for long periods on one's fanny; and if you sit on anything for a long time it is liable to get broader. But I doubt if one learns much about the rest of the world from hotels and airports.

Modern travel is obviously designed for people in a hurry. One international airline acknowledges, in a glossy ad in a foreign magazine, that a business trip halfway around the world 'can be the most hectic part of your hectic life,' and undertakes to make it as relaxed and enjoyable as the hectic circumstances permit. In this crowded shrinking, hurrying world, even relaxation is something that has to be taken at the gallop.

There are no quiet corners left for quiet people; no undiscovered lands for explorers; no unmapped territories for adventurers; no lonely stretches of beach, no mysterious hidden rivers... Romance died with Lord Jim.

Still, if it's a hectically relaxed business trip that you want, then by all means travel. But if it's your mind that you intend broadening, you would do better to stay at home and tend your orchids or geraniums. Nero Wolfe, Rex Stout's great armchair detective, was convinced that, in nine cases out of ten, the places that people go to are no improvement upon the places that they come from.

Lao Tzu, who lived in the sixth century B.C., was even more succinct. 'The further one goes,' he said, 'the less one knows.'

~

The Road to Anjani Sain

Fog, mist, cloud, rain and mildew—these were the things the British must have looked for when selecting suitable sites for the hill stations they set up in the Himalayan foothills 150 years ago: Simla, Mussoorie, Darjeeling, Dalhousie, Nainital, all soggy with monsoon or winter mist and dripping oaks and deodars. The climate must have reminded them of their homes on the English moors or the Scottish highlands.

I have survived all that some thirty mountain monsoons have thrown at me; and having gone through the annual ritual of wiping the mildew from my books and a certain green fungus from my one and only suit, I decided to leave cloud country behind for a few days and be the guest of Cyril Raphael, at the Bhuvneshwari Mahila Ashram (a social service organization), at Anjani Sain in Tehri Garhwal.

Pine country this, dry and bracing, with the scent of pine resin in the air. I have always thought 5,000 to 6,000 feet a healthier altitude to live at, but perhaps I'm prejudiced, having been born in Kasauli, which is pine rather than deodar country. Anjani Sain is about the same height and gets the sun all day. Given adequate food and pure water, it's a healthy place to live. Contrary to what most people think, Garhwal is not a poverty-stricken area. Almost everyone has a bit of land and does at least have the traditional do-roti for sustenance, which is more than can be said for the urban unemployed in other parts of northern India. But medical facilities are certainly lacking.

This area has always been known as Khas-patti, probably because it was special in several ways—climate-wise and probably economy-wise too. Down in the flat valley, there are green fields and even mango trees, the descent to lower altitudes being quite sudden in these parts. The small Anjani Sain bazaar, with its single bank, post office and chemist's shop, shimmers in the noonday sun; it looks like a set for the gunfight at the OK Corral. But this is, generally, a peaceful area.

At the ashram, I am in time for an early lunch—thick rotis made from mandwa (millet)—two of these are more than enough for me! Endless glasses of milky tea will see me through till supper time.

Towering over Anjani Sain, and blessing all who live or pass beneath, is the Chanderbadni temple, dedicated to one of the incarnations of the goddess Parvati. As this is not one of the main pilgrim routes, the temple does not get as many visitors as some of the other sacred shrines in the hills. Below the Chanderbadni peak is a rest house, for those who wish to break their journey here.

Anjani Sain lies midway between Tehri and Devprayag—a two-hour bus ride from either place. I came via Tehri, the road climbing steeply above the hot, dusty town that is destined to be submerged by the waters of the Tehri dam. The dam should have been ready by now, but having been the subject of a great deal of controversy, work on it has progressed in fits and starts.

I am told that this entire region is 'eco-fragile', one of those words bandied around at seminars all over the world. Well, I am not an expert in these matters (and who is, I wonder?) but I should think most of our earth is 'eco-fragile', having had to put up with hundreds of thousands of years of human civilization.

Do we stop all development in the name of preserving the environment? Or do we move on regardless? Proceed with caution would be the rational person's answer. But are human beings really rational?

Old Tehri was no beauty spot, and New Tehri (growing rapidly above it) is even uglier; from a distance it looks like a gaint cemetery. When the architecture of suburban Delhi is brought to the hills, what is there to say? You just look the other way.

Fortunately the defaced mountain is soon left behind, and as it slips out of sight and we ascend into the pine regions, the eye is soothed by the pretty, slate-covered houses of the villages and their little gardens ablaze with marigolds and yellow and bronze chrysanthemums. Chrysanthemums love this climate. Down in the fields there are patches of crimson cholai (amaranth) interspersed with the fresh green of young wheat.

And here be leopards! My companion tells me of one that strolls down the motor road every evening, forcing the local bus to go around him. His presence also accounts for the absence of stray dogs.

Suddenly in the distance I see what at first glance appears to be a cloud or a large white sailing ship. On approaching, it turns out to be the freshly whitewashed buildings of the Bhuvneshwari Mahila Ashram, clinging to the steep slopes of the mountain.

Here, for two or three days, I find rest and sustenance. The manifold activities of the ashram (directed mainly towards the welfare of widows and small children) are there for all to see, and I recall the relief work undertaken by its young fieldworkers after the Uttarkashi earthquake last year—they had rushed to the area before the government agencies could swing into action.

However, as a social worker I am somewhat inept. I am just a frazzled old writer who never made it to the bestseller lists and who now seeks a refuge from the all-pervasive clutter of tourism that makes ordinary life almost impossible in our hill stations.

I hope the land-grabbers and the real estate 'developers' never get this far. They are welcome to their malls and artificial lakes and concrete parks. Just so long as I am free to escape from it all, to sit here at Anjani Sain contemplating a large white rose in Cyril's garden, while the rest of the world watches videos.

~

A Village in Garhwal

I wake to what sounds like the din of a factory buzzer, but is in fact the music of a single vociferous cicada in the lime tree near my window.

Through the open window, I focus on a pattern of small, glossy lime leaves; then through them I see the mountains, the Himalayas, striding away into an immensity of sky.

'In a thousand ages of the gods I could not tell thee of the glories of Himachal.' So confessed a Sanskrit poet at the dawn of Indian history and he came closer than anyone else to capturing the spell of the Himalayas. The sea has had Conrad and Stevenson and Masefield, but the mountains continue to defy the written word. We have climbed their highest peaks and crossed their most difficult passes, but still they keep their secrets and their reserve; they remain remote, mysterious, spirit-haunted.

No wonder, then, that the people who live on the mountain slopes in the mist-filled valleys of Garhwal have long since learned humility, patience and a quiet resignation. Deep in the crouching mist lie their villages, while climbing the mountain slopes are forests of rhododendron, spruce and deodar, soughing in the wind from the ice-bound passes. Pale women plough, they laugh at the thunder as their men go down to the plains for work; for little grows on the beautiful mountains in the north wind.

When I think of Manjari village in Garhwal I see a small river, a tributary of the Ganga, rushing along the bottom of a steep, rocky valley. On the banks of the river and on the terraced hills above, there are small fields of corn, barley, mustard, potatoes and onions. A few fruit trees grow near the village. Some hillsides are rugged and bare, just masses of quartz or granite. On hills exposed to wind, only grass and small shrubs are able to obtain a foothold.

This landscape is typical of Garhwal, one of India's most northerly regions with its massive snow ranges bordering on Tibet. Although thinly populated, it does not provide much of a living for its people. Most Garhwali cultivators are poor, some are very poor. 'You have beautiful scenery,' I observed after crossing the first range of hills.

'Yes,' said my friend, 'but we cannot eat the scenery.'

And yet these are cheerful people, sturdy and with wonderful powers of endurance. Somehow they manage to wrest a precarious living from the unhelpful, calcinated soil. I am their guest for a few days.

My friend Gajadhar has brought me to his home, to his village above the little Nayar River. We took a train into the foothills and then we took a bus and finally, made dizzy by the hairpin bends devised in the last century by a brilliantly diabolical road-engineer, we alighted at the small hill station of Lansdowne, chief recruiting centre for the Garhwal Regiment.

Lansdowne is just over 6,000 feet high. From there we walked, covering 25 miles between sunrise and sunset, until we came to Manjari village, clinging to the terraced slopes of a very proud, very permanent mountain.

This is my fourth morning in the village. Other mornings I was woken by the throaty chuckles of the red-billed blue magpies, as they glided between oak trees and medlars; but today the cicada has drowned all birdsong. It is a little out of season for cicadas but perhaps this sudden warm spell in late September has deceived him into thinking it is mating season again.

Early though it is I am the last to get up. Gajadhar is exercising in the courtyard, going through an odd combination of Swedish exercises and yoga. He has a fine physique with the sturdy legs that most Garhwalis possess. I am sure he will realize his ambition of joining the Indian army as a cadet. His younger brother Chakradhar, who is slim and fair with high cheekbones, is milking the family's buffalo. Normally, he would be on his long walk to school, five miles distant; but this is a holiday, so he can stay at home and help with the household chores.

His mother is lighting a fire. She is a handsome woman, even though her ears, weighed down by heavy silver earrings, have lost their natural shape. Garhwali women usually invest their savings in silver ornaments. And at the time of marriage it is the boy's parents who make a gift of land to the parents of an attractive girl; a dowry system in reverse. There are fewer women than men in the hills and their good looks and sturdy physique give them considerable status among the menfolk.

Chakradhar's father is a corporal in the Indian army and is away for most of the year. When Gajadhar marries, his wife will stay in the village to help his mother and younger brother look after the fields, house, goats and buffalo. Gajadhar will see her only when he comes home on leave. He prefers it that way; he does not think a simple hill-girl should be exposed to the sophisticated temptations of the plains.

The village is far above the river and most of the fields depend on rainfall. But water must be fetched for cooking, washing and drinking. And so, after a breakfast of hot sweet milk and thick chapattis stuffed with minced radish, the brothers and I set off down the rough track to the river.

The sun has climbed the mountains but it has yet to reach the narrow valley. We bathe in the river. Gajadhar and Chakradhar dive off a massive rock; but I wade in circumspectly, unfamiliar with the river's depths and currents. The water, a milky blue, has come from the melting snows; it is very cold. I bathe quickly and then dash for a strip of sand where a little sunshine has spilt down the mountainside in warm, golden pools of light.

A little later, buckets filled, we toil up the steep mountain. We must go by a better path this time if we are not to come tumbling down with our buckets of water. As we climb we are mocked by a barbet which sits high up in a spruce calling feverishly in its monotonous mournful way.

The path leads us past a primary school, a small temple and a single shop in which it is possible to buy salt, soap and a few other necessities. It is also the post office. And today it is serving as a lock-up.

The villagers have apprehended a local thief, who specializes in stealing jewellery from women while they are working in the fields. He is awaiting escort to the Lansdowne police station, and the shop-keeper-cum-postmaster-cum-constable brings him out for us to inspect. He is a mild-looking fellow, clearly shy of the small crowd that has gathered round him. I wonder how he manages to deprive the strong hill-women of their jewellery; it could not be by force! In any case crimes of violence are rare in Garhwal; and robbery too, is uncommon, for the simple reason that there is very little to rob.

The thief is rather glad of my presence, as it distracts attention from him. Strangers seldom come to Manjari. The crowd leaves him, runs to me, eager to catch a glimpse of the stranger in its midst. The children exclaim, point at me with delight, chatter among themselves. I might be a visitor from another planet instead of just an itinerant writer from the plains.

The postman has yet to arrive. The mail is brought in relays from Lansdowne. The Manjari postman who has to cover eight miles and delivers letters at several small villages on his route, should arrive around noon. He also serves as a newspaper, bringing the villagers news of the outside world. Over the years he has acquired a reputation for being highly inventive, sometimes creating his own news; so much so that when he told the villagers that men had landed on the moon, no one believed him. There are still a few sceptics.

Gajadhar has been walking out of the village every day, anxious to meet the postman. He is expecting a letter giving the results of his army entrance examination. If he is successful he will be called for an interview. And then, if he is accepted, he will be trained as an officer-cadet. After two years he will become a second lieutenant. His father, after twelve years in the army, is still only a corporal. But his father never went to school. There were no schools in the hills during the father's youth.

The Manjari school is only up to Class 5 and it has about forty pupils. If these children (most of them boys) want to study any further, then, like Chakradhar, they must walk the five miles to the high school at the next big village.

'Don't you get tired walking ten miles every day?' I ask Chakradhar.

'I am used to it,' he says. 'I like walking.'

I know that he only has two meals a day—one at seven in the morning when he leaves home and the other at six or seven in the evening when he returns from school—and I ask him if he does not get hungry on the way.

'There is always the wild fruit,' he replies.

It appears that he is an expert on wild fruit: the purple berries of the thorny bilberry bushes ripening in May and June; wild strawberries like drops of blood on the dark green monsoon grass; small sour cherries and tough medlars in the winter months. Chakradhar's strong teeth and probing tongue extract whatever tang or sweetness lies hidden in them. And in March there are the rhododendron flowers. His mother makes them into jam. But Chakradhar likes them as they are: he places the petals on his tongue and chews till the sweet juice trickles down his throat.

He has never been ill.

'But what happens when someone is ill?' I ask, knowing that in Manjari there are no medicines, no dispensary or hospital.

'He goes to bed until he is better,' says Gajadhar. 'We have a few home remedies. But if someone is very sick, we carry the person to the hospital at Lansdowne.' He pauses as though wondering how much he should say, then shrugs and says: 'Last year my uncle was very ill. He had a terrible pain in his stomach. For two days he cried out with the pain. So we made a litter and started out for Lansdowne. We had already carried him fifteen miles when he died. And then we had to carry him back again.'

Some of the villages have dispensaries managed by compounders but the remoter areas of Garhwal are completely without medical aid. To the outsider, life in the Garhwal hills may seem idyllic and the people simple. But the Garhwali is far from being simple and his life is one long struggle, especially if he happens to be living in a high-altitude village snowbound for four months in the year, with cultivation coming to a standstill and people having to manage with the food gathered and stored during the summer months.

Fortunately, the clear mountain air and the simple diet keep the Garhwalis free from most diseases, and help them recover from the more common ailments. The greatest dangers come from unexpected disasters, such as an accident with an axe or scythe, or an attack by a wild animal. A few years back, several Manjari children and old women were killed by a man-eating leopard. That leopard was finally killed by the villagers who hunted it down with spears and axes. But the leopard that now sometimes prowls round the village at night looking for a stray dog or goat slinks away at the approach of a human.

For Gajadhar, impatient to know the result of his army entrance examination, the following day is a trial of his patience.

First, we hear that there has been a landslide and that the postman cannot reach us. Then, we hear that although there has been a landslide, the postman has already passed the spot in safety. Another alarming rumour has it that the postman disappeared with the landslide. This is soon denied. The postman is safe. It was only the mailbag that disappeared.

And then, at two in the afternoon, the postman turns up. He tells us that there was indeed a landslide but that it took place on someone else's route. Apparently, a mischievous urchin who passed him on the way was responsible for all the rumours. But we suspect the postman of having something to do with them…

Gajadhar has passed his examination and will leave with me in the morning. We have to be up early in order to reach Lansdowne before dark. But Gajadhar's mother insists on celebrating her son's success by feasting her friends and neighbours. There is a partridge (a present from a neighbour who had decided that Gajadhar will make a fine husband for his daughter), and two chickens: rich fare for folk whose normal diet consists mostly of lentils, potatoes and onions.

After dinner, there are songs, and Gajadhar's mother sings of the homesickness of those who are separated from their loved ones and their home in the hills. It is an old Garhwali folk song:

Oh, mountain-swift, you are from my father's home;
Speak, oh speak, in the courtyard of my parents,
My mother will hear you; she will send my brother to fetch me.
A grain of rice alone in the cooking pot cries,
'I wish I could get out!'
Likewise I wonder: 'Will I ever reach my father's house?'

The hookah is passed round and stories are told. Tales of ghosts and demons mingle with legends of ancient kings and heroes. It is almost midnight by the time the last guest has gone. Chakradhar approaches me as I am about to retire for the night.

'Will you come again?' he asks.

'Yes, I'll come again,' I reply. 'If not next year, then the year after. How many years are left before you finish school?'

'Four.'

'Four years. If you walk ten miles a day for four years, how many miles will that make?'

'Four thousand and six hundred miles,' says Chakradhar after a moment's thought, 'but we have two months' holiday each year. That means I'll walk about 12,000 miles in four years.'

The moon has not yet risen. Lanterns swing in the dark.

The lanterns flit silently over the hillside and go out one by one. This Garhwali day, which is just like any other day in the hills, slips quietly into the silence of the mountains.

I stretch myself out on my cot. Outside the small window the sky is brilliant with stars. As I close my eyes, someone brushes against the lime tree, bruising its leaves; and the fresh fragrance of limes comes to me on the night air, making the moment memorable for all time.

India:
People and Places

At Home in India

There are many among us who, given the opportunity to leave India, are only too happy to go. But whenever I have had the chance to go away, I have held back. Or something has held me back.

What is it that has such a hold on me, but leaves others free to go where they will, sometimes never to come back?

A few years ago I was offered a well-paid job on a magazine in Hong Kong. I thought about it for weeks, worried myself to distraction, and finally, with a great sigh of relief, turned it down.

My friends thought I was crazy. They still do. Most of them would have jumped at a comparable offer, even if it had meant spending the rest of their lives far from the palm-fringed coasts or pine-clad mountains of this land. Many friends have indeed gone away, never to return, except perhaps to get married, very quickly, before they are off again! Don't they feel homesick, I wonder.

I am almost paranoid at the thought of going away and then being unable to come back. This almost happened to me when, as a boy, I went to England, longed to return to India, and did not have the money for the passage. For two years I worked and slaved like a miser (something I have never done since) until I had enough to bring me home.

And 'home' wasn't parents and brothers and sisters. They were no longer here. Home, for me, was India.

So what is it that keeps me here? My birth? I take too closely after a Nordic grandparent to pass for a typical son of the soil. Hotel receptionists often ask me for my passport.

'Must I carry a passport to travel in my own country?' I ask.

'But you don't look like an Indian,' they protest.

'I'm a Red Indian,' I say.

India is where I was born and went to school and grew to manhood. India was where my father was born and went to school and worked and died. India is where my grandfather lived and died. Surely that entitles me to a place in the Indian sun? If it doesn't, I can revert to my mother's family and go back to the time of Timur the Lame. How far back does one have to go in order to establish one's Indianness?

It must be the land itself that holds me. But so many of my fellow Indians have been born (and reborn) here, and yet they think nothing of leaving the land. They will leave the mountains for the plains; the villages for the cities; their country for another country; and if other countries were a little more willing to open their doors, we would have no population problem—mass emigration would have solved it.

But it's more than the land that holds me. For India is more than a land. India is an atmosphere. Over thousands of years, the races and religions of the world have mingled here and produced that unique, indefinable phenomenon, the Indian: so terrifying in a crowd, so beautiful in himself.

And oddly enough, I'm one too. I know that I'm as Indian as the postman or the paanwala or your favourite MP.

Race did not make me an Indian. Religion did not make me an Indian. But history did. And in the long run, it's history that counts.

~

Blossoms in the Dust

Sometimes young readers ask me, 'How old were you at the time of Independence, and what do you remember of it?' And then I realize that I am now classified as an 'old-timer', a relic from the days of the Raj, one of a dwindling number of people who witnessed some of the momentous events of 1947.

Well, you would have to be about eighty plus to have any clear memories of August '47, and the months and years leading up to it. I was thirteen at the time, tucked away in a boarding school in Simla, and I remember the day when we were all marched up to town to witness the Indian flag being raised for the first time. Simla was still the summer capital of India, so it was quite an event.

Of course, it was raining, as you would expect in the middle of the monsoon, and we were in our raincoats and gum-boots, while a sea of umbrellas covered the mall. What did I feel, as I saw the Union

Jack being lowered and the Indian tricolours replacing it? I had lost my father three years previously. He had been an officer in the Royal Air Force. He had, of course, been aware of the coming of Indian Independence, for he had been born and raised in the country; but he seldom spoke about it, except to say that we would be going away once the war (meaning World War II) was over.

I was still a small boy and I don't think I had strong feelings about the issue, one way or the other. I remember being more interested in the colours and design of the Indian flag than in the speeches that were being made from the rostrum. Two years later, as a school prefect, it become my duty to raise the Indian flag on the school flat. It seemed quite natural to be doing so. I was also a member of the N.C.C., the National Cadet Corps. Whatever happened to it, I wonder. Or is it still a part of school life?

At school, geography was my favourite subject and I liked poring over maps. As a result of two World Wars, maps kept changing. And in 1947 the map of India changed too, and quite dramatically. No one seemed quite prepared for Partition and its aftermath. Suddenly, after decades of endeavour, Independence had arrived. The War had changed everything. The British were in a hurry to leave; our leaders (or most of them) were in a hurry to take over. Lines were drawn across maps, and the Punjab and Bengal were torn asunder— divided according to religion—and entire populations were faced with the prospect of being uprooted and being resettled far from their ancestral homes. Violence spread over northern India, and almost everywhere, in small towns, large cities, villages, mobs went on the rampage, killing indiscriminately and burning the properties of rural communities. There were not enough soldiers, Indian or British, to handle the situation.

About one-third of the boys in my school came from Lahore and Peshawar, now in Pakistan, and they had to be evacuated. Overnight, they were whisked away in Army trucks, two of my best friends among them; no time to say goodbye. All got home safely. Not so the servants who accompanied them; they strayed from the party and were killed in the bazaars of Kalka.

Back in my home town of Dehradun there was considerable carnage. Old residents talk nostalgically of the canal that ran down the East Canal Road. My mother, who was then living just behind the

Karanpur police station, told me of how the little canal was choked with the bodies of riot victims. My stepfather, a Hindu gentleman, helped Muslim friends to escape by driving them to the border in his old Ford convertible. There were humanitarians on both sides.

Even violence wears itself out. In December I came home to Dehra for my winter holidays. It was a peaceful, sleepy little town again. I went to the pictures twice a week, walking home after dark, across the lonely Parade Ground; no one bothered me. Late January, I had just settled down to see a film called *Blossoms in the Dust*—they had begun showing the credits—when the manager stopped the show and informed us that news had just come in that Mahatma Gandhi had been shot.

It was some time before the country recovered from all these catastrophes, but recover it did. The 1950s were a relatively tranquil period, with an educated middle class gradually growing in numbers and prosperity. After I had finished school, my mother packed me off to the UK. But four years later I came back on my own steam, determined to see if I could find my own place under the Indian sun.

Someone took me to see a new city coming up. A wilderness near Kalka where not a tree could be seen for miles. But some strange-looking edifices were coming up. It was the beginning of Chandigarh.

A few years later, when I came again, there were trees and parks and gardens—a green city! And people were thriving in it.

I had seen history happening. And geography too. And I am lucky enough to see it still happening.

~

Children of India

They pass me every day on their way to school—boys and girls from the surrounding villages and the outskirts of the hill station. There are no school buses plying for these children: they walk.

For many of them, it's a very long walk to school.

Ranbir, who is ten, has to climb the mountain from his village, four miles distant and 2,000 feet below the town level. He comes in all weathers, wearing the same pair of cheap shoes until they have almost fallen apart.

Ranbir is a cheerful soul. He waves to me whenever he sees me at my window. Sometimes he brings me cucumbers from his father's field. I pay him for the cucumbers; he uses the money for books or for small things needed at home.

Many of the children are like Ranbir: poor, but slightly better off than their parents were at the same age. They cannot attend the expensive residential and private schools that abound here, but must go to the government-aided schools with only basic facilities. Not many of their parents managed to go to school. They spent their lives working in the fields or delivering milk in the hill station. The lucky ones got into the army. Perhaps Ranbir will do something different when he grows up.

He has yet to see a train but he sees planes flying over the mountains almost every day.

'How far can a plane go?' he asks.

'All over the world,' I tell him. 'Thousands of miles in a day. You can go almost anywhere.'

'I'll go round the world one day,' he vows. 'I'll buy a plane and go everywhere!'

And maybe he will. He has a determined chin and a defiant look in his eye.

The following lines in my journal were put down for my own inspiration or encouragement, but they will do for any determined young person:

> *We get out of life what we bring to it. There is not a dream which may not come true if we have the energy which determines our own fate. We can always get what we want if we will it intensely enough. So few people succeed greatly because so few people conceive a great end, working towards it without giving up. We all know that the man who works steadily for money gets rich; the man who works day and night for fame or power reaches his goal. And those who work for deeper, more spiritual achievements will find them too. It may come when we no longer have any use for it, but if we have been willing it long enough, it will come!*

Up to a few years ago, very few girls in the hills or in the villages of India went to school. They helped in the home until they were old enough to be married, which wasn't very old. But there are now just as many girls as there are boys going to school.

Bindra is something of an extrovert—a confident fourteen-year-old who chatters away as she hurries down the road with her companions. Her father is a forest guard and knows me quite well. I meet him on my walks through the deodar woods behind Landour. And I had grown used to seeing Bindra almost every day. When she did not put in an appearance for a week, I asked, her brother if anything was wrong.

'Oh, nothing', he says, 'she is helping my mother cut grass. Soon the monsoon will end and the grass will dry up. So we cut it now and store it for the cows in winter.'

'And why aren't you cutting grass too?'

'Oh, I have a cricket match today,' he says, and hurries away to join his teammates. Unlike his sister, he puts pleasure before work!

Cricket, once the game of the elite, has become the game of the masses. On any holiday, in any part of this vast country, groups of boys can be seen making their way to the nearest field or open patch of land, with bat, ball and any other cricketing gear that they can cobble together. Watching some of them play, I am amazed at the quality of talent, at the finesse with which they bat or bowl. Some of the local teams are as good, if not better, than any from the private schools, where there are better facilities. But the boys from these poor or lower-middle-class families will never get the exposure that is necessary to bring them to the attention of those who select state or national teams. They will never get near enough to the men of influence and power. They must continue to play for the love of the game, or watch their more fortunate heroes' exploits on television.

~

As winter approaches and the days grow shorter, those children who live far away must quicken their pace in order to get home before dark. Ranbir and his friends find that darkness has fallen before they are halfway home.

'What is the time, uncle?' he asks, as he trudges up the steep road past Ivy Cottage.

One gets used to being called uncle by almost every boy or girl one meets. I wonder how the custom began. Perhaps it has its origins in the folktale about the tiger who refrained from pouncing on you if you called him uncle. Tigers don't eat their relatives! Or do they?—

the ploy may not work if the tiger happens to be a tigress. Would you call her aunty as she (or your teacher!) descends on you?

Its dark at six and Ranbir likes to be out of the deodar forest and on the open road to the village by then. The moon and the stars and the village lights are sufficient, but not in the forest, where it is dark even during the day. And the silent flitting of bats and flying foxes and the eerie hoot of an owl, can be a little disconcerting for the hardiest of children. Once Ranbir and the other boys were chased by a bear.

When he told me about it, I said, 'Well, now we know you can run faster than a bear!'

'Yes, but you have to run downhill when chased by a bear,' He spoke as one having long experience of escaping from bears. 'They run much faster uphill!'

'I'll remember that,' I said, 'thanks for the advice.' And I don't suppose calling a bear 'uncle' would help.

Usually Ranbir has the company of other boys, and they sing most of the way, for loud singing by small boys will silence owls and frighten away the forest demons. One of them plays a flute, and flute music in the mountains is always enchanting.

~

Not only in the hills, but all over India, children are constantly making their way to and from school, in conditions that range from dust storms in the Rajasthan desert to blizzards in Ladakh and Kashmir.

In the larger towns and cities, there are school buses, but in remote rural areas, getting to school can pose a problem. Most children are more than equal to any obstacles that may arise. Like the youngsters in the Ganjam district of Orissa. In the absence of a bridge, they swim or wade across the Dhanei river every day in order to reach their school. I have a picture of them in my scrapbook. Holding books or satchels aloft in one hand, they do the breast stroke or dog paddle with the other; or form a chain and help each other across.

Wherever you go in India, you will find children helping out with the family's source of livelihood, whether it be drying fish on the Malabar coast, or gathering saffron buds in Kashmir **or** grazing camels or cattle in a village in Rajasthan or Gujarat.

Only the more fortunate can afford to send their children to English-medium private or public schools, and those children really are fortunate, for some of these institutions are excellent schools, as good, and often better, than their counterparts in Britain or the USA. Whether it's in Ajmer or Bangalore, New Delhi or Chandigarh, Kanpur or Kolkata, the best schools set very high standards. The growth of a prosperous middle class has led to an ever-increasing demand for quality education. But as private schools proliferate, standards suffer, too, and many parents must settle for the second-rate.

The great majority of our children still attend schools run by the state or municipality. These vary from the good to the bad to the ugly, depending on how they are run and where they are situated. A classroom without windows, or with a roof that lets in the monsoon rain, is not uncommon. Even so, children from different communities learn to live and grow together. Hardship makes brothers of us all.

The census tells us that two in every five of the population is in the age group of five to fifteen. Almost half our population is on the way to school!

And here I stand at my window, watching some of them pass by—boys and girls, big and small, some scruffy, some smart, some mischievous, some serious, but all going somewhere—hopefully towards a better future.

~

Ghosts of a Peepul Tree

The villages of India have always harboured a large variety of ghosts, some of them good, some evil. There are the prets and bhuts, both the spirits of dead men; and the churels, ghosts of women who change their shape after death. Then there is the pisach, a sort of hobgoblin; and the munjia, a mischievous and sometimes sinister evil spirit. They have one thing in common; nearly all of them choose to live in the peepul tree.

There is not much difference between the bhut and the pret: the latter is simply a better class of ghost, less inclined to indulge in malicious activities. It is usually the spirit of one who has loved the earth so much that he cannot bear to take final leave of it. The pret lives either in its former home or in a peepul tree, and is sometimes honoured with the title of Purwaj Dev, an ancestor god. Prets often take the form of snakes, living in the garden, where they are fed with milk and honoured by the household.

There is a story of a villager who was in the habit of beating his son unceasingly. One day the villager visited a garden where a Purwaj Dev in the form of a snake was living. The snake threatened to bite and kill the villager unless he promised to give his son better treatment. The villager went away a chastened man. The lady of the house was very fond of the snake and gave it milk every day; and in return for this favour the snake would often guard her baby and rock its cradle.

~

A ghost which in the past was often responsible for the desertion of a house or even of a village was the churel.

A churel is full of animosity towards men, probably because in life she was unfairly treated by them. She is covered with hair, has the ears of an ape, and her toes are two or three feet in length. Sometimes her feet face backwards. During the day the churel has no power, but at night she lies along the branches of a peepul tree, directly over a footpath. Should any man pass beneath the tree, the churel's prehensile toes stretch out, grip the man by the neck and throttle him.

The pisach can be a malignant, sometimes amorous ghost. It has no body or shape, but dwells in a peepul tree or a graveyard. In the *Vetal Panchvishi* there is the story of a young wife who, while her husband is in another town, falls in love with a young man. On her husband's return, the wife would have nothing to do with him; as soon as he was asleep, she ran to join her lover near the house of her maidservant. But the lover, who had arrived first, was bitten by a cobra, and died before the woman arrived. A pisach (who had seen everything from a nearby peepul tree) now entered the dead man's body and began to play the lover to the errant wife. After some time, out of sheer wickedness, the pisach bit off the woman's nose, left the corpse and went back to the peepul tree.

The unfortunate lady, now without a nose, ran home screaming that her husband had bitten it off. The husband was arrested and his execution ordered; but a stranger suggested that a search might be made at the maidservant's cottage. There they found the lover's body on the bed, and between his teeth was the wife's nose. Finally the husband was acquitted and the wife placed on a donkey and driven out of the city.

~

The Mahrattas used to be familiar with an evil spirit known as a munjia.

A munjia is said to be the disembodied spirit of a Brahmin youth who has died before his marriage. Like other spirits, it lives in a peepul tree, often rushing out at tongas, bullock carts and bicycles, and upsetting them. (No instance has as yet been recorded of its trying collisions with a bus.) When passing a peepul tree at night, should anyone be so careless as to yawn without snapping his fingers in front of his mouth, a munjia will dash down his throat and completely ruin him. It is quite possible that people suffering from indigestion have made the mistake of yawning under a peepul tree.

It is not surprising that in villages, after dark, everyone, even the blind, is supposed to carry a lamp. And if you ask the blind man what use a lamp is to him, he will reply: 'Fool, the lamp is not for my benefit, but for yours, lest you stumble against me in the dark.'

Great Spirits of the Trees

Explore the history and mythology of almost any Indian tree, and you will find that at some period of our civilization it has held an important place in the minds and hearts of the people of this land.

During the rains, when the neem pods are crushed underfoot, they give out a strong refreshing aroma which lingers in the air for days. This is because the neem gives out more oxygen than most trees. When the ancient herbalists held that the neem was a great purifier of the air, and that its leaves, bark and sap had medicinal qualities, they were quite right, for the neem is still used in medicine today.

From the earliest times it was connected with the gods who protect us from disease. Some castes regarded the tree as sacred to Sitala, the smallpox goddess. When children fell ill, a branch of the neem was waved over them. The tree is said to have sprung from the nectar of the gods, and people still chew the leaves as a means of purification, both spiritual and physical.

The tree is also connected with the sun, as in the story of neem-barak, 'The Sun in the Neem Tree'. The Sun God invited to dinner a man of the Bairagi tribe whose rules forbade him to eat except by daylight. Dinner was late, and as darkness fell, the Bairagi feared he would have to go hungry. But Suraj Narayan, the Sun God, descended from a neem tree and continued shining till dinner was over.

Why have so many trees been held sacred, not only in India but the world over?

To early man they were objects of awe and wonder. The mystery of their growth, the movement of their leaves and branches, the way they seemed to die and then come to life again in spring, the sudden growth of the plant from the seed, all these happenings appeared as miracles—as indeed they are! And because of the wonderful growth of a tree, people began to suppose that it was occupied by spirits, and devotion to a tree became devotion to the spirit or tree god who occupied it.

In *Puck of Pook's Hill*, Kipling wove some wonderful stories, around Puck, the tree spirit, and the sacred trees of Old England— oak, ash and thorn: 'I came into England with Oak, Ash and Thorn, and when Oak, Ash and Thorn are gone, I shall go too.' Among the Gonds of central India, before a man cut a tree he had to beg its pardon for the injury he was about to inflict on it. He would not shake a tree at night because the tree spirit was asleep and might be disturbed. When a tree had to be felled, the Gonds would pour ghee on the stump, saying: 'Grow thou out of this, O Lord of the Forest, grow into a hundred shoots! May we grow with a thousand shoots.'

The beautiful mahua is a forest tree held sacred by a number of tribes. Early on the wedding morning, before he goes to fetch his bride, the Bagdi bridegroom goes through a mock marriage with a mahua tree. He embraces it and daubs it with vermilion, his right wrist is bound to it with thread, and after he is released from the tree the thread is used to attach a bunch of mahua leaves to his wrist.

There is a beautiful tradition connected with the sal tree. It is said that at the time of the Buddha's birth, his mother stretched out her hand to take hold of a branch of the sal and was delivered. Sal trees are also said to have rendered homage to the Buddha at his death, letting fall on him their flowers out of season, and bending their branches to shade him.

Special respect is paid to trees growing near the graves of Muslim saints. Near the tomb of a famous saint, Musa Sohag, at Ahmedabad, there used to be a large old champa tree—perhaps it is still there—the branches of which were hung with glass bangles. Those anxious to have children came and offered bangles to the saint—the number of bangles depending on the means of the supplicant. If the saint favoured a wish, the champa tree snatched up the bangles and wore them on its arms.

Another spectacular tree which has its place in our folklore is the dhak, or palasa, which gave its name to the battlefield of Plassey. It has the habit of dropping its leaves when it flowers, the upper and outer branches standing out in sprays of scarlet and orange. The flowers are sometimes used to dye the powder scattered at Holi, and the wood, said to contain the seed of fire, is used in lighting the Holi bonfire. Legend tells us that the Sun God aimed an arrow at the earth, and that it took root and became the palasa tree.

The babul (or keekar) is not very impressive to look at but it will grow almost anywhere in the plains, and there are a number of old beliefs associated with it. For instance, you can cure fever and headache at a babul tree if you tie seven cotton threads from your left big toe to your head, and from your head to a branch of the tree. Then you must embrace the trunk seven times. Try it sometime. You will be so busy tying threads that you will forget you ever had a headache! And there are no after-effects.

Another belief concerning the babul is that if you water it regularly for thirteen days, you acquire control over the spirit who occupies it. There is a story about a man at Saharanpur who did this, and when he died and his corpse was taken away for cremation, no sooner was his pyre lit than he got up and walked away!

In the folklore of India, the mango is the 'wish-fulfilling tree.' When you want to make a wish on a mango tree, shut your eyes and get someone to lead you to the tree; then rub mango blossoms in your hands, and make your wish. The favour granted lasts only for a year, and the charm must be performed again at the next flowering of the tree. In the spring, the young leaves and buds symbolize the darts of Manmatha, or Kamadeva, God of Love.

Whole forests have been held sacred, such as that in Berar which was dedicated to a particular temple; no one dared to buy or cut the trees. The sacred groves near Mathura, where Lord Krishna sported as a youth, were also protected for centuries. But now, alas, even the hallowed groves are disappearing, making way for the demands of an ever-increasing population. A pity, because every human needs a tree of his own. Even if you do not worship the tree spirit, you can love the tree.

~

People of the Snows

Stories of the Abominable Snowman, or Yeti, are common enough. Fully-equipped expeditions have gone out in search of this creature, while so-called Yeti scalps have been taken abroad for scientific examination, and famous personalities have clashed over the question of whether the Snowman is myth or reality.

All this fuss about a Snowman would seem to have obscured the fact that there is also an Abominable Snow-woman, as well known to the Nepalese (who call her the Lidini) as the Yeti is to the Tibetans.

The Lidini, like the Yeti, is said to be heavy and long-haired. She differs in that her feet are turned in the usual direction and not inward like the Yeti's. She has been known to attack on sight, and one can only escape from her by running downhill, because the Lidinis progress is slowed down by her huge body, and the long hair that covers her eyes. This should be remembered by anyone setting out in search of the Snow-woman. If you meet her, and try running uphill, she will soon overtake you (she is very fast going uphill), and then you will be at the mercy of her long nails and sharp teeth.

The husband of the Lidini, known as the Banjakhiri, is said to be gifted with supernatural powers. Waking at dawn, he leaves his forest lair for a large cave in the mountains which he has converted into a shrine. Unlike his wife, he does not attack human beings with intent to kill, but is said to entirely ignore grown-ups, preferring to capture children, whom he hides in his long hair. He takes the children to his cave-shrine, where he looks after them very carefully, feeding them on fruit, rice and earthworms. (The earthworms may be thrown over the shoulder when the Banjakhiri isn't looking!)

The Banjakhiri has a great school where he teaches children Black Magic. So careful is he in choosing his disciples that only children of the highest intelligence are captured by him. When the youngsters are fully versed in magic, they are taken back to where they were captured, and then sent out into the world to practice their magic on all evil-doers.

There is another couple said to live in the forests of the higher Himalayas: the Sagpa and Sagpani.

In appearance they resemble the Banjakhiri and Lidini, but they are much smaller. They, too, attack on sight (though their feet are turned inwards); but beyond the desire to capture living creatures and eat them, their greatest ambition is to sleep as much as possible. You are therefore quite safe if you allow them to sleep undisturbed; but if you wake them, they become very ferocious and do not give you much time in which to start running uphill or downhill. But as a rule the Sagpanis avoid human habitation, and are only to be found in the very heart of the great oak and rhododendron forests.

Then there are the Kasundas—wild, curly-headed creatures, usually seen at great heights well above the snowline. Nobody has got close to a Kasunda. There is a story that many years ago some Mongol soldiers caught one in Tibet. Finding it to be of an imitative disposition, a soldier gave it a tin containing kerosene oil, while he himself filled a similar tin with water. The soldier poured the water over his own head, and the Kasunda immediately imitated his action, pouring the oil over itself. The soldier then took a box of matches, and giving a match to the Kasunda, lit one himself and pretended to set fire to his clothes. The Kasunda immediately did the same, set his curly hair on fire, and went up in smoke.

Since then, the Kasundas have kept well away from human beings. And who can blame them?

The Lady of Sardhana

The bus that took us to Sardhana was prehistoric. I do believe it was kept from falling apart by a liberal use of sellotape. The noise and rattle made by its nuts and bolts and shaky chassis reminded me of

Kipling's story 'The Ship that Found Herself'. Every part seemed alive and complaining. The bus conductor found the crank handle under somebody's seat, and, panting and sweating in the sun, kept turning it until, reluctantly, the engine spluttered into life. The bus moved of its own volition, and the conductor just had time to get on and collect our tickets. Most of the passengers were rural folk, descendants of those Jats and Rohillas who made this fertile Doab region (the Doab is the area between the Ganges and the Jumna) one of the richest granaries of India, only to have it plundered by marauding Marathas, Sikhs and Afghans. They smoked bidis or chewed paan, shooting the coloured spittle out of the open windows; and, seeing my watch, asked me the time every few minutes.

The Sardhana bus stop, when we got to it, was the usual unexciting swamp of churned-up mud, with a tea stall, and several stray dogs and pigs nosing about in a garbage heap. We hailed a cycle rickshaw and told the man to take us to the church.

The Sardhana church was built at the expense of Begum Samru by an Italian architect. Upon her husband's death she had become a devout Catholic, and earned from the Pope the title of 'Joanna Nobilis'. The Emperor at Delhi, grateful to her for services rendered in the battlefield, gave her another title: Zeb-un-Nissa, the 'Ornament of Her Sex'. Her life, until she reached old age, was a succession of love affairs, intrigue and petty warfare. It was never a dull life. She had certain admirable qualities which made her attractive to men. As a young girl, she was beautiful; in middle age, rather plump. She was a courageous woman, and rode into battle at the head of her troops, something which few women have done before or since. But we must begin at the beginning, and in the beginning was Sombre, alias Samru, alias Walter Reinhardt...

Sombre's real name was Walter Reinhardt, but due to a dusky complexion he acquired the name of Sombre, which in Hindustani was soon corrupted to Samru. He was perhaps the most notorious of foreign adventurers, and this notoriety was acquired when he was in the service of the Nawab of Bengal, Kassim Ali, who, warring with the English, had attacked and captured a large number of English residents at Patna and ordered them to be executed.

None of Kassim's own native officers came forward to undertake this, but Sombre, wishing to ingratiate himself with his new employer, agreed to carry out the execution. Details of the murders are given in the Annual Register:

'Somers invited about forty officers and other gentlemen, who were amongst these unfortunate prisoners, to sup with him on the day he had fixed for the execution, and when his guests were in full security, protected as they imagined by the laws of hospitality, as well as by the right of prisoners, he ordered the Indians under his command to fall upon them and cut their throats. Even these barbarous soldiers revolted at the orders of this savage European. They refused to obey, and desired that arms should be given to the English, and that they would then engage them. Somers, fixed in his villainy, compelled them with blows and threats to the accomplishment of that odious service. The unfortunate victims, though thus suddenly attacked and wholly unarmed, made a long and brave defence, and with their plates and bottles even killed some of their assailants, but in the end they were all slaughtered... Proceeding then, with a file of sepoys, to the prison where a number of prisoners then remained, he directed the massacre, and with his own hands assisted in the inhuman slaughter of 148 defenceless Europeans confined within its walls—an appalling act of atrocity that has stamped his name with infamy for ever.'

Sombre left Kassim Ali's service before an avenging British army could catch up with him, and by the end of his subsequent career he had served twelve to fourteen masters. He finally tendered his services to Shah Alam, the Emperor of Delhi, who agreed to pay him 65,000 rupees for his services and those of his two battalions. He remained in the service of the Delhi Court and was assigned a rich jagir, or estate, at Sardhana, a district forty miles north of the capital, where he built and fortified his headquarters and settled down. He had adopted native dress, and the custom of keeping a harem.

At Sardhana he fell in love with a very beautiful woman. One historian asserts that she was the daughter of a decadent Moghul nobleman, another that she was a Kashmiri dancing girl, and a third that she was a lineal descendant of the Prophet. In due course she became Sombre's Begum. He died at Agra on the fourth of May 1778, aged fifty-eight years; infamous, unloved even by his own followers, but successful to the end.

After his death the command of his troops, their pay and the jagir of Sardhana became the property of his Begum, who, on being baptized and received into the Roman Catholic faith, was christened 'Joanna Nobilis'. By means of rare ability and force of character, she proved equal to her responsibilities; but she was unfortunate in her officers. Only the most dissolute had cared to join Sombre, and their conduct often incited the troops to mutiny. She gave the command to a German named Pauly 'perhaps because he was a countryman of her husband, but, it has been suggested, for more tender reasons'; Pauly was murdered 'by a bloody process' in 1783; and those who succeeded him did not remain long in command.

It was at this time that George Thomas, the Irish freelance, rose to a position of some importance in the army of Begum Samru.

When the Begum saw Thomas, it did not take her long to decide to give him a command. He had the pleasing, honeyed speech of the Irishman; he was tall, handsome, virile; far more attractive physically than most of the Europeans in her service. How could the Begum resist him? For months he would remain her most trusted officer, her lover, and then, seeking some other novelty, she would transfer her affections to another, only appealing to Thomas for help in time of distress.

This arrangement suited Thomas. He was willing to make love to the Begum without making the mistake of falling in love with her. He used her as she used him; but he never betrayed her, as she was often to betray him.

Several years after Thomas had left her service and had established himself at Panipat and Karnal, Begum Samru, faced with a mutiny, appealed to him for help. She must have known Thomas's character well, for she had only recently raided his territory; any other person would have shown retaliation instead of succour; but when beauty was in distress Thomas always forsook his own interests to become the gallant knight-errant.

The Begum was now forty-five, inclined to plumpness, but her skin was still very smooth and fair, and her eyes 'black, large and animated'. The trouble at Sardhana had arisen from her having taken a new husband, a Frenchman named Le Vassoult.

Le Vassoult was no friend of Thomas's and had in fact proposed marriage to the Begum earlier, in order to gain an advantage over the Irishman who was then in her service. He was well educated and from an aristocratic family, but aloof by nature and unpopular with his men. A free and easy roisterer like Thomas got more from his troops than the conventional disciplinarian. Both officers and troops resented the fact that Le Vassoult, after his marriage to the Begum, refused to eat with them or treat them as equals; they planned on deposing the Begum and transferring their allegiance to Balthazar Sombre, a debauched son of Sombre by his first wife. This first wife was still alive, and when she died in 1838 she must have been over a hundred years old. (The Sardhana cemetery contains the remains of many centenarians.)

Another officer named Legois, a friend of George Thomas, had tried to dissuade the Begum from raiding Thomas's territory in Hariana, and for this had been badly treated by Le Vassoult. The troops, who had served Legois for a long time, and obviously liked him, broke into mutiny, and the Begum and her husband had no alternative but to try and reach Anupshahr, then the last outpost of British territory in northern India.

The troops had sent for Balthazar Sombre from Delhi. Le Vassoult and the Begum slipped away, but were soon pursued and overtaken. The lovers had agreed that rather than fall into the hands of the mutineers they would first kill themselves. While Le Vassoult, an unimaginative man of honour, was quite serious about this pact, the Begum treated it lightly. On being surrounded, she drew a dagger and made a half-hearted attempt at stabbing herself; but all she did was nick her breast and bespatter her blouse with blood. Le Vassoult was more thorough. On hearing that the Begum was bleeding to death, he drew his pistol, put the muzzle to his mouth, and pulled the trigger.

'The ball passed through his brain, and he sprang from the saddle a full foot in the air, before he fell dead to the ground. His corpse was subjected to every indignity and insult that the gross and bestial imagination of his officers and men could conceive, and left to rot, unburied, on the ground.'

However, the Begum did not get off too lightly. She was taken back to Sardhana and chained between two guns, occasionally being placed astride one of them at midday, when it was nearly red hot. The only food she received was smuggled to her by her maidservants. This was the Begum's plight when Thomas, by forced marches, reached Sardhana and quelled the mutiny.

The command of the Begum's force was now given to Colonel Saleur (the only European who could write) and he and the others signed or affixed their seals to a document in which they swore allegiance to their mistress. This was drawn up by a Mohammedan scribe in Persian, and as his religion prevented him from acknowledging Christ as God, the document was superscribed: 'In the name of God, and of His Majesty Christ!'

In 1803, after the British had defeated the Marathas, and established themselves in Hindustan (then the name for most of northern India) the Begum submitted to General Lake near Agra. James Skinner, the famous Eurasian adventurer, left a description of her meeting with the General: 'When the Begum came in person to pay her respects to General Lake, an incident occurred of a curious and characteristic description. She arrived at headquarters just after dinner, and being carried in her palanquin at once to the reception tent, the General came out to meet and receive her. As the adhesion of every petty chieftain was, in those days, of consequence, Lord Lake was not a little pleased at the early demonstration of the Begum's loyalty, and being a little elevated by the wine which had just been drunk, he forgot the novel circumstance of its being a native female, instead of some well-bearded chief, so he gallantly advanced, and, to the utter dismay of her attendants, took her in his arms and kissed her. The mistake might have been awkward, but the lady's presence of mind put all right. Receiving courteously the proffered attention, she turned calmly around to her astonished attendants and observed, "It is the salute of a priest to his daughter."'

When the Begum accepted British protection, her income increased, and she disbanded most of her troops. Bishop Heber saw her in 1825 and described her as a 'very queer-looking old woman, with brilliant but wicked eyes, and the remains of beauty in her features'.

She became very rich and philanthropic. She sent the Pope at Rome 150,000 rupees, and the Archbishop of Canterbury 50,000 rupees. She built a church at Meerut—less pretentious but more handsome than the one at Sardhana—where the Roman Catholic bishop was an Italian named Julius Caesar. At Meerut she often entertained Governors-General and Commanders-in-Chief, and when she died in 1836, at the age of ninety, she left behind a fortune of £700,000 and an immense army of pensioners.

The Sardhana church hasn't changed much over the years. The dome is nobly proportioned, but the twin spires on either side somehow spoil the effect. They are not spires actually, but pyramidal structures that serve no purpose, aesthetic or practical. The interior of the church is handsome, and has several new additions; but the centre of interest are the eleven life-size statues and three panels in bas-relief. This marble monument is the work of an Italian sculptor, Adamo Tadolini of Bologna. The Begum in her rich dress is seated on a chair of state holding in her right hand a folded scroll, the Emperor's firman conferring on her the jagir of Sardhana. On her right stands Dyce Sombre, her stepson, and on her left Dewan Rae Singh, her minister. Immediately behind are Bishop Julius Caesar and Innayat Uliah, her commandant of cavalry.

Of the three panels one represents an incident in the consecration of the church when she presented rich vestments to the Bishop (these are still in existence). The other panel shows the Begum holding a durbar, surrounded by European officers; and the third shows the Begum mounted on an elephant in triumphant procession.

We felt like intruders, our footsteps resounding in the silent church, and we did not stay long. There was nothing else to see except the Begum's palace, now a school, and a few old houses and graves. The spirit of the Begum's time has left Sardhana, and it is just another district town, hot and dusty and malarious. It is difficult to believe that there was drama here once, intrigue, battle and romance. The place is a backwater, cut off somehow from the mainstream of life. A few nuns pass through the church cloisters, and a bullock cart trundles along the road. The fields are waterlogged.

We went away before sunset, afraid that if we stayed too long we might meet the ghost of a queer-looking old woman with brilliant and wicked eyes, lurking in the mango grove near the church.

Kipling's Simla

Every March, when the rhododendrons stain the slopes crimson with their blooms, a sturdy little steam engine goes huffing and puffing through the 103 tunnels between Kalka and Simla.

This is probably the most picturesque and romantic way of approaching the hill station, although the journey by road is much quicker. But quite recently I went to Simla by a little-used route, the road from Dehradun via Nahan and Solan. It takes one first through the subtropical Siwaliks, and then after Nahan into the foothills and some beautiful and extensive pine forests, before joining the main highway near Solan. By bus it is a tedious ten-hour journey, but by car it is a picturesque ride, and there is very little traffic to contend with.

But those train journeys stand out in memory—the little restaurant at Barog, just before the train reaches Dharampur, where the roads for Sanawar and Kasauli branch off; and the gorge at Tara Devi, opening out to give the weary traveller the splendid and uplifting panorama of the city of Simla straddling the side of the mountain.

~

In Rudyard Kipling's time (that is, in the 1870s and '80s), travellers spent the night at Kalka and then covered the sixty-odd hill miles by tonga, a rugged and exhausting journey. It was especially hard on invalids who had travelled long distances to recuperate in the cool clear air of the mountains.

In his story 'The Other Man' (*Plain Tales from the Hills*), Kipling describes the unhappy results of the tonga ride on one such visitor:

'Sitting on the back seat, very square and firm, with one hand on the awning stanchion and the wet pouring off his hat and moustache, was the Other Man—dead. The sixty-mile uphill jolt had been too much for his valve, I suppose. The tonga driver said, "This Sahib died two stages out of Solan. Therefore, I tied him with a rope, lest he should fall out by the way, and so we came to Simla. Will the Sahib give me *bakshish*? It," pointing to the Other Man, "should have given one rupee."'

Today's visitor to Simla need have no qualms about the journey by road, which is swift and painless (provided you drive carefully), but the coolies at the Simla bus stand will be found to be as, adamant as Kipling's tonga driver in claiming their bakshish.

Simla is worth a visit at any time of the year, even during the monsoon. The monsoon season is one of the most beautiful times of the year in the Himalayas, with the mist trailing up the valleys, and the hill slopes a lush green, thick with ferns and wild flowers. The call of the kastura, or whistling thrush, can be heard in every glen, while the barbet cries insistently from the treetops.

Not far from Christ Church is the corner where a great fictional character, Lurgan Sahib, had his shop—Lurgan being the curio dealer who took the young Kim in hand and trained him as a spy. He was based on a real-life character, who had his shop here. Kipling wrote *Kim* a few years after he had left India. His nostalgia for India, and in particular for the hills, come through in his description of Kim's arrival in Simla in the company of the Afghan horse-dealer, Mahbub Ali.

> "'A fair land—a most beautiful land is this of Hind—and the land of the Five Rivers is fairer than all,' Kim half-chanted. "Into it I will go again... Once gone, who shall find me? Look, Hajji, is yonder the city of Simla? Allah! What a city!'"

They led their horses below the main road into the lower Simla bazaar—'the crowded rabbit warren that climbs up from the valley to the Town Hall at an angle of forty-five!' And then together they set off 'through the mysterious dusk, full of the noises of a city below the hillside and the breath of a cool wind in deodar-crowned Jakko, shouldering the stars.'

Shouldering the stars! That is how I always think of Simla—standing on the Ridge and looking up through the clear air into the vault of the heavens, where the stars seem so much nearer... And they are reflected below, in the myriad lights of the shops and houses.

For those who want a bit of history, Simla came into being at the end of the Anglo-Gurkha War (1814-16), when most of the surrounding district—captured by the Gurkhas during their invasion—was restored to various states; but the land on which Simla stands was retained by the British—'for services rendered'! Lieutenant Rose built the first house, a thatched wooden cottage, in 1819. His successor, Lieutenant Kennedy, in 1822 built a permanent house, which survived until it was destroyed in a fire in the 1970s. In 1827 Lord Amherst spent several months at Kennedy House and from then on Simla grew in favour with the British. Its early history can be read in more detail in Sir Edward Buck's *Simla Past and Present,* copies of which sometimes turn up in second-hand bookshops.

From 1865 until World War II, Simla was the summer capital of the Government of India. Later it served as the capital of East Punjab pending the construction of Chandigarh, and today of course it is the capital of Himachal Pradesh.

It is not, however, as a capital city that Simla attracts the visitor but as a place of lovely winding walks, magnificent views, and romantic links with the past. Compared with some of our other hill stations, it is well looked after; the streets are clean and uncluttered, the old Georgian-style buildings still stand. And the trees are more in evidence than at other hill resorts.

Simla has a special place in my affections. It was there that I went to school, and it was there that my father and I spent our happiest times together.

We stayed on Elysium Hill; took long walks to Kasumpti and around Jakko Hill; sipped milkshakes at Davico's; saw plays at the Gaiety Theatre (happily still in existence); fed the monkeys at the temple on Jakko; picnicked in Chhota Simla. All this during the short summer break when my father (on leave from the Air Force) came up to see me. He told me stories of phantom rickshaws and enchanted forests and planted in me the seeds of my writing career. I was only ten when he died. But he had already passed on to me his love for the hills. And even after I had finished school and grown to manhood, I was to return to the hills again and again—to Simla and Mussoorie, Himachal and Garhwal—because once the mountains are in your blood, there is no escape.

~

Simla beckons. I must return. And, like Kim, I will take the last bend near Summer Hill and look up and exclaim: 'Ah! What a city!'

'Romance brought up the nine-fifteen,' wrote Kipling and there is still romance to be found on trains and at lonely stations. Small wayside stations have always fascinated me. Manned sometimes by just one or two men, and often situated in the middle of a damp subtropical forest, or clinging to the mountainside on the way to Simla or Darjeeling, these little stations are, for me, outposts of romance, lonely symbols of the spirit that led a certain kind of pioneer to lay tracks into the remote corners of the earth.

Recently I was at such a wayside stop, on a line that went through the Terai forests near the foothills of the Himalayas. At about ten at night, the khilasi, or station watchman, lit his kerosene lamp and started walking up the track into the jungle. He was a Gujar, and his true vocation was the keeping of buffaloes, but the breaking up of his tribe had led him into this strange new occupation.

'Where are you going?' I asked.

'To see if the tunnel is clear,' he said. 'The Mail train comes in twenty minutes.'

So I went with him, a furlong or two along the tracks, through a deep cutting which led to the tunnel. Every night, the khilasi walked though the dark tunnel, and then stood outside to wave his lamp to the oncoming train as a signal that the track was clear. If the engine driver did not see the lamp, he stopped the train. It always slowed down near the cutting. Having inspected the tunnel, we stood outside, waiting for the train. It seemed a long time coming. There was no moon, and the dense forest seemed to be trying to crowd us into the narrow cutting. The sounds of the forest came to us on the night wind—the belling of a sambar, the cry of a fox, told us that perhaps a tiger or a leopard was on the prowl. There were strange nocturnal bird and insect sounds; and then silence.

The khilasi stood outside the tunnel, trimming his lamp, listening to the faint sounds of the jungle—sounds which only he, a Gujar who had grown up on the fringe of the forest, could identify and understand. Something made him stand very still for a few moments, peering into the darkness, and I could sense that everything was not as it should be.

'There is something in the tunnel,' he said.

I could hear nothing at first; but then there came a regular sawing sound, just like the sound of someone sawing through the branch of a tree.

'Baghera!' whispered the khilasi. He had said enough to enable me to recognize the sound—that of a leopard trying to find its mate.

I thought how fortunate we were that it had not been there when we walked through the tunnel. A leopard is unpredictable. But so is a khilasi.

'The train will be coming soon,' he whispered urgently, 'we must drive the animal out of the tunnel, or it will be killed.'

He must have sensed my astonishment, because he said, 'Do not worry, sahib. I know this leopard well. We have seen each other many times. He has a weakness for stray dogs and goats, but he will not harm us.'

He gave me his small hand axe to hold, and, raising his lamp high, started walking into the tunnel, shouting at the top of his voice to try and scare away the animal. I followed close behind him.

We had gone about twenty yards into the tunnel when the light from the khilasi's lamp fell on the leopard, who was crouching between the tracks, only about fifteen feet from us.

He was not a big leopard, but he was lithe and sinewy. Baring his teeth in a snarl, he went down on his belly, tail twitching, and I felt sure he was going to spring.

The khilasi and I both shouted together. Our voices rang and echoed through the tunnel. And the frightened leopard, uncertain of how many human beings were in there with him, turned swiftly and disappeared into the darkness.

As we returned to the tunnel entrance, the rails began to hum and we knew the train was coming.

I put my hand to one of the rails and felt its tremor. And then the engine came round the bend, hissing at us, scattering sparks into the darkness, defying the jungle as it roared through the steep sides of the cutting. It charged straight at the tunnel and into it, thundering past us like some beautiful dragon from my childhood dreams. And when it had gone the silence returned, and the forest breathed again. Only the rails still trembled with the passing of the train.

As they tremble now to the passing of my own train, rushing through the night with its complement of precious humans, while somewhere at a lonely cutting in the foothills, a small thin man, who must always remain a firefly to these travelling thousands, lights up the darkness for steam engines and panthers.

And yet, for the khilasi himself, the incident I have recalled was not an adventure; it was a duty, a job of work, an everyday incident.

For me, all are significant: the lighted compartment with its farmers, shopkeepers, artisans, clerks and occasional pickpockets; and the lonely wayside stop, with its uncorrupted lamplighter.

Romance still rides the nine-fifteen.

To See a Tiger

Mr Kishore drove me out to the forest rest house in his jeep, told me he'd be back in two days, and left me in the jungle. The caretaker of the rest house, a retired Indian Army corporal, made me a cup of tea.

'You have come to see the animals, sir?'

'Yes,' I said, looking around the clearing in front of the house, where a few domestic fowls scrabbled in the dust. 'Will I have to go far?'

'This is the best place, sir,' said the caretaker. 'See, the river is just below.'

A stream of clear mountain water ran through a shady glade of sal and shisham trees about fifty yards from the house.

'The animals come at night,' said the caretaker. 'You can sit in the verandah, with a cup of tea, and watch them. You must be very quiet, of course.'

'Will I see a tiger?' I asked. 'I've come to see a tiger.'

'Perhaps the tiger will come, sir,' said the caretaker with a tolerant smile. 'He will do his best, I am sure.'

He made me a simple lunch of rice and lentils, flavoured with a mango pickle. I spent the afternoon with a book taken from the rest house bookshelf. The small library hadn't been touched for over twenty years, and I had to make my choice from Marie Corelli, P.C. Wren, and early Wodehouse. I plumped for a Wodehouse—*Love Among the Chickens*. A peacock flaunted its tail feathers on the lawn, but I was not distracted. I had seen plenty of peacocks.

When it grew dark, I took up my position in the verandah, on an old cane chair. Bhag Singh, the caretaker, brought me dinner on a brass thali with two different vegetables in separate katoris. The chapatis came in relays, brought hot from the kitchen by Bhag Singh's ten-year-old son. Then, sustained by more tea, sweet and milky, I began my vigil. It took an hour for Bhag Singh's family to settle down for the night in their outhouse. Their pi-dog stood outside, barking at me for half an hour, before he too fell asleep. The moon came up over the foothills, and the stream could be seen quite clearly.

And then a strange sound filled the night air. Not the roar of a tiger, nor the sawing of a leopard, but a rising crescendo of noise— *wurk, wurk, wurk*—issuing from the muddy banks near the stream.

All the frogs in the jungle seemed to have gathered there that night. They must have been having a sort of an old boys' reunion, because everyone seemed to have something to say for himself. The speeches continued for about an hour. Then the meeting broke up, and silence returned to the forest.

A jackal slunk across the clearing. A puff of wind brushed through the trees. I was almost asleep when a cicada burst into violent music in a nearby tree. I started, and stared out at the silver, moon-green stream; but no animals came to drink that night.

~

The next evening Bhag Singh offered to sit up with me. He placed a charcoal burner on the verandah, and topped it with a large basin of tea.

'Whenever you feel sleepy, sir, I'll give you a glass of tea.'

Did we hear a panther—or was it someone sawing wood? The sounds are similar, in the distance. The frogs started up again. The old boys must have brought their wives along this time, because instead of speeches there was general conversation, exactly like the natter of a cocktail party.

By morning I had drunk over fifteen cups of tea. Out of respect for my grandfather, a pioneer tea planter in India, I did not complain. Bhag Singh made me an English breakfast—toast, fried eggs and more tea.

The third night passed in much the same way, except that Bhag Singh's son stayed up with us and drank his quota of tea.

In the morning, Mr Kishore came for me in his jeep. 'Did you see anything?'

'A jackal,' I said.

'Never mind, you'll have better luck next time. Of course, the jungles aren't what they used to be...'

I said goodbye to Bhag Singh, and got into the jeep.

We had gone barely a hundred yards along the forest road when Mr Kishore brought the jeep to a sudden, jolting halt.

Right in the middle of the road, about thirty yards in front of us, stood a magnificent full-grown tiger.

The tiger didn't roar. He didn't even snarl. But he gave us what appeared to be a quick, disdainful glance, and then walked majestically across the road and into the jungle.

'What luck!' exclaimed Mr Kishore. 'You can't complain now, can you? You've seen your tiger!'

'Yes,' I said, 'three sleepless nights, and I've seen it—in broad daylight!'

'Never mind,' said Mr Kishore. 'If you're tired, I know just the thing for you—a nice cup of tea!'

I think it was Malcolm Muggeridge who said that the only real Englishmen left in the world were to be found in India.

The Last Days of the Tonga

Tongas, along with tramcars, haircuts and the Indian rhinoceros, will soon be extinct. In many towns where, ten years ago, there were two or three hundred tongas on the roads, there are now some twenty or thirty. Buses, taxis, above all the ubiquitous scooter-rickshaws, are slowly but surely putting the pony-drawn carriage out of business and out of existence.

This is nowhere more apparent than in Delhi. During World War II, when I was a small boy, the Delhi tonga was the accepted mode of conveyance for high-ranking officers and officials, and for their wives and families. My father and I thought nothing of taking a tonga from Humayun Road to Connaught Place in order to visit a cinema or the famous Davicos restaurant. There was no bus service then, cars were few, the scooter had not been invented, and the only public transport, the tramcar (now obsolete) plied exclusively in Chandni Chowk and environs. In today's Delhi, no one of any standing would think of taking a tonga; it would be *infra dig*. And if a foreign tourist should find a tonga-ride exhilarating, we look on him with the tolerant amusement reserved for eccentrics.

This is all very sad for those who, like this writer, grew up in a tonga-driven world.

When I was very small, I travelled some thirty miles from Dehradun to Hardwar in a tonga. There were a few cars about in those days but a tonga was considered just as good, almost as fast, and certainly more dependable when it came to crossing the Song River—a small tributary of the Ganga.

During the rains, when the river flowed strong and deep, it was impossible to get across except by a hand-operated ropeway (which is still in use in some areas); but during the dry months, when the river was a small stream, the tonga-pony went splashing through, carriage wheels churning through the clear mountain water. If the pony found the going difficult, we removed our shoes, rolled up our trousers and waded across, while the driver led his pony by the muzzle.

Long before my time, in fact before the turn of the century, when the 'Scinde, Punjab and Delhi Railway' went no further than Saharanpur, the only way of getting to Dehra was by the night-mail, better known as the dak-ghari.

Dak-ghari ponies were difficult animals, always attempting to turn around and get into the carriage with the passengers. It was only when the coachman used his whip liberally, and reviled the ponies' ancestors as far back as their third and fourth generations, that the beasts could be persuaded to move. And once they started, there was no stopping them; it was a gallop all the way to the first stage, where the ponies were changed to the accompaniment of a bugle blown by the coachman in true Dickensian fashion.

The journey through the Siwaliks really began—as it still does today—at the Mohand Pass. The ascent starts with a gradual gradient, which increases as the road becomes more steep and winding. The hills are abrupt and perpendicular on the southern side, but slope gently away to the north.

At this stage of the journey, drums were beaten (if it was day) and torches were lit (if it was night), because sometimes wild elephants resented the approach of the dak-ghari and, trumpeting a challenge, would throw the ponies into confusion and panic, and send them racing back to the plains.

There are no wild elephants to be found near Mohand today, and very few other animals. Poachers have seen to that. Tigers, once a fairly common sight, are now almost as rare as dak-gharis.

And now it is the tonga that is nearing extinction. With the emergence of a fairly prosperous middle class in many cities, the machine has taken precedence as a means of conveyance. Trucks, buses, cars, motorcycles and scooters now ply on routes that were once the monopoly of cycles and tongas. If this can be taken as a measure of a country's progress, then we have certainly forged ahead; but our roads, never meant for such heavy traffic, are frequently cracking.

Tongas are still to be found, but they are usually confined to roads where buses and taxis do not penetrate. Most tonga-drivers refuse to change with the times, despite a diminishing income. Their ponies seem to have more traffic sense than some of our taxi drivers, and are involved in fewer accidents.

But give a tonga a straight clear stretch of road, and it will go into action, racing at breakneck speed while the passengers cling to their seats for their lives, and the exhilarated driver, shouting his challenge to the machine-age, cracks his whip, calls an endearment to his pony and bursts into song.

Tonga-drivers vary according to the towns they belong to. In Lucknow they are courteous, garrulous, self-styled descendants of Nawabs. In Delhi they are aggressive and shrewd, matching the temper of the city. Some of them are selling their ponies and buying scooters. Everywhere, tongas are fading away, becoming part of our nostalgia for the past.

Pedestrian in Peril

I think it was really my love of walking that first took me to the hills, and then kept me there for two decades. It had become increasingly difficult for me to walk about in Delhi, and I resented this, because I had been walking about Delhi before most of my readers were born. As a youth I walked from Connaught Place to Humayun's Tomb, and from Paharganj to Pusa, and although as the years passed I still covered these distances occasionally, it was so longer a pleasurable activity. Rather it became an obstacle race, an exercise in survival.

Now whenever I visit Delhi, I do not even try covering long distances. Even crossing a road is something of a feat for me. Usually I wedge myself between two well-built women and cross over in their company. No Maruti owner would risk damage to his car by colliding with us.

But being a compulsive walker, I stay out of Delhi as much as possible and do most of my walking in the hills. Even hill stations are congested these days, but as I live on the outskirts of one, I have no difficulty in marching off for a few miles with only myself and a circling eagle for company. Here, too, motor roads have multiplied. But it is possible to leave them at will, taking any old path that leads through fields of maize or mustard, or through oak and rhododendron forest, until a village is reached.

Here there is always hospitality if you are not the arrogant or fastidious sort. And occasionally you might come across a mountain stream where you can rest on a bed of ferns. And if there is no stream, you will eventually find a spring, perhaps a mere trickle of water but welcome all the same. Some springs dried up last year when the rains failed. Let us hope for the sake of bird and beast and thirsty trekker that it rains this winter.

~

Although I have given up walking in Delhi, it is still possible to do so in some of the smaller towns in the plains. But only just. When growing up in Dehradun, I walked all over that town, and all around it, and I tried again last week but it wasn't the same.

My maternal grandfather once taught me the art of zigzagging. If you take a zigzag walk, he said, you will see more of a place and also have some interesting encounters. Distrust the straight and narrow, that was his philosophy.

In those days one zigzagged from choice; now one does so out of necessity. One zigzags between scooters, tempos, buses, trucks, cars, bicycles, bullock-carts and various forms of locomotion. When a town of forty thousand people has, over a period of forty years, become a city of over a hundred thousand, the resultant traffic congestion may well be imagined. And even as you struggle to make your way along one of those overburdened roads, you are helped along by the stench from overflowing drains and piles of refuse that seems never to shrink or go away.

One cannot really blame anyone. It must happen when a small town acquires the population of a large city. And no one seems to mind. Perhaps it was all part of what Swami Vivekananda once called our 'kitchen mentality', the attitude that as long as the kitchen is clean, what happens on the road is none of our business.

~

Anyway, I need to walk in order to live, and although I have been defeated by Delhi, I am not going to let Dehra do the same. If I walk to the old cemetery, I might enjoy a reasonably quiet stroll. My maternal grandfather, he who taught me to zigzag, is buried there, and it would be nice to locate his grave. But it is thirty years since I last visited the cemetery. Will I find it without difficulty?

It took me the better part of the morning. Two of the busiest roads had to be crossed, and there were no Amazons to get between. As I stood on the curb, wondering how I was going to get across, a partially blind man carrying a stick tapped me on the arm and asked me if I could take him across. This put me in a quandary. It would have been churlish of me to refuse, but I was hardly the best choice for the task.

'I don't see too well myself,' I said, which was perfectly true. 'But I will see what I can do.' A frail old lady now approached us, I knew she was going to ask me to take her across the road, so I got in first. 'Could you lead two blind men across the road, madam?' I asked. Well, she got us safely across, and then looked back and asked me, 'Where is the second blind man?'

'Don't worry,' I said, 'he probably changed his mind.'

~

When I did get to the cemetery, I found it was no longer the quiet place of yore. A line of motor workshops had sprung up in front, while a slum colony had spread along one of the boundary walls. Once reputed to be the most beautiful cemetery in northern India, it still had its trees, but of the garden only traces remained. Quite obviously, funds were lacking.

I did not think I would find my grandfather's grave in the wilderness of worn and weathered tombs. Many had lost their inscriptions. They represented the presence in the Doon Valley of well over a thousand Europeans, from the first soldiers and settlers of the early nineteenth century to the more recent few who 'stayed on'—and passed on. Strangely enough, I had barely begun my search when I found myself before my grandfather's grave. The inscription, placed there by my grandmother, stood out more clearly than most. *'In memory of my beloved husband, William Dudley Clerke, died 9th January 1935'.*

And this was the 9th of January, too. It was becoming a day of coincidences. Or had something more than coincidence led me here on the anniversary of my grandfather's death? And if so, why? Perhaps the coming months will give me the answer.

~◠

A Station for Scandal

'Seeds of the potato-berries should be sown in adapted places by explorers of new countries.' So declared a botanically-minded empire-builder. And among those who took this advice was Captain Young of the Sirmur Rifles, Commandant of the Doon from the end of the Gurkha War in 1815 to the time of the Mutiny (1857).

It has to be said that the good captain was motivated by self-interest. He was an Irishman and fond of potatoes. He liked his Irish stew. So he grew his own potatoes and encouraged the good people of Garhwal to grow them too. In 1823 he received a supply of superior Irish potatoes and was considering where to plant them. The northern hill districts had been in British hands for almost ten years, but as yet no one had thought of resorting to them for rest or relaxation. The hills of central India, covered with jungle, were known to be extremely unhealthy. The Siwaliks near Dehradun were malarious. It was supposed that the Himalayan foothills, also forest clad, would be equally unhealthy. But Captain Young was to discover otherwise.

Carrying his beloved Irish potatoes with him, Captain Young set out on foot and soon left the sub-tropical Doon behind him. Above 4,000 feet he came to forests of oak and rhododendron, and above 6,000 feet they found cedars, known in the Himalayas as deodars. He found a climate so cool and delightful that not only did he plant potatoes, he built himself a small hunting lodge facing the snows.

Captain Young was to make a number of visits to his little hut on the mountain. No one lived nearby. The villages were situated in the valleys, where water was available. Bears, leopards and wild boar roamed the forests. There were pheasants in the shady ravines and small trout in the little Aglar river. Young and his companions could hunt and fish to their hearts' content. In 1826 Young, now a colonel, built the first large house, 'Mullingar' (I see its remnants from my window every morning), on the way up to what became the convalescent depot and cantonment. Others soon began to follow

Young's example, settling as far away as Cloud's End and The Abbey. By 1830, the twin hill stations of Landour and Mussoorie had come into being.

Those early pleasure-seeking residents took little or no interest in potato growing, but Young certainly did, and the slope beneath his house became known as Colonel Young's potato field. You won't find potatoes there now, only Professor Saili's dahlias and cucumbers; but potato-growing had caught on in the surrounding villages, and soon everyone in Garhwal and beyond was growing potatoes.

The potato, practically unknown in India before its introduction in the nineteenth century, was soon to become a popular and vital ingredient of so many Indian dishes. The humble aloo made life much more interesting for chefs, housewives, gourmands and gourmets. The writers of cookery books would have a hard time filling out their pages without the help of the potato.

> *For aloo-mutter and aloo-dhum,*
> *Our heartfelt thanks to Captain Young!*

~

Shimla became the capital of British India, Nainital the capital of the United Provinces. These towns were soon teeming with officials and empire-builders. But Mussoorie remained non-official, the pleasure capital of princes, wealthy Indians, European entrepreneurs and the wives and mistresses of all of them. Mussoorie was smaller than Shimla, all length and not much width, but there was room enough for private lives, for discreet affairs conducted over picnic baskets beneath the whispering deodars.

Ah, those picnics! They seem to be a thing of the past, now that you can drive almost anywhere and find a line of dhabas awaiting you. Few people today bother to prepare those delicate sandwiches or delicious parathas when packets of potato chips and other fast foods are to be found at every bend of the road. Stop at any dhaba in the hills and an instant meal of chow mein will be ready for you. Professor Saili tells me that chow mein is now the national dish of Uttaranchal. I believe him. My own family members demand it whenever we are out for the day.

But to return to Mussoorie's easy-going early days, before the missionaries arrived and made their own rules, imposing their ideas of morality upon the inhabitants.

The station's reputation was well established as far back as October 1884, when the local correspondent of the Calcutta *Statesman* wrote to his paper: 'Last Sunday, a sermon was delivered by the Rev Mr Hackett, belonging to the Church Mission society; he chose for his text Ezekiel 18th and 2nd verse, the latter clause: "The fathers have eaten sour grapes and set their children's teeth on edge." The reverend gentleman discoursed upon the highly immoral tone of society up here, that it far surpassed any other hill station in the scale of morals; that ladies and gentlemen after attending church proceeded to a drinking shop, a restaurant adjoining the library and there indulged freely in pegs, not one but many; that at a Fancy Bazaar held this season, a lady stood up on a chair and offered her kisses to gentlemen at Rs 5 each. What would they think of such a state of society at Home?' But this was not all. 'Married ladies and married gents formed friendships and associations, which tended to no good purpose, and set a bad example.'

Adultery under the pines? Mussoorie was well ahead of the times. The poor reverend preached to no purpose. And it was just as well that he was not alive in the year 1933, when a lady stood up at a benefit show and auctioned a single kiss, for which a gentleman paid Rs 300, a substantial amount seventy years ago. (A year's house rent, in fact.) The *Statesman's* correspondent had nothing to say on this latter occasion; his silence was in itself a comment on the changing times.

~

A few years ago I received a letter from a reader in England, wanting to know if there were any Maxwells still living in Mussoorie. He was a Maxwell himself, he said, by his father's first marriage. From what he knew of the family history, there ought to have been several Maxwells by the second marriage, and he wanted to get in touch with them.

He was very frank and mentioned that his father had given up a brilliant career in the Indian Civil Service to marry a fourteen-year-old Muslim girl. He had met her in Madras, changed his religion to facilitate the marriage, and then—to avoid 'scandal'—had made his home with her in Mussoorie.

Although there are no longer any Maxwells living in Mussoorie, my former neighbour, Miss Bean, confirmed that Mr Maxwell's children from his second wife had grown up on the hillside, each inheriting a considerable property. The children emigrated, but one grand-daughter returned to Mussoorie not so long ago, on a honeymoon with her fourth husband, thus keeping up the family tradition.

~

Mussoorie was probably at its brightest and gayest in the 1930s. Ballrooms, skating-rinks and cinema halls flourished. Beauty saloons sprang up along the Mall. An old advertisement in my possession announces the superiority of Madame Freda in the art of 'permanent waving'. Another old ad recommends Holloway's Ointment as a 'certain remedy for bad legs, bad breasts, and ulcerations of all kinds.'

Darlington's Pain-Curer was another certain remedy for all manner of ailments. It was even recommended by His Highness Raja Pratap Sah of Tehri-Garhwal State, whose domains bordered Mussoorie: 'It affords me much pleasure in informing you that the two bottles of Darlington's Pain-Curer, which I took from you, has given extraordinary relief from the rheumatism I have been suffering since last six months. Therefore I request you to send me two bottles more (large size) as I wish to take this valuable medicine with me on my tour through the Himalaya mountains.'

Neither the ad nor his Highness tells us whether you were supposed to apply the potion or drink the stuff. Perhaps you could do both.

By the time Independence came to India, most of the British and Anglo-Indian residents of our hill stations had sold their homes and left the country. Only a few stayed on—elderly folks like Miss Bean who had spent all their lives here and whose meagre incomes did not allow them to settle abroad.

~

I wonder what really brought me to Mussoorie in the 1960s. True, I had been here as a child, and my mother's people had lived in Dehradun, in the valley below. When I returned to India, still a young man in my twenties (I had spent only four years in England), I lived in Delhi and Dehradun for a few years; and then, on an impulse, I found myself revisiting the hill station, calling on the oldest resident, Miss Bean, and being told by her that the upper portion of her cottage, Maplewood, was to let. On another impulse, I rented it.

Always a creature of impulse, my life has been shaped more by a benign providence than by any system of foresight or planning.

Well, that was more than fifty years ago, and Miss Bean has long since gone to her Maker, and here I am in the midst of a large family, living in another cottage and doing my best to keep it from falling down.

Perhaps I really wanted to come back to my beginnings. Because it was in Mussoorie in 1933 (the Year of Kissing!) that my parents met each other and were married.

I have a photograph of them, on horseback, riding on the Camel's Back Road. He was thirty-six then and had just given up a tea-estate manager's job; she was barely twenty, taking a nurse's training at the Cottage Hospital, just below Gun Hill.

A few months later they were living in the heat and dust of Alwar, in Rajasthan, and then Jamnagar in Kathiawar, where my father conducted a small palace school. I was not born in Mussoorie but I am pretty sure I had my conception there!

There is something in the air of the place—especially in October— that is conducive to love and passion and desire. Miss Bean told me that as a girl she'd many suitors, and if she did not marry it was more from procrastination than from being passed over. While on all sides elopements and broken marriages were making hill station life exciting, and providing orphans and illegitimate children for the mission schools, Miss Bean contrived to remain single and childless. She was probably helped by the fact of her father being a retired police officer with a reputation for being a good shot with the pistol and Lee-Enfield rifle.

She taught elocution in one of the many schools that flourished (and still flourish) in Mussoorie. There is a protective atmosphere about a residential school, an atmosphere which, although it protects one from the outside world, often exposes one to the hazards within the system.

The schools were not without their own scandals. Mrs Fennimore, the wife of a headmaster at Oak Grove, got herself entangled in a defamation suit, each hearing of which grew more and more distasteful to her husband. Unable to stand the whole weary and sordid business, Mr Fennimore hit upon a solution. Loading his revolver, he moved to his wife's bedside and shot her through the head. For no accountable reason he put the weapon under her pillow—obviously no one could have mistaken the death for suicide—and then, going to his study, he leaned over his rifle and shot himself.

Ten years later, in the same school, another headmaster's wife was arrested for attempted murder. She had fired at, and wounded a junior mistress. The motive remained obscure and the case was hushed up.

In the St Fidelis' School, circa 1941, a boy asleep in the dormitory had his throat slit by another boy, it was said at the instigation of one of the teachers. This too was hushed up, but the school closed down a year later.

In recent years, there has been a suicide in one public school, and murders (involving students) in two others; also an accidental death by way of a drug overdose. Tom Brown's school days were pretty dull when compared to the goings-on in some of our residential schools.

These affairs usually get hushed up, but there was no hushing up the incidents that took place on 25th July 1927, at the height of the season and in the heart of the town—a double tragedy that set the station agog with excitement. It all happened in broad daylight and in a full boarding house, Zephyr Hall.

Shortly after noon the boarders were startled into brisk activity when a shot rang out from one of the rooms, followed by screams. Other shots followed in quick succession. Those boarders who happened to be in the lounge or on the verandah dived for the safety of their own rooms and bolted the doors. One unhappy boarder however, ignorant of where the man with the gun might be, decided to take no chances and came round the corner with his hands held well above his head—only to run straight into the levelled pistol! Even the man who held it, and who had just shot his wife and daughter, couldn't help laughing.

Mr Owen, the maniac with the gun, after killing his wife and wounding his daughter finally shot himself. His was the first official Christian cremation in Mussoorie, performed apparently in compliance with wishes expressed long before his dramatic end.

A couple of years ago I had a letter from an old Mussoorie resident, Col. Cole, now retired in Pune, who recalled the event: 'Mrs Owen ran Zephyr Hall as a boarding house. It was the last Saturday of the month, and Mrs Owen's son Basil was with me at the 11a.m.—1 p.m. session at the skating rink and so escaped the tragedy that took place about mid-day, when Mr Owen shot Mrs Owen and one daughter and then shot himself. I do not know what happened to Basil but he was withdrawn from school and an uncle took him over. This was not the end of the family tragedy. An older sister of Basil's in her early twenties was boating on the river Gumpti at Lucknow with her fiance, when a flash flood took place and the strong current drowned them both.'

~

This was not the end of the story, at least not for me.

A few summers ago, while I was walking along the Mall, I was stopped by a stranger, a small man with pale blue eyes and thinning hair. He must have been over sixty. Accompanying him was a much younger woman, whom he introduced as his wife. He apologized for detaining me, and said: 'You look as though you have been here a long time. Do you know if any of the Gantzers still live here? I believe they look after the cemetery.'

I gave him the necessary directions and then asked him if he was visiting Mussoorie for the first time. He seemed to welcome the inquiry and showed a willingness to talk.

'It's well over fifty years since I was last here', he said. 'I was just a boy at the time'. And he gestured towards the ruins of Zephyr Hall, now occupied by postmen and their families. 'That was my mother's boarding house. That was where she died.'

'Not—not Mr Owen?' I ventured to ask.

'That's right. So you've heard about it. My father had a sudden brainstorm. He shot and killed Mother. My sister was badly wounded. I was out at the time. Now I have come to revisit her grave. I know she'd have wanted me to come.'

He took my telephone number and promised to look me up before he left Mussoorie. But I did not see him again. After a few days, I began to wonder if I had really met a survivor of this old tragedy, or if he had been just another of the hill station's ghosts. But one day, while I was walking along the cemetery's lowest terrace, I found confirmation that Mrs Owen's son had indeed visited his mother's grave. Set into the tombstone was a new stone plaque with the inscription: *Mother Dear, I am Here.*

In Search of John Lang

I had lived in Mussoorie just over four years without realizing that someone of literary distinction might be buried in the old English cemetery. Just as I was about to return to Delhi, a friend in Australia sent me a newspaper clipping which made mention of the first Australian-born novelist, John Lang, who spent the last years of his life in Mussoorie and was known to have been buried here. There is still an unsolved mystery about Lang's manuscripts. He left his papers to his second wife, née Margaret Watter, but neither they, nor any trace of her after his death, have ever been found.

John Lang was born in Sydney in 1816. His father, a young soldier turned merchant, died before his birth. His mother was Elizabeth Harris, born on Norfolk Island, the daughter of two convicts. Lang proved a brilliant Latin scholar at Sydney College, then went to England to study law. He was expelled from Cambridge for *Botany Bay Tricks*—believed to be the writing of blasphemous litanies—but was admitted to the Society of the Middle Temple and called to the bar in 1841. He returned to Sydney shortly afterwards, but his convict connections stood in the way of his advancement, and it was only when he went to India that he began to lead a successful legal and literary life. *The Forger's Wife*—a robust tale of Australian outlaws—was published in England in 1855; *Botany Bay*—a collection of stories based on life in Sydney in the early years of the century—was written for Charles Dickens' magazine *Household Words* and published in 1859. The best of his books on India are *The Weatherbys* (1853) and *The Ex-Wife* (1859). These take a lightly satirical look at English social life in India, and are precursors of Kipling's stories of Simla society.

Lang practised at the Bar in Calcutta, and represented the Rani of Jhansi in her legal battles against the East India Company. He did well both as a barrister and as a newspaper proprietor. But none of his manuscripts, and no portrait of him, have ever been discovered. When he died he left everything to his second wife, whom he married in Mussoorie in 1861: but what happened to her after his death remains a mystery.

Although Lang's books are elusive, I decided that his grave should not be so hard to find, and set out in search of it on a crisp

October morning. This is the best time of year in the hills, with the grass still fresh and green, the horse chestnut leaves yellowing, the hillsides sprinkled with wild geranium and umbrella-fronds of lady's lace.

I take Camel's Back Road that leads round the northern and more forested face of Gun Hill, which is a rocky outcrop in the centre of the hill station. Gun Hill is so named because in Lang's time it boasted a cannon which boomed out at noon each day. The gun was a mixed blessing. Once on a Sunday morning during service in the Anglican Church of St Thomas (built in 1834 and now beginning to crumble), one of the straw cannon balls shot through the open door, bounced off a pew, and landed in the lap of a stout lady who had been sleeping through the sermon. The cannon was shifted to the municipal godowns where, for all I know, it may still be gathering rust.

Although Mussoorie's Camel's Back Road was not as high in social hierarchy as Scandal Point in Simla, it was, until the 1930s, almost exclusively a European preserve; and so was the cemetery, where most of the names on the tombstones are of Anglo-Saxon vintage. The graves occupy terraced slopes which face the snow-covered Nilkanth and Bandarpoonchh ranges.

I am unable to enter at the gate which is securely padlocked and encircled by barbed wire, making the two large noticeboards—'No Trespassing' and 'Visitors Should Leave Their Dogs Behind'—seem rather unnecessary. I walk along the railing until I notice a small footpath leading off the verge. Climbing over the railings, I start down the path; but it is steep and slippery with pine needles, and I end by tobogganing down the slope into a thicket of myrtle.

Brushing dust, burrs and pine needles from my clothes, I stand up and survey the hillside, my eyes finally coming to rest on a small knoll where several bulky obelisks rise from the ground. Obelisks were all the rage in the late nineteenth century, and it is just possible that John Lang's grave will be among them.

The knoll does seem to be the oldest part of the cemetery; it is certainly the prettiest. The sunlight penetrating the gaps in the tall trees plays chess on the gravestones, shifting slowly and thoughtfully across the worn old stones. The wind, like a hundred violins, plays perpetually in the topmost branches of the deodar. The only living thing in sight is an eagle, wheeling high overhead. The snows are just a great dazzle in the sky. This is a romantic spot, a fit burial ground for adventurers and pioneers. Here are the graves of soldiers, merchants, evangelists. The largest of the graves belongs to Mr Henry Bohle, who died in 1852. The financial benefits accruing to the hill station from Bohle's Brewery (now a ruin) led to Mackinnon going one better by building a cart road for his produce, and this road formed the basis for the present motor road from Dehra to Mussoorie.

There are a number of Mackinnons buried here. But unless John Lang left his widow in a generous mood, the chances of my finding his grave here are rather remote. Only the more expensive gravestones with marble insets have retained their inscriptions. The sandstone graves are now just anonymous slabs. Over a hundred monsoons have worn away the lettering on many old tombs.

I am still searching the knoll when I am hailed by a man holding a bundle of sticks in one hand and an axe in the other. He calls out to me in a belligerent tone:

'What are you doing here? And how did you get in?'

'I am looking for a grave,' I reply mildly.

'You may come across your own grave if you walk in here without permission!'

This must be the mali, who is both gardener and caretaker. I have been warned about him; a fierce man who has been known to eject intruders at the point of a lathi. I am told he is short-sighted; and, like a bear, which is also short-sighted, believes that there is no point in trying to identify an intruder until he has been finished off.

It is only when the mali comes closer, and finds that I look fairly respectable, that his bluster disappears.

'Some people come here to rob the graves,' he explains in an injured tone. 'And every time an arm or a head or a piece of marble goes,' he says, gesturing towards a decapitated angel, 'the Committee memsahibs take me to task for carelessness.'

'Well, I'll tell the memsahibs how vigilant you are. I am looking for an old grave. Over a hundred years old.'

'There are some old ones near my house,' he says, beginning to mellow. 'But you should look at the register, sahib. That will help you find your relative's grave.'

I am about to tell him that it is not a relative's grave, then decide not to as I do not want to raise his suspicions again. And it is pleasant to invent a relationship with another writer, a fellow Indo-Anglian, who lived, loved, died and was buried here over a hundred years ago.

'Who has the register?'

'The Garlah miss-sahib. She will tell you everything.'

'All right, I'll see her and come again tomorrow.'

'If you bring a chit from the miss-sahib, I can open the gate for you.'

I continue searching on my own for a while, to the evident unease of the mali. Does he really think I shall make off with a headstone?

~

That evening I visit Miss Garlah. She is a tubby little Anglo-Indian lady with a hearty manner and a strong constitution. Forty of her sixty years have been spent in Mussoorie.

'Did you have trouble with the mali?' she asks with apparent relish. Evidently she looks forward to getting complaints about him.

'He was a bit aggressive,' I say. 'He needs glasses to help him separate grave robbers from other people.'

'Well, he saw you climbing the railings, and that made him wonder what you were up to.'

'So he's been to you already?'

'Yes, he's very good. We keep him because he's so tough. The last man used to let in all sorts of people, including some hippies who thought the cemetery would be just the right place for smoking pot.'

When I tell her the object of my search, she says: 'Yes, I have a register. Give me the name and date of your author's death and we'll look him up.'

'John Lang, 1864.'

'Ah, that's going too far back. There must have been a register for those years, but if there was, it's long since lost. I can help you from 1910 onwards.'

I make no attempt to hide my disappointment. 'Nothing earlier? If only I had an idea of where the grave might be situated, I might be able to identify it.'

'Well, young man, I can only suggest that you keep hunting. Try the graves near the mali's house. I'll ask him to clean them up for you. You may be lucky. We do our best to maintain them because the British High Commission makes us a small grant towards their upkeep. But we're short-handed, and the heavy monsoon rains don't help.'

~

The next day I am back at the cemetery, determined to make one more attempt at finding John Lang's grave. I am leaving for Delhi in a day or two, and it may be months, perhaps years, before I can return to Mussoorie.

This time I find the gate open. A small boy with little on goes skipping over the graves, like some mischievous cupid trying to resurrect dead lovers. His father, the mali, appears from behind a placid buffalo and gives me an elaborate salaam. Apparently Miss Garlah has already sent word of my coming.

The mali apologizes for the condition of some of the graves near his outhouse. His buffalo is tethered to a crumbling obelisk. A cow and calf are tied to a slanting stone cross. Several graves are half-buried under straw and offal. Others appear to have vanished into a small ploughed field which now contains mustard. The strangest sight of all is a memorial tablet, commemorating a certain Captain Jones of Her Majesty's 30th Foot, which lies flat on the step of the mali's shack and provides an ideal platform for the gardener's tall and ornate hookah pipe.

The chances of finding John Lang's grave in this tumbled, crumbling heap now seem remote. But the mali offers to help me in my search and he is so anxious to please that I am loath to disappoint him. He starts scraping the mud off partly obscured inscriptions and tells his small son, a merry little fellow with bright eyes and a disarming smile, to do the same. It is a glorious day, but the wind is from behind the mali's house, and there is no escape from the odour of sour milk and cow dung. I came in search of the dead, only to find the living.

We find several graves dating from 1864 and earlier, but John Lang's is not one of them. I begin to harbour mean thoughts about his wife. If she could disappear so suddenly and mysteriously with his manuscripts, it is unlikely that she would have bothered to give him an expensive and permanent grave.

'There were a few on this northern slope, sahib,' says the mali after some time, 'but we had a landslide a few years ago and the graves went down the khud.'

This is enough to make me give up all hope. For all I know, John Lang's remains may well be at the foot of the mountain. My search becomes desultory, and I find myself muttering, 'What does it matter, anyway? If a writer's any good, his books will be his monument. What need have we of tombstones to commemorate our passage on earth?'

But all the same I am disappointed. And seeing my disappointment, the mali makes renewed efforts to clean up some of the graves near the cattle shed. He cannot understand my whim, or anyone's sentimentality over old graves, but he has warmed towards me, wants to please me, and would be quite willing to chisel 'John Lang, died 1864' into any grave I choose, if it will make me happy.

~

Three weeks after leaving Mussoorie, I receive a letter from Miss Garlah, informing me that the old register had turned up and that John Lang had indeed been buried in the Mussoorie cemetery, on 'C' terrace.

On a subsequent visit I made my way to the spot and found the grave quite easily, under a covering of moss and ferns; shaded by the deodars, it was just a mound of earth and foliage. Prem and I cleared away a hundred years of detritus, and there on a plain stone slab was the simple inscription—'John Lang, Barrister at law. Died Landour, 1864, aged 47.'

Grandfather's Earthquake

'If ever there's a calamity,' Grandmother used to say, 'it will find Grandfather in his bath.' Grandfather loved his bath—which he took in a large round aluminium tub, and sometimes spent as long as an hour in it, wallowing, as he called it and splashing around like a boy.

He was in his bath during the earthquake that convulsed Bengal and Assam on 12 June 1897—an earthquake so severe that even today the region of the great Brahmaputra river basin hasn't settled down. Not long ago it was reported that the entire Shillong plateau had moved an appreciable distance away from the Brahmaputra towards the Bay of Bengal. According to the Geological Survey of India, this shift has been taking place gradually over the past eighty years.

Had Grandfather been alive, he would have added one more clipping to his scrapbook on the earthquake. The clipping goes in anyway, because the scrapbook is now with the children. More than newspaper accounts of the disaster, it was Grandfather's own letters and memoirs that made the earthquake seem recent and vivid; for he, along with Grandmother and two of their children (one of them my father), was living in Shillong, a picturesque little hill station in Assam,* when the earth shook and the mountains heaved.

As I have mentioned, Grandfather was in his bath, splashing about, and did not hear the first rumbling. But Grandmother was in the garden, hanging out or taking in the washing (she could never remember which) when, suddenly, the animals began making a hideous noise—a sure intimation of a natural disaster, for animals sense the approach of an earthquake much more quickly than humans.

The crows all took wing, wheeling wildly overhead and cawing loudly. The chickens flapped in circles, as if they were being chased. Two dogs sitting in the verandah suddenly jumped up and ran out with their tails between their legs. Within half a minute of her noticing the noise made by the animals, Grandmother heard a rattling, rumbling noise, like the approach of a train.

The noise increased for about a minute, and then there was the first trembling of the ground. The animals by this time all seemed to have gone mad. Treetops lashed backwards and forwards, doors banged and windows shook, and Grandmother swore later that the house actually swayed in front of her. She had difficulty in standing straight, though this could have been due more to the trembling of her knees than to the trembling of the ground.

The first shock lasted for about a minute and a half. 'I was in my tub having a bath,' Grandfather wrote for posterity, 'which for the first time in the last two months I had taken in the afternoon instead of in the morning. My wife and children and the ayah were downstairs. Then the shock came, accompanied by a loud rumbling sound under the earth and a quaking which increased in intensity every second. It

---

* This, of course, was a long time before the state of Meghalya, of which Shillong is now the capital, was created.

was like putting so many shells in a basket and shaking them up with a rapid sifting motion from side to side.

'At first I did not realize what it was that caused my tub to sway about and the water to splash. I rose up, and found the earth heaving, while the washstand, basin, sewer, cups and glasses danced and rocked about in the most hideous fashion. I rushed to the inner door to open it and search for wife and children, but could not move the dratted door as boxes, furniture and plaster had come up against it. The back door was the only way of escape. I managed to burst it open, and thank God, was able to get out. Sections of the thatched roof had slithered down on the four sides like a pack of cards and blocked all the exits and entrances.

'With only a towel wrapped around my waist, I ran out into the open to the front of the house, but found only my wife there. The whole front of the house was blocked by the fallen section of thatch from the roof. Through this I broke my way under the iron railings and extricated the others. The bearer had pluckily borne the weight of the whole thatched-roof section on his back as it had slithered down, and in this way saved the ayah and children from being crushed beneath it.'

After the main shock of the earthquake had passed, minor shocks took place at regular intervals of five minutes or so, all through the night. But during that first shake-up the town of Shillong was reduced to ruin and rubble. Everything made of masonry was brought to the ground. Government House, the post office, the jail, all tumbled down. When the jail fell, the prisoners, instead of making their escape, sat huddled on the road waiting for the superintendent to come to their aid.

'The ground began to heave and shake,' wrote a young girl in a newspaper called the *Englishman*[*]. 'I stayed on my bicycle for a second, and then fell off and got up and tried to run, staggering about from side to side of the road. To my left I saw great clouds of dust, which I afterwards discovered to be houses falling and the earth slipping from the sides of the hills. To my right I saw the small dam at the end of the lake torn asunder and the water rushing out, the

---

[*] This later became the *Statesman*.

wooden bridge across the lake break in two and the sides of the lake falling in; and at my feet the ground cracking and opening. I was wild with fear and didn't know which way to turn.'

The lake rose up like a mountain, and then totally disappeared, leaving only a swamp of red mud. Not a house was left standing. People were rushing about, wives looking for husbands, parents looking for children, not knowing whether their loved ones were alive or dead. A crowd of people had collected on the cricket ground, which was considered the safest place; but Grandfather and the family took shelter in a small shop on the road outside his house. The shop was a rickety wooden structure, which had always looked as though it would fall down in a strong wind. But it withstood the earthquake.

And then the rain came and it poured. This was extraordinary, because before the earthquake there wasn't a cloud to be seen; but, five minutes after the shock, Shillong was enveloped in cloud and mist. The shock was felt for more than a hundred miles on the Assam-Bengal Railway. A train was overturned at Shamshernagar; another was derailed at Mantolla. Over a thousand people lost their lives in the Cherrapunji Hills, and in other areas, too, the death toll was heavy.

The Brahmaputra burst its banks and many cultivators were drowned in the flood. A tiger was found drowned. And in North Bhagalpur, where the earthquake started, two elephants sat down in the bazaar and refused to get up until the following morning.

Over a hundred men who were at work in Shillong's government printing press were caught in the building when it collapsed, and though the men of a Gurkha regiment did splendid rescue work only a few were brought out alive. One of those killed in Shillong was Mr McCabe, a British official. Grandfather described the ruins of Mr McCabe's house: 'Here a bedpost, there a sword, a broken desk or chair, a bit of torn carpet, a well-known hat with its Indian Civil Service colours, battered books, all speaking reminiscences of the man we mourn.'

While most houses collapsed where they stood, Government House, it seems, 'fell backwards'. The church was a mass of red stones in ugly disorder. The organ was a tortured wreck.

A few days later the family, with other refugees, were making their way to Calcutta to stay with friends or relatives. It was a slow, tedious journey, with many interruptions, for the roads and railway lines had been badly damaged and passengers had often to be transported in trolleys. Grandfather was rather struck at the stoicism displayed by an assistant engineer. At one station a telegram was handed to the engineer informing him that his bungalow had been destroyed. 'Beastly nuisance,' he observed with an aggrieved air. 'I've seen it cave in during a storm, but this is the first time it has played me such a trick on account of an earthquake.'

The family got to Calcutta to find the inhabitants of the capital in a panic; for they too had felt the quake and were expecting it to recur. The damage in Calcutta was slight compared to the devastation elsewhere, but nerves were on edge, and people slept in the open or in carriages. Cracks and fissures had appeared in a number of old buildings, and Grandfather was among the many who were worried at the proposal to fire a salute of sixty guns on Jubilee Day (the Diamond Jubilee of Queen Victoria); they felt the gunfire would bring down a number of shaky buildings. Obviously Grandfather did not wish to be caught in his bath a second time. However, Queen Victoria was not to be deprived of her salute. The guns were duly fired, and Calcutta remained standing.

~

The Kipling Road

As boys we would often trudge up from Rajpur to Mussoorie by the old bridle path, the road that used to serve the hill station in the days before the motor road was built. Before 1900, the traveller to Mussoorie took a tonga from Saharanpur to Dehradun, spent the night at a Rajpur hotel, and the following day came up the steep seven-mile path on horseback, or on foot, or in a dandy (a crude palanquin) held aloft by two sometimes four, sweating coolies.

The railway came to Dehradun in 1904, and a few years later the first motor car made it to Mussoorie, the motor road following the winding contours and hairpin bends of the old bullock-cart road. Rajpur went out of business; no one stopped there any more, the hotels became redundant, and the bridle path was seldom used except by those of us who thought it would be fun to come up on foot.

For the first two or three miles you walked in the hot sun, along a treeless path. It was only at Jharipani (at approximately 4,000 ft.) that the oak forests began, providing shade and shelter. Situated on a spur of its own, was the Railways School Oakgrove, still there today, providing a boarding school education to the children of Railway personnel. My mother and her sisters came from a Railway family, and all of them studied at Oakgrove in the 1920s. So did a male cousin, who succumbed to cerebral malaria during the school term. In spite of the salubrious climate, mortality was high amongst school children. There were no cures then for typhoid, cholera, malaria, dysentery and other infectious diseases.

Above Oakgrove was Fairlawn, the palace of the Nepali royal family. There was a sentry box outside the main gate, but there was never any sentry in it, and on more than one occasion I took shelter there from the rain. Today it's a series of cottages, one of which belongs to *Outlook's* editor, Vinod Mehta, who seeks shelter there from the heat and dust of Delhi.

From Jharapani we climbed to Barlowganj, where another venerable institution, St George's College, crowns the hilltop. Then on to Bala Hissar, once the home-in-exile of an Afghan king, and now the grounds of Wynberg-Allen, another school. In later years I was to live near this school, and it was its then Principal, Rev W. Biggs, who told me that the bridle path was once known as the Kipling Road.

Why was that, I asked. Had Kipling ever come up that way? Rev Biggs wasn't sure, but he referred me to *Kim,* and the chapter in which Kim and the Lama leave the plains for the hills. It begins thus:

> They had crossed the Siwaliks and the half-tropical Doon, left Mussoorie behind them, and headed north along the narrow hill-roads. Day after day they struck deeper into the huddled mountains, and day after day Kim watched the lama return to a man's strength. Among the terraces of the Doon he had leaned on the boy's shoulder, ready to profit by wayside halts. Under the great ramp to Mussoorie he drew himself together as an old hunter faces a well remembered bank, and where he should have sunk exhausted swung his long draperies about him, drew a deep double lungful of the diamond air, and walked as only a hill-man can.

This description is accurate enough, but it is not evidence that Kipling actually came this way, and his geography becomes quite confusing in the subsequent pages—as Peter Hopkirk discovered when he visited Mussoorie a few years ago, retracing Kim's journeys for his book *Quest for Kim*. Hopkirk spent some time with me in this little room where I am now writing, but we were unable to establish the exact route that Kim and the Lama took after traversing Mussoorie. Presumably they had come up the bridle path. But then? After that, Kipling becomes rather vague.

Mussoorie does not really figure in Rudyard Kipling's prose or poetry. The Simla Hills were his beat. As a journalist he was a regular visitor to Simla, then the summer seat of the British Raj.

But last year my Swiss friend, Anilees Goel, brought me proof that Kipling had indeed visited Mussoorie. Among his unpublished papers and other effects in the Library of Congress, there exists an album of photographs, which includes two of the Charleville Hotel, Mussoorie, where he had spent the summer of 1888. On a photograph of the office he had inscribed these words:

> 'And there were men with a thousand wants
> And women with babes galore
> But the dear little angels in Heaven know
> That Wutzler never swore.'

Wutzler was the patient, long-suffering manager of this famous hotel, now the premises of the Lal Bahadur Shastri National Academy of Administration.

A second photograph is inscribed with the caption 'Quarters at the Charleville, April-July 88,' and carries this verse:

> 'A burning sun in cloudless skies
> and April dies,
> A dusty Mall—three sunsets splendid
> and May is ended,
> Grey mud beneath—grey cloud o'erhead
> and June is dead.
> A little bill in late July
> and then we fly.'

Pleasant enough, but hardly great verse, and I'm not surprised that Kipling did not publish these lines.

However, we now know that he came to Mussoorie and spent some time here, and that he would have come up by the old bridle path (there was no other way except by bullock-cart on the long and tortuous cart road), and Rev Biggs and others were right in calling it the Kipling Road, although officially that was never its name.

~

As you climb up from Barlowganj, you pass a number of pretty cottages—May Cottage, Wakefield, Ralston Manor, Wayside Hall— and these old houses all have stories to tell, for they have stood mute witness to the comings and goings of all manner of people.

Take Ralston Manor. It was witness to an impromptu cremation, probably Mussoorie's first European cremation, in the late 1890s. There is a small chapel in the grounds of Ralston, and the story goes that a Mr and Mrs Smallman had been living in the house, and Mr Smallman had expressed a wish to be cremated at his death. When he died, his widow decided to observe his wishes and had her servants build a funeral pyre in the garden. The cremation was well underway when someone rode by and looked in to see what was happening. The unauthorized cremation was reported to the authorities and Mrs Smallman had to answer some awkward questions. However, she was let off with a warning (a warning not to cremate any future husbands?) and later she built the little chapel on the site of the funeral pyre— in gratitude or as penance, or as a memorial, we are not told. But the chapel is still there, and this little tale is recorded in *Chowkidar* (Autumn 1995), the journal of the British Association for Cemeteries in South Asia (BACSA).

As we move further up the road, keeping to the right, we come to Wayside Hall and Wayside Cottage, which have the advantage of an open sunny hillside and views to the north and east. I lived in the cottage for a couple of years, back in 1966-67, as a tenant of the Powell sisters who lived in the Hall.

There were three sisters, all in their seventies; they had survived their husbands. Annie, the eldest, had a son who lived abroad, Martha, the second, did not have children; Dr Simmonds, the third sister, had various adopted children who came to see her from time to time. They were God-fearing, religious folk, but not bigots; never chided me for not going to church. Annie's teas were marvellous; snacks and savouries in abundance. They kept a beautiful garden.

'Why go to church?' I said. 'Your garden is a church.'

In spring and summer it was awash with poppies, petunia, phlox, larkspur, calendula, snapdragons and other English flowers. During the monsoon, the gladioli took over, while magnificent dahlias reared up from the rich foliage. During the autumn came zinnias and marigolds and cosmos. And even during the winter months there would be geraniums and primulae blooming in the verandah.

Honeysuckle climbed the wall outside my window, filling my bedroom with its heady scent. And wisteria grew over the main gate. There was perfume in the air.

Annie herself smelt of freshly baked bread. Dr Simmonds smelt of Pears' baby soap. Martha smelt of apples. All good smells, emanating from good people.

Although they lived on their own, without any men on the premises, they never felt threatened or insecure. Mussoorie was a safe place to live in then, and still is to a great extent—much safer than towns in the plains, where the crime rate keeps pace with the population growth.

Annie's son, Gerald, then in his sixties, did come out to see them occasionally. He had been something of a shikari in his youth—or so he claimed—and told me he could call up a panther from the valley without any difficulty. To do this, he made a contraption out of an old packing-case, with a hole bored in the middle, then he passed a length of thick wire through the hole, and by moving the wire backwards and forward produced a sound not dissimilar to the sawing, coughing sound made by a panther during the mating season. (Incidentally, a panther and a leopard are the same animal.)

Gerry invited me to join him on a steep promontory overlooking a little stream. I did so with some trepidation. Hunting had never been my forte, and normally I preferred to go along with Ogden Nash's dictum, 'If you meet a panther, don't anther!'

However, Gerry's gun looked powerful enough, and I believed him when he told me he was a crack shot. I have always taken people at their word. One of my failings I suppose.

Anyway, we positioned ourselves on this ledge, and Gerry started producing panther noises with his box. His Master's Voice would have been proud of it. Nothing happened for about twenty minutes, and I was beginning to lose patience when we were answered by the cough and grunt of what could only have been a panther. But we couldn't see it! Gerry produced a pair of binoculars and trained them on some distant object below, which turned out to be a goat. The growling continued—and then it was just above us! The panther had made a detour and was now standing on a rock and staring down, no doubt wondering which of us was making such attractive mating calls.

Gerry swung round, raised his gun and fired. He missed by a couple of feet, and the panther bounded away, no doubt disgusted with the proceedings.

We returned to Wayside Hall, and revived ourselves with brandy and soda.

'We'll get it next time, old chap', said Gerry. But although we tried, the panther did not put in another appearance. Gerry's panther call sounded genuine enough, but neither he nor I nor the panther thought that his wired box looked anything like a female panther.

The Old Names Linger On

'Stand still for ten minutes, and they'll build a hotel on top of you', said one old-timer, gesturing towards the concrete jungle that had sprung up along Mussoorie's Mall, the traditional promenade.

This hill station in northern India is now one long, ugly bazaar, but if you leave the mall and walk along some of the old lanes and byways, you would come across many of the old houses, most of them still bearing their original names from the mid-nineteenth century.

Mussoorie, like other hill resorts in India, came into existence in the 1820s or thereabouts, when the families of British colonials began making for the hills in order to escape the scorching heat of the plains. Small settlements grew into large 'stations' and were soon vying with each other for the title of 'Queen of the Hills'.

Mussoorie's name derives from the mansur shrub (*Cororiana nepalensis*), common in the Himalayan foothills; but many of the house-names derive from the native places of those who first built and lived in them. Today, the old houses and estates are owned by well-to-do Indians, many of whom enjoy the lifestyle of the former colonial rulers. In most cases, the old names have been retained.

The Mullingar is not one of the better preserved buildings, having been under litigation for some years; but it was a fine mansion once, and it has the distinction of being the oldest building in Mussoorie. It was the home of an Irish cavalry officer from Mullingar, Captain Young, who commanded the first Gurkha battalion when it was in its infancy. It was to Ireland that he finally returned when he gave up his sword and saddle, but there is a story that on moonlit nights a ghostly rider can be seen on the Mullingar flat—Captain Young revisiting old haunts.

There must have been a number of Irishmen settling and building in Mussoorie in those pioneering days, for there are houses with names such as Tipperary, Killarney, Shamrock Cottage and Tara Hall.

In Mussoorie, as everywhere, the Scots were also great pioneers and were quick to identify the Himalayan hills and meadows with their own glens and braes. There are over a dozen house-names prefixed with 'Glen' and close to where I live there is a Scottsburn, a Wolfsburn and a Redburn. A 'burn' is a small stream, but there are none in the vicinity, so the names must have been given for purely sentimental reasons. The Welsh were not far behind, with Ellengowan and Chynoweth.

The English, of course, went in for castles—there is Connaught Castle and Grey Castle and the Castle Hill, home for a time to the young Sikh prince, Dalip Singh, before he went to England to become a protégé of Queen Victoria.

Sir Walter Scott must have been a very popular writer with the British expatriates, for there are many houses in Mussoorie that were named after his novels and romances—*Kenilworth, Ivanhoe, Woodstock* (later an American mission school), *Rokeby, Waverley, The Monastery*—and there is also Abbotsford, named after Scott's own home.

Dickens' lovers must have felt frustrated, because they could hardly name their house *Nicholas Nickleby* or *Martin Chuzzlewit;* but one Dickens fan did come up with *Bleak House* for a name, and bleak it is, even to this day. I have never had the money to buy or build a house of my own, but I am ever the optimist, and if ever I do, I shall call it *Great Expectations*.

Mussoorie did have a Dickens' connection in the 1850s, when Charles Dickens was publishing his magazine *Household Words*. His correspondent in India was John Lang, a popular novelist and newspaper proprietor who spent the last years of his life in Mussoorie. His diverting account of a typical Mussoorie 'season', called *The Himalaya Club*, appeared in *Household Words* in the issue of 21 March, 1857. Recently, I was able to obtain a copy from the British Museum.

I have not been able to locate the house in which Lang lived, but from one of his descriptions it may have been White Park Forest, now practically a ruin. The name is another puzzle, because of park or forest there is no trace. But on looking up an old guide, I discovered that it had been named after its joint owners, Mr White, Mr Park and Mr Forest.

Another name that puzzled me for a time was that of the old Charleville Hotel, now an academy for young civil servants. Was it French in its origins? Most of the locals always referred to it as the 'Charley-Billy' Hotel, which I thought was an obvious mispronunciation; but the laugh was on me. According to the records, the original owner had two sons, Charley and Billy, and he had named the hotel after them.

This naming of places is never as simple as it seems. I shall end this piece with Mossy Falls, a small waterfall on the outskirts of the hill station. You might think it was named after the moss that is so plentiful around it, but you would be wrong. It was really named after Mr Moss, the owner of the Alliance Bank, who was affectionately known as 'Mossy' to his friends. When at the turn of the century the Alliance Bank collapsed, Mr Moss also fell from grace. 'Poor old Mossy,' said his friends, and promptly named the falls after him.

A Hill Station's Vintage Murder

There is less crime in the hills than in the plains, and so the few murders that do take place from time to time stand out as landmarks in the annals of a hill station.

Among the gravestones in the Mussoorie cemetery there is one which bears the inscription: 'Murdered by the hand he befriended.' This is the grave of Mr James Reginald Clapp, a chemist's assistant, who was brutally done to death on the night of 31 August 1909.'

Miss Ripley-Bean, who has spent most of her eighty-seven years in this hill station, remembers the case clearly, though she was only a girl at the time. From the details she has given me, and from a brief account in *A Mussoorie Miscellany,* now out of print, I am able to reconstruct this interesting case and a couple of others which were the sensations of their respective 'seasons'.

Mr Clapp was an assistant in the chemist's shop of Messrs. J.B. & E. Samuel (no longer in existence), situated in one of the busiest sections of the Mall. At that time the adjoining cantonment of Landour was an important convalescent centre for British soldiers. Mr Clapp was popular with the soldiers, and he had befriended some of them when they had run short of money. He was a steady worker and sent most of his savings home, to his mother in Birmingham; she was planning to use the money to buy the house in which she lived.

At the time of the murder, Clapp was particularly friendly with a Corporal Allen, who was eventually to be hanged at the Naini Jail. The murder was brutal, the initial attack being launched with a soda-water bottle on the victim's head. Clapp's throat was then cut from ear to ear with his own razor, which was left behind in the room. The body was discovered on the floor of the shop the next morning by the proprietor, Mr Samuel, who did not live on the premises.

Suspicion immediately fell on Corporal Allen because he had left Mussoorie that same night, arriving at Rajpur, in the foothills (a seven-mile walk by the bridle path) many hours later than he was expected at a boarding house. According to some, Clapp had last been seen in the corporal's company.

There was other circumstantial evidence pointing to Allen's guilt. On the day of the murder, Mr Clapp had received his salary, and this sum, in sovereigns and notes, was never traced. Allen was alleged to have made a payment in sovereigns at Rajpur. Someone had give Allen a biscuit tin packed with sandwiches for his journey down, and it was thought that perhaps the tin had been used by the murderer as a safe for the money. But no tin was found, and Allen denied having had one with him.

Allen was arrested at Rajpur and brought back to Mussoorie under escort. He was taken immediately to the victim's bedside, where the body still lay, the police hoping that he might confess his guilt when confronted with the body of the victim; but Allen was unmoved, and protested his innocence.

Meanwhile, other soldiers from among Mr Clapp's friends had collected on the Mall. They had removed their belts and were ready to lynch Allen as soon as he was brought out of the shop. The situation was tense, but further mishap was averted by the resourcefulness of Mr Rust, a photographer, who, being of the same build as the corporal, put on an army coat with a turned-up collar, and arranged to be handcuffed between two policemen. He remained with them inside the shop, in partial view of the mob, while the rest of the police party escorted the corporal out by a back entrance. Mr Rust did not abandon his disguise or leave the shop until word arrived that Allen was secure in the police station.

Corporal Allen was eventually found guilty, and was hanged. But there were many who felt that he had never really been proved guilty, and that he had been convicted on purely circumstantial evidence; and looking back on the case from this distance in time, one cannot help feeling that the soldier may have been a victim of circumstances, and perhaps of local prejudice, for he was not liked by his fellows. Allen himself hinted that he was not in the vicinity of the crime that night but in the company of a lady whose integrity he was determined to shield. If this was true, it was a pity that the lady prized her virtue more than her friend's life, for she did not come forward to save him. The chaplain who administered to Allen during his last days in the 'condemned cell' was prepared to absolve the corporal and could not accept that he was a murderer.

~~

Landour Bazaar

In most north Indian bazaars, there is a clock tower. And like most clocks in clock towers, this one in Landour works in fits and starts: listless in summer, sluggish during the monsoon, stopping altogether when it snows in January. Almost every year the tall brick structure gets a coat of paint. It was pink last year. Now it's a livid purple.

From the clock tower at one end to the mule sheds at the other, this old Mussoorie bazaar is a mile long. The tall, shaky three-storey buildings cling to the mountainside, shutting out the sunlight. They are even shakier now that heavy trucks have started rumbling down the narrow street, originally made for nothing heavier than a rickshaw. The street is narrow and damp, retaining all the bazaar smells—sweetmeats frying, smoke from wood or charcoal fires, the sweat and urine of mules, petrol fumes—all these mingle with the smell of mist and old buildings and distant pines.

The bazaar sprang up about 150 years ago to serve the needs of British soldiers who were sent to the Landour convalescent depot to recover from sickness or wounds. The old military hospital, built in 1827, now houses the Defence Institute of Work Study (renamed the Institute of Technologic Management}. One old resident of the bazaar, a ninety-year-old tailor, can remember the time, in the early years of the century, when the Redcoats marched through the small bazaar on their way to the cantonment church. And they always carried their rifles into church, remembering how many had been surprised in churches during the 1857 uprising.

Today, the Landour bazaar serves the local population, Mussoorie itself being more geared to the needs and interest of tourists. There are a number of silversmiths in Landour. They fashion silver nose-rings, earrings, bracelets and anklets, which are bought by the women from the surrounding Jaunpuri villages. One silversmith had a chest full of old silver rupees. These rupees are sometimes hung on thin silver chains and worn as pendants. I have often seen women in Garhwal wearing pendants or necklaces of rupees embossed with the profiles of Queen Victoria or King Edward VII.

At the other extreme there are the kabari shops, where you can pick up almost everything—a tape recorder discarded by a Woodstock student, or a piece of furniture from Grandmother's time in the hill station. Old clothes, Victorian bric-a-brac and bits of modern gadgetry vie for your attention.

The old clothes are often more reliable than the new. Last winter I bought a new pullover marked 'Made in Nepal' from a Tibetan pavement vendor. I was wearing it on the way home when it began to rain. By the time I reached my cottage, the pullover had shrunk inches and I had some difficulty getting out of it! It was now just the right size for Bijju, the milkman's twelve-year-old son, and I gave it to the boy. But it continued to shrink at every wash, and it is now being worn by Teju, Bijju's younger brother, who is eight.

At the dark windy corner in the bazaar, one always found an old man hunched up over his charcoal fire, roasting peanuts. He'd been there for as long as I could remember, and he could be seen at almost any hour of the day or night, in all weathers.

He was probably quite tall, but I never saw him standing up. One judged his height from his long, loose limbs. He was very thin, probably tubercular, and the high cheekbones added to the tautness of his tightly stretched skin.

His peanuts were always fresh, crisp and hot. They were popular with small boys, who had a few coins to spend on their way to and from school. On cold winter evenings, there was always a demand for peanuts from people of all ages.

No one seemed to know the old man's name. No one had ever thought of asking. One just took his presence for granted. He was as fixed a landmark as the clock tower or the old cherry tree that grew crookedly from the hillside. He seemed less perishable than the tree, more dependable than the clock. He had no family, but in a way all the world was his family because he was in continuous contact with people. And yet he was a remote sort of being; always polite, even to children, but never familiar. He was seldom alone, but he must have been lonely.

Summer nights he rolled himself up in a thin blanket and slept on the ground beside the dying embers of his fire. During winter he waited until the last cinema show was over, before retiring to the rickshaw-coolies' shelter where there was protection from the freezing wind.

Did he enjoy being alive? I often wondered. He was not a joyful person; but then neither was he miserable. Perhaps he was one of those who do not attach overmuch importance to themselves, who are emotionally uninvolved in the life around them, content with their limitations, their dark corners; people on whom cares rest lightly, simply because they do not care at all.

I wanted to get to know the old man better, to sound him out on the immense questions involved in roasting peanuts all one's life; but it's too late now. He died last summer.

That corner remained very empty, very dark, and every time I passed it, I was haunted by visions of the old peanut vendor, troubled by the questions I did not ask; and I wondered if he was really as indifferent to life as he appeared to be.

Then, a few weeks ago, there was a new occupant of the corner, a new seller of peanuts. No relative of the old man, but a boy of thirteen or fourteen. The human personality can impose its own nature on its surroundings. In the old man's time it seemed a dark, gloomy corner. Now it's lit up by sunshine—a sunny personality, smiling, chattering. Old age gives way to youth; and I'm glad I won't be alive when the new peanut vendor grows old. One shouldn't see too many people grow old.

Leaving the main bazaar behind, I walk some way down the Mussoorie-Tehri road, a fine road to walk on, in spite of the dust from an occasional bus or jeep. From Mussoorie to Chamba, a distance of some 35 miles, the road seldom descends below 7,000 feet, and there is a continual vista of the snow ranges to the north and valleys and rivers to the south. Dhanaulti is one of the lovelier spots, and the Garhwal Mandal Vikas Nigam has a rest house here, where one can spend an idyllic weekend. Some years ago I walked all the way to Chamba, spending the night at Kaddukhal, from where a short climb takes one to the Surkhanda Devi temple.

Leaving the Tehri road, one can also trek down to the little Aglar river and then up to Nag Tibba, 9,000 feet, which has good oak forests and animals ranging from barking deer to Himalayan bear; but this is an arduous trek and you must be prepared to spend the night in the open or seek the hospitality of a village.

On this particular day I reach Suakholi and rest in a tea shop, a loose stone structure with a tin roof held down by stones. It serves the bus passengers, mule drivers, milkmen and others who use this road.

I find a couple of mules tethered to a pine tree. The mule drivers, handsome men in tattered clothes, sit on a bench in the shade of the tree, drinking tea from brass tumblers. The shopkeeper, a man of indeterminate age—the cold dry winds from the mountain passes having crinkled his face like a walnut—greets me enthusiastically, as he always does. He even produces a chair, which looks a survivor from one of Wilson's rest houses, and may even be a Sheraton. Fortunately the Mussoorie kabaris do not know about it or they'd have snapped it up long ago. In any case, the stuffing has come out of the seat. The shopkeeper apologizes for its condition: 'The rats were nesting in it.' And then, to reassure me: 'But they have gone now.

I would just as soon be on the bench with the Jaunpuri mule drivers, but I do not wish to offend Mela Ram, the tea shop owner; so I take his chair into the shade and lower myself into it.

'How long have you kept this shop?'

'Oh, ten, fifteen years, I do not remember.' He hasn't bothered to count the years. Why should he? Outside the towns in the isolation of the hills, life is simply a matter of yesterday, today and tomorrow. And not always tomorrow.

Unlike Mela Ram, the mule drivers have somewhere to go and something to deliver—sacks of potatoes! From Jaunpur to Jaunsar, the potato is probably the crop best suited to these stony, terraced fields. They have to deliver their potatoes in the Landour bazaar and return to their village before nightfall; and soon they lead their pack animals away, along the dusty road to Mussoorie.

'Tea or lassi?' Mela Ram offers me a choice, and I choose the curd preparation, which is sharp, sour and refreshing. The wind soughs gently in the upper branches of the pine trees, and I relax in my Sheraton chair like some eighteenth-century nawab who has brought his own furniture into the wilderness. I can see why Wilson did not want to return to the plains when he came this way in the 1850s. Instead he went further and higher into the mountains and made his home among the people of the Bhagirathi valley.

Having wandered some way down the Tehri road, it is quite late by the time I return to the Landour bazaar. Lights still twinkle on the hills, but shop fronts are shuttered and the little bazaar is silent. The people living on either side of the narrow street can hear my footsteps, and I hear their casual remarks, music, a burst of laughter.

Through a gap in the rows of buildings I can see Pari Tibba outlined in the moonlight. A greenish phosphorescent glow appears to move here and there about the hillside. This is the 'fairy light' that gives the hill its name Pari Tibba, Fairy Hill. I have no explanation for it, and I don't know anyone else who has been able to explain it satisfactorily; but often from my window I see this greenish light zigzagging about the hill.

A three-quarter moon is up, and the tin roofs of the bazaar, drenched with dew, glisten in the moonlight. Although the street is unlit, I need no torch. I can see every step of the way. I can even read the headlines on the discarded newspaper lying in the gutter.

Although I am alone on the road, I am aware of the life pulsating around me. It is a cold night, doors and windows are shut; but through the many chinks, narrow fingers of light reach out into the night. Who could still be up? A shopkeeper going through his accounts, a college student preparing for his exams, someone coughing and groaning in the dark.

Three stray dogs are romping in the middle of the road. It is their road now, and they abandon themselves to a wild chase, almost knocking me down.

A jackal slinks across the road, looking to the right and left—he knows his road-drill—to make sure the dogs have gone. A field rat wriggles through a hole in a rotting plank on its nightly foray among sacks of grain and pulses.

Yes, this is an old bazaar. The bakers, tailors, silversmiths and wholesale merchants are the grandsons of those who followed the mad sahibs to this hilltop in the thirties and forties of the last century. Most of them are plainsmen, quite prosperous, even though many of their houses are crooked and shaky.

Although the shopkeepers and tradesmen are fairly prosperous, the hill people—those who come from the surrounding Tehri and Jaunpur villages—are usually poor. Their small holdings and rocky fields do not provide them with much of a living, and men and boys have to often come into the hill station or go down to the cities in search of a livelihood. They pull rickshaws, or work in hotels and restaurants. Most of them have somewhere to stay.

But as I pass along the deserted street under the shadow of the clock tower, I find a boy huddled in a recess, a thin shawl wrapped around his shoulders. He is wide awake and shivering.

I pass by, my head down, my thoughts already on the warmth of my small cottage only a mile away. And then I stop. It is almost as though the bright moonlight has stopped me, holding my shadow in thrall.

> *If I am not for myself,*
> *Who will be for me?*
> *And if I am not for others,*
> *What am I?*
> *And if not now, when?*

The words of an ancient sage beat upon my mind. I walk back to the shadows where the boy crouches. He does not say anything, but he looks up at me, puzzled and apprehensive. All the warnings of well-wishers crowd in upon me—stories of crime by night, of assault and robbery, 'ill met by moonlight'.

But this is not northern Ireland or Lebanon or the streets of New York. This is Landour in the Garhwal Himalayas. And the boy is no criminal. I can tell from his features that he comes from the hills beyond Tehri. He has come here looking for work and has yet to find any.

'Have you somewhere to stay?' I ask.

He shakes his head; but something about my tone of voice has given him confidence, because now there is a glimmer of hope, a friendly appeal in his eyes.

I have committed myself. I cannot pass on. A shelter for the night, that's the very least one human should be able to expect from another.

'If you can walk some way,' I offer, 'I can give you a bed and blanket.'

He gets up immediately, a thin boy, wearing only a shirt and part of an old tracksuit. He follows me without any hesitation. I cannot now betray his trust. Nor can I fail to trust him.

~~

Up at Sisters Bazaar

A few years ago I spent a couple of summers up at Sisters Bazaar, at the farthest extremity of Mussoorie's Landour cantonment—an area as yet untouched by the tentacles of a bulging, disoriented octopus of a hill station.

There were a number of residences up at Sisters, most of them old houses, but they were at some distance from each other, separated by clumps of oak or stands of deodar. After sundown, flying foxes swooped across the roads, and the nightjar set up its nocturnal chant. Here, I thought, I would live like Thoreau at Walden Pond—alone, aloof, far from the strife and cacophony of the vast amusement park that was now Mussoorie. How wrong I was proved to be!

To begin with, I found that almost everyone on the hillside was busily engaged in writing a book. Was the atmosphere really so conducive to creative activity, or was it just a conspiracy to put me out of business? The discovery certainly put me out of my stride completely, and it was several weeks before I could write a word.

There was a retired brigadier who was writing a novel about

World War II, and a retired vice-admiral who was writing a book about a rear admiral. Mrs S, who had been an actress in the early days of the talkies, was writing poems in the manner of Wordsworth; and an ageing (or rather, resurrected) ex-maharani was penning her memoirs. There was also an elderly American who wrote salacious best-selling novels about India. It was said of him that he looked like Hemingway and wrote like Charles Bronson.

With all this frenzied literary activity going on around me, it wasn't surprising that I went into shock for some time.

I was saved (or so I thought) by a 'far-out' ex-hippie and ex-Hollywood scriptwriter who decided he would produce a children's film based on one of my stories. It was a pleasant little story, and all would have gone well if our producer friend hadn't returned from some high-altitude poppy fields in a bit of a trance and failed to notice that his leading lady was in the family way. Although the events of the story all took place in a single day, the film itself took about four months to complete, with the result that her figure altered considerably from scene to scene until, by late evening of the same day, she was displaying all the glories of imminent motherhood.

Naturally, the film was never released. I believe our producer friend now runs a health food restaurant in Sydney.

I shared a large building (it had paper-thin walls) with several other tenants, one of whom, a French girl in her thirties, was learning to play the sitar. She and her tabla-playing companion would sleep by day, but practise all through the night, making sleep impossible for me or anyone else in my household. I would try singing operatic arias to drown her out, but you can't sing all night and she always outlasted me. Even a raging forest fire, which forced everyone else to evacuate the building for a night, did not keep her from her sitar any more than Rome burning kept Nero from his fiddle. Finally I got one of the chowkidar's children to pour sand into her instrument, and that silenced her for some time.

~

Another tenant who was there for a short while was a Dutchman (yes, we were a cosmopolitan lot in the 1980s, before visa regulations were tightened) who claimed to be an acupuncturist. He showed me his box of needles and promised to cure me of the headaches that bothered me from time to time. But before he could start the treatment, he took a tumble while coming home from a late-night party and fell down the khud into a clump of cacti, the sharp-pointed kind, which punctured the more tender parts of his anatomy. He had to spend a couple of weeks in the local mission hospital, receiving more conventional treatment, and he never did return to cure my headaches.

~

How did Sisters Bazaar come by its name?

Well, in the bad old, good old days, when Landour was a convalescent station for sick and weary British soldiers, the nursing sisters had their barracks in the long, low building that lines the road opposite Prakash's Store. On the old maps this building is If called 'The Sisters'. For a time it belonged to Dev Anand's family, hut I believe it has since changed hands.

Of a 'bazaar' there is little evidence, although Prakash's Store must be at least a hundred years old. It is famous for its home-made cheese, and tradition has it that several generations of the Nehru family have patronized the store, from Motilal Nehru in the 1920s, to Rahul and his mother in more recent times.

I am more of a jam-fancier myself, and although I no longer live in the area, I do sometimes drop into the store for a can of raspberry or apricot or plum jam, made from the fruit brought here from the surrounding villages.

Further down the road is Dahlia Bank, where dahlias once covered the precipitous slope (known as the 'Eyebrow') behind the house. The old military hospital (which was opened in 1827) has Men altered and expanded to house the present Defence Institute of Work Study. Beyond it lies Mount Hermon, with the lonely grave of a lady who perished here one wild and windy winter, 150 years ago. And close by lies the lovely Oakville Estate, where at least three generations of the multitalented Alter family have lived. They do everything from acting in Hindi films to climbing greasy poles, Malkhumb style. From wise old Bob to Steve and Andy, those Alter boys are mighty handy.

It is cold up there in winter, and I now live about 500 feet lower down, where it is only slightly warmer. But my walks take me up the hill from time to time. Most of the unusual eccentric people I have written about have gone away, but others, equally interesting, have taken their place. But for news of them you'll have to wait for my autobiography. The Mussoorie gossips will then get a dose of their own medicine. Let them start having sleepless nights.

~

'Let's Go to the Pictures!'

My love affair with the cinema began when I was five and ended when I was about fifty. Not because I wanted it to, but because all my favourite cinema halls were closing down—being turned into shopping malls or garages or just disappearing altogether.

There was something magical about sitting in a darkened cinema hall, the audience silent, completely focused on the drama unfolding on the big screen. You could escape to a different world—run away to Dover with David Copperfield, sail away to a treasure island with Long John Silver, dance the light fantastic with Fred Astaire or Gene Kelly, sing with Saigal or Deanna Durbin or Nelson Eddy, fall in love with Madhubala or Elizabeth Taylor. And until the lights came on at the end of the show you were in their world, far removed from the troubles of one's own childhood or the struggles of early manhood.

Watching films on TV cannot be the same. People come and go, the power comes and goes, other viewers keep switching the channels, food is continually being served or consumed, family squabbles are ever present, and there is no escape from those dreaded commercials that are repeated every ten or fifteen minutes or even between overs if you happen to be watching cricket.

~

No longer do we hear that evocative suggestion: 'Let's go to the pictures!' Living in Mussoorie where there are no longer any functioning cinemas, the invitation is heard no more. I'm afraid there isn't half as much excitement in the words 'Let's put on the TV!'

For one thing, going to the pictures meant going out—on foot, or on a bicycle, or in the family car. When I lived on the outskirts of Mussoorie it took me almost an hour to climb the hill into town to see a film at one of our tiny halls—but walk I did, in hot sun or drenching rain or icy wind, because going to the pictures was an event in itself, a break from more mundane activities, quite often a social occasion. You would meet friends from other parts of the town, and after the show you would join them in a cafe for a cup of tea and the latest gossip. A stroll along the Mall and a visit to the local bookshop would bring the evening to a satisfying end. A long walk home under the stars, a drink before dinner, something to listen to on the radio... 'And then to bed,' as Mr Pepys would have said.

Not that everything went smoothly in our small-town cinemas. In Shimla, Mussoorie and other hill stations, the roofs were of corrugated tin sheets, and when there was heavy rain or a hailstorm it would be impossible to hear the sound-track. You had then to imagine that you were back in the silent film era.

Mussoorie's oldest cinema, the Picture Palace, did in fact open early in the silent era. This was in 1912, the year electricity came to the town. Later, its basement floor was also turned into a cinema, the Jubilee, which probably made it India's first multiplex hall. Sadly, both closed down, along with the Rialto, the Majestic and the Capitol (below Halman's Hotel).

In Shimla, we had the Ritz, the Regal and the Rivoli. This was when I was a schoolboy at Bishop Cotton's. How we used to look forward to our summer and autumn breaks. We would be allowed into town during these holidays, and we lost no time in tramping up to the Ridge to take in the latest films. Sometimes we'd arrive wet or perspiring, but the changeable weather did not prevent us from enjoying the film. One-and-a-half hours escape from the routine and discipline of boarding-school life. Fast foods had yet to be invented, but roasted peanuts or bhuttas would keep us going. They were cheap too. The cinema ticket was just over a rupee. If you had five rupees in your pocket you could enjoy a pleasant few hours in the town.

~

It was during the winter holidays—three months of time on my hands—that I really caught up with the films of the day.

New Delhi, the winter of 1943. World War II was still in progress. The halls were flooded with British and American movies. My father would return from Air Headquarters, where he'd been working on cyphers all day. 'Let's go to the pictures,' he'd say, and we'd be off to the

Regal or Rivoli or Odeon or Plaza, only a short walk from our rooms on Atul Grove Road.

Comedies were my favourites. Laurel and Hardy, Abbot and Costello, George Formby, Harold Lloyd, the Marx Brothers... And sometimes we'd venture further afield, to the old Ritz at Kashmere Gate, to see Sabu in *The Thief of Baghdad* or *Cobra Woman*. These Arabian Nights-type entertainments were popular in the old city.

The *Statesman*, the premier newspaper of that era, ran ads for all the films in town, and I'd cut them out and stick them in a scrapbook. I could rattle off the cast of all the pictures I'd seen, and today, sixty years later, I can still name all the actors (and sometimes the director) of almost every 1940s film.

My father died when I was ten and I went to live with my mother and stepfather in Dehradun. Dehra too, was well served with cinemas, but I was a lonely picture-goer. I had no friends or companions in those years, and I would trudge all on my own to the Orient or Odeon or Hollywood, to indulge in a few hours of escapism. Books were there, of course, providing another and better form of escape, but books had to be read in the home, and sometimes I wanted to get away from the house and pursue a solitary other-life in the anonymous privacy of a darkened cinema hall.

It has gone now, the little Odeon cinema opposite the old Parade Ground in Dehra. Many of my age, and younger, will remember it with affection, for it was probably the most popular meeting place for English cinema buffs in the '40s and '50s. You could get a good idea of the popularity of a film by looking at the number of bicycles ranged outside. Dehra was a bicycle town. The scooter hadn't been invented, and cars were few. I belonged to a minority of walkers. I have walked all over the towns and cities I have lived in—Dehradun, New and Old Delhi, London, St Helier (in Jersey), and our hill stations. Those walks often ended at the cinema!

The Odeon was a twenty-minute walk from the Old Survey Road, where we lived at the time, and after the evening show I would walk home across the deserted parade ground, the starry night adding to my dreams of a starry world, where tap-dancers, singing cowboys, swashbuckling swordsmen and glamorous women in sarongs reigned supreme in the firmament. I wasn't just a daydreamer; I was a star-dreamer.

During the intervals (five-minute breaks between the shorts and the main feature), the projectionist or his assistant would play a couple of gramophone records for the benefit of the audience. Unfortunately the management had only two or three records, and the audience would grow restless listening to the same tunes at every show. I must have been compelled to listen to *Don't Fence Me In* about a hundred times, and felt thoroughly fenced in.

At home I had a good collection of gramophone records, passed on to me by relatives and neighbours who were leaving India around the time of Independence. I decided it would be a good idea to give some of them to the cinema's management so that we could be provided with a little more variety during the intervals. I made a selection of about twenty records—mostly dance music of the period—and presented them to the manager, Mr Suri.

Mr Suri was delighted. And to show me his gratitude, he presented me with a Free Pass which permitted me to see all the pictures I liked without having to buy a ticket! Any day, any show, for as long as Mr Suri was the manager! Could any ardent picturegoer have asked for more?

This unexpected bonanza lasted for almost two years with the result that during my school holidays I saw a film every second day. Two days was the average run for most films. Except *Gone With the Wind*, which ran for a week, to my great chagrin. I found it so boring that I left in the middle.

Usually I did enjoy films based on famous or familiar books. Dickens was a natural for the screen. *David Copperfield, Oliver Twist, Great Expectations, Nicholas Nickleby, A Tale of Two Cities, Pickwick Papers, A Christmas Carol* (Scrooge) all made successful films, true to the originals. Daphne du Maurier's novels also transferred well to the screen. As did Somerset Maugham's works: *Of Human Bondage, The Razor's Edge, The Letter, Rain* and several others.

Occasionally I brought the management a change of records. Mr Suri was not a very communicative man, but I think he liked me (he knew something about my circumstances) and with a smile and a wave he would indicate that the freedom of the hall was mine.

Eventually, school finished. I was packed off to England, where my picture-going days went into a slight decline. No Free Passes any more. But on Jersey island, where I lived and worked for a year, I found an out-of-the-way cinema which specialized in showing old comedies, and here I caught up with many British film comedians such as Tommy Trinder, Sidney Howard, Max Miller, Will Hay, Old Mother Riley (a man in reality) and Gracie Fields. These artistes had been but names to me, as their films had never come to India. I was thrilled to be able to discover and enjoy their considerable talents. You would be hard put to find their films today; they have seldom been revived.

In London for two years I had an office job and most of my spare time was spent in writing (and rewriting) my first novel. All the same, I took to the streets and discovered the Everyman cinema in Hampstead, which showed old classics, including the films of Jean Renoir and Orson Welles. And the Academy in Leicester Square, which showed the best films from the continent. I also discovered a couple of seedy little cinemas in the East End, which appropriately showed the early gangster films of James Cagney and Humphrey Bogart.

I also saw the first Indian film to get a regular screening in London. It was called *Aan,* and was the usual extravagant mix of music and melodrama. But it ran for two or three weeks. Homesick Indians (which included me) flocked to see it. One of its stars was Nadira, who specialized in playing the scheming sultry villainess. Some time ago she came out of retirement to take the part of Miss Mackenzie in a TV serial based on some of my short stories set in Mussoorie. A sympathetic role for a change. And she played it to perfection.

~

It was four years before I saw Dehra again. Mr Suri had gone elsewhere. The little cinema had closed down and was about to be demolished, to make way for a hotel and a block of shops.

We must move on, of course. There's no point in hankering after distant pleasures and lost picture palaces. But there's no harm in indulging in a little nostalgia. What is nostalgia, after all, but an attempt to preserve that which was good in the past?

And last year I was reminded of that golden era of the silver screen. I was rummaging around in a kabari shop in one of Dehradun's bazaars where I came across a pile of old 78 rpm records, all looking a little the worse for wear. And on a couple of them I found my name scratched on the labels. *Pennies from Heaven* was the title of one of the songs. It had certainly saved me a few rupees. That and the goodwill of Mr Suri, the Odeon's manager, all those years ago.

I bought the records. Can't play them now. No wind-up gramophone! But I am a sentimental fellow and I keep them among my souvenirs as a reminder of the days when I walked home alone across the silent, moonlit parade ground, after the evening show was over.

~~~

The Old Lama

I meet him on the road every morning, on my walk up to the Landour post office. He's a lean, old man in a long maroon robe, a Tibetan monk of uncertain age. I'm told he's about eighty-five. But age is really immaterial in the mountains. Some grow old at their mother's breasts, and there are others who do not age at all.

If you are like this old lama, you go on forever. For he is a walking man, and there is no way you can stop him from walking.

The lama in Rudyard Kipling's *Kim*, rejuvenated by the mountain air, strode along with 'steady, driving strokes', leaving his disciple far behind. My lama, older and feebler than Kim's, walks very slowly, with the aid of an old walnut walking stick. The ferrule keeps coming off the end of the stick, but he puts it back with coal tar left behind by the road repairers.

He plods and shuffles along. In fact, he's very like the tortoise in the story of the hare and the tortoise. I see him walking past my window, and five minutes later when I start out on the same road, I feel sure of overtaking him halfway up the hill. But invariably I find him standing near the post office when I get there.

He smiles when he sees me. We are always smiling at each other. His English is limited, and I speak absolutely no Tibetan. He knows a few words of Hindi, enough to make his needs known, but that's about all. He is quite happy to converse silently with all the creatures and people who take notice of him on the road.

It's the same walk he takes every morning. At nine o'clock, if I look out of my window, I can see a line of Tibetan prayer flags fluttering over an old building in the cantonment. He emerges from beneath the flags and starts up the steep road. Ten minutes later he is below my window and sometimes he stops to sit and rest on my steps, or on a parapet farther along the road. Sooner or later, coming or going, I shall pass him on the road or up near the post office. His eyes will twinkle behind thick-lensed glasses, and he will raise his walking stick slightly in salutation. If I say something to him, he just smiles and nods vigorously in agreement.

An agreeable man.

He was one of those who came to India in 1959, fleeing the Chinese occupation of Tibet. The Dalai Lama found sanctuary in India, and lived here in Mussoorie for a couple of years; many of his followers settled here. A new generation of Tibetans has grown up in the hill station, and those under thirty have never seen their homeland.

But for almost all of them, and there are several thousand in this district alone, Tibet is their country, their real home, and they are quick to express their determination to go back when their land is free again.

Even a twenty-year-old girl like Tseten, who has grown up knowing English and Hindi, speaks of the day when she will return to Tibet with her parents. She has given me a painting of Milarepa, the Buddhist monk-philosopher, meditating beneath a fruit-laden tree, the eternal snows in the background. This is, perhaps, her vision of the Tibet which she would like to see, some day. Meanwhile, she works as a typist in the office of the Tibetan Homes Foundation.

My old lama will, I am sure, be among the first to return, even if he has to walk all the way over the mountain passes. Maybe that's why he plods up and around this hill every day. He is practising for the long walk back to Tibet.

Here he is again, pausing at the foot of my steps. It's a cool, breezy morning, and he does not feel the need to sit down.

'Tashi-tilay! Good day!' I greet him, in the only Tibetan I know.

'Tashi-tilay!' he responds, beaming with delight.

'Will you go back to Tibet one day?' I ask him for the first time.

In spite of his limited Hindi, he understands me immediately, and nods vigorously.

'Soon, soon!' he exclaims, and raises his walking stick to emphasize his words.

Yes, if the Tibetans are able to return to their country, he will be among the first to go back. His heart is still on that high plateau. And like the tortoise, he'll be there waiting for the young hares to catch up with him.

If he goes, I shall certainly miss him on my walks.

~~○

The Hill of the Fairies

Fairy Hill, or Pari Tibba as the paharis call it, is a lonely uninhabited mountain lying to the east of Mussoorie, at a height of about 6,000 feet. I have visited it occasionally, scrambling up its rocky slopes where the only paths are the narrow tracks made by goats and the small hill cattle. Rhododendrons and a few stunted oaks are the only trees on the hillsides, but at the summit is a small, grassy plateau ringed by pine trees.

It may have been on this plateau that the early settlers tried building their houses. All their attempts met with failure. The area seemed to attract the worst of any thunderstorm, and several dwellings were struck by lightning and burnt to the ground. People then confined themselves to the adjacent Landour hill, where a flourishing hill station soon grew up.

Why Pari Tibba should be struck so often by lightning has always been something of a mystery to me. Its soil and rock seem no different from the soil or rock of any other mountain in the vicinity. Perhaps a geologist can explain the phenomenon; or perhaps it has something to do with the fairies.

'Why do they call it the Hill of the Fairies?' I asked an old resident, a retired schoolteacher. 'Is the place haunted?'

'So they say,' he said.

'Who say?'

'Oh, people who have heard it's haunted. Some years after the site was abandoned by the settlers, two young runaway lovers took shelter for the night in one of the ruins. There was a bad storm and they were struck by lightning. Their charred bodies were found a few days later. They came from different communities and were buried far from each other, but their spirits hold a tryst every night under the pine trees. You might see them if you're on Pari Tibba after sunset.'

There are no ruins on Pari Tibba, and I can only presume that the building materials were taken away for use elsewhere. And I did not stay on the hill till after sunset. Had I tried climbing downhill in the dark, I would probably have ended up as the third ghost on the mountain. The lovers might have resented my intrusion; or, who knows, they might have welcomed a change. After a hundred years together on a windswept mountaintop, even the most ardent of lovers must tire of each other.

Who could have been seeing ghosts on Pari Tibba after sunset? The nearest resident is a woodcutter who makes charcoal at the bottom of the hill. Terraced fields and a small village straddle the next hill. But the only inhabitants of Pari Tibba are the langurs. They feed on oak leaves and rhododendron buds. The rhododendrons contain an intoxicating nectar, and after dining—or wining—to excess, the young monkeys tumble about on the grass in high spirits.

The black bulbuls also feed on the nectar of the rhododendron flower, and perhaps this accounts for the cheekiness of these birds. They are aggressive, disreputable little creatures, who go about in rowdy gangs. The song of most bulbuls consists of several pleasant tinkling notes; but that of the Himalayan black bulbul is musical as the bray of an ass. Men of science, in their wisdom, have given this bird the sibilant name of *Hypsipetes psaroides*. But the hill-men, in their greater wisdom, call the species the ban bakra, which means the 'jungle goat'.

Perhaps the flowers have something to do with the fairy legend. In April and May, Pari Tibba is covered with the dazzling yellow flowers of St John's Wort (wort meaning herb). The paharis call the flower a wild rose, and it does resemble one. In Ireland it is called the Rose of Sharon.

In Europe this flower is reputed to possess certain magical and curative properties. It is believed to drive away all evil and protect you from witches. But do not tread on St John's Wort after sunset, lest a fairy horseman come and carry you off, landing you almost anywhere.

By day, St John's Wort is kindly. Are you insane? Then drink the sap from the leaves of the plant, and you will be cured. Are you hurt? Take the juice and apply it to your wound—and if at first this doesn't help, just keep applying juice until you stop bleeding, or breathing. Are you bald? Then rise early and bathe your head with the dew from St John's Wort, and your hair will grow again—if you don't catch pneumonia.

Can St John's Wort be connected with the fairy legend of Pari Tibba? It is said that most flowers, when they die, become fairies. This might be especially true of St John's Wort.

There is yet another legend connected with the mountain. A shepherd boy, playing on his flute, discovered a beautiful silver snake basking on a rock. The snake spoke to the boy, saying, 'I was a princess once, but a jealous witch cast a spell over me and turned me into a snake. This spell can only be broken if someone who is pure in heart kisses me thrice. Many years have passed, and I have not been able to find one who is pure in heart.' Then the shepherd boy took the snake in his arms, and he put his lips to its mouth, and at the third kiss he discovered that he was holding a beautiful princess in his arms. What happened afterwards is anybody's guess.

There are snakes on Pari Tibba, and though they are probably harmless, I have never tried taking one of them in my arms. Once, near a spring, I came upon a checkered water snake. Its body was a series of bulges. I used a stick to exert pressure along the snake's length, and it disgorged five frogs. They came out one after the other, and, to my astonishment, hopped off, little the worse for their harrowing experience. Perhaps they, too, were enchanted. Perhaps shepherd boys, when they kiss the snake-princess, are turned into frogs and remain inside the snake's belly until a writer comes along with a magic stick and releases them from bondage.

Biologists probably have their own explanation for the frogs, but I'm all for perpetuating the fairy legends of Pari Tibba.

◦◦◦

At the End of the Road

Choose your companions carefully when you are walking in the hills. If you are accompanied by the wrong person—by which I mean someone who is temperamentally very different to you—that long hike you've been dreaming of could well turn into a nightmare.

This has happened to me more than once. The first time was many years ago, when I accompanied a businessman friend to the Pindari Glacier in Kumaon. He was in such a hurry to get back to his executive's desk in Delhi that he set off for the glacier as though he had a train to catch, refusing to spend any time admiring the views, looking for birds or animals, or greeting the local inhabitants. By the time we had left the last dak bungalow at Phurkia, I was ready to push him over a cliff. He probably felt the same way about me.

On our way down, we met a party of Delhi University boys who were on the same trek. They were doing it in a leisurely, good-humoured fashion. They were very friendly and asked me to join them. On an impulse, I bid farewell to my previous companion—who was only too glad to dash off downhill to where his car was parked at Kapkote—while I made a second ascent to the glacier, this time in better company.

Unfortunately, my previous companion had been the one with the funds. My new friends fed me on the way back, and in Nainital I pawned my watch so that I could have enough for the bus ride back to Delhi. Lesson Two: always carry enough money with you; don't depend on a wealthy friend!

Of course, it's hard to know who will be a 'good companion' until you have actually hit the road together. Sharing a meal or having a couple of drinks together is not the same as tramping along on a dusty road with the water bottle down to its last drop. You can't tell until you have spent a night in the rain, or lost the way in the mountains, or finished all the food, whether both of you have stout hearts and a readiness for the unknown.

I like walking alone, but a good companion is well worth finding. He will add to the experience. 'Give me a companion of my way, be it only to mention how the shadows lengthen as the sun declines,' wrote Hazlitt.

~

Pratap was one such companion. He had invited me to spend a fortnight with him in his village above the Nayar river in Pauri-Garhwal. In those days, there was no motor-road beyond Lansdowne and one had to walk some thirty miles to get to the village.

But first, one had to get to Lansdowne. This involved getting into a train at Dehradun, getting out at Luxor (across the Ganga), getting into another train, and then getting out again at Najibabad and waiting for a bus to take one through the Tarai to Kotdwara.

Najibabad must have been one of the least inspiring places on earth. Hot, dusty, apparently lifeless. We spent two hours at the bus stand, in the company of several donkeys, also quartered there. We were told that the area had once been the favourite hunting ground of a notorious dacoit, Sultana Daku, whose fortress overlooked the barren plain. I could understand him taking up dacoity—what else was there to do in such a place—and presumed that he looked elsewhere for his loot, for in Nazibabad there was nothing worth taking. In due course he was betrayed and hanged by the British, when they should instead have given him an OBE for stirring up the sleepy countryside.

There was a short branch line from Nazibabad to Kotdwara but the train wasn't leaving that day, as the engine driver was unaccountably missing. The bus driver seemed to be missing too, but he did eventually turn up, a little worse for some late-night drinking. I could sympathize with him. If in 1940, Nazibabad drove you to dacoity, in 1960 it drove you to drink.

Kotdwara, a steamy little town in the foothills, was equally depressing. It seemed to lack any sort of character. Here we changed buses, and moved into higher regions, and the higher we went, the nicer the surroundings; by the time we reached Lansdowne, at 6,000 feet, we were in good spirits.

The small hill station was a recruiting centre for the Garhwal Rifles (and still is), and did not cater to tourists. There were no hotels, just a couple of tea-stalls where a meal of dal and rice could be obtained. I believe it is much the same forty years on. Pratap had a friend who was the caretaker of an old, little used church, and he bedded us down in the vestry. Early next morning we set out on our long walk to Pratap's village.

I have covered longer distances on foot, but not all in one day. Thirty miles of trudging uphill and down and up again, most of it along a footpath that traversed bare hillsides where the hot May sun beat down relentlessly. Here and there we found a little shade and a freshet of spring water, which kept us going; but we had neglected to bring food with us apart from a couple of rock-hard buns probably dating back to colonial times, which we had picked up in Lansdowne. We were lucky to meet a farmer who gave us some onions and accompanied us part of the way.

Onions for lunch? Nothing better when you're famished.

~

In the West they say, 'Never talk to strangers.' In the East they say, 'Always talk to strangers.' It was this stranger who gave us sustenance on the road, just as strangers had given me company on the way to the Pindar Glacier. On the open road there are no strangers. You share the same sky, the same mountain, the same sunshine and shade. On the open road we are all brothers.

The stranger went his way, and we went ours. 'Just a few more bends,' according to Pratap, always encouraging to the novice plains-man. But I was to be a hill-man by the time we returned to Dehra! Hundreds of 'just a few more bends,' before we reached the village, and I kept myself going with my off-key rendering of the old Harry Lauder song—

> 'Keep right on to the end of the road,
> Keep right on to the end.
> If your way be long, let your heart be strong,
> So keep right on round the bend.'

By the time we'd done the last bend, I had a good idea of how the expression 'going round the bend' had came into existence. A maddened climber, such as I, had to negotiate one bend too many....

But Pratap was the right sort of companion. He adjusted his pace to suit mine; never lost patience; kept telling me I was a great walker. We arrived at the village just as night fell, and there was his mother waiting for us with a tumbler of milk.

Milk! I'd always hated the stuff (and still do) but that day I was grateful for it and drank two glasses. Fortunately it was cold. There was plenty of milk for me to drink during my two-week stay in the village, as Pratap's family possessed at least three productive cows. The milk was supplemented by thick rotis, made from ground maize, seasonal vegetables, rice, and a species of lentil peculiar to the area and very difficult to digest. Health food friends would have approved of this fare, but it did not agree with me, and I found myself constipated most of the time. Still, better to be constipated than to be in free flow.

The point I am making is that it is always wise to carry our own food on a long hike or treks in the hills. Not that we could have done so, as Pratap's guest; he would have taken it as an insult. By the time I got back to Dehra—after another exhausted trek, and more complicated bus and train journeys—I felt quite famished and out of sorts. I bought some eggs and bacon rashers from the grocery store across the road from Astley Hall, and made myself a scrumptious breakfast. I am not much of a cook, but I can fry an egg and get the bacon nice and crisp. My needs are simple really. To each his own!

On another trek, from Mussoorie to Chamba (before the motor road came into existence) I put two tins of sardines into my knapsack but forgot to take along a can-opener. Three days later I was back in Dehra, looking very thin indeed, and with my sardine tins still intact. That night I ate the contents of both tins.

Reading an account of the same trek undertaken by John Lang about a hundred years earlier, I was awestruck by his description of the supplies that he and his friends took with them. Here he is, writing in Charles Dickens' magazine, *Household Words,* in the issue of January 30, 1858:

> *In front of the club-house our marching establishment had collected, and the one hundred and fifty coolies were laden with the baggage and stores. There were tents…camp tables, chairs, beds, bedding, boxes of every kind, dozens of cases of wine—port, sherry and claret—beer, ducks, fowls, geese, guns, umbrellas, great coats and the like.*

He then goes on to talk of lobsters, oysters and preserved soups.

I doubt if I would have got very far on such fare. I took the same road in October, 1958, a century later; on my own and without provisions except for the afore-mentioned sardine tins. By dusk I had reached the village of Kaddukhal, where the local shopkeeper put me up for the might.

I slept on the floor, on a sheepskin infested by fleas. They were all over me as soon as I lay down, and I found it impossible to sleep. I fled the shop before dawn.

'Don't go out before daylight,' warned my host. 'There are bears around.'

But I would sooner have faced a bear than that onslaught from the denizens of the sheepskin. And I reached Chamba in time for an early morning cup of tea.

~

Sleeping out, under the stars, is a very romantic conception. 'Stones thy pillow, earth thy bed,' goes an old hymn, but a rolled up towel or shirt will make a more comfortable pillow. Do not settle down to sleep on sloping ground, as I did once when I was a Boy Scout during my prep-school days. We had camped at Tara Devi, on the outskirts of Shimla, and as it was a warm night I decided to sleep outside our tent. In the middle of the night I began to roll. Once you start rolling on a steep hillside, you don't stop. Had it not been for a thorny dog rose bush, which halted my descent, I might well have rolled over the edge of a precipice.

I had a wonderful night once, sleeping on the sand on the banks of the Ganga above Rishikesh. It was a balmy night with just a faint breeze blowing across the river, and as I lay there looking up at the stars, the lines of a poem by R.L. Stevenson kept running through my head:

> *Give to me the life I love,*
> *Let the lave go by me,*
> *Give the jolly heaven above*
> *And the byway nigh me.*
> *Bed in the bush with stars to see,*
> *Bread I dip in the river—*
> *There's the life for a man like me,*
> *There's the life for ever.*

The following night I tried to repeat the experience, but the jolly heaven above opened up in the early hours, the rain came pelting down, and I had to run for shelter to the nearest ashram. Never take Mother Nature for granted!

~

The best kind of walk, and this applies to the plains as well as to the hills, is the one in which you have no particular destination when you set out.

'Where are you off?' asked a friend of me the other day, when he met me on the road.

'Honestly, I have no idea,' I said, and I was telling the truth.

I did end up in Happy Valley, where I met an old friend whom I hadn't seen for years. When we were boys, his mother used to tell us stories about the bhoots that haunted her village near Mathura. We reminisced and then went our different ways. I took the road to Hathipaon and met a schoolgirl who covered ten miles every day on her way to and from her school. So there were still people who used their legs, though out of necessity rather than choice.

Anyway, she gave me a story to write and thus I ended the day with two stories, one a memoir and the other based on a fresh encounter. And all because I had set out without a plan. The adventure is not in getting somewhere, it's the on-the-way experience. It is not the expected; it's the surprise. Not the fulfilment of prophecy, but the providence of something better than that prophesied.

Walking the Streets of Delhi

I made my home in Mussoorie in 1963, but of course I was to revisit Delhi many times, even spending a couple of winters there.

On one of these visits, in 1971, I reached my friend Kamal's house in Rajouri Garden, and mentioned that I had walked from Connaught Place, a distance of some eight miles. His family greeted me with a pained and bewildered silence.

Finally my friend's mother, a practical Punjabi lady, asked, 'How did you lose your money?' She kept hers knotted in the end of her sari, and firmly believed that people who kept their money in easily snatched handbags and wallets were asking for trouble.

'I haven't lost anything,' I said.

'Aren't the buses running?'

'Oh, the buses are running. One nearly ran over me.'

'Then why did you walk?'

'I thought I'd see more that way.'

The rest of the story is told in my journal: The consensus of opinion in my friend's house is that I am a little mad. They have never heard of anyone in Delhi walking from choice. They prefer to wait long periods for overcrowded buses and hang on by their eyebrows, even if the distance to be covered is only a furlong. As in big cities the world over, the people of Delhi are rapidly losing the use of their legs.

I suppose Delhi is one of the least attractive cities in which to walk about. Crossing roads can be hazardous. Single- and double-decker buses (many emitting smokescreens of diesel fumes), wildly driven taxis, unpredictable scooter-rickshaws, slow-moving cars and tongas, and thousands of wavering, wayward cyclists, make for chaos on the streets. On the main roads the traffic is fast and furious, and cyclists are frequently knocked over and killed. But Delhi has an acute transport problem, and the cycle is the poor man's only guarantee of getting to work in time. He cannot afford a scooter, and he cannot wait for a bus. And yet, in this city bursting with the Punjabi nouveau riche there are thousands who do have their own scooters and cars, and the number and variety of vehicles on the road increase at an alarming rate.

Setting out on another long walk, I realized that the pavement is meant for almost every purpose except walking. I am on the Najafgarh Road, heading in the general direction of central Delhi. It is a straight road, but this is no straight walk. To find a thirty-yard stretch of unoccupied pavement is most unlikely. In a territory where every square foot of land has a high price, why should so much good pavement go to waste?

The first two wayside stalls belong to sellers of lottery tickets. Theirs is a thriving business. All over Delhi, at almost every street corner, there is someone selling lottery tickets. The prizes are attractive enough. The owner of the winning ticket collects Rs 150,000—sometimes more—and there are a number of other prizes. And the income accruing to the state is also tremendous—so much so that almost every state in the country, including Delhi, has climbed on the lottery bandwagon. After all, it is easier than collecting taxes. No one, not even the street sweeper, grudges giving a rupee to the government if there is a chance in a million of his winning a fortune.

While the poor man is quite willing to part with his rupee, it is the rich man, the thriving businessman, who often goes in for lottery tickets in a big way, sometimes buying up forty or fifty tickets at a time. He believes that while it is great to be rich, there is nothing like getting richer.

How times have changed. Ten years ago, if I asked a Sikh boy what he would like to be on growing up, he would unhesitatingly have said, 'I'll join the Army'—or the Navy, or the Air Force. He was proud of his martial traditions. Yesterday, while talking to an intelligent twelve-year-old Sikh, I asked the same question, and received this reply: 'I'll open a cinema, or deal in spare parts.'

No spirit of adventure, no vision of faraway places—unless it be of a cloth shop in Bangkok! The boy confessed that what he really wanted in life was a television set bigger and better than his neighbour's.

~

But Delhi is not entirely Punjabi. Here on the Najafgarh Road I find a community of Lohiawalas, a gypsy tribe of blacksmiths, who have wandered into Delhi, camped on the pavement, and gone about their ancient and traditional way of living, supremely indifferent to the fast pace, the noise of traffic, the neon signs and Western clothes that surround them on all sides. Their bullock carts (in which they travel and sleep and live and die and have their babies) stand just off the pavement; these are lined with old iron stamped with decorative patterns and studded with coloured stones.

A charcoal fire has been made in a hole in the ground, and this is kept alive by a bellows worked by a wheel turned by an attractive woman wearing a black blouse and black skirt. This sombre attire is set off by heavy silver anklets and a pair of very lively eyes. Another pair of bellows has been fashioned out of goat's skin. A man is beating out a strip of red-hot tin on his anvil. A boy is filling a bent bicycle pump with sand (to keep it firm) before straightening it out with his hammer. The entire family, including bearded old men, wizened old women ready to take off on broomsticks and naked grandchildren, is at work. Handsome people these; and although they live in dirt and squalor, they seem quiet and dignified.

A little farther along the road are some people making what appear to be straw mats. These turn out to be roofs for the small shacks belonging to the Rajasthani labourers who live on the other side of an open drain. The walls of these shacks are about four feet high, the rooms about six feet square. There is no sanitation. People use the drain. They bathe at a public tap. During the rains, water moves sluggishly along this drain, but now it is dry except for pools of stagnant, slimy water, a grey liquid tinged with green. It must hold treasures for anyone searching for biological specimens. (And indeed, the enterprising Delhiwala has not ignored this possibility, for farther along, on Link Road, frogs are on sale to biology students.)

At this side of the road lies a dead pony, knocked down at night by a speeding truck. A portion has been eaten away by dogs and jackals. It is now being pecked at by crows; when these birds tire of the stinking carcass they move on to a nearby fruit stall. No one seems to notice this, least of all the fruit vendors. Well-dressed people pass by without a glance at dead horse or open drain. Is it apathy, or is it that Delhi people—city people—are unobservant by nature? Does city life dull the perceptions? Are the giant cinema hoardings so overpowering, so dazzling, that everything else pales into insignificance beside them?

Some of the shack dwellers have tried to make their homes attractive. They have whitewashed their walls, adorned them with crude but colourful drawings of birds and animals. But what a contrast there is between these humble homes and the elegant villas and bungalows of Kirti Nagar, Patel Road and Pusa Road, three prosperous areas of Delhi which lie on my route.

I went flat hunting once, but I was turned away by the house owners—not because of race, colour or religion, but because I was a bachelor. In India, staying single is something of a crime against society. Bachelors have a rough time; they seldom get invited into homes where there are girls of marriageable age.

'Are Delhi bachelors such monsters?' I asked a house agent in Rajinder Nagar.

'Most of them are very well behaved,' he said. 'But you see, parents no longer have much confidence in their daughters. A girl sees too many films, and then she wants to have a tragic affair with the first good-looking male who comes along.'

~

It has taken me two hours of foot slogging to reach Connaught Place, which is still the premier shopping centre of New Delhi, I remember it well from my childhood, in the war years, when my father was stationed at Air Headquarters in New Delhi. The capital was a small, sparsely populated town in those days. We lived in temporary R.A.F. hutments on Wellesley Road. A multi-storeyed hotel now occupies the site. The jungle where I hunted rabbits has long since been cleared to make way for the expensive residential area of Sunder Nagar. But the central vista, leading from India Gate up to Lutyens's complex of

Parliament House and the President's Estate, is still a lovely stretch of green grass, still water and shady jamun trees.

Connaught Place has not changed much. The milk bar I frequented as a boy is still there, although they do not sell milk any more; now it is espresso coffee and hamburgers. The Regal cinema has switched over to Hindi films. In its cellar is a discotheque. Shopfronts are more flashy, but service lanes have not altered. And of course the faces and clothes are different. The British uniforms of the war years have given way to the uniforms of the hippies, who slouch about in beads and togas, unaccepted and even scorned by the local citizens. Indians are not impressed by people who do not dress well. Their concept of the true Englishman is of the sahib who dresses for dinner even when there is no dinner; they *like* that kind of Englishman. No one is as clothes-conscious as a Punjabi. He likes his shoes polished, his shirt pressed, his suit spotless—a difficult business in Delhi, where the dust, even in winter, is as thick as in the time of Emperor Shah Jahan who, proud of his new capital, asked the Persian Ambassador how it compared with his Isphahan, and received the double-edged reply: 'By God! Isphahan cannot be compared with the dust of your Delhi!'

But Shah Jahan's Delhi, the old walled city near the Yamuna, is not on my route today. I am tired and hungry, and I lunch at a dhaba, a cheap eating house, one of many lining the outer pavements round Connaught Place. If one does not mind the filthy surroundings, there is good meat to be had in these little restaurants, most of them run by Punjabis who learned their cooking in Lahore. Certainly the food here is better and cheaper than the watered-down dishes served in some of the smart restaurants in the inner circle. The dishwashers and servers are barefooted hill boys, working in the city because their small fields in the hills do not provide a sufficient living for their families. They work quite cheerfully (for they are cheerful by nature), in spite of hard words, cuffs and meagre wages.

Outside, on the road, a small crowd has gathered round a turbaned Pathan. For a moment I fear violence to this exotic stranger; then I realize that the crowd is merely curious, even in good humour. The Pathan is extolling the virtues of an aphrodisiac mixture which he is trying to sell. 'Be happy!' he cries. 'And make your bulbul happy!'

In spite of the family planning hoarding directly behind him, he appears to be doing good business.

It is, after all, the marriage season.

I am forcibly reminded of this on my way home in the evening. The roads in and out of every residential area are blocked by shamianas put up for marriage receptions. This is illegal, but the fine is a small one, and when a father is spending thousands on his daughter's wedding, he doesn't mind paying a few more rupees. He accepts the summons with good humour, and carries on with the reception. This is the month most propitious for marriages. After the 15th of January, four months must pass before a Hindu will marry off his daughter. Astrology plays as great a part in the lives of the people today as it did three hundred years ago when the traveller Francois Bernier observed that no one in Delhi, Hindu or Muslim, undertook any project without first consulting his astrologer. Today, matchmakers must still study the stars in their courses before pairing a boy with a girl.

Most fathers love to give their daughters a good send-off, and Delhi marriages are splendid, glittering affairs. The bridegroom traditionally arrives on a white horse, but Delhiwalas, who like being up to date, often use cars, jeeps, or even tractors (because of the high perch they provide).

I find myself involved in a procession on Pusa Road. It is impossible to get past the throng of people, so I must remain with them for some distance. If I choose to attend the reception, no one will turn me away. The bride's people will be under the impression that I am one of the bridegroom's guests, and the bridegroom's group will feel sure that I belong to the bride's party. As most of the guests are seeing each other for the first time, it is possible for any well-dressed person to join the festivities. This frequently happens.

There has, of course, to be a band, and bands are chosen mainly on the strength of the volume of noise they are able to produce and sustain. A trumpet, sounding a foot away from my ear, sends me reeling to the rear of the procession. Drums, bugles, clarinets and saxophones burst into a great profanity of sound. It is not Indian music they play, but an admixture of military marches and popular Hindi film tunes. There is nothing like it anywhere else on earth.

The bandsmen wear red coats and white spats, but shoes are optional. On their heads they wear what appear to be Salvation Army caps. They will play on their instruments (often independently of each other) for as long as they are paid to play, and must deliver a final burst at daybreak when the bride leaves her father's house.

It is a colourful procession, headed by small urchin boys carrying gas lamps. After them comes the band; then the bridegroom's beautifully clothed friends and relatives; and finally the bridegroom, enthroned on top of a gaily caparisoned jeep.

I take a side road and leave the procession, but find my way blocked by another marriage party. This time a heavily built Sikh, slightly tipsy, embraces me as a long-lost brother. He seems to know me. Quite possibly I knew him when he was a smooth cheeked lad of fifteen; but now, disguised by a magnificent beard, he reminds me of no one I have ever known. But he wants me to join his party, and so, to humour him, I accompany him for about hundred yards, when he suddenly forgets me and rushes at some other old acquaintance.

I have to reconnoitre another three processions, and four more shamianas, before I reach Rajouri Garden. I keep going by eating boiled eggs. These are sold on the roadside, and the egg seller will even peel the egg for you, and serve it sliced, with pepper and salt, on a piece of newspaper. Unfortunately all the egg sellers disappear when summer comes, because people believe that eggs are 'heating' and should only be eaten during the winter months. I suppose the same reasoning applies to the Pathan's tonic mixture.

I am almost home. It does not look as though anyone in Delhi sleeps at night, but I am ready for bed, and all the brass bands in the city (and there must be over a hundred of them) will not keep me from sleeping.

But there is something I must do first.

The seller of lottery tickets has been staring hopefully at me, and I hate to disappoint him last thing at night. So I produce a rupee and buy a ticket; and, in doing so, I feel that I have finally identified myself with the good people of Delhi.

~~~

Bhabiji's House

(My neighbours in Rajouri Garden back in the 1960s were the Kamal family. This entry from my journal, which I wrote on one of my later visits, describes a typical day in that household.)

At first light there is a tremendous burst of birdsong from the guava tree in the little garden. Over a hundred sparrows wake up all at once and give tongue to whatever it is that sparrows have to say to each other at five o'clock on a foggy winter's morning in Delhi.

In the small house, people sleep on; that is, everyone except Bhabiji—Granny—the head of the lively Punjabi middle-class family with whom I nearly always stay when I am in Delhi.

She coughs, stirs, groans, grumbles and gets out of bed. The fire has to be lit, and food prepared for two of her sons to take to work. There is a daughter-in-law, Shobha, to help her; but the girl is not very bright at getting up in the morning. Actually, it is this way: Bhabiji wants to show up her daughter-in-law; so, no matter how hard Shobha tries to be up first, Bhabiji forestalls her. The old lady does not sleep well, anyway; her eyes are open long before the first sparrow chirps, and as soon as she sees her daughter-in-law stirring, she scrambles out of bed and hurries to the kitchen. This gives her the opportunity to say: 'What good is a daughter-in-law when I have to get up to prepare her husband's food?'

The truth is that Bhabiji does not like anyone else preparing her sons' food. She looks no older than when I first saw her ten years ago. She still has complete control over a large family and, with tremendous confidence and enthusiasm, presides over the lives of three sons, a daughter, two daughters-in-law and fourteen grandchildren. This is a joint family (there are not many left in a big city like Delhi), in which the sons and their families all live together as one unit under their mother's benevolent (and sometimes slightly malevolent) autocracy. Even when her husband was alive, Bhabiji dominated the household.

The eldest son, Shiv, has a separate kitchen, but his wife and children participate in all the family celebrations and quarrels. It is a small miracle how everyone (including myself when I visit) manages to fit into the house; and a stranger might be forgiven for wondering where everyone sleeps, for no beds are visible during the day. That is because the beds—light wooden frames with rough string across—are brought in only at night, and are taken out first thing in the morning and kept in the garden shed.

As Bhabiji lights the kitchen fire, the household begins to stir, and Shobha joins her mother-in-law in the kitchen. As a guest I am privileged and may get up last. But my bed soon becomes an island battered by waves of scurrying, shouting children, eager to bathe, dress, eat and find their school books. Before I can get up, someone brings me a tumbler of hot sweet tea. It is a brass tumbler and burns my fingers; I have yet to learn how to hold one properly. Punjabis like their tea with lots of milk and sugar—so much so that I often wonder why they bother to add any tea.

Ten years ago, 'bed tea' was unheard of in Bhabiji's house. Then, the first time I came to stay, Kamal, the youngest son, told Bhabiji: 'My friend is Angrez. He must have tea in bed.' He forgot to mention that I usually took my morning cup at seven; they gave it to me at five. I gulped it down and went to sleep again. Then, slowly, others in the household began indulging in morning cups of tea. Now everyone, including the older children, has 'bed tea'. They bless my English forebears for instituting the custom; I bless the Punjabis for perpetuating it.

Breakfast is by rota, in the kitchen. It is a tiny room and accommodates only four adults at a time. The children have eaten first; but the smallest children, Shobha's toddlers, keep coming in and climbing over us. Says Bhabiji of the youngest and most mischievous: 'He lives only because God keeps a special eye on him.'

Kamal, his elder brother Arun and I sit cross-legged and barefooted on the floor while Bhabiji serves us hot parathas stuffed with potatoes and onions, along with omelettes, an excellent dish. Arun then goes to work on his scooter, while Kamal catches a bus for the city, where he attends an art college. After they have gone, Bhabiji and Shobha have their breakfast.

By nine o'clock everyone who is still in the house is busy doing something. Shobha is washing clothes. Bhabiji has settled down on a cot with a huge pile of spinach, which she methodically cleans and chops up. Madhu, her fourteen-year-old granddaughter, who attends school only in the afternoons, is washing down the sitting room floor. Madhu's mother is a teacher in a primary school in Delhi, and earns a pittance of Rs 150 a month. Her husband went to England ten years ago, and never returned; he does not send any money home.

Madhu is made attractive by the gravity of her countenance. She is always thoughtful, reflective; seldom speaks, smiles rarely (but looks very pretty when she does). I wonder what she thinks about as she scrubs floors, prepares meals with Bhabiji, washes dishes and even

finds a few hard-pressed moments for her school work. She is the
Cinderella of the house. Not that she has to put up with anything like
a cruel stepmother. Madhu is Bhabiji's favourite. She has made herself
so useful that she is above all reproach. Apart from that, there is a
certain measure of aloofness about her—she does not get involved
in domestic squabbles—and this is foreign to a household in which
everyone has something to say for himself or herself. Her two young
brothers are constantly being reprimanded; but no one says anything
to Madhu. Only yesterday morning, when clothes were being washed
and Madhu was scrubbing the floor, the following dialogue took
place.

Madhu's mother (picking up a school book left in the courtyard):
'Where's that boy Popat? See how careless he is with his books! Popat!
He's run off. Just wait till he gets back. I'll give him a good beating.'

Vinod's mother: 'It's not Popat's book. It's Vinod's. Where's Vinod?'

Vinod (grumpily): 'It's Madhu's book.'

Silence for a minute or two. Madhu continues scrubbing the floor;
she does not bother to look up. Vinod picks up the book and takes it
indoors. The women return to their chores.

Manju, daughter of Shiv and sister of Vinod, is averse to
housework and, as a result, is always being scolded—by her parents,
grandmother, uncles and aunts.

Now, she is engaged in the unwelcome chore of sweeping the front
yard. She does this with a sulky look, ignoring my cheerful remarks.
I have been sitting under the guava tree, but Manju soon sweeps me
away from this spot. She creates a drifting cloud of dust, and seems
satisfied only when the dust settles on the clothes that have just been
hung up to dry. Manju is a sensuous creature and, like most sensuous
people, is lazy by nature. She does not like sweeping because the boy
next door can see her at it, and she wants to appear before him in a
more glamorous light. Her first action every morning is to turn to the
cinema advertisements in the newspaper. Bombay's movie moguls
cater for girls like Manju who long to be tragic heroines. Life is so
very dull for middle-class teenagers in Delhi that it is only natural
that they should lean so heavily on escapist entertainment. Every
residential area has a cinema. But there is not a single bookshop in
this particular suburb, although it has a population of over twenty
thousand literate people. Few children read books; but they are adept

at swotting up examination 'guides'; and students of, say, Hardy or Dickens read the guides and not the novels.

Bhabiji is now grinding onions and chillies in a mortar. Her eyes are watering but she is in a good mood. Shobha sits quietly in the kitchen. A little while ago she was complaining to me of a backache. I am the only one who lends a sympathetic ear to complaints of aches and pains. But since last night, my sympathies have been under severe strain. When I got into bed at about ten o'clock, I found the sheets wet. Apparently Shobha had put her baby to sleep in my bed during the afternoon.

While the housework is still in progress, cousin Kishore arrives. He is an itinerant musician who makes a living by arranging performances at marriages. He visits Bhabiji's house frequently and at odd hours, often a little tipsy, always brimming over with goodwill and grandiose plans for the future. It was once his ambition to be a film producer, and some years back he lost a lot of Bhabiji's money in producing a film that was never completed. He still talks of finishing it.

'Brother,' he says, taking me into his confidence for the hundredth time, 'do you know anyone who has a movie camera?'

'No,' I say, knowing only too well how these admissions can lead me into a morass of complicated manoeuvres. But Kishore is not easily put off, especially when he has been fortified with country liquor.

'But you knew someone with a movie camera?' he asks.

'That was long ago.'

'How long ago?' (I have got him going now.)

'About five years back.'

'Only five years? Find him, find him!'

'It's no use. He doesn't have the movie camera any more. He sold it.'

'Sold it!' Kishore looks at me as though I have done him an injury. 'But why didn't you buy it? All we need is a movie camera, and our fortune is made. I will produce the film, I will direct it, I will write the music. Two in one, Charlie Chaplin and Raj Kapoor. Why didn't you buy the camera?'

'Because I didn't have the money.'

'But we could have borrowed the money.'

'If you are in a position to borrow money, you can go out and buy another movie camera.'

'We could have borrowed the camera. Do you know anyone else who has one?'

'Not a soul.' I am firm this time; I will not be led into another maze.

'Very sad, very sad,' mutters Kishore. And with a dejected, hangdog expression designed to make me feel that I am responsible for all his failures, he moves off.

Bhabiji had expressed some annoyance at his arrival, but he softens her up by leaving behind an invitation to a marriage party this evening. No one in the house knows the bride's or bridegroom's family, but that does not matter; knowing one of the musicians is just as good. Almost everyone will go.

While Bhabiji, Shobha and Madhu are preparing lunch, Bhabiji engages in one of her favourite subjects of conversation, Kamal's marriage, which she hopes she will be able to arrange in the near future. She freely acknowledges that she made grave blunders in selecting wives for her other sons—this is meant to be heard by Shobha—and promises not to repeat her mistakes. According to Bhabiji, Kamal's bride should be both educated and domesticated; and of course she must be fair.

'What if he likes a dark girl?' I ask teasingly.

Bhabiji looks horrified. 'He cannot marry a dark girl,' she declares.

'But dark girls are beautiful,' I tell her.

'Impossible!'

'Do you want him to marry a European girl?'

'No foreigners! I know them, they'll take my son away. He shall have a good Punjabi girl, with a complexion the colour of wheat.'

Noon. The shadows shift and cross the road. I sit beneath the guava tree and watch the women at work. They will not let me do anything, but they like talking to me and they love to hear my broken Punjabi. Sparrows flit about at their feet, snapping up the grain that runs away from their busy fingers. A crow looks speculatively at the empty kitchen, sidles towards the open door; but Bhabiji has only to glance up and the experienced crow flies away. He knows he will not be able to make off with anything from this house.

One by one the children come home, demanding food. Now ii is Madhu's turn to go to school. Her younger brother Popat, an intelligent but undersized boy of thirteen, appears in the doorway and asks for lunch.

'Be off!' says Bhabiji. 'It isn't ready yet.'

Actually the food is ready and only the chapatis remain to be made. Shobha will attend to them. Bhabiji lies down on her cot in the sun, complaining of a pain in her back and ringing noises in her ears. 'I'll press your back,' says Popat. He has been out of Bhabiji's favour lately, and is looking for an opportunity to be rehabilitated.

Barefooted he stands on Bhabiji's back and treads her weary flesh and bones with a gentle walking-in-one-spot movement. Bhabiji grunts with relief. Every day she has new pains in new places. Her age, and the daily business of feeding the family and running everyone's affairs, are beginning to tell on her. But she would sooner die than give up her position of dominance in the house. Her working sons still hand over their pay to her, and she dispenses the money as she sees fit.

The pummelling she gets from Popat puts her in a better mood, and she holds forth on another favourite subject, the respective merits of various dowries. Shiv's wife (according to Bhabiji) brought nothing with her but a string cot; Kishore's wife brought only a sharp and clever tongue; Shobha brought a wonderful steel cupboard, fully expecting that it would do all the housework for her.

This last observation upsets Shobha, and a little later I find her under the guava tree, weeping profusely. I give her the comforting words she obviously expects; but it is her husband Arun who will have to bear the brunt of her outraged feelings when he comes home this evening. He is rather nervous of his wife. Last night he wanted to eat out, at a restaurant, but did not want to be accused of wasting money; so he stuffed fifteen rupees into my pocket and asked me to invite both him and Shobha to dinner, which I did. We had a good dinner. Such unexpected hospitality on my part has further improved my standing with Shobha. Now, in spite of other chores, she sees that I get cups of tea and coffee at odd hours of the day.

Bhabiji knows Arun is soft with his wife, and taunts him about it. She was saying this morning that whenever there is any work to be done Shobha retires to bed with a headache (partly true). She says even Manju does more housework (not true). Bhabiji has certain talents as an actress, and does a good take-off of Shobha sulking and grumbling at having too much to do.

While Bhabiji talks, Popat sneaks off and goes for a ride on the bicycle. It is a very old bicycle and is constantly undergoing repairs. 'The soul has gone out of it,' says Vinod philosophically and makes his way on to the roof, where he keeps a store of pornographic literature. Up there, he cannot be seen and cannot be remembered, and so avoids being sent out on errands.

One of the boys is bathing at the handpump. Manju, who should have gone to school with Madhu, is stretched out on a cot, complaining of fever. But she will be up in time to attend the marriage party…

Towards evening, as the birds return to roost in the guava tree, their chatter is challenged by the tumult of people in the house getting ready for the marriage party.

Manju presses her tight pyjamas but neglects to darn them. She wears a loose-fitting, diaphanous shirt. She keeps flitting in and out of the front room so that I can admire the way she glitters. Shobha has used too much powder and lipstick in an effort to look like the femme fatale which she indubitably is not. Shiv's more conservative wife floats around in loose, old-fashioned pyjamas. Bhabiji is sober and austere in a white sari. Madhu looks neat. The men wear their suits.

Shobha is happy. She loves going out, especially to marriages, and she always takes her two small boys with her, although they invariably spoil the carpets.

Popat is holding up a mirror for his Uncle Kishore, who is combing his long hair. (Kishore kept his hair long, like a court musician at the time of Akbar, before the hippies had been heard of.) He is nodding benevolently, having fortified himself from a bottle labelled 'Som Ras' ('Nectar of the Gods'), obtained cheaply from an illicit still.

Kishore: 'Don't shake the mirror, boy!'

Popat: 'Uncle, it's your head that's shaking.'

Only Kamal, Popat and I remain behind. I have had more than my share of marriage parties.

The house is strangely quiet. It does not seem so small now, with only three people left in it. The kitchen has been locked (Bhabiji will not leave it open while Popat is still in the house), so we visit the dhaba, the wayside restaurant near the main road, and this time I pay the bill with my own money. We have kababs and chicken curry.

Yesterday Kamal and I took our lunch on the grass of the Buddha Jayanti Gardens (Buddha's Birthday Gardens). There was no college for Kamal, as the majority of Delhi's students had hijacked a number of corporation buses and headed for the Pakistan High Commission, with every intention of levelling it to the ground if possible, as a protest against the hijacking of an Indian plane from Srinagar to Lahore. The students were met by the Delhi police in full strength, and a pitched battle took place, in which stones from the students and teargas shells from the police were the favoured missiles. There were two shells fired every minute, according to a newspaper report. And this went on all day. A number of students and policemen were injured, but by some miracle no one was killed. The police held their ground, and the Pakistan High Commission remained inviolate. But the Australian High Commission, situated to the rear of the student brigade, received most of the teargas shells, and had to close down for the day.

Kamal and I attended the siege for about an hour, before retiring to the Gardens with our ham sandwiches. A couple of friendly squirrels came up to investigate, and were soon taking bread from our hands. We could hear the chanting of the students in the distance. I lay back on the grass and opened my copy of *Barchester Towers*. Whenever life in Delhi, or in Bhabiji's house (or anywhere, for that matter), becomes too tumultuous, I turn to Trollope. Nothing could be further removed from the turmoil of our times than an English cathedral town in the nineteenth century. But I think Jane Austen would have appreciated life in Bhabiji's house.

By ten o'clock, everyone is back from the marriage. (They had gone for the feast, and not for the ceremonies, which continue into the early hours of the morning.) Shobha is full of praise for the bridegroom's good looks and fair complexion. She describes him as being 'gora-chitta'—very white! She does not have a high opinion of the bride.

Shiv, in a happy and reflective mood, extols the qualities of his own wife, referring to her as The Barrel. He tells us how, shortly after their marriage, she had threatened to throw a brick at the next-door girl. This little incident remains fresh in Shiv's mind, after eighteen years of marriage.

He says: 'When the neighbours came and complained, I told them, "It is quite possible that my wife will throw a brick at your daughter. She is in the habit of throwing bricks." The neighbours held their peace.'

I think Shiv is rather proud of his wife's militancy when it comes to taking on neighbours; recently she vanquished the woman next door (a formidable Sikh lady) after a verbal battle that lasted three hours. But in arguments or quarrels with Bhabiji, Shiv's wife always loses, because Shiv takes his mother's side. Arun, on the other hand, is afraid of both wife and mother, and simply makes himself scarce when a quarrel develops. Or he tells his mother she is right, and then, to placate Shobha, takes her to the pictures.

Kishore turns up just as everyone is about to go to bed. Bhabiji is annoyed at first, because he has been drinking too much; but when he produces a bunch of cinema tickets, she is mollified and asks him to stay the night. Not even Bhabiji likes missing a new picture.

Kishore is urging me to write his life story.

'Your life would make a most interesting story,' I tell him. 'But it will be interesting only if I put in everything—your successes and your failures.'

'No, no, only successes,' exhorts Kishore. 'I want you to describe me as a popular music director.'

'But you have yet to become popular.'

'I will be popular if you write about me.'

Fortunately we are interrupted by the cots being brought in. Then Bhabiji and Shiv go into a huddle, discussing plans for building an extra room. After all, Kamal may be married soon.

One by one, the children get under their quilts. Popat starts massaging Bhabiji's back. She gives him her favourite blessing: 'God protect you and give you lots of children.' If God listens to all Bhabiji's prayers and blessings, there will never be a fall in the population.

The lights are off and Bhabiji settles down for the night. She is almost asleep when a small voice pipes up: 'Bhabiji, tell us a story.'

At first Bhabiji pretends not to hear; then, when the request is repeated, she says: 'You'll keep Aunty Shobha awake, and then she'll have an excuse for getting up late in the morning.' But the children know Bhabiji's one great weakness, and they renew their demand.

'Your grandmother is tired,' says Arun. 'Let her sleep.'

But Bhabiji's eyes are open. Her mind is going back over the crowded years, and she remembers something very interesting that happened when her younger brother's wife's sister married the eldest son of her third cousin …

Before long, the children are asleep, and I am wondering if I will ever sleep, for Bhabiji's voice drones on, into the darker reaches of the night.

~~⌒

Street of the Red Well

The sun beats down on the sweltering city of Old Delhi. Not a breath of air stirs in the narrow, winding streets. This old Walled City, now over 300 years old, has no open spaces, no sidewalks, no shady avenues. During the reign of Emperor Shah Jahan, a canal ran down the centre of the main thoroughfare, Chandni Chowk (street of the silversmiths), but the canal has long since been covered over, and the Yamuna river, from which water has been channelled, lies beyond the emperor's fort, the Red Fort of Delhi, where the Prime Minister speaks to the multitude every year on Independence Day.

It is not water that I seek most, but shelter from the heat and glare of the overhead sun. I have chosen what is quite possibly the hottest day in May, the temperature over 105 degrees Fahrenheit, to go walking in search of—what? A story, perhaps, and adventure. Or that is what I set out to do. The heat of the day has willed otherwise. I may be ready for an adventure, but no one else is interested. I am the only one walking the streets from choice.

Shopkeepers nod drowsily beneath whirring ceiling-fans. The pavement barber has taken his customer into the shelter of an awning. A fortune-teller has decided that there is nothing to predict and has fallen asleep under the same awning. A vegetable seller sprinkles water on his vegetables in a dispirited fashion. Those cauliflowers were fresh an hour ago: they look old already. Even the flies are drowsy. Instead of buzzing feverishly from place to place, they stagger about on tired legs.

It is the pigeons who have found all the coolest places. These birds have made the old city their own. New Delhi is for the crows who like to have a tree to sleep in, even if they take their meals from out of kitchens and verandahs. But the pigeons prefer buildings, and the older the buildings the better. They are familiar with every cool alcove or shady recess in the crumbling walls of neglected mosques and mansions.

A fat, supercilious pigeon watches me from the window ledge above a jeweller's shop. The pigeon's forebears settled here long before the British thought of taking Delhi. Conquerors have come and gone, Nadir Shah the Persian, Madhav Rao the Maratha, Gulam Kadir the Rohilla and generations of goldsmiths and silversmiths. Hindus and Muslims have made and lost fortunes in the city, but nothing has disturbed the tranquil life of these pigeons. Their gentle cooing can always be heard when there is a lull in the jagged symphony of traffic noise. How do they manage to sound so cool?

But here's welcome relief for humans; a shady corner in Lal Kuan bazaar (street of the Red Well), where an old man provides drinking water to thirsty wayfarers such as myself. His water is stored in a surahi, an earthenware jug which keeps the water sweet and cool. I bend down, cup my hands, and receive the sparkling liquid as my benefactor tilts the surahi towards me.

Lal Kuan. The Red Well. Of course it is no longer here, but the street still bears its name. And I like to think that here, in the middle of the street, where a bullock has gone to sleep, forcing the cyclists to make a detour, there was once a well, made of dark red brick, where the water bubbled forth all day. Imprisoned beneath the soil, held down by the crowded commercial houses of this old quarter, the water must still be there; it gives nourishment to an old peepul tree that grows beside a temple. It is the only tree in the street. It juts out from the temple wall growing straight and tall, dwarfing the two-storeyed houses. One of its roots, breaking throughout the ground, has curled up to provide a smooth, well-worn seat. And it is cool here, beneath the peepul.

On the other side of the road, a tall iron doorway is set in a high wall. Doors like this were only built in the previous century, when a wealthy merchant's house had to be a miniature fortress as well as a residence. I cannot see over the wall and I would like to know what lies behind the door. Perhaps a side street, perhaps a market, perhaps a garden, perhaps....

The door opens, not easily, because it had been left closed for a long time, but slowly and with much complaint. And beyond the door there is only an empty courtyard, covered with rubble, the ruins of the old house. I am about to turn away when I hear a deep tremendous murmur.

It is the cooing of many pigeons. But where are they?

I advance further into the ruin, and there, opening out in front of me, ready to receive me as the rabbit-hole was ready to receive Alice, is an old, disused well. I peer down into its murky depths. It is dark, very dark down there; but that is where the pigeons live, in the walls of this lost, long-forgotten well shut away from the rest of the city. I cannot see any water, so I drop a pebble over the side. It strikes the wall, and then, with a soft plop, touches water. At that instant there is a rush of air and a tremendous beating of wings, and a flock of pigeons. Thirty or forty of them fly out of the well, streak upwards, circle the building, and then falling into formation, wheel overhead, the sun gleaming white on their underwings.

I have discovered their secret. Now I know why they look so cool, so refreshed, while we who walk the streets of Old Delhi do so with parched mouths and drooping limbs. The pigeons are the only ones who still know about the Red Well.

Bird Life in the City

Having divided the last ten years of my life between Delhi and Mussoorie, I have come to the heretical conclusion that there is more bird life in the cities than there is in the hills and forests around our hill stations.

For birds to survive, they must learn to live with and off humans; and those birds, like crows, sparrow and mynas, who do this to perfection, continue to thrive as our cities grow; whereas the purely wild birds, those who depend upon the forests for life, are rapidly disappearing, simply because the forests are disappearing.

Recently, I saw more birds in one week in a New Delhi colony than I had seen during a month in the hills. Here, one must be patient and alert if one is to spot just a few of the birds so beautifully described in Salim Ali's *Indian Hill Birds*. The babblers and thrushes are still around, but the flycatchers and warblers are seldom seen or heard.

In Delhi, if you have just a bit of garden and perhaps a guava tree, you will be visited by innumerable bulbuls, tailorbirds, mynas, hoopoes, parrots and tree pies. Or, if you own an old house, you will have to share it with pigeons and sparrows, perhaps swallows or swifts. And if you have neither garden nor rooftop, you will still be visited by the crows.

Where the man goes, the crow follows. He has learnt to perfection the art of living off humans. He will, I am sure, be the first bird on the moon, scavenging among the paper bags and cartons left behind by untidy astronauts.

Crows favour the densest areas of human population, and there must be at least one for every human. Many crows seem to have been humans in their previous lives; they possess all the cunning and sense of self-preservation of man. At the same time, there are many humans who have obviously been crows; we haven't lost their thieving instincts.

Watch a crow sidling along the garden wall with a shabby genteel air, cocking a speculative eye at the kitchen door and any attendant humans. He reminds one of a newspaper reporter, hovering in the background until his chance comes—and then pouncing! I have even known a crow to make off with an egg from the breakfast table. No other bird, except perhaps the sparrow, has been so successful in exploiting human beings.

The myna, although he too is quite at home in the city, is more of a gentleman. He prefers fruit on the tree to scraps from the kitchen, and visits the garden as much out of a sense of sociability as in expectation of hand-outs. He is quite handsome, too, with his bright orange bill and the mask around his eyes. He is equally at home on a railway platform as on the ear of a grazing buffalo, and, being omnivorous, has no trouble in coexisting with man.

The sparrow, on the other hand, is not a gentleman. Uninvited, he enters your home, followed by his friends, relatives and political hangers-on, and proceeds to quarrel, make love and leave his droppings on the sofa-cushions, with a complete disregard for the presence of humans. The party will then proceed into the garden and destroy all the flower-buds. No birds have succeeded so well in making fools of humans.

Although the bluejay, or roller, is quite capable of making his living in the forest, he seems to show a preference for the haunts of men, and would rather perch on a telegraph wire than in a tree. Probably he finds the wire a better launching pad for his sudden rocket-flights and aerial acrobatics.

In repose he is rather shabby; but in flight, when his outspread wings reveal his brilliant blues, he takes one's breath away. As his food consists of beetles and other insect pests, he can be considered man's friend and ally.

Parrots make little or no distinction between town and country life. They are the freelances of the bird world—sturdy, independent and noisy. With flashes of blue and green, they swoop across the road, settle for a while in a mango tree, and then, with shrill, delighted cries, move on to some other field or orchard.

They will sample all the fruit they can, without finishing any. They are destructive birds but, because of their bright plumage, graceful flight and charming ways, they are popular favourites and can get away with anything. No one who has enjoyed watching a flock of parrots in swift and carefree flight could want to cage one of these virile birds. Yet so many people do cage them.

After the peacock, perhaps the most popular bird in rural India is the sarus crane—a familiar sight around the jheels and river banks of northern India and Gujarat. The sarus pairs for life and is seldom seen without his mate. When one bird dies, the other often pines away and seemingly dies of grief. It is this near-human quality of devotion that has earned the birds their popularity with the villagers of the plains. As a result, they are well protected.

In the long run, it is the 'common man', and not the scientist or conservationist, who can best give protection to the birds and animals living around him. Religious sentiment has helped preserve the peacock and a few other birds. It is a pity that so many other equally beautiful birds do not enjoy the same protection.

But the wily crow, the cheeky sparrow and the sensible myna will always be with us. Quite possibly they will survive the human species.

And it is the same with other animals. While the cringing jackal has learnt the art of survival, his master, the magnificent tiger, is on his way to extinction.

Cold Beer at Chutmalpur

Just outside the small market town of Chutmalpur (on the way back from Delhi) one is greeted by a large signboard with just two words on it: Cold Beer. The signboard is almost as large as the shop from which the cold beer is dispensed; but after a gruelling five-hour drive from Delhi, in the heat and dust of May, a glass of chilled beer is welcome—except, of course, to teetotallers who will find other fizzy ways to satiate their thirst.

Chutmalpur is not the sort of place you'd choose to retire in. But it has its charms, not the least of which is its Sunday Market, when the varied produce of the rural interior finds its way onto the dusty pavements, and the air vibrates with noise, colour and odours. Carpets of red chillies, seasonal fruits, stacks of grain and vegetables, cheap toys for the children, bangles of lac, wooden artefacts, colourful underwear, sweets of every description, churan to go with them…

Lakar hajam, pather hajam cries the churan-seller. Translated: Digest wood, digest stones! That is, if you partake of this particular digestive pill which, when I tried it, appeared to be one part hing (asafoetida) and one part gunpowder.

Things are seldom what they seem to be. Passing through the small town of Purkazi, I noticed a signboard which announced the availability of 'Books'—just that. Intrigued, I stopped to find out more about this bookshop in the wilderness. Perhaps I'd find a rare tome to add to my library. Peeping in I discovered that the dark interior was stacked from floor to ceiling with exercise books! Apparently the shopowner was the supplier for the district.

Rare books can be seen in Roorkee, in the University's old library. Here, not many years ago, a First Folio Shakespeare turned up and was celebrated in the Indian press as a priceless discovery. Perhaps it's still there.

Also in the library is a bust of Sir Proby Cautley, who conceived and built the Ganga Canal, which starts at Hardwar and passes through Roorkee on its way across the Doab. Hardly anyone today has heard of Cautley, and yet surely his achievement outstrips that of many Englishmen in India—soldiers and statesmen who became famous for doing all the wrong things.

Cautley's Canal

Cautley came to India at the age of seventeen and joined the Bengal Artillery. In 1825, he assisted Captain Robert Smith, the engineer in charge of constructing the Eastern Yamuna Canal. By 1836 he was Superintendent-General of Canals. From the start, he worked towards his dream of building a Ganga Canal, and spent six months walking and riding through the jungles and countryside, taking each level and measurement himself, sitting up all night to transfer them to his maps. He was confident that a 500-kilometre canal was feasible. There were many objections and obstacles to his project, most of them financial, but Cautley persevered and eventually persuaded the East India Company to back him.

Digging of the canal began in 1839. Cautley had to make his own bricks—millions of them—his own brick kiln, and his own mortar. A hundred thousand tonnes of lime went into the mortar, the other main ingredient of which was surkhi, made by grinding over-burnt bricks to a powder. To reinforce the mortar, ghur, ground lentils and jute fibres were added to it.

Initially, opposition came from the priests in Hardwar, who felt that the waters of the holy Ganga would be imprisoned. Cautley pacified them by agreeing to leave a narrow gap in the dam through which the river water could flow unchecked. He won over the priests when he inaugurated his project with aarti, and the worship of Ganesh, God of Good Beginnings. He also undertook the repair of the sacred bathing ghats along the river. The canal banks were also to have their own ghats with steps leading down to the water.

The headworks of the Canal are at Hardwar, where the Ganga enters the plains after completing its majestic journey through the Himalayas. Below Hardwar, Cautley had to dig new courses for some of the mountain torrents that threatened the canal. He collected them into four streams and took them over the Canal by means of four passages. Near Roorkee, the land fell away sharply and here Cautley had to build an aqueduct, a masonry bridge that carries the Canal for half a kilometre across the Solani torrent—a unique engineering feat. At Roorkee the Canal is 25 metres higher than the parent river which flows almost parallel to it.

Most of the excavation work on the canal was done mainly by the Oads, a gypsy tribe who were professional diggers for most of northwest India. They took great pride in their work. Through extremely poor, Cautley found them a happy and carefree lot who worked in a very organized manner.

When the Canal was formally opened on 8th April 1854, its main channel was 348 miles long, its branches 306 and the distributaries over 3,000. Over 767,000 acres in 5,000 villages were irrigated. One of its main branches re-entered the Ganga at Kanpur; it also had branches to Fatehgarh, Bulandshahr and Aligarh.

Cautley's achievements did not end there. He was also actively involved in Dr Falconer's fossil expedition in the Siwaliks. He presented to the British Museum an extensive collection of fossil mammalia—including hippopotamus and crocodile fossils, evidence that the region was once swampland or an inland sea. Other animal remains found here included the sabre-toothed tiger; *Elephis ganesa,* an elephant with a trunk ten-and-a-half feet long; a three-toed ancestor of the horse; the bones of a fossil ostrich; and the remains of giant cranes and tortoises. Exciting times, exciting finds.

Nor did Cautley's interests and activities end in fossil excavation. My copy of Surgeon General Balfour's *Cyclopedia of India* (1873) lists a number of fascinating reports and papers by Cautley. He wrote on a submerged city, twenty feet underground, near Behut in the Doab; on the coal and lignite in the Himalayas; on gold washings in the Siwalik Hills, between the Jamuna and Sutlej rivers; on a new species of snake; on the mastodons of the Siwaliks; on the manufacture of tar; and on Panchukkis or corn mills.

How did he find time for all this, I wonder. Most of his life was spent in tents, overseeing the canal work or digging up fossils. He had a house in Mussoorie (one of the first), but he could not have spent much time in it. It is today part of the Manav Bharti School, and there is still a plaque in the office stating that Cautley lived there. Perhaps he wrote some of his reports and expositions during brief sojourns in the hills. It is said that his wife left him, unable to compete against the rival attractions of canals and fossil remains.

I wonder, too, if there was any follow up on his reports of the submerged city—is it still there, waiting to be rediscovered—or his findings on gold washings in the Siwaliks. Should my royalties ever dry up, I might just wonder off into the Siwaliks, looking for 'gold in them thar hills'. Meanwhile, whenever I travel by road from Delhi to

Hardwar, and pass over that placid Canal at various places en route, I think of the man who spent more than twenty years of his life in executing this magnificent project, and others equally demanding. And then, his work done, walking away from it all without thought of fame or fortune.

～✺

A Wayside Tea Shop

The Jaunpur range in Garhwal is dry, brown and rocky. Water is hard to find, and green fields are to be seen only far down in the valley, near the Aglar or some smaller stream. Elsewhere only monsoon crops are grown.

I have walked five miles without finding a spring or even a shady spot along the sun-blistered path, and I am beginning to wonder if the only living creatures in the area are the big lizards, who slither about on the hot surface of the rocks and stare at me with unwinking eyes. Just as I am asking myself if it is better to be a lizard than a thirsty trekker, I round a bend and discover a small mountain oasis: a crooked little shack tucked away in a cleft of the hillside. Growing beside the shack is a single pine tree, humming softly in the faint breeze that drifts across the mountains.

When one tree suddenly appears in this way, lonely and dignified in the midst of a vast treeless silence, it can be more beautiful than a forest.

There is no glamour about the shack, a loose stone structure with a tin roof held down by stones. But it is a tea shop, one of those little pockets of pioneering mankind that spring up in the mountain wilderness to serve the weary traveller. Go where you will in Garhwal, you will always find a tea shop to sustain you just when you feel you have reached the end of your tether.

The shopkeeper, Megh Chand, a man of indeterminate age—the cold dry winds from the snows have crinkled his face like a walnut but his teeth are sound and his eyes are clear—greets me as a long-lost friend, although we are meeting for the first time.

'Do you live here alone?' I ask.

'Sometimes I am alone,' he says. 'My family is down in the village, looking after the fields. It is quite far, six miles. So I go home once a week, and then my son comes up to look after the shop.'

Megh Chand tells me that he has been starved of good conversation. 'Next year,' he says, sitting down on the steps of his shop, 'the government will be widening the road, and then the buses will be able to stop here. For many years I have depended on the mule drivers, but they do not have much money to spend. Once the buses come, I will have many customers. Then perhaps I can afford to go to Delhi to have my operation.'

'What operation?'

'Oh, a rasoli—a growth—in my stomach. Sometimes the pain is very bad. I went to the hospital in Mussoorie, but they told me I would have to go to Delhi for an operation. Whenever someone is seriously ill, they say, "Go to Delhi!" Does the whole world go to Delhi to get treated? My uncle was told to go to Delhi for an operation. He went from one hospital to another until his money was finished, and then he came back to the village and died within a week. So maybe I won't go for the operation. The money is needed here. Once the buses come, I will have to keep sweets and biscuits and other things, and also a boy to help me cook a few meals. All I can offer you today is a bun. It was made in Delhi, I am told.'

'I'd rather have your lassi than a Delhi bun,' I protest. 'But where do you get your water?' I ask.

'Come, I will show you,' he says, and takes me round to the back of the shack and through an unexpected gap in the hillside. It gives me a breathtaking glimpse of snow-clad mountains striding into the sky. It is cool and shady on the northern face of the hill, and here, issuing from a rock, is a trickle of water. Yellow primulae grow in clusters along the edges of a damp, dripping rock face. The water collects in a small stone trough.

'There is no other cheshma (spring) along this road,' he says, 'and the buses can't go down into the ravine, unless they fall into it. So they will have to stop here!' He is triumphant.

We return to the shopfront, where a milkman has just arrived with a container of milk. He too sits down for rest, refreshment and conversation. Next year, if the road is ready (and it is a big if, because with hill roads you can never be sure), and if he can afford the fare (an even bigger if), the milkman will be able to use the bus. But there are some who will walk anyway, because they have always been walking. Or ride mules, because they have been doing it all their lives.

Still, when the road comes, time will take on new dimensions for Megh Chand. Even in remote mountain areas, buses must keep to some sort of schedule, and Megh Chand will have to be sure that his pot is on the boil, and be on the lookout for arrivals and departures. He will be better off than he is today but he is aware that prosperity has its pitfalls. He remembers a cousin, who opened a small grocery shop on a new bus route near Devprayag. One day, some young hooligans got off the bus, looted his shop, and left him battered and bruised. It was the sort of thing that had never happened before...

It is time for me to be on my way. 'I hope the road will soon be ready,' I say in parting. 'I hope you will make lots of money. I hope you will be able to go to Delhi for your operation. And I hope I can come this way again.'

Hill-man or plains-man, we have only our hopes to keep us going.

The Nautch Girl's Curse

At the other end of the Doon, far to the west, the Yamuna comes down from the mountains and forms the boundary between the states of Himachal and Uttaranchal. Today, there's a bridge across the river, but many years ago, when I first went across, it was by means of a small cable car, and a very rickety one at that.

During the monsoon, when the river was in spate, the only way across the swollen river was by means of this swaying trolley, which was suspended by a steel rope to two shaky wooden platforms on either bank. There followed a tedious bus journey, during which some sixty-odd miles were covered in six hours. And then you were at Nahan, a small town a little over 3,000 feet above sea level, set amidst hill slopes thick with sal and shisham trees. This charming old town links the sub-tropical Siwaliks to the first foothills of the Himalaya, a unique situation.

The road from Dagshai and Shimla runs into Nahan from the north. No matter in which direction you look, the view is a fine one. To the south stretches the grand panorama of the plains of Saharanpur and Ambala, fronted by two low ranges of thickly forested hills. In the valley below, the pretty Markanda river winds its way out of the Kadir valley.

Nahan's main street is curved and narrow, but well-made and paved with good stone. To the left of the town is the former Raja's palace. Nahan was once the capital of the state of Sirmur, now part of Himachal Pradesh. The original palace was built some three or four hundred years ago, but has been added to from time to time, and is now a large collection of buildings mostly in the Venetian style.

I suppose Nahan qualifies as a hill station, although it can be quite hot in summer. But unlike most hill stations, which are less than two hundred years old, Nahan is steeped in legend and history.

~

The old capital of Sirmur was destroyed by an earthquake some seven to eight hundred years ago. It was situated some 24 miles from present day Nahan, on the west bank of the Giri, where the river expands into a lake. The ancient capital was totally destroyed, with all its inhabitants, and apparently no record was left of its then ruling family. Little remained of the ancient city, just a ruined temple and a few broken stone figures.

As to the cause of the tragedy, the traditional story is that a nautch girl happened to visit Sirmur, and performed some wonderful feats. The Raja challenged the girl to walk safely over the Giri on a rope, offering her half his kingdom if she was successful.

The girl accepted the challenge. A rope was stretched across the river. But before starting out, the girl promised that if she fell victim to any treachery on the part of the Raja, a curse would fall upon the city and it would be destroyed by a terrible catastrophe.

While she was on her way to successfully carrying out the feat, some of the Raja's people cut the rope. She fell into the river and was drowned. As predicted, total destruction came to the town.

The founder of the next line of the Sirmur Raja came from the Jaisalmer family in Rajasthan. He was on a pilgrimage to Hardwar with his wife when he heard of the catastrophe that had immolated every member of the state's ancient dynasty. He went at once with his wife into the territory, and established a Jaisalmer Raj. The descent from the first Rajput ruler of Jaisalmer stock, some seven hundred years ago, followed from father to son in an unbroken line. And after much initial moving about, Nahan was fixed upon as the capital.

The territory was captured by the Gurkhas in 1803, but twelve years later they were expelled by the British after some severe fighting, to which a small English cemetery bears witness. The territory was restored to the Raja, with the exception of the Jaunsar Bawar region.

Six or seven miles north of Nahan lies the mountain of Jaitak, where the Gurkhas made their last desperate stand. The place is worth a visit, not only for seeing the remains of the Gurkha fort, but also for the magnificent view the mountain commands.

From the northernmost of the mountain's twin peaks, the whole south face of the Himalayas may be seen. From west to north you see the rugged prominences of the Jaunsar Bawar, flanked by the Mussoorie range of hills. It is wild mountain scenery, with a few patches of cultivation and little villages nestling on the sides of the hills. Garhwal and Dehradun are to the east, and as you go downhill you can see the broad sweep of the Yamuna as it cuts its way through the western Siwaliks.

When the Monsoon Breaks

I was staying at a small hotel in Meerut, in north India. There had been no rain for a month, but the atmosphere was humid, and there were clouds overhead, dark clouds burgeoning with moisture. Thunder blossomed in the air.

The monsoon was going to break that day. I knew it; the birds knew it; the grass knew it. There was the smell of rain in the air. And the grass, the birds and I responded to this odour with the same longing.

A large drop of water hit the windowsill, darkening the thick dust on the woodwork. A faint breeze had sprung up, and again I felt the moisture, closer and warmer.

Then the rain approached like a dark curtain. I could see it moving down the street, heavy and remorseless. It drummed on the corrugated tin roof and swept across the road and over the balcony of my room. I sat there without moving, letting the rain soak my sticky shirt and gritty hair.

Outside, the street rapidly emptied. The crowd disappeared. Then buses, cars and bullock carts plowed through the suddenly rushing water. A group of small boys, gloriously naked, came romping along a side street, which was like a river in spate. A garland of marigolds, swept off the steps of a temple, came floating down the middle of the road. The rain stopped as suddenly as it had begun.

The day was dying, and the breeze remained cool and moist. In the brief twilight that followed, I was witness to the great yearly flight of insects into the cool, brief freedom of the night.

Termites and white ants, which had been sleeping through the hot season, emerged from their lairs. Out of every hole and crack, and from under the roots of trees, huge winged ants emerged, at first fluttering about heavily on this, the first and last flight of their lives. There was only one direction in which they could fly—toward the light—toward the street lights and the bright neon tubelight above my balcony.

The light above my balcony attracted a massive, quivering swarm of clumsy termites, giving the impression of one thick, slowly revolving mass. A frog had found its way through the bathroom and came hopping across the balcony to pause beneath the light. All he had to do was gobble, as insects fell around him.

This was the hour of the geckos, the wall lizards. They had their reward for weeks of patient waiting. Plying their sticky pink tongues, they devoured insects as swiftly and methodically as children devour popcorn. For hours they crammed their stomachs, knowing that such a feast would not come their way again. Throughout the entire hot season the insect world had prepared for this flight out of darkness into light, and the phenomenon would not happen again for another year.

~

In hot up-country towns in India, it is good to have the first monsoon showers arrive at night, while you are sleeping on the verandah. You wake up to the scent of wet earth and fallen neem leaves, and find that a hot and stuffy bungalow has been converted into a cool, damp place. The swish of the banana fronds and the drumming of the rain on broad-leaved sal trees will soothe any brow.

During the rains, the frogs have a perfect country music festival. There are two sets of them, it seems, and they sing antiphonal chants all evening, each group letting the other take its turn in the fairest manner. No one sees or hears them during the hot weather, but the moment the monsoon breaks, they swarm all over the place. When night comes on, great moths fly past, and beetles of all shapes and sizes come whirring in at the open windows. The fireflies also light up their lamps, flashing messages to each other through the mango groves. Some nocturnal insects thrive mainly at the expense of humans, and sometimes one wakes up to find thirty or forty mosquitoes looking through the netting in a hungry manner. If you are sleeping out, you'll need that mosquito-netting.

The road outside is lined with nine babul trees, now covered with powdery little balls of yellow blossom, filling the air with a faint scent. After the first showers, there is a great deal of water about, and for many miles the trees are standing in it.

The common sights along an up-country road are often picturesque-—the wide plains with great herds of smoke-colored, delicate-limbed cattle being driven slowly home for the night, accompanied by troops of ungainly buffaloes, and flocks of goats and black long-tailed sheep. Then you come to a pond, where the buffaloes are indulging in a wallow, no part of them visible but the tips of their noses.

Within a few days of the first rain, the air is full of dragonflies, crossing and re-crossing, poised motionless for a moment, then darting away with that mingled grace and power that is unmatched among insects. Dragonflies are the swallows of the insect world; their prey is the mosquitoes, the gnats, the midges and the flies. These swarms, therefore, tell us that the moistened surface of the ground, with its mouldering leaves and sodden grass, has become one vast incubator teeming with every form of ephemeral life.

After the monotony of a fierce sun and a dusty landscape quartering in the dim distance, one welcomes these days of mild light, green earth and purple hills coming near in the clear and transparent air.

And later on, when the monsoon begins to break up and the hills are dappled with light and shade, dark islands of clouds moving across the bright green sea, the effect on one's spirit is strangely exhilarating. For in India the true spring, the beginning of things, the birthday of nature, is not in March but in June.

At Home under the Big Top

The big circus tent looms up out of the monsoon mist, standing forlorn in a quagmire of mud and slush. It has rained ceaselessly for two days and nights. The chairs stand about in deep pools of water. One or two of them float around with their legs in the air. There will be no show for the third night running, and tomorrow there will be problems, with the ring-hands to be fed and the ground rent to be paid: a hundred odd bills to be settled, and no money at the gate.

Nina, a dark, good-looking girl—part Indian, part Romanian, who has been doing the high-wire act for several years—sits at the window of a shabby hotel room and gazes out at the heavy downpour.

At one time, she tells me, she was with a very small circus, touring the remote areas of the Konkan on India's west coast. The tent was so low that when she stood on her pedestal her head touched the ceiling-cloth. She can still hear the hiss of the Petromax lamps. The band was a shrill affair: it made your hair stand on end!

The manager of a big circus happened to be passing through, and he came in and saw Nina's act, and that was the beginning of a life of constant travel.

She remembers her first night with the new circus, and the terrible suspense she went through. Suddenly feeling like a country bumpkin, she looked about her in amazement. There were more than twenty elephants, countless horses and a menacing array of lions and tigers. She looked at the immense proportions of the tent and wanted to turn and run. The lights were a blinding brilliance—she had never worked in a spotlight before.

As the programme ran through, she stood at the rear curtains waiting for her entrance. She peeped through the curtains and felt sure she would be lost in that wide circus ring. Though her costume was new, she suddenly felt shabby. She had spangled her crimson velvet costume with scarlet sequins so that the whole thing was a red blaze. Her feet were sweating in white kid boots.

She cannot recall how she entered the ring. But she remembers standing on her pedestal and looking over her shoulder to see if the supporting wires were pulled taut. Her attention was caught by the sea of faces behind her. All the artists, the ring-hands, and the stable boys were there, eager to look over the new act.

Her most critical audience was the group of foreign artists who stood to one side in a tight, curious knot. There were two Italian brothers, a family of Belgians, and a half-Russian, half-English aerial ballet artist, a tiny woman who did a beautiful act on the single trapeze.

Nina has no recollection of how she got through her act. She did get through it somehow and was almost in tears when she reached the exit gate. She hurried to the seclusion of her dressing room tent, and there she laid her head upon her arms and sobbed. She did not hear the tent flaps open and was surprised at the sudden appearance of the tiny woman at her side.

'Ah, no!' exclaimed the little trapeze-artist, laying a hand on the girl's head. 'Never tears on your first night! It was a lovely act, my child. Why do you cry? You are sensitive and beautiful in the ring.'

Nina sobbed all the more and would not be comforted by the kind woman's words. Yet it was the beginning of a friendship that lasted for several years. The woman's name was Isabella. She took the young girl under her wing with deep maternal care.

She showed Nina how to use ring makeup and what colours looked best at night. She was nimble-fingered and made costumes and coronets for the girl, and taught her grace in the ring. Once she made a blue and silver outfit. The first night Nina wore it, she performed solely for her friend, although the circus tent was crowded and appreciative.

The circus was kind to Nina, and she grew used to its ways. It was the outside world that puzzled her sometimes. What did her audiences think, she wondered. Did they see more than a winged stranger, green and gold and blue, hovering above them? Did they know that once she returned to the solitary square of her small dressing-room, she often crept outside the tent to hear the wind singing in the trees? Did they know that she wrote poetry?

Whenever she glanced at a map of India, the towns were not merely dots with names. They were familiar to her because the circus had been there, and she called each name softly. They sprang alive, clothed in the mood in which she had committed them to her memory. She loved the smaller towns and villages, she liked the dusty roads and the damp smell of the fields, the tall swaying stalks of sugarcane, the bright yellow carpets of mustard.

As the rain streams down outside, she sits at the window of her small hotel room, remembering all these things, bringing them to life for me. The room has bright green walls and cobwebs in the corners. The open window frames the sky and solitary peepul tree, and she is grateful for both. At twilight the birds come to roost.

There is an old bedraggled crow that comes faithfully to perch on the parapet opposite the window. He has seen a good deal of life, this crow, for his feathers have long since lost their gloss. He cocks his head to one side and regards the girl intently.

'Hello, old crow,' she says. At the sound of her voice he grows uneasy, spreads his wings and dives into the rain with his scrawny neck stretched taut. Nina, too, is restless. She is longing for the high, bright, private world above the circus ring.

The ring, she tells me, has a way of welcoming its people back. And the tent, faded and old, drenched as it is at present, is a better home than a lonely room in a shabby hotel.

~

The Box Man

Sitting outside my cottage, in the summer shade of an old plum tree, I can see a path leading through the deodars towards the next tree-darkened mountain. On this morning, I saw an old man coming down the path, walking very slowly, carrying a small tin trunk on his head.

He stopped at the gate and asked me if I would buy something. I could think of nothing I wanted, but the old man looked so tired, so very old, that I thought he would collapse if he moved any further along the path without resting. So I asked him to step in and show me his wares. He had a snow-white beard, crinkled brown skin, and bright intelligent eyes. He was thin and bandy-legged and wore a patched, black waistcoat.

He couldn't get the box off his head by himself, but together we managed to set it down in the shade and the old man insisted on spreading the entire contents out on the grass: bangles, combs, shoelaces, safety-pins, cheap stationery, buttons, pomades, elastic, and scores of other minor household necessities.

When I refused buttons because there was no one to sew them on for me, he plied me with safety-pins. I said no; but, as he moved from article to article, his querulous, persuasive voice slowly broke down my sales resistance, and I ended up buying envelopes, a letter pad (pink roses on bright blue paper), a one-rupee fountain pen, and several yards of elastic. I had no idea what I would use the elastic for, but the old man convinced me that I could no longer live without it.

He then produced a small plastic glass from his waistcoat pocket, and I thought it was another item for sale. But he only wanted a drink of water. I readily brought him some. He drank the water slowly, then leant back against the trunk of the plum tree, making no effort to pack his things. He closed his eyes. I had a sudden panicky feeling that he would die in my garden!

'I am very tired, hazoor,' he said. 'Please do not mind if I rest here for a while.' 'Rest for as long as you like,' I said. 'That's a heavy load to carry on a hot day.' He opened his eyes at the chance of a conversation and said, 'When I was a young man, it was nothing. I could carry my box up from Rajpur to Mussoorie by the bridle path—seven steep miles! But now I find it difficult to cover even one mile from the bazar to the Mall.'

'Naturally, you are old.' 'Seventy years old, sahib.' 'You are very fit for your age. You do not look more than sixty-five.' Though he was frail, he had a wiry frame and his skin still had a healthy colour. 'Don't you have anyone to help you?' I asked.

'I had a boy last month, but he stole my earnings and ran off to Dilli. I wish my son was alive—he would not have permitted me to work like a mule for a living. But he died five years ago, of a cough.' By a 'cough', I presume, he meant tuberculosis. 'Have you no relatives, then?' 'None. I have outlived them all. That is the curse of a healthy life. Your friends, your loved ones, all go before you and at the end you are left alone. But I must go too, before long. The road seems more difficult each day. I feel as though it has added a mile to its length. The stones are harder. The sun is hotter. Even some of the trees that were here in my youth have grown old and died. I have outlived the trees.'

He had outlived the trees. And I was certain that if he fell asleep in my garden he would strike root there, sending out crooked branches. I could imagine a small bent tree with a black waistcoat. He closed his eyes again, but kept on talking.

'Yes, there were times when the memsahibs bought great quantities of elastic. Today it is ribbons and bangles for the girls, and combs for the boys. But I do not make so much. Not because people do not buy from me, but because I cannot walk as far. How many houses do I reach in a day? Ten, fifteen. But twenty years ago I could walk to fifty houses. That makes a difference.'

'Have you always been here?'

'Most of my life, hazoor. Except when I went to Najibabad to get married. I was here before they built the motor road, when gentlemen came up on ponies, and their women in dandies borne by coolies. I was here when the Prince of Welles came from across the sea. And I was here during the earthquake—when that was, I cannot remember exactly, I was only a boy—but the hills shook and many houses fell. Oh, I have been here a long time, hazoor. I was here when this house was built. Fifty, sixty years ago, it must have been. I cannot remember exactly. What is ten years when you have lived seventy? It was a Major Sahib who built your house. I remember, because he did not live in it for long. He was thrown from his horse one day, and was killed. Then came—I forget the name—and his wife and children. Beautiful children. But they went away many years ago. Everyone has gone away.'

'But others have come,' I said. 'True, and that is as it should be. That is not my complaint. My complaint is that I have been left behind.' He produced his little glass again. 'I am sorry, hazoor, but talking has made me thirsty.'

I took the glass and went indoors to fill it. By the time I returned to the garden the old man had miraculously put away all his odds and ends. He stood over his old blue tin box, gazing down at it with a mixture of disdain and affection.

I helped him lift it, and placed it on the flattened cloth on his head. I opened the gate, and the box man tottered out. He did not have the energy to turn and make a salutation of any kind; but, setting his sights on the mountain ahead, he walked up the path with steps that were shaky and slow but wonderfully straight.

I watched him until he was far along the path. I wondered how long he could last. Perhaps a year or two, perhaps a day, perhaps an hour. But whenever or however he died, it wouldn't be death. He was too old to die. He could only sleep. He could only fall gently, like an old brown leaf.

Humour

Flattery Will Get You Everywhere

When I was a boy in Dehra, there was a mango grove just opposite the bungalow. It belonged to someone called Seth Govind Ram (may his soul rest in peace), and, during the mango season, it was fiercely guarded by a giant of a man called Phambiri. All my efforts to get into the grove were repulsed, and on one occasion I received a mild lathi-blow on my backside.

'I just wanted to climb the tree,' I pleaded.

'Come back when the mango season is over,' said Phambiri with a vicious smile copied from a filmi villain.

And then I discovered that he was an ex-wrestler, that he had been a champion in his youth, and had even thrown the great King Kong, a famous wrestler from about forty years ago. (I did not know at the time that King Kong, in his bad years, was constantly being thrown out of the ring.) So, whenever I passed the grove and saw Phambiri, I would remark on his great strength, his superb condition (going to fat, really), his muscles like cricket balls, and his bull-like neck and shoulders. Gradually he warmed to me, and began to tell me of his exploits. I acclaimed them. Then he showed me feats of strength, like picking up rocks and hurling them across the road. I applauded. Before long, he had invited me into the mango grove, and by the end of the week I could have all the mangoes I wanted. The guardian of the grove actually pressed them upon me.

Flattery will get you everywhere.

One of the first lessons learnt by school children is that the majority of teachers are susceptible to the most blatant forms of flattery. Hard work helps a little, but the child at the top of the class is often held in esteem by the teacher as being so polite, so sweet, 'such a little gentleman', etc. This paragon of virtue wears an adoring smile, and always waits till the teacher is out of hearing before slandering her. 'They do but flatter with their lips, and dissemble in their double heart.' The Psalmist was speaking of political hangers-on, but he could have been talking of school children. Their power games are played out on similar lines.

There is of course that cynical old ploy of telling a woman she looks ten years younger than her actual age. This doesn't always work. I once told a woman (who looked fifty) that she looked an attractive forty, and she hit me over the ear with her handbag. It turned out she was thirty.

Be careful when you flatter. The results can sometimes be unexpected.

Getting Rid of Guests

There is something we all want to do, although few of us will readily admit it: Get rid of our guests.

For nine months in the year, only my closest friends come to see me. Then, when temperatures start soaring in the plains, long-lost acquaintances suddenly remember that I exist, and people whom I am barely able to recognize appear at the front door, willing to have me put them up for periods ranging from six days to six weeks.

This is what comes of living in a hill station. I am a forgotten man until the holidays begin. Then, suddenly, I am at the top of the popularity poll.

Occasionally I am the master of the situation. I inform the hopeful visitors that the cottage is already bursting, that people are sleeping on the floor. If the hopefuls start looking around for signs of these uncomfortable guests, I remark that they have all gone out for a picnic.

The other day I received visitors who proved to be more thick-skinned than most. The man was a friend of a friend of an acquaintance of mine. I'd never seen him before. But on the strength of this distant relationship, he'd brought his family along, together with their bedding-rolls and enough luggage for a long stay.

I tried the usual ploy but it didn't work. The man and his family were perfectly willing to share the floor with any others who might be staying with me.

So I made my next move. 'I must warn you about the scorpions,' I said. 'Only yesterday I found a nest of scorpions beneath the carpet.'

The scorpion-scare is effective with most people. But I was dealing with professionals. The man set his son to rolling up the carpet, saying that carpets were the reason for scorpions. The lady turned on her transistor.

'Sometimes centipedes fall from the ceiling,' I said desperately. 'And with the next shower of rain there'll be leeches crawling in at the window.'

They must have thought I was talking about the litchis that grow in Dehradun, because they looked quite pleased. The woman had begun to unpack. We were now interrupted by someone knocking on the front door. It was the postman, with a rejected manuscript: his arrival inspired me to greater inventiveness.

'I'm terribly sorry,' I said, staring hard at a rejection slip. 'I'm afraid I have to leave immediately for Rishikesh. A paper wants me to interview the Maharishi. I hope you won't mind. Would you like the name of a good hotel?'

'Oh don't worry about us,' said the woman expansively. 'We'll look after the house while you're away. It will be very hot in Rishikesh, but I suppose you have to earn a living. You must return soon. Only do let us know when you're coming!'

Monkeying About

1

I am fairly tolerant of monkeys doing the bhangra on my roof, but I do resent it when they start invading my rooms. Not so long ago, I opened the bathroom door to find a very large Rhesus monkey sitting on the potty. He wasn't actually using the potty—monkeys prefer parapet walls—but he had obviously found it a comfortable place to sit, and he showed no signs of vacating the throne when politely requested to do so. Bullies seldom do. So I had to give him a fright by slamming the door as loudly as I could, and he took off through the open window and found his cousins on the hillside.

On another occasion, a female of the species sat on my desk, lifted the telephone receiver and appeared to be making an STD call to some distant relative. Some ladies are apt to linger long over their calls, and I hated to interrupt, but I was anxious to get in touch with my publisher, who took priority; so I pushed her off my desk with a feather-duster. She was so resentful of this intrusion that she made off with my telephone directory and tore it to shreds, scattering pages along the road. As this was something that I had wanted to do for a long time, I could not help admiring her audacity.

The kitchen area of our flat is closely guarded, as I resent sharing my breakfast with creatures great and small. But the other day a wily crow flew in and made off with my boiled egg. I know crows are fond of eggs—other birds' eggs that is—but I did not know that they like them boiled. Anyway, this egg was still piping hot, and the crow had to drop it on the road, where it was seized upon by one of the stray dogs who police this end of the road.

Barking furiously, the dogs run after the monkeys, who simply leap onto the nearest tree or rooftop and proceed to throw insults at the frustrated pack. The dogs never succeed in catching anything except their own kind. Canine intruders from another area are readily attacked and driven away.

~

Having dressed, breakfasted and written the morning's two or three pages (early morning is the best time to do this), I am free to walk up the road to the bank or post office or tea shop at the top of the hill. If it's springtime, I shall look out for wild flowers. If it's monsoon time; I shall look out for leeches.

Well, it's monsoon time, and we haven't seen the sun for a couple of weeks. Clouds envelop the hills, and a light shower is falling. I have unfurled my bright yellow umbrella, as a gesture of defiance. At least it provides some contrast to the grey sky and the dark green of the hillside. You cannot see the snows or even the next mountain. There's no one else on the road today, only a few intrepid tourists from Amritsar. I overhead one robust Punjabi complain to his guide: 'You've brought us all the way to the top of this forsaken mountain, and what have you shown us? The kabristan!'

True, the old British graves are all that one can see through the fog. Some of the tombstones have been standing there for close on two centuries. The old abandoned parsonage next door to the cemetery is now the home of Victor Banerjee, the celebrated actor. He enjoys living next door to the graveyard, and one night he defied me to walk home alone past the graves. I am not a superstitious person but I did feel rather uneasy as those old graves loomed up through the mist. I was startled by the cry of a night bird emanating from behind one of the tombstones. Then a weird, blood-chilling cry rose from a clump of bushes. It was Victor, trying to frighten me—or possibly practicing for his next role as Dracula. I was about to break into a run when a large dog—one of our strays—appeared beside me and accompanied me home. On a dark and scary night, even a half-starved mongrel is welcome company.

By day, the road holds no terrors. But there are other hazards. On the road near Char Dukan, several small boys are kicking a football around. The ball rolls temptingly towards me. Remembering my football skills of fifty or more years ago, I cannot resist the temptation to put boot to ball. I give it a mighty kick. The ball sails away, the children applaud, I am left hopping about on the road in agony, I had quite forgotten my gout!

I'm glad I stuck to writing instead of taking up professional football. At seventy I can still write without inflicting damage on myself.

~

When I am feeling good, and have the road to myself, I do occasionally break into song. This is the only opportunity I have to sing. Otherwise my musical abilities turn friends into foes.

I am not permitted to sing in the homes of my friends. If I am being driven about in their cars, I am told to remain silent unless we veer off the road or hit an oncoming vehicle. Even at home, the sound of my music causes the girls to drop dishes and the children to find an excuse to stop doing their homework.

'Dada is ill again,' says Gautam, when all I am trying to do is emulate Caruso singing *Che Gelida Manina* (Your Tiny Hand is Frozen) from *La Boheme*. Our tiny hands do freeze up here in the winter, and there's nothing like an operatic aria to get the blood circulating freely. Of course Caruso was a tenor, but I can also sing baritone like Domingo or Nelson Eddy and bass like Chaliapin the great Russian singer. Sometimes I combine all three voices—tenor, baritone, bass—and that's when the window glass shatters and cars come to a screeching halt.

It was a boyhood ambition to be an opera star, but I'm afraid I never made it beyond the school choir. Our music teacher did not appreciate the wide range of my voice.

'Too loud!' she would screech. 'Too flat!'

'Caruso sings in A-flat,' I replied.

'You sound like a warbling frog,' she snapped.

'And you look like one,' I responded.

And that was the end of my brief appearance in cassock and surplice.

But when I'm on the open road—especially when it's raining and I have the road to myself—I am free to sing as loud and as flat as I like, and if flat tyres on passing cars are the result, it's the fault of the tyres and not my singing. So here we go:

> 'When you are down and out,
> Lift up your head and shout—
> It's going to be a great day!'

There's nothing like a spirited song to raise the flagging spirit. Whenever I feel down and out—and that's often enough—I recall some old favourite and share it with the trees, the birds, and even those pesky monkeys.

> 'Just like a sunflower
> After a summer shower
> My inspiration is you!'

Sloppy, sentimental stuff, but it works. And there's always the likelihood of a little romance around the corner.

> 'Some enchanted evening
> You will see a stranger
> Across a crowded room...'

Actually, I prefer the winding road to a crowded room. Romantic encounters are more likely when there are not too many people around. Such as the other day, when I had unfurled my new umbrella and was sauntering up the road, singing my favourite rain song, *Singing in the Rain*.

I had gone some distance when I noticed a young lady struggling up the road a little way ahead of me. My glasses were wet and misty, but I was determined to share my umbrella with any damsel in distress. So, huffing and puffing, I caught up with her.

'Do share my umbrella,' I offered.

No, she wasn't sweet twenty-one, as I'd hoped. She was nearer eighty. But she was munching on a bhutta, so her teeth were in good order. She took the umbrella from me and marched on ahead, leaving me to get drenched. A retired headmistress, as I discovered later!

She returned the umbrella when we got to Char Dukan, but in future I shall make a frontal approach before making any gallant overtures on the road. Those crowded rooms are safer.

Monsoon time, and umbrellas are taken out and frequently lost. I lost three last year. One was borrowed, and as you know, borrowed books and umbrellas are seldom returned. By some mysterious process they become the permanent property of the borrower. Another disappeared while I was cashing a cheque in the bank. And the third was wrecked in the following fashion.

Coming down from Char Dukan, I found two hefty boys engaged in furious combat in the middle of the road. One was a kick-boxer, the other a kung-fu exponent. Afraid that one of them would be badly hurt, I decided to intervene, and called out, 'Come on boys, break it up!'

I thrust my umbrella between them in a bid to end the fracas. My umbrella received a mighty kick, and went sailing across the road and over the parapet. The boys stopped fighting in order to laugh at my discomfiture. One of them retrieved my umbrella, minus its handle.

In a way, I'd been successful as a peacemaker—certainly more successful than the United Nations—although at some cost to my personal property. Well, we peacemakers must be prepared to put up with a little inconvenience.

I'm a great believer in the Law of Compensation (as propounded by Emerson in his famous essay)—that what we do, good or bad, is returned in full measure in this life rather than in the hereafter. Not long after the incident just described, there was my old friend Vipin Buckshey standing on the threshold with a seasonal gift—a beautiful blue umbrella!

He did not know about the street-fighters, but had read my story 'The Blue Umbrella'—a simple tale about greed being overcome by generosity—and had bought me a blue umbrella in appreciation. I shall be careful not to lose it.

2

Those monkeys are at the bank too. They are there before it opens, doing their best to damage the roof; and they are there when it closes, tearing up the geraniums so lovingly planted by the manager.

I am also there when it opens, having, as usual, run short over the weekend, with the result that all I have in my pocket is a damaged fifty rupee note which I have attempted to repair with Sellotape. The bank opens promptly at 10 a.m. Unfortunately, it doesn't have any money. No, it has not collapsed like the old Mansaram Bank, for which Ganesh Saili still has his father's chequebook showing a balance of three hundred rupees in 1957; the taxi with the cash (which comes from the main branch) has been caught in a traffic jam due to an unprecedented influx of tourists. This happens occasionally, as there are only two ways in and out of Mussoorie and only one way to Char Dukan.

Anyway, I pass the time by having a cup of tea with the manager and discussing the latest cricket test match with the cashier. He is of the opinion that the result of a match depends on who wins the toss, while I maintain that the game is won by the team that has slept better the night before.

The cash arrives safely and I emerge into the sunshine to be met by several small boys who demand money for a cricket ball. I part with a new fifty rupee note (the old one having been obligingly changed by the cashier) and then run into several members of Tom Alter's cricket team, who insist that I join their Invitation XI in a game against the Dhobi Ghat Team, about to be played up at Chey-Tanki flat. (This was before the area got fenced off by the Defence establishment as cricket balls kept sailing into their offices and smashing their computers.)

Forgetting my age, but remembering my great days as a twelfth man for the Doon Heroes, I consented on condition that a substitute would field in my place. (No longer would I be a twelfth man.)

Well, the Dhobi Ghat Team put up a good score, and Tom's Invitation XI was trailing by some sixty or seventy runs, when I came in to bat at number seven. Tom was at the other end, holding the innings together.

The bowler (who ran a dry-cleaner's in town) was a real speedster, and his first ball caught me in the midriff. I am well padded there (by nature) but I resolved not to use that dry-cleaner's shop again. The second ball took the edge of my bat and sped away for four.

'Well played, Ruskin!' called Tom encouragingly, and I resolved to write a part for him in my next story. I tapped the third ball into the covers and set off for a run, completely forgetting that I hadn't taken a run in fifty years. Still, I got to the other end, gasping for breath and trembling in the legs. Next, Tom tapped the ball away and called me for a run! There was no way I was going to join the brave souls sleeping in Jogger's Park (the name for the Landour cemetery), so I held up my hand and remained rooted to the crease. Tom was halfway down the pitch when the ball hit his stumps and he was run out. The look he gave me as he marched back to the pavilion was as effective as any that he had essayed in his more villainous roles.

I managed another streaky four before being bowled, and when I returned to the 'pavilion' (the gardener's shed), Tom sportingly said, 'You should stick to writing, Ruskin'—quite forgetting that I had out-scored him!

After that, I had to pay for the refreshments and contribute towards the prize money (won by the Dhobi Ghat Team), and all this necessitated another trip to the bank before closing time.

~

I was home well in time for lunch. My favourite: rajma curry with hot chapattis and mango pickle. As it was a Saturday, the kids were home from school, and we all tucked in—except for Gautam who was on a hunger strike because his promised Saturday ice cream was missing. Then his father arrived and took us for a drive to Dhanaulti, where there was ice cream aplenty.

Gone are the days when a picnic involved preparing and packing a lunch basket, and then trudging off into the wilderness on a hot and dusty road. People don't walk anymore. They get into their cars and drive out to a crowded 'picnic spot' where dhabas will provide you with national dishes such as chow mein or pizza. While Indian cuisine has taken over Britain, Chinese and Italian dishes have conquered Indian palates. There's globalization for you.

But I miss those picnics of old. They were leisurely, strung-out affairs. We seemed to have more time on our hands and a picnic meant an entire day's outing.

In Shimla we picnicked at the Brockhurst tennis courts (now

apartment buildings), or out at Jutogh or Summer Hill, or beyond Chota Shimla; but not at Jakko, where the monkeys—hundreds of them—were inclined to join in.

In Dehradun we picnicked at Sulphur Springs, or in the hills near Rajpura, or on the banks of the Tons or Suswa rivers. You could also go fishing at Raiwala, just before the Song joins the Ganga. Equipped with rod and line, some friends and I went fishing there, but being inexpert, caught nothing. Some soldiers who were camping there had caught dozens of fish (by stunning them with explosives, I'm afraid) and were generous enough to give us a couple of large singharas. We returned to Dehra with our 'catch', and impressed friends and neighbours with our prowess as anglers.

Here in Mussoorie, there was Mossy Falls, and other more distant falls: the Company Bagh, Cloud's End, Haunted Houses and the banks of the little Aglar river.

I won't go down to the Aglar again, at least not on foot. Climbing up, ascending from 2,000 to 7,000 feet within a distance of three or four miles takes it out of you. On my first visit, some thirty years ago, I was accompanied by several school children. On our way back, we took the wrong path and lost our way (a frequent occurrence when I'm put in charge), and it was past ten o'clock when we were located by a bunch of anxious and angry parents accompanied by villagers who'd seen me going down. Fortunately, there was a full moon and there were no mishaps on the steep and stony path.

We went to bed hungry that night.

On another occasion, well provisioned with parathas, various sabzi, pickles, boiled eggs and bananas, two young friends—Kuku and Deepak—and I, tramped down to the Aglar and spread ourselves out on a grassy knoll. A pool of limpid water looked cool and inviting. We removed our clothes and plunged into the water. Great fun! We romped about, quite oblivious to what might be happening to our provisions. Then one of us looked up and yelled, 'Monkeys!' At least six of them were tucking into our lunch. We scrambled up the bank, and the monkeys fled, taking with them the remains of the parathas, the last bananas and most of our underwear. They had left the pickle for us.

We were a sorry-looking threesome by the time we returned to the town. But we did not go to bed hungry. We had enough money between us for a meal at Neelam's—then the most popular restaurant on the Mall—and we did full justice to various kababs, koftas, tikkas and tandoori rotis.

~

By now, my readers will have come to the conclusion that I am perpetually persecuted by monkeys. And you would not be far wrong, gentle reader. Even as I write, I see one grinning at me from my window. Fortunately the window is closed and he cannot get in. I stick my tongue out at him, and he takes off, finding me far more hideous than his friends and relations.

But it wasn't always like that. Some years ago, when I lived in Maplewood, on the edge of the forest, a little girl monkey would sometimes perch shyly on the windowsill and study me with friendly curiosity. The rest of her tribe showed no interest in me as a person, but this little girl—and I think of her as a human rather than as a monkey—would turn up every morning while I was at my typewriter, and sit there quietly, her eyes intent on me as I tapped out a story or article. Perhaps it was the typewriter that fascinated her. I like to think it was my blue eyes. She had blue eyes too!

Now it isn't often that girls take a fancy to me, but I like to think that the little monkey had a crush on me. Her eyes had a gentle, appealing look, and she would make little chuckling sounds that I took for intimate conversation. If I approached, she would leap onto the walnut tree just outside the window and gesture to me to join her there. But my tree-climbing days were already over; and besides, I was afraid of her peers and parents.

One day I came into the room and found her at the typewriter, playing with the keys. When she saw me, she returned to the window and looked guilty. I looked down at the sheet in my machine. Had she been trying to give me a message? It read something like this—*!;!_1;:0—and there it broke off. I'm convinced she was trying to write the word 'love'.

However, I never did find out for sure, and the tribe went away, taking my girl-friend with her. I never saw her again. Perhaps they married her off.

~

Talking of marriages, I am often asked by sympathetic readers why I never married. Now that's a long, sad story which would be out of place here, but I can tell you the story of my Uncle Bertie and why he never married.

As a young man, Uncle Bertie worked at the Ishapore rifle factory, which is just outside Kolkata. In pre-Independence days, Ishapore had a large Anglo-Indian and European community, many of whom were employed in the factory. Uncle Bertie was an impetuous fellow. He had a bit of a fling with a girl who lived across the road, and after a romp in the nearest mango-grove, he asked her to marry him. She agreed with alacrity. She was older than him, much taller, and her figure—46, 46, 46—would have been the envy of Marlene Dietrich or Marilyn Monroe. The girl's parents were agreeable, and everything had been arranged when Bertie Bond began to have second thoughts. He was always one for second thoughts. His brief infatuation over, he began to wonder what he had seen in the girl in the first place. She liked going to dances and Bertie couldn't dance. Her reading was limited to film magazines such as *Hollywood Romance*, while Bertie read Maxim Gorky and Emile Zola. She could not cook. Nor could Bertie. And khansamas were expensive. She liked to go shopping and Bertie's salary was three hundred rupees per month.

The banns were announced, the great day came around, and the church filled up with friends, relatives and well-wishers. The padre put on his gown and prepared to take the wedding service. The bride was present, arrayed in the white wedding dress in which her mother had been married. But there was no sign of Bertie. Half an hour, an hour, two hours passed. The bridegroom could not be found.

He had, in fact, fled to Calcutta, and had gone underground. He remained underground for some time, emerging from hiding only in order to take a job at the docks in Ishapore. Everyone was waiting for him to return. They had varied and interesting ideas of what they would do to him. Some of them are still waiting.

'Marriage,' said Oscar Wilde, 'is a romance in which the hero dies in the first chapter.'

Uncle Bertie made his exit in the Preface.

~~

Frogs in the Fountain

Marigolds grow almost everywhere in our beautiful country, and they are constantly in demand—at festivals, marriages, religious ceremonies, arrivals and departures, functions of all kinds. If you happen to be a guest of honour on a public occasion, be prepared to be smothered in garlands of marigolds. I am a little wary of these welcoming garlands because on one occasion a slumbering bee, nestling between the petals, flew out and stung me under my chin. It made for a very short speech.

When I told young Gautam about this incident, he asked, 'Is that how you got your double chin?'

Actually the double chin came from my grandmother, who was a large, generously proportioned lady with a number of chins. Gautam and his sister Shrishti like to play with my double chin, but I would never have dared touch my old Granny on her chin or anywhere else. She was a stern, reserved woman, with a strict Victorian upbringing, who believed that little boys should speak only when spoken to.

She fed us reasonably well—she kept a great khansama—but she did not believe in second helpings, with the result that I spent the rest of my life indulging in second helpings.

Two mutton koftas were all that I was allowed with my plate of rice. I liked koftas—still do—and it was painful for a small boy to have to stop at two. Now that I am a grown man with an independent source of income, I help myself to four! Who can stop me?

Dr Bhist, who drops in to see me once a year, remarked that I looked overweight and that I should cut down on my food intake.

'What did you have for lunch?' he asked.

'Kofta curry and rice.'

'How much rice?'

'Just two small helpings.'

'And how many koftas?'

'Only four.'

'Don't have more than two,' he advised.

'Yes, Granny,' I said.

Dr Bhist gave me a puzzled look.

'Sorry,' I said, 'I thought you were my grandmother.' Now he thinks I've got Alzheimer's.

~

Talking of marigolds, Granny surrounded her house with them, as she believed they kept snakes away. Apparently snakes do not like their pungent aroma. I, too, believed in this folklore until I was told (by an expert on reptiles) that snakes do not have a strong sense of smell and would be impervious to the scent of flowers or other odours. Maybe so, but I don't recall ever seeing a snake in Granny's garden, although I did see them elsewhere. However, we did have plenty of frogs, thanks to the disused fountain installed by my grandfather but neglected after his death.

The fountain hadn't functioned for a couple of years, but the little reservoir in which it stood had filled up with rain water and was now covered with water lilies.

One day, after an expedition to the Canal Head Works, I brought home some small fish in a bucket and introduced them to the lily pond. I hadn't paid much attention to the tadpoles swimming around in the bucket.

Well, the fish died as they were used to fresh running water, not stagnant water; but the tadpoles did very well, and before long we had frogs leaping all over the place. Very soon the frogs multiplied. They would come into the verandah at night and keep us awake with their incessant singing and warbling.

'I can't sleep a wink,' complained Aunt Mabel, who was very sensitive to noise and allergic to choirs made up entirely of bass singers.

'They're serenading you,' I said. It was a long time since anyone had serenaded Aunt Mabel, a confirmed spinster in her early forties.

'They'll go away once the rains finish,' said Granny hopefully. But they did not go away. One day screams came from the bathroom— Aunt Mabel screaming for help! Granny, the khansama and I ran to her aid, and discovered that the cause of her distress was a large frog swimming around in the potty.

I pulled the flush chain. There was a loud gurgling sound, a combination of frog and flush, and out jumped the frog straight into Aunt Mabel's arms. She left for Lucknow that day, saying she would be safer in a zoo, where her cousin was the superintendent.

Well, Granny hired some labourers to empty the lily pond and round up as many frogs as they could. They were put into baskets and taken to some mysterious destination.

'Perhaps they've been exported to China,' I mused, 'or even to France. They eat frogs there, don't they?'

'Only the legs,' said Granny.

But they hadn't been exported. The khansama told me later that the baskets had been opened and dumped near a pond behind the railway station and before long they were all over the station waiting-rooms and platforms, until the stationmaster had a brilliant idea. He had the frogs rounded up by a number of street urchins who wanted to make a little pocket money; he then had them packed firmly into several well-ventilated boxes.

The crates were labelled 'To Lucknow Zoo—Attn: Superintendent Sahib', and dispatched as a free gift.

'A zoo is the best place for creatures great and small,' opined our philosophical stationmaster, who had previously sent them a consignment of stray station dogs.

~

Strangely enough, Aunt Mabel would have preferred a crate of frogs to a bouquet of flowers. She was allergic to flowers. Apparently the pollen brought on sneezing fits.

A fear of flowers is called anthophobia, and Aunt Mabel suffered from it. She lived in constant terror of flowers. An innocent pansy made her think of the devil; a snapdragon reminded her of real dragons; the spear-like leaves of the iris were as real spears to her; and the goldenrod sent shivers down her spine. The ones that made her sneeze the most were hollyhock, cosmos, calendula, daisies of all kinds and chrysanthemums.

It was more than an allergy, it was an irrational but very real fear of flowers. Their very names terrified her. If I shouted 'thunder lily!' she would turn pale and tremble like a leaf. If I whispered 'gladioli', she would let out a shriek. If I said 'dandelion!' she would get a rash. And if I exclaimed 'convolvulus!' she'd go into convulsions.

Small boys can be cruel, especially to aunts, and I was no exception. But teasing Aunt Mabel with flowers had a limited appeal for me. Instead, I used them for blackmail. If I needed money for the cinema, I would take Aunt Mabel a bunch of larkspur or candytuft. She would turn pale at my approach, push me out of her room and hurriedly give me the price of a cinema ticket.

In Lucknow, she lived in a flat and was able to keep flowers at bay. But in Dehra she had to put up with Granny's garden, and Granny had no intention of doing away with her flower garden. After all, she was acknowledged to have the most luxuriant display of sweet peas in town. Also Aunt Mabel stayed indoors most of the time, venturing out only in a tonga. She felt quite safe in Paltan Bazaar where there were no flowers apart from the cauliflowers on sale in the sabzi mandi, and even these she avoided.

So engraved was my aunt's phobia that she made everyone in the family promise that when she died there would be no flowers at her funeral. However, she did not really trust us to carry out her wishes, and this may have been the reason why she left India and chose to settle in Arizona, in an area where even the cacti had a hard time surviving. She'd found happiness at last.

I, on the other hand, cannot live without flowers. A little vase of bright yellow and orange nasturtiums rests on the corner of my desk, and every now and then I look up to refresh my eyes and mind by gazing at them. I have never been able to afford a large house with a garden (like Granny's, which was sold when she died) but I grow geraniums in my window and nasturtiums on the roof, and in the spring I throw cosmos seed on the hillside and some of them come up and reward me and others with autumn flowers.

Of course we all have our phobias, and some of the most interesting include bacteriophobia, a fear of germs; mysophobia, a fear of dirt (I knew someone who would wash her hands thirty to forty times a day, even when she was at home and unoccupied); xenophobia, a fear of strangers; nyctophobia, a fear of darkness; agoraphobia, a fear of open spaces. The trouble is, most of us—men especially—hate to admit being afraid of anything. This fear of showing fear is a phobia in itself. The word for it is phobophobia.

My own particular phobia is a fear of lifts. As far as possible I will avoid entering a building where it is necessary to use a lift. If I do go in, I take the stairs. On one occasion I was incarcerated in a five-star hotel where there was no staircase. My room was on the seventeenth floor. I was forced to use the fire-escape! Now you know why I prefer to stay at the India International Centre whenever I'm in New Delhi: not because I have any intellectual pretensions, but because the building (God bless the architect) has only two floors.

Perhaps the best way of dealing with a phobia is to give in to it, admit it, tell everyone about your weakness, and enlist their support. I can tell people that I'm afraid of lifts. As most fellow humans are sympathetic by nature, they crowd into the lift to keep me company, and press all the right buttons—something I have never been able to do successfully in lifts, on cell phones or with ladies' corsets.

Company in a lift always makes me feel much better. I know I won't be alone when it crashes.

~

My Failed Omelettes—And Other Disasters

In nearly fifty years of writing for a living, I have never succeeded in writing a bestseller. And now I know why. I can't cook. Had I been able to do so, I could have turned out a few of those sumptuous-looking cookery books that brighten up the bookstore windows before being snapped up by folk who can't cook either.

As it is, if I were forced to write a cook book, it would probably be called *Fifty Different Ways of Boiling an Egg, and Other Disasters*.

I used to think that boiling an egg would be a simple undertaking. But when I came to live at 7,000 feet in the Himalayan foothills, I found that just getting the water to boil was something of an achievement. I don't know if it's the altitude or the density of the water, but it just won't come to the boil in time for breakfast. As a result my eggs are only half-boiled. 'Never mind,' I tell everyone; 'half-boiled eggs arc more nutritious than full-boiled eggs.'

'Why boil them at all?' asks Gautam, who is my Mr Dick, always offering good advice. 'Raw eggs are probably healthier.'

'Just you wait and see,' I told him. 'I'll make you a cheese omelette you'll never forget.' And I did. It was a bit messy, as I was over-generous with the tomatoes, but I thought it tasted rather good. Gautam, however, pushed his plate away, saying, 'You forgot to put in the egg.'

101 Failed Omelettes might well be the title of my bestseller. I love watching other people cook—a habit that I acquired at a young age, when I would watch my granny at work in the kitchen, turning out delicious curries, koftas and custards. I would try helping her, but she soon put a stop to my feeble contributions. On one occasion, she asked me to add a cup of spices to a large curry dish she was preparing, and absent-mindedly I added a cup of sugar. The result—a very sweet curry! Another invention of mine.

I was better at remembering Granny's kitchen proverbs. Here are some of them:

'There is skill in all things, even in making porridge.'
'Dry bread at home is better than curried prawns abroad.'
'Eating and drinking should not keep men from thinking'
'Better a small fish than an empty dish.'

And her favourite maxim, with which she reprimanded me whenever I showed signs of gluttony: 'Don't let your tongue cut your throat.'

And as for making porridge, it's certainly no simple matter. I made one or two attempts, but it always came out lumpy.

'What's this?' asked Gautam suspiciously, when I offered him some.

'Porridge!' I said enthusiastically. 'It's eaten by those brave Scottish Highlanders who were always fighting the English!'

'And did they win?' he asked.

'Well—er—not usually. But they were outnumbered!'

He looked doubtfully at the porridge. 'Some other time,' he said.

So why not take the advice of Thoreau and try to simplify life? Simplify, simplify! Or simply sandwiches...

These shouldn't be too difficult, I decided. After all, they are basically bread and butter. But have you tried cutting bread into thin slices? Don't. It's highly dangerous. If you're a pianist, you could be putting your career at great risk.

You must get your bread ready sliced. Butter it generously. Now add your fillings. Cheese, tomato, lettuce, cucumber, whatever. Gosh, I was really going places! Slap another slice of buttered bread over this mouth-watering assemblage. Now cut in two. Result: Everything spills out at the sides and onto the tablecloth.

'Now look what you've gone and done,' says Gautam, in his best Oliver Hardy manner.

'Never mind,' I tell him. 'Practice makes perfect!'

And one of these days you're going to find *Bond's Book of Better Sandwiches* up there on the bestseller lists.

Voting at Barlowganj

I am standing under the deodars, waiting for a taxi. Devilal, one of the candidates in the civic election, is offering free rides to all his supporters to ensure that they get to the polls in time. I have assured him that I prefer walking but he does not believe me; he fears that I will settle down with a bottle of beer rather than walk the two miles to the Barlowganj polling station to cast my vote. He has gone to the expense of engaging a taxi for the day just to make certain of lingerers like me. He assures me that he is not using unfair means—most of the other candidates are doing the same thing.

It is a cloudy day, promising rain, so I decide I will wait for the taxi. It has been plying since 6 a.m., and now it is ten o'clock. It will continue plying up and down the hill till 4 p.m. and by that time it will have cost Devilal over a hundred rupees.

Here it comes. The driver—like most of our taxi drivers, a Sikh—sees me standing at the gate, screeches to a sudden stop and opens the door. I am about to get in when I notice that the windscreen carries a sticker displaying the Congress symbol of the cow and calf. Devilal is an Independent, and has adopted a cock bird as his symbol.

'Is this Devilal's taxi?' I ask.

'No, it's the Congress taxi,' says the driver.

'I'm sorry,' I say. 'I don't know the Congress candidate.'

'Thats all right,' he says agreeably; he isn't a local man and has no interest in the outcome of the election. 'Devilal's taxi will be along any minute now.'

He moves off, looking for the Congress voters on whose behalf he has been engaged. I am glad that the candidates have had to adopt different symbols; it has saved me the embarrassment of turning up in a Congress taxi, only to vote for an Independent. But the real reason for the symbols is to help illiterate voters know whom they are voting for when it comes to putting their papers in the ballot box. All through the hill station's mini-election campaign, posters have been displaying candidates' symbols—a car, a radio, a cock bird, a tiger, a lamp—and the narrow, winding roads resound to the cries of children who are paid to shout, 'Vote for the Radio!' or 'Vote for the Cock!'

Presently my taxi arrives. It is already full, having picked up others on the way, and I have to squeeze in at the back with a stout lalain and her bony husband, the local ration-shop owner. Sitting up front, near the driver, is Vinod, a poor, ragged, quite happy-go-lucky youth, who contrives to turn up wherever I happen to be, and frequently involves himself in my activities. He gives me a namaste and a wide grin. 'What are you doing here?' I ask him.

'Same as you, Bond sahib. Voting. Maybe Devilal will give me a job if he wins.'

'But you already have a job. I thought you were the games-boy at the school.'

'That was last month, Bond sahib.'

'They kicked you out?'

'They asked me to leave.'

The taxi gathers speed as it moves smoothly down the winding hill road. The driver is in a hurry; the more trips he makes, the more money he collects. We swerve round sharp corners, and every time the lalain's chubby hands, covered with heavy bangles and rings, clutch at me for support. She and her husband are voting for Devilal because they belong to the same caste; Vinod is voting for him in the hope of getting a job; I am voting for him because I like the man. I find him simple, courteous and ready to listen to complaints about drains, street lighting and wrongly assessed taxes. He even tries to do something about these things. He is a tall, cadaverous man, with paan-stained teeth; no Nixon, Heath or Indira Gandhi; but he knows that Barlowganj folk care little for appearances.

Barlowganj is a small ward (one of four in the hill station of Mussoorie); it has about 1,000 voters. An election campaign has, therefore, to be conducted on a person-to-person basis. There is no point in haranguing a crowd at a street corner; it would be a very small crowd. The only way to canvass support is to visit each voter's house and plead one's cause personally. This means making a lot of promises with a perfectly straight face.

The bazaar and village of Barlowganj crouch in a vale on the way down the mountain to Dehra. The houses on either side of the road are nearly all English-looking, most of them built before the turn of the century. The bazaar is Indian, charming and quite prosperous: tailors sit cross-legged before their sewing machines, turning out blazers and tight trousers for the well-to-do students who attend the many public schools that still thrive here; halwais—potbellied sweet vendors—spend all day sitting on their haunches in front of giant frying pans; and coolies carry huge loads of timber or cement or grain up the steep hill paths.

Who was Barlow, and how did the village get his name? A search through old guides and gazetteers has given me no clue. Perhaps he was a revenue superintendent or a surveyor, who came striding up from the plains in the 1830s to build a hunting lodge in this pleasantly wooded vale. That was how most hill stations began. The police station, the little Church of the Resurrection, and the ruined brewery were among the earliest buildings in Barlowganj.

The brewery is a mound of rubble, but the road that came into existence to serve the needs of the old Crown Brewery is the one that now serves our taxi. Buckle and Co.'s 'Bullock Train' was the chief means of transport in the old days. Mr Bohle, one of the pioneers of brewing in India, started the 'Old Brewery' at Mussoorie in 1830. Two years later he got into trouble with the authorities for supplying beer to soldiers without permission; he had to move elsewhere.

But the great days of the brewery business really began in 1876. when everyone suddenly acclaimed a much-improved brew. The source was traced to Vat 42 in Whympers Crown Brewery (the one whose ruins we are now passing), and the beer was retasted and retested until the diminishing level of the barrel revealed the perfectly brewed remains of a soldier who had been reported missing some months previously. He had evidently fallen into the vat and been drowned and, unknown to himself, had given the Barlowganj beer trade a real fillip. Apocryphal though this story may sound, I have it on the authority of the owner of the now defunct *Mafasalite Press* who, in a short account of Mussoorie, wrote that 'meat was thereafter recognized as the missing component and was scrupulously added till more modem, and less cannibalistic, means were discovered to satiate the froth-blower'.

Recently, confirmation came from an old India hand now living in London. He wrote to me reminiscing of early days in the hill station and had this to say:

> Uncle Georgie Forster was working for the Crown Brewery when a coolie fell in. Coolies were employed to remove scum etc. from the vats. They walked along planks suspended over the vats. Poor devil must have slipped and fallen in. Uncle often told us about the incident and there was no doubt that the beer tasted very good.

What with soldiers and coolies falling into the vats with seeming regularity, one wonders whether there may have been more to these accidents than met the eye. I have a nagging suspicion that Whymper and Buckle may have been the Burke and Hare of Mussoorie's beer industry.

But no beer is made in Mussoorie today, and Devilal probably regrets the passing of the breweries as much as I do. Only the walls of the breweries remain, and these are several feet thick. The roofs and girders must have been removed for use in other buildings. Moss and sorrel grow in the old walls, and wildcats live in dark corners protected from rain and wind.

We have taken the sharpest curves and steepest gradients, and now our taxi moves smoothly along a fairly level road which might pass for a country lane in England were it not for the clumps of bamboo on either side.

A mist has come up the valley to settle over Barlowganj, and out of the mist looms an imposing mansion, Sikander Hall, which is still owned and occupied by the Skinners, descendants of Colonel James Skinner who raised a body of Irregular Horse for the Marathas. This was absorbed by the East India Company's forces in 1803. The cavalry regiment is still known as Skinner's Horse, but of course it is a tank regiment now. Skinner's troops called him 'Sikander' (a corruption of both Skinner and Alexander), and that is the name his property bears. The Skinners who live here now have, quite sensibly, gone in for keeping pigs and poultry.

The next house belongs to the Raja of K but he is unable to maintain it on his diminishing privy purse, and it has been rented out as an ashram for members of a saffron-robed sect who would rather meditate in the hills than in the plains. There was a time when it was only the sahibs and rajas who could afford to spend the entire 'season' in Mussoorie. The new rich are the industrialists and maharishis. The coolies and rickshaw pullers are no better off than when I was a boy in Mussoorie. They still carry or pull the same heavy loads, for the same pittance, and seldom attain the age of forty. Only their clientele has changed.

One more gate, and here is Colonel Powell in his khaki bush shirt and trousers, a uniform that never varies with the seasons. He is an old shikari; once wrote a book called *The Call of the Tiger*. He is too old for hunting now, but likes to yarn with me when we meet on the road. His wife has gone home to England, but he does not want to leave India.

'Its the mountains,' he was telling me the other day. 'Once the mountains are in your blood, there is no escape. You have to come back again and again. I don't think I'd like to die anywhere else.'

Today there is no time to stop and chat. The taxi driver, with a vigorous blowing of his horn, takes the car round the last bend, and then through the village and narrow bazaar of Barlowganj, stopping about a hundred yards from the polling stations.

There is a festive air about Barlowganj today, I have never seen so many people in the bazaar. Bunting, in the form of rival posters and leaflets, is strung across the street. The tea shops are doing a roaring trade. There is much last-minute canvassing, and I have to run the gamut of various candidates and their agents. For the first time I learn the names of some of the candidates. In all, seven men are competing for this seat.

A schoolboy, smartly dressed and speaking English, is the first to accost me. He says: 'Don't vote for Devilal, sir. He's a big crook. Vote for Jatinder! See, sir, that's his symbol—the bow and arrow.'

'I shall certainly think about the bow and arrow.' I tell him politely. Another agent, a man, approaches, and says, 'I hope you are going so vote for the Congress candidate.'

'I don't know anything about him,' I say.

'That doesn't matter. It's the party you are voting for. Don't forget it's Mrs Gandhi's party.'

Meanwhile, one of Devilal's lieutenants has been keeping a close watch on both Vinod and me, to make sure that we are not seduced by rival propaganda. I give the man a reassuring smile and stride purposefully towards the polling station, which has been set up in the municipal schoolhouse. Policemen stand at the entrance, to make sure that no one approaches the voters once they have entered the precincts.

I join the patient queue of voters. Everyone is in good humour, and there is no breaking of the line; these are not film stars we have come to see. Vinod is in another line, and grins proudly at me across the passageway. This is the one day in his life on which he has been made to feel really important. And he *is*. In a small constituency like Barlowganj, every vote counts.

Most of my fellow voters are poor people. Local issues mean

something to them, affect their daily living. The more affluent can buy their way out of trouble, can pay for small conveniences; few of them bother to come to the polls. But for the 'common man'—the shopkeeper, clerk, teacher, domestic servant, milkman, mule driver—this is a big day. The man he is voting for has promised him something, and the voter means to take the successful candidate up on his promise. Not for another five years will the same fuss be made over the local cobblers, tailors and laundrymen. Their votes are indeed precious.

And now it is my turn to vote. I confirm my name, address and roll number. I am down on the list as 'Rusking Bound', but I let it pass: I might forfeit my right to vote if I raise any objection at this stage! A dab of marking-ink is placed on my forefinger—this is so that I do not come round a second time—and I am given a paper displaying the names and symbols of all the candidates. I am then directed to the privacy of a small booth, where I place the official rubber stamp against Devilal's name. This done, I fold the paper in four and slip it into the ballot box.

All has gone smoothly. Vinod is waiting for me outside. So is Devilal.

'Did you vote for me?' asks Devilal.

It is my eyes that he is looking at, not my lips, when I reply in the affirmative. He is a shrewd man, with many years' experience in seeing through bluff. He is pleased with my reply, beams at me and directs me to the waiting taxi.

Vinod and I get in together, and soon we are on the road again, being driven swiftly homewards up the winding hill road.

Vinod is looking pleased with himself; rather smug, in fact. 'You did vote for Devilal?' I ask him. 'The symbol of the cock bird?'

He shakes his head, keeping his eyes on the road. 'No, the cow,' he says.

'You ass!' I exclaim. 'Devilals symbol was the cock, not the cow!"

'I know,' he says, 'but I like the cow better.'

I subside into silence. It is a good thing no one else in the taxi has been paying any attention to our conversation. It would be a pity to see Vinod turned out of Devilal's taxi and made to walk the remaining mile to the top of the hill. After all, it will be another five years before he gets another free taxi ride.

Escape to Nowhere

By the end of August, the hill-dweller has got the monsoon blues. Heartily sick of cloud and fog, drizzle and downpour, he longs for a little sunshine, some dryness in the air.

Forsaking my jammed typewriter, and mildewed books and files, I set out for Dehradun in the valley. It was damp there too, and sultry, but at least there were occasional bursts of sunshine. I took a room in a small hotel and lay beneath a whirring fan, waiting for the cool of the evening.

Evening walks in Dehra are not what they used to be. Speeding vehicles stop for no one, and you take your life in your hands every time you cross a road. Most of the roads came into existence over a hundred years ago, and were originally meant for pedestrians and pony-drawn tongas. Now, neither pedestrians nor ponies have any rights.

Wait until dark and the hazards are even greater, for street lights do not exist on the smaller roads, while open ditches and other obstacles are there in abundance, just waiting to trap you. Returning to my room muddied and dishevelled, I was consoled by the old man who brought me a cup of tea. Things were much worse in Agra, he told me.

'And what were you doing in Agra?' I asked.

'I was in the madhouse, the pagal-khana, for ten years. Then one day, when no one was looking, I slipped away.'

He burst into laughter, and naturally I had to join in.

'Inside or outside, there's no difference,' he added. 'The roads are full of pagals these days.'

Next day, going out in search of a little sanity, I decided I'd call on Nergis Dalal, a fellow writer whom I hadn't seen for some years.

As I approached the Dilawar Bazaar, the area where she lived, I noticed that the traffic on the main road had come to a standstill and that smoke was issuing from a couple of small shops. A crowd had gathered and now, as a police van arrived, people began to scatter, most of them running in my direction. I always seem to be standing in the way of advancing hordes.

Looking for some avenue of escape, I found a gap in a wall, leading into an old orchard of litchi trees. I sat beneath a litchi tree, recalling the days when Dehra was famous for its litchis. Now only a few gardens remain, for owners find it more profitable to sell their land for buildings. Will litchis vanish forever? They don't grow anywhere else.

When the main road seemed normal again, I left the protection of the trees and took another chance with my fellow humans. Two boys were discussing the recent incident. One said the shop had been burnt down because it had been selling brown sugar. The other said it had been burnt down because it had *refused* to sell brown sugar.

My own blood-sugar level was by now distinctly low, so I hurried along to Nergis Dalal's flat, knowing she would give me sustenance. Hadn't she written half-a-dozen cookery books?

Nor was I disappointed. Pullau rice, kofta curry and a chocolate souffle awaited me. I was on the right track again!

When I got back to my hotel, I found Mr Arora of the Green Bookshop waiting for me in the verandah. He had a surprise for me, he said. He wouldn't tell me what it was until I got into his car.

Ten minutes later we drove in at the gates of Welham Girls' School. And within minutes I found myself trapped in a classroom, surrounded by some two hundred girls, their ages ranging from fourteen to eighteen. And I was expected to talk to them! Usually tongue-tied in front of one girl, how was I to converse with two hundred? Jules Verne had a similar problem, I believe. No wonder he preferred to be 20,000 leagues under the sea—which was where I wanted to be just then!

Bright-eyed and eager they were, waiting for words of wisdom to flow from my lips. I had none to impart! I looked around the sea of faces. Here was beauty and intelligence combined! I was struck dumb.

Their principal, Mrs Verma, came to my rescue and said nice things about my writing. I answered a few questions, trying to be witty if not wise. The girls were kind and indulgent.

When it was all over, I found myself back in my hotel room. A smart young Gurkha brought me a cup of tea.

'Where's the old man?' I asked.

'One of his sons came for him,' he said. 'They've taken him back to Agra.'

So that was the end of *his* great escape. Was it the end of mine?

Thoughts from a Window

Best of All Windows

Those who advertise rooms or flats to let often describe them as 'Room with bath' or 'Room with tea and coffee-making facilities'. A more attractive proposition would be 'Room with window', for without a view a room is hardly a living place—merely a place of transit.

As an itinerant young writer, I lived in many single room apartments, or bedsitters as they were called, and I have to admit that the quality of my life was certainly enhanced if my window looked out on something a little more inspiring than a factory wall or someone's backyard. We cherish a romantic image of a starving young poet living in a garret and writing odes to skylarks, but, believe me, garrets don't help. For six months in London I lived in a small attic room which had no view at all, except for the roofs of other houses—an endless vista of grey tiles and blackened chimneys, without so much as a proverbial cat to relieve the monotony. I did not write a single ode, for no self-respecting nightingale or lark ever found its way up there.

My next room, somewhere near Clapham Junction, had a view of the railway, but you couldn't actually see the railway lines because of the rows of washing that were hung out to dry behind the building. It was a working class area and there were no laundries round the corner. But if you couldn't see the railway, you could certainly hear it. Every time a train thundered past, the building shuddered, and ornaments, crockery and dishes rattled and rocked as though an earthquake was in progress. It was impossible to hang a picture on the wall, the nail (and with it the picture) fell out after a couple of days. But it reminded me a bit of my Uncle Fred's railway quarters just near Delhi's main railway station, and I managed to write a couple of train stories while living in this particular room.

Train windows, naturally, have no equal when it comes to views, especially in India, where there's an ever-changing panorama of mountain, forest and desert, village, town and city, along with the colourful crowds at every railway station.

But good, personal windows—windows to live with—these were to prove elusive for several years. Even after returning to India, I had some difficulty in finding the ideal window.

Moving briefly to a small town in north India, I was directed to the Park View lodging house. There did happen to be a park in the vicinity, but no view of it could be had from my room or, indeed, from any room in the house. But I found, to my surprise, that the bathroom window actually looked out on the park. It provided a fine view! However, there is a limit to the length of time one can spend in the bath, gazing out at palm fronds waving in the distance. So I moved on again.

After a couple of claustrophobic years in New Delhi, I escaped to the hills, fully expecting that I would immediately find rooms or a cottage with widows facing the eternal snows. But it was not to be! To see the snows I had to walk four miles from my lodgings to the highest point in the hill station. My window looked out on a high stone rampart, built to prevent the steep hillside from collapsing. True, a number of wild things grew in the wall—bunches of red sorrel, dandelions, tough weeds of various kinds, and, at the base, a large clump of nettles. Now I am sure there are people who can grow ecstatic over nettles, but I am not one of them. I find that nettles sting me at the first opportunity. So I gave my nettles a wide berth.

And then, at last, fortune smiled, or rather, persistence was rewarded. I found my present abode, a windswept, rather shaky old house on the edge of a spur. My bedroom window opened on to blue skies, mountains striding away into the far distance, winding rivers in the valley below, and, just to bring me down to earth, the local television tower. Like The Red Shadow in *The Desert Song*, I could stand at my window and sing 'Blue heaven, and you and I', even if the only listener was a startled policeman.

The window was so positioned that I could lie on my bed and look at the sky, or sit at my desk and look at the hills, or stand at the window and look at the road below.

Which is the best of these views?

Some would say the hills, but the hills never change. Some would say the road, because the road is full of change and movement—

tinkers, tailors, tourists, salesmen, cars, trucks and motorcycles, mules, ponies and even, on one occasion, an elephant. The elephant had no business being up here, but I suppose if Hannibal could take them over Alps, an attempt could also be made on the Himalayan passes. (It returned to the plains the next day.)

The road is never dull, but, given a choice, I'd opt for the sky. The sky is never the same. Even when it's cloudless, the sky's colours are different. The morning sky, the daytime sky, the evening sky, the moonlit sky, the starry sky, there are all different skies. And there are almost always birds in the sky—eagles flying high, mountain swifts doing acrobatics, cheeky myna birds nesting under the eaves of the roof, sparrows flitting in and out of the room at will. Sometimes a butterfly floats in on the breeze. And on summer nights, great moths enter at the open window, dazzled by my reading-light. I have to catch them and put them out again, lest they injure themselves.

When the monsoon rains arrive, the window has to be closed, otherwise cloud and mist fill the room, and that isn't good for my books. But the sky is even more fascinating at this time of the year. From my desk I can, at this very moment, see the clouds advancing across the valley, rolling over the hills, ascending the next range. Raindrops patter against the windowpanes, drum on the corrugated iron roof. The mynas line up on the window ledge, waiting for the rain to stop.

And when the shower passes and the clouds open up, the heavens are a deeper, darker blue. Truly magic casements these... For every time I see the sky I am aware of belonging to the universe rather than to just one corner of the earth.

～◦

From a Window

The sitting-room window opened out on to the forest, but my bedroom window faced the hillside and offered a more limited though equally interesting view.

A wild cherry tree had grown out of the pushta, or retaining wall, and in a strong wind its branches would beat against the window as though it wanted to get in. Unlike most fruit trees, it blossomed in November—pale pink blossoms that covered the tree for about a fortnight. Later, when the fruit appeared, small birds would arrive to feast on the sour wild cherries. Bulbuls, warblers, brightly coloured finches. The tree inspired me to write a story in which little Rakesh, Prem's three-year-old son, featured. Prem's family was to grow steadily over the years, and today Rakesh is a married man with three children of his own. There is also Mukesh and his family; and their sister Dolly… All my family over the years…

But to return to the window. From my bed I could see the tree and beyond it, the little path that came down the steep hillside up to my front door. I couldn't see the entire pathway, but far enough to know who was approaching—tradesman, or postman, or neighbour, or casual visitor.

If I was not in the mood for a casual visitor, there would be time to warn Prem and he would meet the caller and say I was out for the day. People who did not know me always seemed to call in the afternoon, in the middle of my siesta. It still happens. I don't mind being disturbed while I'm eating or working or bathing, but siesta time is sacred and I'm very grumpy then—like a bear disturbed during his long winter sleep.

And yet, I'm happy to be up at four or five in the morning to watch the coming of the dawn.

In some earlier life (if there was one) I might well have been a worshipper of Usha, the goddess of the dawn. In the *Rig Veda*, that first pale flush of light is compared to a mother awakening her children; to a lovely maiden awakening a sleeping world. She is described as the giver of light, ever youthful, ever receiving.

If, today, we all become worshippers of Usha, everyone would rise at dawn, start the day's work at six or seven, and come home to rest at noon. Then we would all enjoy afternoon siestas and no one would disturb me.

~

Guests Who Fly in from the Forest

When mist fills the Himalayan valleys, and heavy monsoon rain sweeps across the hills, it is natural for wild creatures to seek shelter.

Any shelter is welcome in a storm—and sometimes my cottage in the forest is the most convenient refuge.

There is no doubt that I make things easier for all concerned by leaving most of my windows open—I am one of those peculiar people who like to have plenty of fresh air indoors—and if a few birds, beasts and insects come in too, they're welcome, provided they don't make too much of a nuisance of themselves.

I must confess that I did lose patience with a bamboo beetle who blundered in the other night and fell into the water jug. I rescued him and pushed him out of the window. A few seconds later he came whirring in again, and with unerring accuracy landed with a plop in the same jug. I fished him out once more and offered him the freedom of the night. But attracted no doubt by the light and warmth of my small sitting room, he came buzzing back, circling the room like a helicopter looking for a good place to land. Quickly I covered the water jug. He landed in a bowl of wild dahlias, and I allowed him to remain there, comfortably curled up in the hollow of a flower.

Last week, as I was sitting down at my desk to write a long deferred article, I was startled to see an emerald green praying mantis sitting on my writing-pad. He peered up at me with his protuberant glass bead eyes, and I stared down at him through my reading glasses. When I gave him a prod, he moved off in a leisurely way. Later I found him examining the binding of Whitman's *Leaves of Grass;* perhaps he had found a succulent bookworm. He disappeared for a couple of days, and then I found him on the dressing table, preening himself before the mirror. Perhaps I am doing him an injustice in assuming that he was preening. Maybe he thought he'd met another mantis and was simply trying to make-contact. Anyway, he seemed fascinated by his reflection.

Out in the garden, I spotted another mantis, perched on the jasmine bush. Its arms were raised like a boxer's. Perhaps they're a pair, I thought, and went indoors and fetched my mantis and placed him on the jasmine bush, opposite his fellow insect. He did not like what he saw—no comparison with his own image!—and made off in a huff.

My most interesting visitor comes at night, when the lights are still burning—a tiny bat who prefers to fly in at the door, should it be open, and will use the window only if there's no alternative.

His object in entering the house is to snap up the moths that cluster around the lamps.

All the bats I've seen fly fairly high, keeping near the ceiling as far as possible, and only descending to ear level (my ear level) when they must; but this particular bat flies in low, like a dive bomber, and does acrobatics amongst the furniture, zooming in and out of chair legs and under tables. Once, while careening about the room in this fashion, he passed straight between my legs.

Has his radar gone wrong, I wondered, or is he just plain crazy?

I went to my shelves of *Natural History* and looked up bats, but could find no explanation for this erratic behaviour. As a last resort, I turned to an ancient volume, Sterndale's *Indian Mammalia* (Calcutta, 1884), and in it, to my delight, I found what I was looking for—

> a bat found near Mussoorie by Captain Hutton, on the southern range of hills at 5,500 feet; head and body, 1.4 inch; skims close to the ground, instead of flying high as bats generally do, Habitat, Jharipani, N.W. Himalayas.

Apparently the bat was rare even in 1884.

Perhaps I've come across one of the few surviving members of the species: Jharipani is only two miles from where I live. And I feel rather offended that modern authorities should have ignored this tiny bat; possibly they feel that it is already extinct. If so, I'm pleased to have rediscovered it. I am happy that it survives in my small corner of the woods. On lonely nights, even a crazy bat is company.

Things I Love Most

Sea-shells. They are among my earliest memories. I was five years old, walking barefoot along the golden sands of a Kathiawar beach, collecting shells and cowries and taking them home to fill up an old trunk. Some of these shells have remained with me through the years. I still have one which I place against my ear to listen to the distant music of the Arabian Sea.

A jackfruit tree. It stood outside my grandfather's house in Dehradun: it was easy to climb and generous with its shade and in its trunk was a large hole where I kept my marbles, sweets, prohibited books and other treasures.

I have always liked the smell of certain leaves, perhaps even more than the scent of flowers. Crushed geranium and chrysanthemum leaves, mint and myrtle, lime and neem trees after the rain, and the leaves of ginger, marigolds and nasturtiums.

Of course, there were other smells which as a boy I especially liked—the smells of pullau and kofta, curry, hot jalebis, roast chicken and fried prawns. But these are smells loved most by gourmets (and most boys) and are not as personal as the smell of leaves and grass.

I have always liked trains and railway stations. I like eating at railway stations—hot gram, peanut, puris, oranges.

As a boy, I travelled to Shimla on a little train that crawls round and through the mountains. In March, the flowers on the rhododendron trees provided splashes of red against the dark green of the hills. Sometimes there would be snow on the ground to add to the contrast.

What else do I love and remember of the hills? Smells again. The smells of fallen pine needles, cow-dung smoke, spring rain, bruised grass, the pure cold water of mountain streams, the depth and blueness of the sky.

In the hills, I have loved forests. In the plains, I have loved single trees. A lone tree on a wide, flat plain—even if it is a thin, crooked, nondescript tree—gains beauty and nobility from its isolation, from the precarious nature of its existence.

Of course, I have had my favourites among trees. The banyan, with its great branches spreading to form roots and intricate passageways. The peepul with its beautiful heart-shaped leaves catching the breeze and fluttering even on the stillest of days. The jacaranda and golmohour bursting into blossom with the coming of summer. The cherries, peaches and apricots flowering in the hills—the tall, handsome chestnuts and the whispering deodars.

Deodars have often inspired me to poetry. One day I wrote:

> *Trees, of God, we call them.*
> *Planted there when the world was young.*
> *The first trees*
> *Their fingers pointing to the stars,*
> *Older than the cedars of Lebanon.*

Several of these trees were cut down recently and I was furious

> *They cut them down last spring*
> *With quick and efficient tools,*
> *The sap was rising still.*
> *The trees bled,*
> *Slaughtered*
> *To make furniture for fools.*

And which flower is most redolent of India? Not for me the lotus or the water lily but the simple marigold, fresh, golden, dew-drenched, kissed by the morning sun.

The smell of the sea. I lived with it for over a year in the Channel Islands, I liked the sea mist and liked the fierce gales that swept across the islands in the winter.

Later, there were the fogs of London; I did not like them but they made me think of Dickens, and I walked to Wapping and the East India Dock Road and watched the barges on the Thames, I had my favourite pub and my favourite fish-and-chips shop. There were always children flying kites from Primrose Hill or sailing boats in the ponds on Hampstead Heath.

Once we visited the gardens at Kew and in a hothouse, moist and smelling of the tropics, I remembered the East and some of the simple things I had known—a field of wheat, a stack of sugarcane, a cow at rest and a boy sleeping in the shade of a long, red-fingered poinsettia. And I knew I would go home to India.

─⋙

Geraniums

I can meditate upon a geranium. That is, I can spend a long time gazing at one.

And while I was gazing at mine, there came a phone call from my accountant informing me that it was time for me to start preparing my income-tax return. And thus, the harsh realities of life intrude upon our poetic fancies—but I shall return to the subject of geraniums at the first opportunity. And as I can get geraniums to flower on my sunny bedroom windowsill, summer and winter, I have every opportunity to do so.

The geranium that has done best is the one I have grown in a large plastic bucket standing on the chest of drawers and facing the early morning sun. Here, protected from wind and rain (both of which are anathema to geraniums), this generous plant has produced no less than eight florets of soft pink confetti. Pastel shades have always appealed to me. And there is something alluring about this sensual pink. Other shades are appealing too—the salmon-pink, the cerise, the flaming red—but this pale pink is restful, intimate. From my bed or desk I can gaze at it and have pleasant thoughts. Is that meditation? Or is it contemplation? The latter, probably. I am really the contemplative type.

But meditation is in fashion—people give and take courses in it!—whereas I have yet to meet someone taking a course in contemplation. I suspect that meditation is something that you do deliberately (hence the need for practise), and contemplation is simply what comes naturally.

When we meditate, we look within, and hopefully there is something to find there. When I look at a flower, I am looking without contemplating at the miracle of creation. I suppose we should do a little of both, just to get the right balance.

~

A Rainy Day in June

A thunderstorm, followed by strong winds, brought down the temperature. That was yesterday. And today it is cloudy, cool, drizzling a little, almost monsoon weather; but it is still too early for the real monsoon.

The birds are enjoying the cool weather. The green-backed tits cool their bottoms in the rainwater pool. A king crow flashes past, winging through the air like an arrow. On the wing, it snaps up a hovering dragonfly. The mynahs fetch crow feathers to line their nests in the eaves of the house. I am lying so still on the window seat that a tit alights on the sill, within a few inches of my head. It snaps up a small dead moth before flying away.

At dusk I sit at the window and watch the trees and listen to the wind as it makes light conversation in the leafy tops of the maples.

There is a whirr of wings as the king crows fly into the trees to roost for the night. But for one large bat it is time to get busy, and he flits in and out of the trees. The sky is just light enough to enable me to see the bat and the outlines of the taller trees.

Up on Landour hill, the lights are just beginning to come on. It is deliciously cool, eight o'clock, a perfect summer's evening. Prem is singing to himself in the kitchen. His wife and sister are chattering beneath the walnut tree. Down the hill, a kakar is barking, alarmed perhaps by the presence of a leopard.

The wind grows stronger and the tall maples bow before it: the maple moves its slender branches slowly from side to side, the oak moves its branches up and down. It is darker now; more lights on Landour. The cry of the barking deer has grown fainter, more distant, and now I hear a cricket singing in the bushes. The stars are out, the wind grows chilly it is time to close the window.

A Good Philosophy

The other day, when I was with a group of students, a bright young thing asked me, 'Sir, what is your philosophy of life?'

She had me stumped.

There I was, a seventy-five-year-old, still writing, and still functioning physically and mentally (or so I believed), but quite helpless when it came to formulating 'a philosophy of life.'

How dare I reach the venerable age of seventy-five without a philosophy; without anything resembling a religious outlook; without arming myself with a battery of great thoughts with which to impress my young interlocutor, who is obviously in need of a little practical if not spiritual guidance to help her navigate the shoals of life?

This morning I was pondering on this absence of a philosophy or religious outlook in my make-up, and feeling a little low because it was cloudy and dark outside, and gloomy weather always seems to dampen my spirits. Then the clouds broke up and the sun came out, large, yellow splashes of sunshine in my room and upon my desk, and almost immediately I felt an uplift of spirit. And at the same time I realized that no philosophy would be of any use to a person so susceptible to changes in light and shade, sunshine and shadow. I was a pagan, pure and simple; a sensualist; sensitive to touch and colour and fragrance and odour and sounds of every description; a creature of instinct, of spontaneous attractions, given to illogical fancies and attachments. As a guide, philosopher and friend I am of no use to anyone, least of all to myself.

I think the best advice I ever had was contained in these lines from Shakespeare which my father had copied into one of my notebooks when I was nine years old:

> *This above all, to thine own self be true,*
> *And it must follow as the night of the day,*
> *Thou can'st not then be false to any man.*

Each one of us is a mass of imperfections, and to be able to recognize and live with our imperfections, our basic natures, defects of genes and birth—hereditary flaws—makes for an easier transit on life's journey.

I am always a little wary of saints and godmen, preachers and teachers, who are ready with solutions for all our problems. For one thing, they talk too much. When I was at school, I mastered the art of sleeping (without appearing to sleep) through a long speech or lecture by the principal or visiting dignitary, and I must confess to doing the same thing today. The trick is to sleep with your eyes half closed; this gives the impression of concentrating very hard on what is being said, even though you might well be roaming happily in dreamland.

In our imperfect world there is far too much talk and not enough thought. The TV channels are awash with TV gurus telling us how to live, and they do so at great length. This verbal diarrhoea is infectious and appears to affect newspersons and TV anchors who are prone to lecturing and bullying the guests on their shows. Too many know-alls. A philosophy for living? You won't find it on your TV sets. You will learn more from a cab driver or street vendor.

~

'And what's *your* philosophy?' I asked my **sabziwalla**, as he weighed out a kilo of onions.

'Philosophy? What's that?' He turned to his assistant. 'Is this gentleman trying to abuse me?'

'No, sir,' I said. 'It's not a term of abuse. I was just asking—are you a happy man?'

'Why do you want to know? Are you from the income-tax department?'

'No, I'm just a storyteller. So tell me—what makes you happy?'

'A good customer,' he said. 'So tell me—what makes *you* happy?'

'The same thing, I suppose,' I had to confess. 'A good publisher!'

I did not tell him about the sunshine, the birdsong, the bedside book, the potted geranium, and all the other little things that make life worth living. It's better that he finds out for himself.

~

On Conquering Depression

Depression.

This is a word that we hear far too often these days. The rich and the famous get depressed. The poor feel depressed. Students suffer from depression. The world's leaders look depressed.

I suppose it's the times we live in: the fast, unrelenting pace of life; the striving for fame, money, power; the ever-increasing dependence on technology; the ascendancy of hate over love in a world of conflicting civilizations and ideologies.

Because people confuse age with wisdom I am sometimes asked if there are ways of combating stress and depression. I am not really the right person to hand out advice, as my periods of depression coincide either with a raging toothache or a bank balance that has fallen below sea level; conditions that apply to most of us from time to time.

But I have been making a short list of people who are immune to deep depression, or appear to be so, and heading the list are our birdwatchers. I am always impressed by the enthusiasm of these good folk who spend their leisure hours tramping about in the woods or on the hillsides or in open country, binoculars in hand, bursting with excitement every time they spot a tree-pippit or a red-bottomed bulbul or a rufous-bellied babbler. I have got the nomenclature wrong, of course, but I am sure my bird-watching friends won't mind, as they are the most tolerant of people. If you want to do away with your depression, go and join the bird-watching fraternity. There is nothing like a spotted fork tail hopping from boulder to boulder, or a kingfisher swooping down upon a startled young trout, to raise the spirits of the most sensitive of souls.

Or you could try bee-keeping. I knew an old lady who was never depressed, she was too busy tending to her bees and making sure their hives were in good order. The first time I visited her I was stung by one of her bees, but she told me bee venom was good for the adrenalin or something like that. Oddly enough, she never got stung. Presumably she had all the adrenalin she needed. You could give it a try.

And then there are my friends, the carpenters. A contented lot, from the look of them—busy making cabinets, cupboards, desks, bookshelves, dining tables, doors and windows, floor boards, rafters, easy chairs, uneasy chairs—like that old rocking-chair in my verandah which creaks every night whenever its ghostly occupant, the late Rani of Lal Tibba, chooses to spend a night in it, rocking herself to sleep while keeping me awake into the early hours.

I have great respect for carpenters, the way they concentrate on their tasks—sawing away, hammering at every little nail, even imaginary ones. I know a young carpenter who just loves to bang away with his hammer, especially when he sees a look of pain cross my face as I try to finish this article.

Here they are, three of them, trying to make sure a new window-frame fits in my window. This is their third or fourth visit, and the frames refuse to fit. An icy wind finds its way through a stubborn little aperture and then makes its way up my pyjamas. They'll fix it tomorrow, they say, and off they go with an advance for nuts and bolts, a happy and contented lot, leaving me just a little depressed.

But I miss the old carpenter who used to have his shop a little way down the road from here. He specialized in making coffins. If anyone on the hillside passed away, he would have a sturdy little coffin (make to size) ready in no time at all. And he always had a coffin or two to spare, if you weren't too fussy about measurements.

A merry soul was our coffin maker. I never saw him looking depressed—except, perhaps, in his later years, when the number of souls departing this hillside decreased dramatically, leading to a drop in the demand for his handiwork.

So forget about being a coffin maker. People are living longer these days.

~

You could try singing.

If I'm down in the dumps, I sing my blues away. If I'm in a romantic trough I'll sing Puccini or Verdi or some great operatic aria, and never mind the neighbours. If I'm broke I'll sing 'Pennies from Heaven'—and hope they'll shower down upon me. If the weather is depressing I'll sing 'Till the Clouds Go By' and hope the depression in the Bay of Bengal has gone by. If I have a headache I'll sing Johny Walker's rendering of 'Tel-Malish' from *Pyaasa*, and give everyone else a headache.

The only trouble is, my singing depresses other people. Friends don't allow me to sing in their company or in their homes. Pictures fall off walls or the rice gets burnt. I burst into song in Victor Banerjee's antique Morris Minor, and the door fell off. It was a battered old car anyway, but he sent me a bill for a new door. Needless to say, I haven't paid it.

This business of preventing me from singing goes back to my school days when our choir mistress, Mrs Whitmarsh-Knight, put me in the school choir but forbade me from singing. She said I looked cute in a cassock and surplice, and that I could open my mouth along with the others but that I must never, never allow any sound to issue forth. So there I was, opening and shutting my mouth like a goldfish, a silent singer in the midst of a gathering of cackling hens.

I got my revenge one day, letting out a bellow in the middle of Mrs Whitmarsh-Knight's favourite carol. I was removed from the choir, but she went into a depression and took to playing the organ late into the night.

And so, over the years, I've learnt to sing on my own, when there's no one around to pass out or take offence. I close my bedroom door, open my window, and give free rein to my vocal chords. Away with depression! Occasionally a car grinds to a halt or veers off the road. A conclave of crows might decide to move elsewhere. Stray dogs will depart, tails between their legs. A wedding band will fall silent.

But I am not to be deterred. No one can prevent me from singing from my second-floor window. Even the langoors watch in awe as I burst into song, belting out an old Nelson Eddy favourite:

'When you are down and out,
Lift up your head and shout—
It's going to be a great day!'

~

When All the Wars Are Done

Time passes, having nothing else to do. But we change, our surroundings change, our country changes. And so I am often being asked: 'You have lived in India for most of your life—almost eighty years—what are the most remarkable changes you have seen?'

Well, change comes slowly, not with a great rush; and although there are certain dramatic events that stand out across the years—Independence, Partition, conflicts with our neighbours, assassinations, communal strife, scientific progress, technological advancement—the actual pace and tenor of everyday life is much as it used to be. Those wedding tents and feasts are still the fulcrum of social life. We follow cricket in preference to other sports, purely out of habit; only we do it courtesy of television rather than through those dear old transistor radios with their running commentaries. The Binaca hit parade is long gone, but Bollywood still provides the hit songs of the day.

The middle class has grown and prospered, and as a result people are better dressed today. The fashion industry barely existed back in the 1950s and '60s. You were 'with it' if you could get into a pair of jeans. I could never find a pair of jeans that would comply with my figure, so I have remained in baggy pants from the Chaplin-Raj Kapoor era to the present day.

Only yesterday a kind soul from Kerala gave me a lungi, saying it would improve my appearance. It does indeed, but as an icy wind from Tibet is at this moment nipping around my ankles, I shall postpone the wearing of the lungi to next summer.

I have never been able to keep up with the fashions in haircuts, still clinging to the short back and sides of my school days. The youngsters in my home are, at present, all looking like porcupines, with their hair standing on end like wire brushes. I believe this is done with the help of some kind of gel which can also be used for sealing envelopes and parcels. I must give it a try. I mean the gel, not the hairstyle.

~

People, people everywhere. This is one change that you can't help noticing if you have been around for some time. The number of human beings on planet earth and in our part of the world in particular has gone up by leaps and bounds. I can't say that this is a bad thing. The loving union of man and woman usually results in human offspring, and, as Tagore said, 'Every child comes with the message that God is not yet tired of man.'

But the earth grows tired. For hundreds of thousands of years it has been sustaining millions, now billions of humankind who, more than bird, beast, reptile or insect, have been helping themselves to the earth's resources without putting anything back. How much longer can this good earth sustain the human race? Already there is talk of mass migration to other planets. All I can say is, the sooner the better!

For one who loves this earth, this land, the prospect is a little depressing, even though I won't be around to see it evolve. What I do see today, in almost every town or city that I visit, are mountains of garbage, growing higher by the day, stagnating in the sun and rain, so foul that even the crows and starving dogs are staying away. A certain amount of rubbish has always been turned out into the streets, but not with the devil-may-care speed and accumulation that is apparent today.

> From plastic bags to polythene
> The prospect now is far from clean.

Oh, for the good old days of paper bags! Those paper bags made from discarded exercise books, exam papers, and unwanted film and fashion magazines. How quickly they would deteriorate, 'dissolve, and resolve themselves into a dew', as Hamlet said about his too too solid flesh.

As a writer I have mixed feelings about paper bags being made from the pages of my books. All those words, so carefully inscribed on paper, are worth no more than a piece of ghur.

Only the other day, on a television show, one of our leaders declared that writers in India were of no consequence, and I can't help feeling that he was right.

Still, if paper bags could replace plastic bags, I would gladly sacrifice the pages on which I have written this essay.

~

I must be one of the few writers still standing, or rather sitting, who writes by hand, that is, with a ballpoint pen. This is not because I am stubborn and out-of-date but simply because I find it more comfortable to write this way, and because I express myself better when I am in close and intimate contact with pen and paper. There are two old, discarded typewriters in the house, in case anyone wants one. There are also two laptops, jealously guarded by my grandchildren, who are up all night on Facebook, keeping in touch with their friends in the 'virtual' world, whatever that may be.

I like to sleep at night. I love the night, and I love gazing at the stars—especially up here in the mountains, where the skies are usually so clear—and I remember romantic moments, when the moon and the stars combined to make those moments more magical. But being a pragmatic fellow, I am also a believer in a good night's sleep. For on the morrow I must face the real world—electricity bills (but no light), school bills, food bills, publishers' deadlines, blocked drainpipes, leaking roofs etc., many of the things that you, dear reader, have to cope with too. Never mind—

When all the wars are done,
And all the garbage gone,
A butterfly will still be beautiful, my son.

~

Thoughts on Reaching Seventy-five

The barbet calls from the top of the spruce tree.

Summer is here again.

The seventy-fifth summer of my life, although I have to admit that I don't remember the first five.

I remember an early summer in Jamnagar, paddling on the beach and staring out at a little steamer making its way across the Gulf of Kutch; an April morning in Dehradun, the air scented with mango blossom; a long hot summer in New Delhi, the bhisti splashing water on the khus-khus seed curtain (no air conditioning then); a summer's day in Shimla, consuming ice creams in the company of my father. All these summers before I was ten.

I was born early one morning in May, hence my prediliction for summer. There's nothing like the sun. In the plains it makes you more appreciative of the shade provided by leafy peepul and banyan trees. In the hills it brings you out of your chilly rooms to bask in its glory. Gardens need sunshine, and I need flowers, so we follow the sun together.

What have I learnt in these seventy-five years on planet earth? Quite frankly, very little. Don't believe the elders and philosophers. Wisdom does not come with age. It is born with you in the cradle. Either you have it or you don't. For the most part I have followed instinct rather than intelligence, and this has resulted in a modicum of happiness.

Happiness is as elusive as a butterfly, and you must never pursue it. If you stay very still, it might come and settle on your hand. But only briefly. Savour those precious moments, for they will not come your way very often.

Contentment is easier to attain. The best example is the small ginger cat who arrives on the balcony every afternoon, to curl up in the sun and slumber peacefully for a couple of hours. There's nothing like an afternoon siesta to help mind and body recuperate from the stress and toil of a busy morning. As Garfield would say: 'Some call it laziness. I call it deep thought.'

To have got to this point in life without the solace of religion says something for all the things that have brought me joy and a degree of contentment. Books, of course. I couldn't have survived without books. And living up here in the hills, where the air is sharp and clean, and you can look at your window and see the mountains marching away into the sunset or sunrise.

Dawn, daybreak, sunrise. They are all different. Twilight, dusk, nightfall. All quite different. We must be aware of these subtle differences in the light around us if we are to appreciate the life around us. There is no harm in sitting in an office and making I money, but sometimes you must look out of the window. And look at the changing light. 'For the night has a thousand eyes and the day but one'. But the light of millions of lives is that fiery sun.

Happiness is also a matter of temperament, and temperament is something you are born with, acquired from near or distant ancestors. Unfortunately we cannot choose our ancestors, and often we are saddled with their worst traits—quarrelsome natures, unmanageable egos, envy, a tendency to grab what isn't ours... 'The fault, dear Brutus, lies not in our stars but in ourselves that we are underlings...' Shakespeare put his finger on it occasionally.

And luck, is there such a thing as luck? Some people seem to have all the luck. Or is that too a matter of temperament? A nature that doesn't sue for happiness often receives it in large measure. A nature that's placid, undemanding, does not suffer the same frustrations as do those who are impatient, ambitious, power-oriented.

Luck would seem to walk beside the healthy and those unencumbered by the daily struggle for survival. We try to summon up Lady Luck, but there are long periods when she stays away and we have to be patient and hope for her return. 'Luck, be my lady tonight!' sings the gambler in the Damon Runyon story, and once in a while she does smile upon us, albeit when least expected.

Luck and Chance are the same thing, I suppose. I have found that Chance gives, and takes away, and gives again. And so, when things are looking dark and gloomy, I know that daybreak is not far off.

I have been extremely fortunate or lucky or blessed by all the gods in that I have lived to this ripe age without too much disappointment or distress. I have made a fair living, doing the thing I enjoy me putting words together and telling stories—and I have been able to find people to love and live for...

Was it all accidental, or was it ordained, or was it in my nature to arrive unharmed at this final stage of life's journey? I love this life passionately, and I wish it could go on and on. But all good things must come to an end, and when the time comes to make my exit I hope I can do so with good grace and humour.

～

Thoughts on Passing Eighty

There is nothing special about living into one's eighties. Many people do it. I can't say that I am any better, or any wiser, for having passed this landmark. But I must say I am a little surprised, because I do not come from a long-lived family (both parents and two grandparents having died quite young); nor have I bothered to take care of myself, health-wise. And I hate all forms of physical exercise!

No jogging for me. No climbing mountain peaks. No dumb-bells or bullworkers or those machines that make you run in one place. I hate running. I will run only when chased by a madman or a mad bull. At school, I came last in the marathon, having stopped along the way to partake of refreshments made available by enterprising vendors of roasted peanuts or bhuttas.

Yoga? No, I am not a yoga enthusiast. I do admire people who can tie themselves into knots, but I am a peculiarly unknotty person, liable to be stuck in one position for hours if I try too ambitious an asana. (is that the right word?) Some years ago I tried looping my right leg over my left shoulder, only to end up calling for help. As ten-year-old Gautam disentangled me, he said: 'You looked like a semi-colon, Dada. You should stuck to writing.'

Stick to writing! Good advice from a pre-teen. And I am frequently taking advice from children. Such as: 'Don't cut your hair too short, Dada. Girls like it long.' These little tips go a long way in helping me to win friends and influence people.

But why am I writing this article? Because only the other day, at our local bookshop, a young man came up to me and said: 'Sir, tell me—what is the secret of happiness?' It was hardly the time for homespun philosophy, as a pretty young thing was trying to take a 'selfie' of the two of us, so all I could say was: 'Signing books for young readers. It would make any writer happy.'

'But I'm not a writer,' he said. 'I'm a psychiatrist.'

'Well then, make your patients happy,' was all I could say.

Which reminds me. When I was a young man and thought I knew the answers to everything, I wrote a piece called 'Thoughts On Reaching Thirty'. It was published in the *Illustrated Weekly of India*, a great magazine now long extinct.

And what were my thoughts at thirty? They couldn't have been very profound, because I can't remember even one of them! And yet, at that enquiring age, I was under the influence of Spiritualism, Theosophy, Tao-sin, Christian Science, and the teachings of Gurdjreff! I suppose the slum of all these things had some effect on me, because the landmark ages of forty, fifty, sixty and seventy passed without any urge to put down my great thoughts—if, indeed, there were any.

Meditation? This was once recommended to me by a gentleman in Rishikesh who had been meditating beside the Ganga for several years. (He had a settled income, which meant he did not have to work for a living.) Well, I do try a little meditation from time to time. The trouble is, after a few minutes I fall asleep.

You see, I have this wonderful ability to fall asleep at any given moment, and it is probably the secret of my happiness. I can sleep by night, I can sleep by day. I can sleep in the sun, I can sleep in the shade. I can sleep in my bed, I can sleep on the back of an elephant. (I have yet to try a camel.)

Perhaps I am meditating in the wrong place. My little room, with the morning sun on my desk, is really meant for writing—or sleeping. In between naps I write stories or little essays like this one. If I am to meditate successfully, I should be down in Rishikesh like my friend in the banks of the Ganga.

When I was a boy I would occasionally visit Hardwar, sometimes in the company of my lost friend Kishen. In my first novel, *The Room on the Roof*, I have described how we crossed the Ganga in a small boat accompanied by a number of pilgrims, all chanting 'Ganga-mai ki jai!' It was a moving experience, both in my story and in reality. And whenever I visited Hardwar, I would sing out 'Ganga-mai ki jai' with whoever was with me.

I am not a religious person, but I have always been moved by the devotion of others. Every evening, after Beena (my grand-daughter) has done her pooja, she brings me prasad, and I accept it humbly and gratefully because it is the symbol of her goodness and devotion. To light a candle is better than to curse the darkness.

And so here I am, in my eighties, trying to gather my thoughts and to see if I have any *great* thoughts. But none come to me. You must do your own thinking, dear reader.

www.ingramcontent.com/pod-product-compliance
Lightning Source LLC
Chambersburg PA
CBHW051058030726
47504CB00006B/1682